本书受昆明理工大学教材项目资助

西方文化中的两希传统

杨 慧 著

Hellenism and Hebraism in Western Culture

社会科学文献出版社
SOCIAL SCIENCES ACADEMIC PRESS (CHINA)

序

　　西方文化中的两希传统是西方文化得以持久发展的原动力，是西方文明在古代独树一帜、在近现代一度引领世界的主要原因。"两希传统"指的是希腊传统（the Greek Tradition；Hellenism）和希伯来传统（the Hebrew Tradition；Hebraism）。希腊传统又包括希腊神话传统和希腊哲学传统，希伯来传统又包括犹太教传统和基督教传统。

　　两希传统的不断冲突与融合是西方文明得以延续两千年并在近代大放异彩的缘由，而其各自内部的冲突与融合为西方文明的发展及近代繁荣提供了保障。其实，西方文明最独特、最值得我们深究和学习的，既不是近现代的科技文明，也不是近现代的制度文明，而是一种自省（self-reflection）、自纠（self-correction）、自我检点（self-criticism）的能力。

　　西方人先有古希腊文明、古罗马文明，之后基督教断送了古罗马帝国，却成就了古罗马文明。基督教思想钳制西方的一千年，通常被认为是"黑暗的中世纪"，然而，恰恰是这"黑暗"的文化，上承古希腊文明，下启西方近代文明。西方近代文明源于对基督教的批判与颠覆，源于对古希腊文明的呼唤与复兴，恰如基督教当年对古希腊文明的批判与颠覆、对古罗马文明的修正与重塑。实际上，古希腊文明早在文艺复兴时期就重新回到西方人的视野，其后更有启蒙主义者、浪漫主义者的热情讴歌与顶礼膜拜。

希腊传统注重的是自由、民主、平等、勇敢、正义，希伯来传统强调的是纪律、顺从、忍耐、博爱。乍一看，这两种传统具有截然不同的特点，似乎针锋相对。然而，这两种看似水火不容的文化却在某些方面惊人的相似，如对"智慧"的热爱、对"正义"的追求，尽管"智慧""正义"这些概念范畴在两种文化中不尽相同，且具有不同的内涵与外延。因为"爱智"的传统，古希腊有了苏格拉底，在大街上见人就谈哲学；因为"爱智"的传统，希伯来人有了约伯的追问。不同的是，苏格拉底关心的是人的正义、城邦的正义，而约伯追问的是神的正义与上帝之城的正义。

在古希腊传统中，柏拉图要把诗人（包括荷马和悲剧家）逐出"理想国"；在希伯来传统中，耶稣在圣殿砸了撒都该人的摊子、颠覆了法利赛人的律法。古希腊的哲学传统是对古希腊神话传统的反思与批判，基督教传统是对犹太教传统的反思与批判。我们所说的"批判性思维"（critical thinking）不是为了"批判"，而是为了"建设"，"批判"不是目的，而是手段。

即使是在希腊神话自身的传统中，也有荷马—赫西俄德—俄耳甫斯的不同。赫西俄德《神谱》对《荷马史诗》的继承与修订，实则是希腊神话走向神学、政治介入神话系统的开始。俄耳甫斯的神话诗（及其日神观、酒神观和灵魂死后受苦以及乐土观等）与赫西俄德的神话诗系统虽不相同，却互相关联，对整个希腊文明的影响是深远巨大的。[①] 即使是荷马的两部史诗《伊利亚特》和《奥德赛》，内容和主题也有很大的不同：《伊利亚特》更接近于神话史诗，而《奥德赛》已经有了神话政治的内涵。举例来说，《伊利亚特》对阿喀琉斯"勇敢"的歌颂与《奥德赛》对奥德修斯"智谋"的肯定显然不同，而奥

---

① 默雷：《古希腊文学史》，孙席珍、蒋炳贤、郭智石译，上海译文出版社，1988，第45页。

德修斯的"智谋"是对阿喀琉斯"勇敢"的否定。实际上，奥德修斯否定的不仅仅是阿喀琉斯的勇敢，还有他的个人主义，在这里我们已然发现后来的悲剧家埃斯库罗斯强调的"爱国主义"。而对于"国家""城邦"的思考，在古希腊无人能够超过索福克勒斯，在古罗马又有斯多葛主义哲学家如塞涅卡等的进一步阐发。至于西方近代思想，其实不外乎对古代思想的进一步阐释、发展和实践。因此，索福克勒斯的思想、斯多葛主义在近代的复兴绝非偶然。

即使是在犹太教自身的传统中，也有先知对自身传统的批判：先知们不仅诅咒、反抗外邦人对希伯来人的侵略与压迫，如《耶利米哀歌》；更有对自己族人的批判与训诫，如《创世记》中对索多玛、蛾摩拉毁灭的记载。先知传统是古犹太教传统中最值得尊重的传统，它反映了希伯来民族敢于自我反思与批判的难能可贵的品质。在《创世记》中，犹太人的拉比记录了祖先的种种劣迹——强奸、乱伦、通奸，甚至亚伯拉罕也做过令人羞耻的事情。但是希伯来人仍然值得我们尊敬，因为他们敢于正视历史、书写历史、揭露历史。更何况希伯来人还有为"义"字牺牲的先知，如施洗约翰和被钉十字架的耶稣。

一部希腊人的历史，是古代先人反思自己、批判自己的历史；一部希伯来人的历史，是犹太民族检点自己、鞭挞自己的历史。"以铜为鉴可以正衣冠，以人为鉴可以明得失，以史为鉴可以知兴替"，我们研究他者及其历史，是为了知"兴替"，包括他者的兴替，也包括自己的兴替。"他山之石可以攻玉"，学习他者，不仅仅是学习他者的优点，也要看清他者的缺点。学习不是崇洋媚外，也不应该妄自尊大。一种先进的文化是一种具有反思批判能力的文化，是一种高度自觉的文化。学习是"祛魅"的过程，既不妖魔化，也不美化。学习是通过反思、审视他者来反思、检点自我，只有这样，路才会越走越宽，前途才会越来越光明。

目　录

第一部分

希腊传统

第一章 宙斯神统

第一节 宙斯爱情神话中的欧洲
中心主义思想

一 "欧洲"的由来

欧洲的全称是欧罗巴洲,英文为 Europe,意为"太阳落下的西方"。关于这个名称的由来,有一个广为流传的希腊神话传说。"众神之王"宙斯看中了腓尼基国王的漂亮女儿欧罗巴,想娶她作为妻子,但又怕她不同意。一天,欧罗巴在一群姑娘的陪伴下在大海边游玩。宙斯见到后连忙变成一头雄健、温顺的公牛,来到欧罗巴面前,欧罗巴看到这可爱的公牛伏在自己身边,便跨上牛背。宙斯一看欧罗巴中计,马上起立前行,腾空而起跳入海中,带着欧罗巴来到一块遥远的陆地上生活。欧罗巴的神话反映了西方人"圣化"自己历史的痕迹。"欧洲"这个词诞生不久,就出现了"欧洲中心主义"思想,那什么是"欧洲中心主义"呢?《牛津英语词典》把"Eurocentric"(欧洲中心主义)解释为以欧洲或视欧洲为中心,认为欧洲文化在世界文化中至高无上。"Euro-centrism"(欧洲中心论)的解释是把欧洲视为世界中心的那种观念或行为 ①。

二 欧洲中心主义思想在宙斯爱情神话中的具体体现

作为宙斯的情人之一，勒托为宙斯生下了太阳神阿波罗和月亮女神阿尔忒弥斯。她的两个子女后来都成为奥林匹斯的主神。有一次，忒拜国王安菲翁的妻子尼俄柏说她的子女比勒托更多，结果勒托大怒，让阿波罗将她的儿子全部射杀，而让阿尔忒弥斯将她的女儿全部射杀。最后直到尼俄柏自杀，宙斯把忒拜的全体居民变成了石头，这一残酷的报复才告结束。从这个故事中可以看到，古希腊神话中神的地位是凡人无法企及的，神的威严不容触犯，哪怕是无心之过。从另一方面来说，这是宙斯所代表的天神文明对凡人文明的鄙视，勒托的子女在某种程度上是天神文明的分支，尼俄柏则是凡人的代表。一个在天上，一个在地下；一个是天神的，一个是凡人的。对应到当时的希腊社会，是希腊文化对其他文化的贬低和鄙视，这无疑是"欧洲中心主义"思想的具体表现。随着时间的流逝，社会的发展，这一思想被赋予了更深的含义，它所代表的地理范围不断扩大，构建的文化意识形态也逐渐增多。欧洲开始作为文化的实体而呈现，其内涵和自我认同是在与非欧洲的比较中实现的。从一开始，有关欧洲与非欧洲的文明特征的认知就同欧洲对非欧洲的偏见相关联。最早的源头可追溯到古希腊文化。

希腊人最初生活在伯罗奔尼撒半岛、爱琴海诸岛和希腊北部的大陆部分，建立了雅典、斯巴达、忒拜等城邦。在同外界的冲突和斗争中，希腊人似乎确认了自我优于其他人，尤其是在公元前 5 世纪，阻止了波斯帝国的入侵使这种优越感更加明显。古希腊人把世界分为欧罗巴、亚细亚和利比亚三部分。其中，欧罗巴是希腊的家园，是优越

---

① John Simpson and Edmund Weiner, *The Oxford English Dictionary* (Vol.5), Second Edition. Oxford: Clarendon Press, 1989, p.442.

的一方。这种思想在当时的著作中多有反映，如希罗多德（公元前484年至公元前430或420年）把世界划分为欧罗巴、亚细亚和利比亚三部分，并多次使用"欧罗巴"指代战争中希腊一方。希波克拉底（公元前430年至公元前338年）也赞同三大陆的分法，他试图用气候和自然环境来说明欧洲的优越性，认为亚洲稳定的气候是亚洲居民缺乏勇气和挑战精神的原因，欧洲多变的气候是欧洲居民积极上进的原因。在希腊人自我优越的思想意识中，不自觉地形成了以希腊为中心的世界。阿那克西曼德的地图把希腊画在图中心，把希腊人所知道的欧洲、亚洲部分画在图的四周①。尽管希罗多德是小亚细亚人，但他受希腊文化影响至深，甚至在其著作中，也把希腊（欧洲）视为主体和中心，而希腊之外的都是附庸。他的《历史》记载了当时所知道的世界，包括希腊、西亚和北非等，有"小百科全书"之称，但实际上，其背景介绍都是为了对比说明希腊地理环境、人性和技术的优越。

三　来自西方的"东方"

18世纪的英国工业革命进一步强化了近代"欧洲中心主义"的论调，使西方各国走上了资本主义道路，大规模的海外殖民由此展开。19世纪时，欧洲已凭其雄厚的经济实力和强大的军事力量奠定了自己的霸权地位，对各殖民地的资源掠夺也慢慢变成了全面占领。将世界踩在脚下的欧洲，认为这种扩张是自身文明的优越性所致。基于这种认识，以欧洲为中心的历史观逐渐形成，这种历史观主要论述的是把西欧的历史进程作为标杆，认为世界各个不同的民族和国家在迈向现代化的进程中，都必须遵循这个模式。尽管这种历史规律后来被抨击得体无完肤，但是在那个时代，这种主张的确在人类社会、经济、政治等各个思想领域造成了深远的影响。黑格尔，作为"欧洲中

---

① 普雷斯顿·詹姆斯：《地理学思想史》，李旭旦译，商务印书馆，1982，第22页。

心论"的标杆学者之一，认为世界历史虽然以东方为起点，但历史的终点在欧洲，特别是落在普鲁士的君主立宪制度之中①。他在《历史哲学》中宣称，世界历史虽然开始于亚洲，但是"旧世界的中央和终极"却是欧洲，而欧洲的"中心"是法兰西、德意志和英格兰。他把中国和印度说成是没有生气而停滞和缺乏内在动力的国家：中国有"一种终古如此的固定的东西代替了一种真正的历史的东西。中国和印度可以说还在历史的局外；而只是预期着、等待着若干因素的结合，然后才能够得到活泼生动的进步"。利奥波德·冯·兰克则无视欧洲以外地区的存在，单纯地将欧洲的历史发展过程视为全球历史发展的主体。他认为世界的发展是以欧洲为主体的，拉丁民族和条顿民族（日耳曼人及其后裔）是这个主体的两个主角；而人类历史发展的过程基本上就是这两个民族相互斗争与融合的过程。兰克更直言："印度和中国根本没有历史，只有自然史。所以世界历史就是西方的历史。"②

但也有许多学者对"欧洲中心论"持批判态度。贡德·弗兰克说："无论自觉与否，我们大家都是这种完全以欧洲为中心的社会科学和历史学的信徒。"他批评一些西方学者，认为"在某些关键性的历史、经济、社会、政治、意识或文化领域里，世界其他地区与西方相比是有欠缺的。他们宣称，正是由于西方拥有所谓在'其他地区'欠缺的东西，才使得'我们'拥有了一种主动内生的发展优势，然后作为'白人身负'的'文明开化使命'，'我们'把这种发展优势向外传播到世界其他地区"③。这段批评是切中"欧洲中心论"要害的。阿诺德·约瑟夫·汤因比认为历史研究的单位应该是社会而不是国家，他激烈抨击了西方"种族主义宣传家"所鼓吹的"欧洲中心论"。

---

① 黑格尔：《历史哲学》，王造时译，上海书店出版社，2006，第144~161页。
② 科林伍德：《艺术原理》，王至元、陈华中译，中国社会科学出版社，1985，第148页。
③ 贡德·弗兰克：《白银资本》，刘北成译，中央编译出版社，2008，导论。

汤因比在他的著作《历史研究》中说道："因为我们西方社会在过去四百年里扩张到了全世界，因此近代西方人的心里也就强调了历史中的种族因素。这种扩张使西方接触到了（常常是不友好的接触）在文化上和体态上同他们迥然不同的人民。这种接触的结果很自然地产生了优越和次劣生物类型的概念。"① 而爱德华·W.赛义德在其所写的《东方主义》一书中所概括的东方话语理论的核心是：西方发现和建造了东方，西方殖民主义者按照西方的意识观念和价值标准对被殖民的东方进行文化建构。换言之，西方在文化层面上对东方进行解构、再现和重构。无疑，"欧洲中心主义"就是如此。《后殖民文化批评和后现代语境及中国知识分子的身份定位》一文对赛氏东方主义话语做了更为详细的表述："赛义德《东方主义》一书的要旨就是揭露西方如何从自己的政治、经济、文化利益出发，用自己的意识形式语言说'东方'……赛义德称这类言说为'东方主义'，认为这种'东方'并不是真实的东方，而是帝国主义意识形态的话语建构文本……"② 可见，赛义德的"东方主义"强调的是，在西方殖民扩张的过程中，处于强势的西方文化渗透到被殖民的东方国家，肢解当地的传统文化和民族文化体系，贬损本土文化的价值观念和思想意识，从而按照西方意识和价值准则重构东方国家的文化体系。波里·怀说："东方主义者把世界分为落后、未开化的'他者'和与之相对立的先进、高度发达的'我们'。"这是一种对立的关系，而这种东西方之间的敌对态度源于人们对自身文化、民族身份的真实性和恒定性的朴素信仰，即朴实的爱国主义和民族主义的情绪。赛义德写《东方主义》的初衷并非要激化东西方之间的矛盾，而是让西方更好地去了解东方、了解世界，消除"欧洲中心主义"的思想偏见。但事实上他的东方主义理论

---

① 汤因比：《历史研究》，刘北成、郭小凌译，上海人民出版社，2005，第 299 页。
② 郭军：《后殖民文化批评和后现代语境及中国知识分子的身份定位》，《外国文学研究》2000 年第 3 期。

对西方批评的态度却迎合了许多长期遭受西方敌视的"非欧洲"人民的抵触情绪。

第二节 从雅典娜神话的变迁探究古希腊的 "文明"与"智慧"

一 雅典娜女神

我们经常看到肩头耸立着猫头鹰的女神像——那就是雅典娜，腰间带蛇的女神像或许也是雅典娜，手持印有蛇发女妖"美杜莎"头像盾牌的女神像还是雅典娜。据记载，自公元前 447 年至公元前 438 年，古希腊著名雕刻家菲狄亚斯 (Phidias) 和他的助手们全身心地为雅典娜神殿雕刻神像。他们为雅典卫城雕塑了三座女神像，其中一座为爱琴海西北部利姆诺斯岛（Lemnos）的护城女神像。这座神像由青铜铸造，比真人稍大，非常精致。另一座是"雅典城守护者"巨型铜像，以雅典城武装保护者的姿态耸立在卫城正门与神殿之间，连基座距地 70 英尺，既是航海者的标志，亦为威慑敌人的堡垒。三座女神像中，最著名的是"雅典娜女神像"，这座神像伫立在雅典娜神殿中，高 38 英尺，象征着智慧与贞洁。

雅典娜是奥林匹斯山十二主神之一，又是宙斯的女儿，地位自然尊贵。她既是战争的保护者（手持长矛和盾牌），又是和平的爱好者（橄榄树是她的象征之一）；既是航海的保护者，又是织布技术的发明者 [她有一个别名叫厄耳伽涅（Ἐργάνη），意思是女工]。她教会人们驯养牛马、制造车船；赐予世人犁和耙、纺锤和织布机（相传雅典娜发明了纺织，曾帮赫拉与赫拉克勒斯编织长袍。在《伊利亚特》中，赫拉披上雅典娜编织的长袍，胸带黄金别针，去约会宙斯；雅典娜还赠送给英雄赫拉克勒斯长袍；据说众英雄寻找金羊毛乘坐的阿耳戈船，就是在雅典娜的指示下建造的）。

雅典娜是智慧的象征（对于有着"爱智"传统的希腊人来说，智慧女神自然有着举足轻重的地位），又是艺术爱好者（相传雅典娜发明的乐器因为吹奏时双颊会鼓起而被众神嘲笑，遂弃之，不料被马耳绪阿斯捡到，其认为使用雅典娜发明的乐器一定能与阿波罗抗衡，于是挑战太阳神，可是阿波罗规定，必须倒着演奏乐器，但是笛子只有前端能吹出声音，所以马耳绪阿斯落败）。

这个受到希腊人顶礼膜拜并充分享受着雅典人盛大祭典的女神，究竟有着怎样的故事？我们沿着女神来时的路，试图找回那个真实的"少女"，拨开笼罩在神话上方的重重迷雾。

二　雅典娜神话的历史变迁

1. 雅典娜名称探源

雅典娜的古希腊语是从 Ἀθῆναα 或 Ἀθήναια 缩略而来的，在伊奥尼亚方言中写成 Ἀθήνη 或 Ἀθηναίη（见于《围困特洛伊城浮雕绘制图》中标记的名字），在多利亚方言中写成 Ἀθάνα 或 Ἀθαναία。如果按照伊奥尼亚的方言 Ἀθήνη，我们可以推测雅典娜是以雅典这座城市命名的——因为在古希腊地名中，有许多城市名字的结尾是 -ήνη，如 Μυκήνη（迈锡尼），也就是说，-ήνη 是一个典型的地名后缀。

但是，雅典娜通常被叫作帕拉斯·雅典娜（Παλλάς Ἀθήνη）。帕拉斯，有人把它解释为"少女"(Maiden)，还有人把它解释为"舞刀弄枪者"(the weapon-brandishing)，但这些说法根据不足，不能得到人们的普遍赞同。在希腊神话中，有几种关于帕拉斯和雅典娜关系的说法。其一，雅典娜为宙斯所生，由河神特里同抚养长大，帕拉斯是特里同的女儿、雅典娜的玩伴，后不幸被雅典娜误杀，为了表示哀悼，她将帕拉斯的名字放在自己的名字之前。其二，帕拉斯是巨灵之一，在众神和巨灵之战中被雅典娜所杀，为显示自己的战功，雅典娜将帕拉斯的名字放在自己的名字之前。其三，在《古代城市：希腊罗马宗教、法律及制度研究》一书中，菲斯泰尔·古朗士曾说帕拉斯是海神。遗憾的是，人们至今还未弄清这个词真正的含义。

2. 雅典娜与克里特岛的"蛇女神"

在《伊利亚特》中，荷马称雅典娜是"猫头鹰眼睛的"(γλαυκῶπιν)（古希腊语直译，γλαυκῶπις 的所有格形式，罗念生将其译作"目光炯炯的"）。维吉尔在《埃涅阿斯纪》中说她是"蛇的保护者"。希罗多德在《历史》卷八中有这样的描述：在雅典的神殿里，有一条巨蟒守护着雅典卫城。雅典娜作为动物神的这些特征源自克里特的"蛇女神"。在克里特神话中，猫头鹰和蛇守卫着弥诺陶洛斯的宫殿。而手持迈锡尼盾牌的女神像，就是后来奥林匹斯的雅典娜的原型。在雅典娜的标志物中，有一件是用饰有美杜莎蛇形头发的羊皮制作的盾牌（即神盾埃癸斯）。

公元前 13 世纪，古尔尼亚家宅小神祠中发现了一尊"蛇女神"陶像：一条蛇缠绕着女神。在古希腊人的观念中，蛇住在地下，是地下神灵和鬼魂的化身。"蛇女神"是家宅的守护神，但米诺的印章和壁画中从未见过"蛇女神"造型。1903 年，在克里特迷宫西翼神殿区的密室发现了三尊"蛇女神"陶像，她们衣着时髦、开放，犹如宫廷贵妇，但缠绕在她们身上的蛇却透露出她们的身份。其中一尊神像呈奶白色，三条有紫褐色花斑的绿蛇缠绕着她的身体。

在米诺人眼中，蛇不是可怕的，而是友善的、保护家庭的。米诺人的家庭供养蛇，将"蛇女神"供奉在家宅神祠中。即使在近代，对家宅蛇的崇拜也未绝迹。把蛇当宠物、给蛇喂奶的风俗在斯拉夫国家、阿尔巴尼亚等国都有记载。蛇是雅典娜的圣物，"花斑蛇"是她的绰号。希罗多德讲述了这样一个故事：希波战争时，波斯大军压境，雅典岌岌可危，将领们决定将全城人民撤退到海岛上；雅典人不愿意撤退，于是雅典娜神庙的女祭司宣称她们亲眼看到一条"花斑蛇"从神庙飞走，雅典人听到护城女神已经飞走，知道城池不保，于是撤退到安全的海岛上。

雕刻家菲狄亚斯曾为帕特农神庙制作了一尊镶嵌着黄金和象牙的雅典娜女神巨像，圣蛇就立于她的身旁。雅典流传着这样一个神话：火神赫菲斯托斯垂涎于雅典娜，后来强奸未遂，雅典娜将火神遗留在身上的精液甩在了地上，使大地母亲受精，并生下了厄里克托尼俄斯。雅典娜把婴儿装在篮子里交给雅典的三位公主看管，嘱咐她们切勿观看。公主好奇，揭开篮子的布，发现了一条蛇（也有一种说法是看到了一个人身蛇腿的小孩），最后被吓疯。这个故事透露的信息是：雅典娜是位"蛇女神"，她的前身可能是位母亲而非处女，是古希腊的生殖女神，蛇是她的亲生儿子。或许，编神话的人为了维护贞洁女神的体面，才将"蛇"改为地母之子。

关于"蛇女神"还有这样一个神话。满头蛇发的女妖美杜莎本是绝色美女，是雅典娜的女祭司。海神波塞冬垂涎于美杜莎的美色，竟在雅典娜的神庙里强奸了她。雅典娜很气恼，遂将美杜莎变成了怪物。后来，英雄珀尔修斯在雅典娜的指使下杀死了美杜莎，并把女妖的头献给雅典娜。雅典娜又将美杜莎的头镶嵌在自己的盾牌上。这个神话透露的信息是：美杜莎是雅典娜的原型，雅典娜变成了美丽的贞女，同时也杀死了她的原型——蛇发女妖。

关于雅典娜与蛇的关联，还有一个故事。特洛伊战争第十年，奥德修斯在雅典娜的帮助下想出了用木马攻城。特洛伊祭司拉奥孔识破此计，极力阻止木马入城。雅典娜遂派出两条毒蛇，将拉奥孔父子三人缠绕致死，这或许可以作为雅典娜是"蛇女神"的证据。[1]除了"蛇女神"的身份，雅典娜还保留着米诺宗教的其他特征：猫头鹰、橄榄树都是她的神圣象征。

---

① 古斯塔夫·施瓦布：《希腊古典神话》，曹乃云译，译林出版社，第415页。

3. 皮拉斯基人的雅典娜

雅典娜从远古时期开始就是一位重要的神祇。线形文字 B 上已出现了她的名字，迈锡尼石板上也曾以"女主宰"来称呼她，后来的一些史诗和祈祷文也常称雅典娜为"女王"（πότνιαν）。按照皮拉斯基人（Pelasgians）的说法[1]，女神雅典娜出生于利比亚的特里同湖畔，因此，雅典娜又被称为特里托革尼亚（Τριτογένεια，意为"诞生于特里同"）。有三位利比亚的水泽神女发现了她，于是给她穿上山羊皮做的衣服，并哺育她成长。她后来取道克里特，来到了雅典。关于这一传说可以参阅《阿波罗尼乌斯》。但是按照克里特的传说，雅典娜女神的家乡就在克里特，她诞生在克诺索斯附近名叫特里同的小溪旁。这段材料是根据皮拉斯基人这个古老民族的传说记载的，因而使许多学者把雅典娜的起源与利比亚的女神联系起来。这种观点还有以下几则旁证材料。

希罗多德的《历史》记载[2]，雅典娜神像所穿的衣服是希腊人从利比亚妇女那里学来的，只有两点除外：利比亚妇女的衣服是皮子制的，她们那山羊皮的埃吉司短衣的穗子不是蛇而是草。除此之外，在所有其他地方，她们的服饰都是相同的。希罗多德在《历史》中还记载了对雅典娜的崇拜：紧邻着玛科律埃斯人的是欧塞埃斯人，他们和玛科律埃斯人隔着特里同河，住在特里托尼斯湖岸边；他们每年为雅典娜举行一次祭典，在举行祭典的时候，少女分成两队，相互用石头和木棒交战，据说，这样做是遵照祖先的方式来敬拜雅典娜女神。

考古发现，利比亚移民早在公元前 4000 年就已进入克里特岛，史料记载与考古发现基本上是一致的。因此，有人认为雅典娜崇拜源于利比亚人，经过克里特文明，才最终进入希腊的神话体系。

---

① 皮拉斯基人：古希腊最早的土著居民，据说来自西亚；生活在大陆上，与生活在海岛上的克里特人都属于地中海族系非希腊语民族。

② 希罗多德：《历史》，王以铸译，商务印书馆，1959，第 101 页。

4. 王室的护家神

宙斯神统的女战神、智慧女神，前身是克里特岛米诺人崇拜的"蛇女神"。"蛇女神"本是家宅保护神，传到希腊本土后，被尚武的迈锡尼人变成了王室的护家神。王室担负着守家卫国的重任，因此，王室的守护神自然成了战神，于是雅典娜具有了护国的职能。

在《伊利亚特》中，雅典娜帮助希腊英雄赢得了战争的胜利：她帮助英雄珀尔修斯杀死美杜莎，帮助柏勒洛丰驾驭飞马战胜了女妖喀麦拉。在《奥德赛》中，雅典娜帮助奥德修斯结束十年的漂泊生活，返回了家园。最重要的是，雅典娜离开奥德修斯后，回到了她在雅典的住所——雅典国王厄瑞克透斯的宫殿。这暗示了女神"王室护家神"的身份。

5. 雅典的保护神

雅典娜成为雅典的守护神，这一传说与雅典娜和海神波塞冬的争斗有关。波塞冬是宙斯的兄弟，掌管着海洋；宙斯的另一个兄弟哈得斯，掌管着冥界。据说雅典建成时，波塞冬与雅典娜争夺为之命名的荣耀。最后他们达成协议：能为人类提供最有用的东西的人将成为该城的守护神。波塞冬用他的三叉戟敲打地面，变出了一匹战马——代表战争与悲伤，而雅典娜变出了一棵橄榄树——象征着和平与富裕，因此雅典就以女神的名字命名（究竟女神以城市的名字命名还是城市以女神的名字命名，我们不得而知，但两者关系的密切程度是毋庸置疑的）。雅典建有希腊宗教艺术的象征——帕特农神庙（Παρθενών，意为贞女的），这是供奉雅典娜女神最大的神殿。神殿坐落在卫城中央最高处，殿内还存放着一尊菲狄亚斯亲手制作的镶嵌着黄金和象牙的雅典娜女神像。

6. 从宙斯头颅中蹦出的雅典娜

赫西俄德的《神谱》这样描述了雅典娜的诞生。诸神之王宙斯首先娶墨提斯为妻，她是神灵和凡人中最聪明的。可是，盖亚和乌拉诺斯说，墨提斯所生的儿子会推翻宙斯，因为墨提斯注定会生下几个绝顶聪明的孩子，第一个就是明眸少女特里托革尼亚（雅典娜），她在力量和智慧两方面都与她的父王不相上下。但这之后，墨提斯将生一位儿子做众神和人类之王。宙斯惧怕预言成真，遂将墨提斯吞入腹中。此后，宙斯得了严重的头痛症，只好要求火神打开他的头颅。令奥林匹斯山诸神惊讶的是，一位披坚执锐的美丽女神从裂开的头颅中跳了出来，这就是雅典娜。

三　俄瑞斯忒斯的审判

希腊人的统帅阿伽门农因为献祭自己的女儿伊菲革涅亚并在战胜特洛伊后带回女战俘卡桑德拉，惹怒了妻子克吕泰涅斯特拉。克吕泰涅斯特拉与情夫合谋在阿伽门农沐浴时杀害了他。代表父权统治的阿波罗对克吕泰涅斯特拉的行为十分愤怒，于是将真相告诉了阿伽门农的儿子——俄瑞斯忒斯，并吩咐他去复仇，杀死自己的母亲。在垂死挣扎之际，克吕泰涅斯特拉诅咒俄瑞斯忒斯：弑母行为必将受到代表母系氏族权力的复仇女神的惩罚。这一诅咒在她死后就应验了，墨该拉的索命之音令俄瑞斯忒斯发了疯，他离开了自己的宫殿和王国，到处寻求阿波罗的保护以躲避复仇女神的追杀。阿波罗知道光凭自己的保护是不够的，因为俄瑞斯忒斯毕竟杀害了自己的母亲，于是吩咐他去雅典，祈求雅典娜的公正判决。雅典娜召集人间的法官共同审理此案，并在黑白石子数目正好相等的情况下投下一枚白石子，最后依据多数票的决定宣布俄瑞斯忒斯无罪。

四　雅典娜神话的历史变迁所反映的希腊文明进程

1. 从"亚细亚"到"大希腊"

从"蛇女神"到"女战神"，我们可以看到古希腊不同宗教信仰融合的某种轨迹。对比皮拉斯基人的传说和希罗多德的考证，再来看赫西俄德《神谱》关于雅典娜诞生的描述，我们可以发现，雅典娜的身份与地位是不断变化的——在宙斯代表的阿卡亚的色雷斯文明入主希腊本土之前（约公元前 4000 年），雅典娜与墨提斯同为希腊的土著神。或许雅典娜的存在还要早于母亲墨提斯——她最早的原型可能是缠死拉奥孔的长蛇，这种"蛇女神"崇拜以一种原始图腾的形式存在。雅典娜被后来的神话杜撰为宙斯的女儿，这可以说是弱势文明对强势文明的屈服，也可以认为是弱势文明对强势文明的认同。

宙斯代表的是阿卡亚人的宗教信仰——阿卡亚人创造了迈锡尼文明与后期的克里特文明，并于公元前 2000 年左右迁入希腊本土。墨提斯则象征着原先希腊本土土著居民的神灵信仰。将墨提斯视为智慧女神，可能意味着当时的希腊本土文明要优于后来的移民者的文明。宙斯将墨提斯吞入肚中，意味着土著居民、阿卡亚人和西亚移民不同宗教信仰与文明的融合，从而形成了新的希腊文明体系。希腊正统宗教的象征仍然是宙斯而不是雅典娜，因为她不是"预言"中的"儿子"，因此最终没有真正取代宙斯，这或多或少地代表了当时被征服民族的屈从。但是，墨提斯留在宙斯的腹中，又象征着这些民族也或多或少地保留着自己的传统。从雅典娜崇拜的演变历史中可以看到，希腊人的神灵世界有着漫长的发展演变过程，是融合了多个民族的神灵观念的结果。

2. 从"女战神"到"智慧女神"

在《伊利亚特》中，雅典娜是一位与阿瑞斯旗鼓相当的战争女神。在特洛伊战场上，雅典娜支持以阿伽门农为首的希腊联军。她急切地挑起希腊联军与特洛伊人之间的矛盾，推动战争的发展，还不断地在战场上鼓动人们作战，帮助英雄们刺杀敌人，甚至自己披挂上阵参加搏杀。她帮助阿喀琉斯杀死了赫克托耳。雅典娜这一女战神赢得了希腊人的崇拜，因为她可以给敌人带来死亡，可以帮希腊人赢得战利品或财富。根据赫西俄德《神谱》的记载，雅典娜是一位在战场上呼啸呐喊的将军，一位渴望喧嚷骚动和战争厮杀的不可战胜的女王。

相比《伊利亚特》中的野蛮好战，《奥德赛》中的雅典娜渐渐远离了女战神形象，虽然仍携带武器（一次她在奥德修斯的家门前手握铜尖长矛，另一次她扮成牧羊少年的模样出现，手握投枪），但是此时的女神不再以全副武装的战斗姿态出现。《奥德赛》中的雅典娜是伴随在奥德修斯父子身边的守护者，是智慧的象征，而战神的品质几乎被这些形象淹没了。

3. 从母系社会到父系社会

雅典娜从宙斯头颅中蹦出的新神话，是父权制全面战胜母权制的结果：当雅典娜希腊化并成为许多城邦的崇拜对象时，描述这位女神的正统的神圣起源的工作就开始了，这一工作也是父权制建立并巩固其统治的需要。宙斯从自己的头颅中生出雅典娜，只有通过这样的方式，才能确定自己永恒的权力。也就是说，宙斯只有结束神祇世界父子传承的繁衍规则，并且把女人兼具身体和心智两方面的繁衍能力占为己有，才能巩固他的父权，或者更确切地说，才能确立他在众神中的统治地位。①

这一神话是根据父权制观点来描写雅典娜出生的，所以雅典娜仿佛是宙斯的延续，是宙斯意志的执行者，是行动中的宙斯。墨提斯的母亲身份逐渐模糊，似乎雅典娜由宙斯一人所生。宙斯从雅典娜身上得到了智慧，就像过去从墨提斯身上得到智慧一样。

雅典娜从宙斯头颅中"诞生"的故事，揭示了雅典娜的身份——她是父权制的代表。她的出生决定了她的立场，为俄瑞斯忒斯投下的一票反映了她必将维护男权社会的统治。

4. 从"少女"到"无性"

伯里克利为雅典娜女神设计的帕特农神庙，是雅典卫城的主建

---

① 居代·德拉孔波：《赫西俄德：神话之艺》，吴雅凌译，华夏出版社，2004，第125页。

筑。"帕特农"意为"贞女""处女的卧室",突出了雅典娜作为处女神的崇高与贞洁。雅典娜作为三处女神之一,极其重视自己的贞洁,有个故事证明了这一点。忒拜城的预言家忒瑞西阿斯的母亲是水泽神女卡里克罗,也是雅典娜的好友。忒瑞西阿斯有一次无意间看到了雅典娜的裸体,雅典娜用双手遮住了忒瑞西阿斯的双眼,之后忒瑞西阿斯就变成了盲人。卡里克罗请求女神帮儿子恢复视力,但是女神做不到。不过,她给忒瑞西阿斯洗净双耳,让他得以听见鸟语,又给了他一把拐杖代替眼睛。不过,这只是忒瑞西阿斯瞎眼由来的传说之一。

这则神话透露的信息是:雅典娜从最初的"蛇女神"到"智慧女神"的性别特征已经渐渐模糊,尤其是从宙斯头颅中蹦出的新神话,更是抹杀了母亲墨提斯的位置,似乎雅典娜非母所生,是无性别的。这一神话通过渲染雅典娜纯洁、崇高的出生来维护男权社会的统治——没有了母亲墨提斯,没有了生殖,也就没有了来自女性的威胁,男权统治才可以稳固。表面看来,雅典娜的出生是纯洁的(无性的),但其实雅典娜已经成为一位男性神;表面看来,雅典娜的出生是高贵的,其实她不过是宙斯神统的一个点缀,是男权统治为女性留下的最后一点位置。

5. 从雅典娜神话看希腊人的"智慧"

(1) 男性智慧与女性智慧

在传入克里特岛和希腊大陆之初,雅典娜是一位少女形象的女战神。她有一个称号是 Areia,意思是"好战的",另一个称号是 Promachus,意思是"勇士",还有一个称号叫作 Sthenias,意思是"强有力的"。[①]这对那些处于游牧时代的民族来说是合适的,然而随着希腊社会文明的发展,雅典娜成为城邦的保护神,进而有了"议事女神"的称呼,于是,"女战神"变成了"智慧女神"。这一转变标志

---

① 郭璇:《希腊女神雅典娜的起源、演变及影响》,《边疆经济与文化》2005 年第 5 期。

着希腊文明在吸收了众多因素之后向更高一级的形态发展。

从父亲宙斯的头颅中蹦出来，让雅典娜具有了男人的智慧。为雅典娜编纂一个新的出生故事，既符合男权社会征服女性的要求，也符合女性主动适应男权社会的需要。雅典娜出生的新神话，是父权社会的衍生物，她的智慧自然也是父权社会的智慧，用于维系父权制的延续。对俄瑞斯忒斯的审判，再次表明了雅典娜的立场：为了维护父权社会的统治，雅典娜必须把自己的那一票投给俄瑞斯忒斯。

在纺织的发明者、航海的保护者雅典娜身上，在发明笛子的雅典娜身上，我们似乎可以看到墨提斯的"智慧"，但是在宙斯的女儿雅典娜身上，我们已经看不到母亲墨提斯的"智慧"，而只能看到宙斯式的"智慧"。

（2）"计谋"与"智慧"

从《伊利亚特》到《奥德赛》，从最初的女战神到后来技艺、准则的发明者，雅典娜作为和平女神的性质似乎掩盖了她作为战争女神的性质。可以说，雅典娜体现了希腊文明的历史进程。

在与海神的较量中，雅典娜胜出，让雅典娜获胜的是她的智慧。当波塞冬用蛮力制服马匹时，雅典娜却用成套的马具对付野马；当波塞冬在大海中兴风作浪时，雅典娜却帮助人们造出舰船；当波塞冬用他的三叉戟使大地冒出咸水时，雅典娜却在周围种上橄榄树。在这里，我们看到的是雅典娜的女性智慧，仿佛是母亲墨提斯智慧的延续。

在对俄瑞斯忒斯的审判中，雅典娜也动用了智慧，然而这里我们看到的是理性的智慧，是男性的智慧，这仿佛是父亲宙斯智慧的延续。虽然是战争女神，但雅典娜并不像阿瑞斯那样好战，而宁愿用法律手段来解决争端。阿瑞斯和雅典娜分别代表了战争的两面性：阿瑞斯所代表的是战争中残酷的一面——生灵涂炭；而雅典娜代表了战争中理性的一面——凭借智谋和力量来取得胜利。例如，在特洛伊战争的最后阶段，雅典娜教导奥德修斯使用木马计，[①] 这也使阿卡亚人最终获得了胜利。

雅典娜的智慧还体现为她养育并帮助过很多英雄。在《希腊宗教研究导论》中，英国著名的古典学家简·艾伦·哈里森描述过雅典娜的事迹：盖亚虽然生了厄里克托尼俄斯，但把他养大成人的是雅典娜；她和赫拉克勒斯也有类似的关系——她是赫拉克勒斯的养母；她帮助伊阿宋建造了阿耳戈船，并完成了寻取金羊毛的远航；她还帮助奥德修斯重返家乡。

雅典娜对奥德修斯之子特勒马科斯的帮助充分显示了她的"智慧"。雅典娜提议特勒马科斯前往皮洛斯和斯巴达去打探他父亲奥德修斯的消息。雅典娜显然知道，奥德修斯的归程已经被众神安排妥当，可是她没有直接告诉特勒马科斯，而是安排他离开舒适的家，踏上危机重重的海上之旅，拜访强大的王公贵族们，去寻找父亲的踪迹。其实，对于奥德修斯的归来，特勒马科斯的旅行不能提供任何帮助。可是为什么雅典娜要做这样的安排？因为雅典娜知道，特勒马科斯需要的是资本——成为史诗时代的贵族，成为奥德修斯真正的儿子，成为与俄瑞斯忒斯相当的人物的资本。之后特勒马科斯学会了自己做决定、自己思考，既了解了他的父亲奥德修斯，也明白了如何成为荷马时代的贵族。当然，所有这一切都是按照女神的意志完成的，作为"在所有的诸神中间以睿智善谋著称的"雅典娜，以其非凡的智慧策划了特勒马科斯的成长之旅，目的在于激发他的智慧——一种随机应变的智慧。

雅典娜对奥德修斯父子二人的宠爱，其实反映了古希腊人对智慧的热爱。雅典娜作为智慧的化身自然也在古希腊人中受到崇拜。人们对奥德修斯的敬重，以及天神对他的庇佑正彰显了希腊人对待智慧的

---

① 古斯塔夫·施瓦布:《希腊古典神话》，曹乃云译，译林出版社，第 409~411 页。

态度。Philosophy（哲学）一词源于希腊文 Philo-sophia，意为"爱智慧的"，是古希腊人"爱智"传统的体现。

然而，我们需要留心的是，古希腊存在"两种智慧"：苏格拉底的"智慧"，也即智者的"智慧"；宙斯、雅典娜、缪斯等神灵的"智慧"，也即普罗米修斯、奥德修斯等的"计谋"（甚至可以说是"诡计"，是为了达到某种目的而施展的才智）；盖亚、墨提斯等女性神的"智慧"，也即宙斯等男性神的"智慧"。在雅典娜身上，我们看到了两种智慧的并存，这里的"智慧"并不单单指代知识。

我们还需要留心的是，希腊人的"爱智"，源于对"无知"的承认。苏格拉底的"自知我无知"是古希腊人的一种普遍认识。或许，只有信仰才能够给人类一种限度，赫西俄德《劳作与时日》的第 649 行与荷马《奥德赛》I 卷第 202 行有着相同的意味：我不是预言家，也不谙鸟飞的秘密。①

五　结语

从克里特岛的"蛇女神"到奥林匹斯山的十二主神之一，从《伊利亚特》的"战争女神"到《奥德赛》的"智慧女神"，从各种技艺的创始人到雅典的守护神，雅典娜拥有太多的身份。

其实，在古希腊宗教中，一位神灵拥有多重形象是很普遍的。由于人口的迁移、新旧宗教的交替、各种宗教的融合，希腊本土的宗教混合了很多外来的神灵观念，这使雅典娜具有了不同的职能、属性和形象；又由于希腊人神灵观念的变化，以及古希腊神—人体验的变化，雅典娜女神形象承载了更多的宗教和文化因素。事实上，雅典娜

---

① 雅典娜借这句话说出奥德修斯重返故土的预言，但雅典娜否认自己是预言家，这是为了符合她的人物身份。这里暗含的意思是：人类是"无知的"，是不知道神的意图的。事实上，无论是《伊利亚特》《奥德赛》还是《神谱》，都旨在对比人类知识的有限与神祇智慧的无限。参见居代·德拉孔波《赫西俄德：神话之艺》，吴雅凌译，华夏出版社，2004，第 15 页。

形象、身份、角色、地位的变化，反映了古希腊文明的进程。

有关雅典娜的种种神话传说，让我们看清了古希腊文明的发展轨迹；而通过分析雅典娜身上蕴含的种种"智慧"，我们似乎对古希腊的"爱智"传统有了新的理解——即便穷尽"智慧"，也是"无知"的，而我们对"无知"的承认，为获得"智慧"铺平了道路。雅典娜的神话还透露出这样的信息：智慧有很多种——善良的智慧、狡诈的诡计，无功利的智慧、急功近利的算计。问题在于：我们需要怎样的智慧？

第三节 古希腊神话中的命运观念

一 敲响命运之门的古希腊神话

古希腊的神与人同形同性，除了有不死性和无比强大的力量，在其他方面都与人没有区别，如具有欲望、感到喜怒哀乐等。命运的形态在希腊神话中得到了形象的展现：宙斯随身携带着小天平，以此作为命运的象征，并支配着自己的判断——即使作为众神之王有时也不得不服从命运的安排。《古典思想》一书中写道："然而，宙斯自己的意志得到贯彻这一点并不总是清楚的。他多少有些模糊地与'命运'相联系。一个人的'命运'或'份额'决定他死亡的时间，而当两个英雄进行决斗时，宙斯称量他们两人的命运，看看哪个英雄必须得死。"[①] 有时宙斯会考虑是否拯救一个特定英雄的命运，但是他从不违抗命运的安排，他最终的决定总是与命运相一致。

除了宙斯，和"命运"关联紧密的神是命运三女神。命运三女神的名字 Moirae 源于 μοίρα，意思是部分、配额，本意为分配者，引申

----

① 特伦斯·欧文：《古典思想》，覃方明译，辽宁教育出版社，1998。

为生活和命运之上，可理解为对人的配给。在希腊神话中，三位命运女神都是面容严肃、忙碌的形象。在赫西俄德的《神谱》中，关于命运女神有如下记载："黑夜还生有司掌命运和无情惩罚的女神——克罗索、拉赫西斯和阿特洛泊斯。克罗索纺生命之线，拉赫西斯为每个人安排命运，阿特洛泊斯是带有可怕剪刀的报复女神。这三位女神在人出生时就给了他们善或恶的命运，并且监察神与人的一切犯罪行为。在犯罪者受到惩罚之前，他们决不停止可怕的愤怒。"①

希腊人将一切都归于命运，命运似乎代表了古希腊人与生俱来的对生命的认识。关于神和英雄的神话传说，形象而深刻地反映了古希腊人对命运的认识。智慧之神普罗米修斯为减轻人类负担，在众神召开的确定人类权利和义务的会议上，用牛油蒙骗众神而受到惩罚。宙斯因此拒绝给予人类火种去构建文明，但普罗米修斯不顾宙斯的愤怒，将偷来的火种送到人间。宙斯大怒，为了报复，令火神赫菲斯托斯、雅典娜、众神使者赫耳墨斯、爱神阿佛洛狄忒共同创造了美丽的女子潘多拉，汇集了世间的罪恶，带给人类数不清的灾难，而普罗米修斯则被惩罚每天都要承受鹫鹰啄食肝脏的痛苦。即使有预知未来的能力，普罗米修斯也无法挣脱命运的摆布。他说："无论谁，只要他学会承认定数的不可动摇的威力，便必须忍受命运女神所判给的痛苦。"②面对命运强大的力量，即使是众神之王宙斯也无可奈何。在《伊利亚特》中，阿喀琉斯在特洛伊城下疯狂追逐赫克托耳，宙斯同情赫克托耳，想鼓动众神来挽救他的生命，却遭到雅典娜的驳斥：

> 抛掷闪电的父亲，聚集云朵的天神，你在说些什么！
> 这个凡人的命运早已被限定，
> 难道你想让他免除可怕的死亡？

---

① 赫西俄德:《神谱》，张竹明译，人民出版社，1991。
② 《埃斯库罗斯悲剧集》，陈中梅译，辽宁教育出版社，2001。

宙斯只好放弃，

当战争双方相持不下之时，

天父取出他的那杆金质天秤，

把两个悲惨的死亡判决放进秤盘，

一个属阿喀琉斯，一个属赫克托耳。

他提起秤杆中央，赫克托耳一侧下倾，

阿波罗立即把他抛弃。[1]

阿喀琉斯无情地杀死了赫克托耳，即使宙斯怜悯他，也无法挽回其死亡的命运。而伟大的阿喀琉斯，即便是神之子，也难逃死亡的命运，最后被帕里斯一箭射中了脚踝而死。在命运面前，我们无法与之对抗，无论是神还是人。然而，普罗米修斯和阿喀琉斯明知自己将要遭受厄运，也没有选择逃避。普罗米修斯自知违背了宙斯的意志，必定会遭到惩罚，但他仍坚持自己的选择，将火种送到人间。阿喀琉斯在开战之前就知道自己将死于特洛伊城下，但还是毫不犹豫地选择了战场，而不是留在故乡。因为选择后者也终将一死，但很不值得。这就是古希腊人的命运观：在不可改变的命运面前，即使粉身碎骨，也要绽放生命的光辉。

二 古希腊神话对"人"的思考

马克思曾说，任何神话都是借助想象以征服自然力、支配自然力，把自然力加以形象化；因而，随着这些自然力在实际上被支配，神话也就消失了。[2]古希腊人用神话来解释他们所处的世界，来探寻"我是谁""从哪里来""到哪里去"的答案，而对"人"的思考与关

---

[1] 《荷马史诗》，罗念生、王焕生译，人民文学出版社，2003。

[2] 马克思：《〈政治经济学批判〉导言》，载《马克思恩格斯选集》第2卷，人民出版社，1972，第113页。

注是古希腊人馈赠给人类的最宝贵的精神财富。俄狄浦斯破解了斯芬克斯之谜，回答出谜底"人"。然而，"人是什么"却是一个永远的斯芬克斯之谜。它是古人未能解决的问题，也是当代未能完成的研究课题。而德尔菲神庙的阿波罗祭台上镌刻着"认识你自己"的警句用来警醒世人，体现了古希腊人对人的本质所做的思考。在索福克勒斯的悲剧《俄狄浦斯王》中，虽然他相信神和命运的力量，相信一切在冥冥之中早已注定，但他将关注点逐渐转移到凡人的身上，开始要求人们有独立自主的精神，这一点在俄狄浦斯身上体现得淋漓尽致：虽然最终承受了弑父娶母的厄运，但他在注定的命运中努力过、对抗过、挣扎过，可谓体现了作为"人"的一大特点——有自己的想法，不甘心做命运的奴隶。作为忒拜国王的俄狄浦斯为了消除忒拜的灾祸，力图寻找杀害老国王的凶手，而当他四处追查凶手的时候，乐队却唱出了命运带来的无法躲避的可怕力量。

俄狄浦斯的悲剧不仅仅是俄狄浦斯个人的悲剧，也是人类的悲剧。俄狄浦斯的命运悲剧在于，他越要摆脱命运的束缚，就越是自投罗网；他越是真诚地为民除害，就越是步步临近灾难与毁灭。但是我们不难发现人性的光辉已经在这部悲剧中有所闪现，古希腊人开始以理性的眼光看待世界。雅典民主制的不断发展，以及公民在城市中的地位和作用不断得到认可，强化了人的价值观念，智者派代表人物普罗泰戈拉提出的"人是万物的尺度"这一命题，成为希腊世界理性思潮的标志。①

三　近代命运观念的发展

14 世纪可以视为人文主义时代的开端，在经历了一千多年的宗教神权统治之后，人们开始挣脱精神枷锁，被禁锢了多年的古典文化再

---

① 崔宜明：《"命运"观念的起源和理性内涵》，《中国哲学史》1996 年第 3 期。

次引起了人们的重视。随着文艺复兴运动的深入，人的中心地位逐步确立，并开始确立自我的人生价值，珍视现实生活的美好。人不愿再默默承受神给他们安排的命运，他们意图通过抗争来获取人生的幸福。

人文主义虽然复兴了古希腊文化，但没有继承古希腊的命运观，人们更多地将"命运"与世俗的人和世俗的成就联系在一起。受基督教思想的影响，虽然上帝至高无上，但上帝在人的命运轨迹中并不起决定性作用。

文艺复兴早期的萨卢塔蒂崇尚斯多葛派哲学，倡导积极生活，他在《论命运、幸运和偶然性》中，强调人运用自由意志积极地对待人生就可以战胜命运。阿尔伯蒂在《论命运和命运女神》一文中对"什么是命运"这一问题做出解释：命运是依次发生的人的生活运动。命运受命运女神的干扰和影响。关于命运女神是什么，他以寓意做了说明：当一个人落入水中时，身旁正好有一块木板或一条船，命运女神就对这个人比较宽厚。相反，对必须依靠自己努力游到河岸的人则严酷无情。从他的譬喻中，我们可以看到他将命运女神理解为偶然性，但又带有一定的规律性：靠近木板或船只，人得救的希望就比较大，而没有这个条件，危险性就比较大。他更希望人们通过主观努力来获取成功，而不是将前途寄托在偶然性上。阿尔伯蒂深信人自身的能力，人能依靠自然赋予的能力去对抗命运女神。自阿尔伯蒂以后，人文主义进入了新的阶段。这一点在莎士比亚的《哈姆雷特》中表现得很明显。不同于俄狄浦斯，哈姆雷特的命运是他自己的命运，不再被凌驾于人之上的神界所规定，也不被复仇所规定，人不再与他人抗争，他人成为虚无，人开始与自身抗争。"生存还是毁灭"，哈姆雷特执着地以生命为代价追寻着"人"生存的意义。虽难逃悲剧性的结局，但这一追问从根本上证明了"人"在现实中自觉寻求生命的永恒价值，这一点难能可贵。

无论是古希腊悲剧，还是莎士比亚悲剧，悲剧英雄们都具有抗争精神，这一点在后来的自由主义悲剧中也有所体现，如易卜生的《玩偶之家》《人民公敌》等剧作。他们不惜用生命向现存秩序挑战来实现自我的全部意义，尽管是以悲剧结束，但那种悲壮美仍然让我们感到震撼。

而19世纪末，以叔本华的悲观哲学、尼采的强力意志、萨特的存在主义、弗洛伊德的精神分析为代表的文化思想瓦解了人类关于无限与永恒的神话——上帝死了，人类失去了精神家园而变得无所适从，所谓的"命运观"开始变得模糊。正是在这种背景下，20世纪的荒诞派戏剧诞生了，其创作的哲学基础主要是萨特的存在主义：否认人类存在的意义，人是在无意义的宇宙中生活。贝克特1953年首演的荒诞剧《等待戈多》展现的是一种人的整体状况，流浪汉与旅行者的两极对立，极大地限制了任何重要的人类行动。"戈多是谁？""为什么要等他？"一切都没有原因也没有结果，一切仿佛都没有进行，但好像一切又都再次发生。

现代戏剧的虚幻与荒诞更多地表现为一种无序与无意义，宿命论的态度与空想主义的乌托邦从来就没有实际意义。即便如此，对人存在的意义和命运的认识仍在继续。

第四节　古希腊神话中的恋母情结与弑父情结

一　俄狄浦斯神话

恋母情结，又称"俄狄浦斯情结"，是弗洛伊德首先创造使用的精神分析术语，指六岁前的儿童对双亲中异性一方无意的眷恋以及对同性一方的敌视。[1] 使弗洛伊德深受启发的是由古希腊著名悲剧家索

---

① 郝澎：《古希腊罗马神话与西方民间传说》，南海出版公司，2007，第108页。

福克勒斯（公元前 496 年至公元前 406 年）创作的悲剧《俄狄浦斯王》。故事讲述的是忒拜国王拉伊俄斯为了避免神谕应验，在儿子出生之后，将其抛到了喀泰戎的荒山中，但婴儿被牧羊人所救，并因受伤的双脚被起名为俄狄浦斯，意为"肿胀的脚"。随后俄狄浦斯成为忒拜邻国国王的养子，由于该国国王没有子嗣，所以俄狄浦斯被认定为王位继承人。长大后，不知道科林斯国王与王后并非其亲生父母的俄狄浦斯为避免神谕成真，便逃了出去，在去特尔斐神庙途中不小心杀死了自己的亲生父亲，后来又因破解了斯芬克斯之谜当了忒拜的国王，娶了自己的母亲。最后，知道真相的俄狄浦斯刺瞎双眼，选择自我放逐。

弑父情结体现得最明显的是时间之神，克洛诺斯用镰刀阉割了自己的父亲乌兰诺斯，成为众神之王。有预言说他将被自己的一个儿子推翻，于是他便吞吃掉自己的每一个孩子。宙斯出生时，其母瑞亚用大石头替换了他，后来他战胜了自己的父亲，解救了自己的兄弟姐妹。

作为诗人的赫西俄德，总是歌颂希腊神话。我们也许很难了解赫西俄德本人对于克洛诺斯和宙斯"弑父"这一在大多数人看来违反伦理常识的事件的看法，但他在《神谱》中所表达的感情却是虔诚和赞美的。"伟大宙斯的能言善辩的女儿们说完这话，便从一棵粗壮的橄榄树上摘给我一根奇妙的树枝，并把一种神圣的声音吹进我的心扉，让我歌唱将来和过去的事情。"[①] 克洛诺斯和宙斯推翻的都是自己的父亲，而为什么不是母亲呢？这是因为在创造相应神话的时期，母权制已荡然无存，取而代之的是对妻子和子女具有统治和支配权的父权制。

从另一方面来看，在克洛诺斯和宙斯"弑父"的过程中不难发现

---

① 赫西俄德：《神谱》，王绍辉译，上海人民出版社，2010，第 27 页。

母亲的身影，他们都是在母亲的授意或帮助下推翻了父亲的统治，那为什么母亲不自己推翻丈夫的统治呢？这是因为她们已经没有能力与之抗衡，也反映了母权制的没落。而从推翻后的结果来看，居于统治地位的仍然是男神，仍然是父权制的代表，这也是当时现实生活的再现。因为希腊神话中的神与人同形同性，既有人的体态美也有人的七情六欲，懂得喜怒哀乐，参与人的活动，神与人的区别仅仅在于前者永生，而后者的生命有限。

二 古希腊社会中的父权制

恩格斯说："母权制的被推翻，乃是女性的具有世界历史意义的失败。丈夫在家中也掌握了权柄，而妻子则被贬低，被奴役，变成丈夫淫欲的奴隶，变成单纯的生孩子的工具了。妇女的这种被贬低了的地位，在英雄时代，尤其是古典时代的希腊人中间，表现得特别露骨……"[1]在父权制社会里，财产、子女和妻子都属于父亲，古希腊社会即是如此，希腊神话便是对古希腊现实生活的真实写照，其中充斥着极其浓厚的男权意识。正是在这种背景下，"恋母情结"和"弑父情结"才得以放大，面对父权的绝对统治，处于弱势的子女和母亲更容易结成联盟来反抗父亲和丈夫的压迫。

按照拉康提出的"菲勒斯中心主义"，男性是主体，女性则被看作为证明男性价值而存在的他者。这使"菲勒斯中心主义"成为人们所说的男权中心主义。在希腊的等级秩序中，"男人与女人的二元对立意味着男性是正面价值，代表男性的'菲勒斯'则是一个超验的能指"[2]。换言之，"她只是用以建构男性主体的一种场所，一种不具有

主体性的物的存在"[1]。古希腊社会正如神话所描绘的那样，整个社会充斥着男性对女性的压迫。从希腊历史中可以发现，古希腊人通过不断的努力，逐渐建立了较为完善的民主制度，由野蛮时期进入文明社会，可是妇女的地位却每况愈下。

在荷马时代（公元前 11 世纪至公元前 9 世纪），城邦是男性公民的主要活动场所，妇女不仅在活动空间上与男性是分开的，在受教育程度上也与男性有很大的差距。此时的她们还没有被完全排除在社会生活之外，而到了公元 4 世纪，政治虽然进步了，但妇女的境遇却变差了，虽然古希腊实行一夫一妻制，但所谓的"一夫一妻"制只是对女性的限制，对男性则没有任何限制。雅典女性被要求严守贞操且不能以任何理由参加公众活动，更别提有政治权利了，此时的她们只能任由男性压迫和欺凌。这一点在希腊神话中有很明显的表现。

《伊利亚特》是以阿喀琉斯的愤怒展开故事情节的。阿喀琉斯之所以愤怒是因为一个女人，这个女人是战争胜利后他的女俘，却被阿伽门农夺去，两人为此展开争夺，这倒不是因为他们到底有多爱布里塞伊斯，而是这个女俘在当时是荣誉的象征。希腊人将战争中获得的女俘当作物品任意处理，并和武器、牲畜一起送人，甚至将其杀死，当然亦可带回家做"床伴"。

苏格拉底也认为妻子仅限于做好配偶，照顾家庭，生育合法的继承人。希腊神话中，希腊统帅阿伽门农为了平息阿尔忒弥斯的愤怒，使远征特洛伊的计划不至受阻，而要亲手杀死自己的女儿。这就是古希腊社会女性的悲惨写照，也是父权制的有力展示。

三 沉默的"羔羊"

正如福柯所说："用不着武器，用不着肉体的暴力和物质上的禁

---

① 张岩冰:《女权主义文论》, 山东教育出版社, 2001, 第 117 页。

止，只需一个凝视，一个监督的凝视，每个人就会在这一凝视的重压下变得卑微，就会使他变成自身的监视者，于是看似自上而下的针对每个人的凝视，其实是由每个人自己加以实施的。"[1] 古希腊社会中，大部分女性处于社会边缘，她们是被父权制忽视的群体。然而，她们却很少起来反抗，原因是父权制下的中心文化、思想意识对女性的统治和压迫，使女性将男性的思想意识进行内化，从而没有察觉到自己所受的不公。

---

[1] 李银河:《女性权力的崛起》，中国社会科学出版社，1997，第61页。

第二章　神话与阐释

第一节　想象与真相——海伦的阐释学意义

一　历史阐释中的海伦

自古红颜多薄命，独留青冢向黄昏。红颜之冢早已无证可考、无迹可寻，红颜之名却与历史的滚滚尘烟一同翻腾不息。海伦只是一个名字，而借其流传的故事，不仅不可计数，而且彼此大相径庭。她到底是伯罗奔尼撒的光明女神，还是特洛伊战争的罪魁祸首？是宙斯与勒达的千金，还是苦苦守候丈夫归来的烈女？海伦是谁？轻纱帷幔，帘卷悲歌，终不见这个倾城倾国的女子之真面目。

1. 古代神话传说中的女神海伦

关于海伦的"有死"和"永生"的问题，正如耶稣的"人性"和"神性"问题一样，受到热议。在最初的传说中，海伦是女神，其生命与植物一样周而复始。后来她成了神与人的女儿，但仍然是永生的：斯巴达王后勒达与宙斯生了四个孩子，其中，海伦和波吕丢刻斯是永生的 (immortal)，克吕泰涅斯特拉和卡斯托尔是有死的 (mortal)。但在后世的文学想象中，海伦更多地以凡间女子的形象出现。

无论是女神，还是女人，无可争辩的是，她有着惊人的美貌，美得倾国倾城，美得败国毁城。海伦如何被理想化成一个永恒的被崇拜、称颂的对象和一个被中伤、诽谤、解构、重构的对象，仍是一个颇值得玩味的话题。她所有的变形 (metamorphoses) 都积淀成西方文化中女性身份演变的化石，积淀成人类历史的集体想象。因此，海伦的故事就是西方女性的故事，是整个人类的故事。

海伦曾是古代米诺斯的植物女神和伯罗奔尼撒的丰产女神与光明女神，与阿佛洛狄忒具有一样的功能，只是影响力不及后者，地位亦有所下降。作为植物女神，其遵循的是一种死而复劫、劫后复归的命运模式。同阿多尼斯一样，海伦与植物的周期性死而复生相契合，所以占有她意味着执掌丰收，意味着对生命（生殖）的肯定与保证。因此，"希腊人远征特洛伊的意义所在——抢回海伦，也就意味着要让富裕重新降临业已面临困境的迈锡尼。作为一个象征，这便是海伦神话的内涵"[1]。

2. 荷马与赫西俄德笔下的海伦

不论是盖亚、潘多拉，还是阿佛洛狄忒、海伦，她们都以不同的名字分享了人类创始神话的同一母题。不论是旧石器时代岩壁上的三角形符号，还是新石器时代的卵形图腾，都将女性与"生殖""死亡"相连。女性可以孕育生命，也可以摧毁生命："子宫即坟墓（womb is tomb）。"[2] 对女性的"妖魔化"与"天使化"，使关于海伦的叙述呈现对抗的态势：她是欢乐的赐予者，也是灾难的制造者。而"官方"叙事则始终处于"厌女传统"(misogyny) 的语境中，这一传统不仅是男性对女性的厌恶，也是女性对女性的厌恶。

在赫西俄德的《神谱》中，海伦本是海洋之神 (Oceanus) 的女

---

① 吕新雨：《神话·悲剧·〈诗学〉》，复旦大学出版社，1995，第32页。

② Robert Emmet Meagher, *Helen: Myth, Legend, and the Culture of Misogyny*. New York: Continuum, 1995, p.73.

儿，后来演变为阿佛洛狄忒的女儿。后来的传说为她找到了父亲——宙斯。宙斯强奸了复仇女神 (Nemesis)，于是女儿海伦作为复仇的种子——"黑夜之女"，成为男权社会永远的威胁。被强奸的复仇女神不断变换形态，作为动物、植物和海洋仙女 (nymph) 被崇拜。后来，她化身为鹅 (goose)，被化身为天鹅 (swan) 的宙斯又一次强暴，而这正是勒达的前身。济慈在《勒达与天鹅》中对海伦身世的重述，使海伦的美丽得到了一个合理的解释。

海伦从蛋中而出，一则传说认为，这个蛋（moon-fallen egg）从月亮上落下，被鱼运送到幼发拉底河岸边，由鸽子孵化而出。女诗人萨福描述了海伦的另一种出身："人们谣传，在荒野风信子花丛下，丽达发现了一个蛋。"从宇宙的蛋 (cosmic egg) 到丽达的蛋 (Leda's egg)，海伦经历了从神到人的身份转变。

海伦作为神赐予凡间的礼物，与潘多拉别无二致。其灾难性表现在两个方面：第一，她的出身与"宙斯的暴力"相连；第二，她的"情欲"与"厄洛斯的暴力"相连。因此，作为礼物，她带来的只能是不幸。

海伦与美神阿佛洛狄忒关系密切，因为阿佛洛狄忒将其许诺给了特洛伊王子帕里斯；海伦也与爱神厄洛斯（情欲）关系密切，因为她与特洛伊王子发生了绝世之恋。在但丁的《神曲》中，她因这种关联被打入地狱。苏格拉底将"情欲"称为"暴君"，如勒内·吉拉尔所说："欲望总是与暴力勾连。"然而，海伦的"暴力"与她的姐姐克吕泰涅斯特拉却完全不同：阿伽门农横尸浴室的血腥与帕里斯温柔乡里的厄运形成了鲜明的对比。原来，不只愤怒可以杀人，爱也能杀人，只不过前者是用"刀"，后者是用"笑"。

虽然都是被强奸，海伦与母亲勒达的结局殊异。勒达不能在屈辱中苟活，遂上吊自尽，而海伦在被劫持的最初暴力之后，竟与劫持者产生了美丽的爱情。海伦没有自我了断，也没有受到诸神的惩罚，相反，她得到了永生，并去往极乐世界。海伦与勒达的选择似乎暗示了"女人"与"暴力"的某种矛盾性关联。

作为宙斯之女，海伦透露出一种神性，一种迥异于人类的"他异性"(otherness)，而这种"他异性"又恰好隐含着"强奸"背后女人与男人和解的秘密。男人想要驯化女人的这种"他异性"，最有效、最直接的方法就是使用暴力。而被"神"强奸的渴望与被"兽"强奸的愤怒，似乎映射出女人对暴力的态度。被强奸的渴望、与强奸者的和解，反映了女性超越现实的冲动与对现实的妥协。

作为一种既定的秩序，宙斯的"暴力"是"残酷"的，但也是"神圣"的，勒达不能忍受"残酷"，也意识不到"神圣"，因此，她选择了死亡。海伦"无耻的智慧"结束了女性对"暴力""无望的对抗"，并将这种"暴力"巧妙地转化成自己的"嫁衣"。男人对这种"无耻的智慧"既喜欢又恐惧无奈，只能将隐藏的纵容掩盖在蔑视的外衣之下。

3. 高尔吉亚、埃斯库罗斯与欧里庇得斯笔下的海伦

智者学派的高尔吉亚在《海伦赞》中为海伦的爱情做了辩护。他强调自然情欲的不可避免性，说海伦的爱属于自然的情欲，是不得已的。不仅如此，他赞美了海伦"神圣的美丽"，因为这激起了如此强烈的"情欲"，以一个"躯体"换来了众多男人的"尸体"。[①]

在埃斯库罗斯的《阿伽门农》中，歌队看到克吕泰涅斯特拉双手沾满鲜血，首先斥责了海伦："为了一个女人，牺牲了那么多男人。他们的生命在特洛伊的阴影中耗尽。"他们将海伦称为"船只的地狱、城邦的地狱、男人的地狱"，但诗人借海伦的姐姐之口为海伦辩解道："你们将愤怒倾泻于海伦，好似特洛伊的希腊人的尸体是她的杰作。

---

① Robert Emmet Meagher, *Helen: Myth, Legend, and the Culture of Misogyny* . New York: Continuum, 1995, p.25.

算了吧。"①

在欧里庇得斯的《特洛伊妇女》中，普里阿摩斯的妻子、特洛伊的老王后赫卡柏也斥责了这场战争的始作俑者："所有已经承受的和将要承受的，难道就为了一个女人和她的床？"奇怪的是，欧里庇得斯又对海伦进行了另一种阐释：《特洛伊妇女》中的这个荡妇竟然摇身一变，成为《海伦》中的贞女，这使人对欧里庇得斯的"女性观"顿生好奇。

欧里庇得斯的《海伦》讲述了一个苦苦等待丈夫归来的烈妇的故事：被帕里斯劫到特洛伊的海伦只是一个幻象，真正的海伦被众神带到埃及，藏在善良的国王普罗透斯家中；特洛伊战争结束后，墨涅拉俄斯漂流到埃及，与海伦相认，并一起逃走。

欧里庇得斯的《海伦》的情节与希罗多德关于海伦留在埃及的故事所反映的古代传说有不可争辩的相似性。② 根据希罗多德在《历史》第 2 卷中的记载，海伦被帕里斯诱拐后在返回特洛伊途中被风暴吹至埃及海岸。国王普罗透斯憎恨帕里斯的不义行为，限期让其离开，而把海伦和宝物留下，准备将来还给墨涅拉俄斯。战争结束后，墨涅拉俄斯发现海伦不在特洛伊。来到埃及后，普罗透斯将海伦还给了他。

欧里庇得斯的《海伦》与希罗多德的叙述有两点相同：第一，海伦没去过特洛伊；第二，海伦的庇护者是埃及国王普罗透斯。至于海伦从斯巴达到埃及，以及在埃及王宫的生活等情节，欧里庇得斯在《海伦》中并未特别提及。其对两种神话传统的采用，足以说明："历史的真相"永远在"历史"之外，而海伦的"幻象"即"历史的真相"。

---

① Rene Girard, *Violence and the Sacred* . Baltimore: Johns Hopkins University Press, 1977, p.145.

② 陈洪文、水建馥选编《古希腊三大悲剧家研究》，中国社会科学出版社，1986，第351 页。

二 "海伦"与"历史"

"海伦是谁"与"海伦何以成为海伦"等问题，彰显了 20 世纪分析主义的历史学与实证主义的历史学之分野。即便新黑格尔主义与新历史主义有滑入"相对主义"和"虚无主义"的危险，狄尔泰的"体验"、克罗齐的"一切历史都是当代史"、科林伍德（也译作"柯林武德"）的"一切历史都是思想史"，以及伽达默尔的"理解即诠释"的历史哲学，也仍然为解释历史知识的可能性问题提供了新的视野。"海伦何以成为海伦"的哲学建构纵然不能代替"海伦是谁"的历史考证，就像上演《哈姆雷特》不能没有丹麦王子一样，但对于探索人类的集体想象来说或许更为重要。

悲剧之所以成为"悲剧"，纵然与"事件"有关，但更重要的是与悲剧的经历者及其观看者的体验有关。对于一个感觉麻木、没有悲剧体验的经历者来说，"悲剧"的意义远不及目睹了这一事件的、具有悲剧意识的旁观者重要。同样，海伦带来的痛苦以及痛苦的记忆如果仅限于荷马笔下的特洛伊人和希腊人，那么追问"海伦是谁"就失去了其可能包含的意义。"海伦之所以成为海伦"，是因为她带来的痛苦以及记忆不断激励着后世的人们进行"鲜活的想象"。[1] 无论是荷马的史诗，还是欧里庇得斯的悲剧，"海伦"作为一种符号都揭示了"历史"的"真相"。

科林伍德的"想象"是"再现历史"的重要手段，"重构"已失去的"问题"，就是一层一层拨开历史的迷雾。尽管海登·怀特的"历史叙事的本质是虚构"[2] 遭到了极大的批判，但他遵循了历史哲学大师们对"想象"与"历史"的分析，或者更确切地说，与"历史叙

---

[1] Robert Emmet Meagher, *Helen: Myth, Legend, and the Culture of Misogyny*. New York: Continuum, 1995, p.12.

[2] 古奇：《十九世纪历史学与历史学家》，耿淡如译，商务印书馆，1989，第 390 页。

事"相关的问题不容回避。关于海伦的"叙事"或许不是"历史",也永远不会成为"历史",因为作为人类集体想象的积淀,"海伦"将永远活跃在不曾停歇的"历史"中。

三　"海伦"的"名字"

作为人,海伦的历史真相无从考察,而作为名字,"海伦"成就了另一种"历史的真相"。对于人的经验史,"海伦是谁"并不重要,重要的是"海伦"这个"名字"。"名字"使无从把握的"海伦"得以"命名",进而被我们感受、追索或者膜拜,对我们产生真实的意义。

意大利符号学家埃柯(Umberto Eco)曾经写过一本畅销小说《玫瑰的名字》。自此,"玫瑰"与"名字"之争成了学术界的焦点。莎士比亚说:"我们用别的名字称呼玫瑰,它也会芳香如故。"这似乎暗示了人们对"名字"的一般理解:"玫瑰"因为可以"经验"而"真实","名字"只是一个"称谓",并非可以经验的实在。然而,真的只有可经验的对象才是真实的吗?"名字"不可以被"真实地"经验吗?"玫瑰"的芳香真的与它的"名字"无关吗?艾柯在小说的结尾写道:"昔日的玫瑰存在于它的名字之中,我们拥有的只是这个名字。"[①]"名字"和"玫瑰"是两种不同的"真实",而在经验史中,作为称谓的"玫瑰的名字"比"玫瑰"更具有真实性。不但如此,"名字"的真实意义,可能恰好是使"玫瑰"成为"玫瑰"的关键。[②]

德里达在《追思》一书中指出:"名字"比"人"的存在更长久,"名字之于他的生命,开始无他而在"(the name begins during his life to get along without him)。[③]"名字"作为德里达的"行为性事

---

① 埃柯:《玫瑰的名字》,闵炳君译,中国戏剧出版社,1988,第 477 页。
② 参见杨慧林《"名字"还是"玫瑰"——"汉语神学"的两种"经验"》,载《现代性、传统变迁与汉语神学》,华东师范大学出版社,2010,第 693 页。
③ Jacques Derrida, *The Work of Mourning*. Chicago: The University of Chicago Press, 2001, p.13.

件"（performative event）[1] 或保罗·利科的"语言的事件"（the event of language）[2]，揭示出"海伦"所具有的意义。"名字"的真实，在于"玫瑰"通过"名字"的符号活动得以延展，在于"玫瑰"作为"名字"而进入历史。关于海伦的想象与阐释包含在"海伦"这个"名字"之中，使"真理在虚构中永生"。作为一个"事件"，"海伦"成全了维特根斯坦的哲学命题："世界的意义在世界之外。"[3]

追问"海伦是谁"，并非要揭示历史的真相，反而能理解历史的虚妄。真理的进程包含在对"名字"的执着追问中，而"海伦何以成为海伦"正是真理得以显现的方式。

第二节　永恒的她者——历史阐释中的美狄亚

一　古希腊神话中的美狄亚母题

美狄亚的故事是西方文学传统中最古老的母题之一，而通过后世的诸多改写和重述，它自身也已经成为一种传统，成为一个"永远的神话"[4] 和"意义生成"的典型过程。特别是在"一切历史"都被视为"当代的历史"[5]、一切"理解"都意味着某种"诠释"[6] 的文化处境中，对美狄亚母题的传承过程进行追溯和梳理的价值必然超出对具体作品

① Paul Ricoeur, *Hermeneutics and the Human Sciences.* Cambridge：Cambridge University Press，1981，p.136.

② 席勒：《美育书简》，徐恒醇译，中国文联出版公司，1984，第62~64页。

③ 维特根斯坦：《逻辑哲学论》，郭英译，商务印书馆，1985，第94页。

④ "永远的神话"之说，参见耿幼壮《永远的神话》，《外国文学研究》2006年第5期，第158~166页。

⑤ 克罗齐：《历史学的理论和实际》，傅任敢译，商务印书馆，1982，第2~3页。

⑥ "诠释学问题是因为浪漫派认识到理解和解释的内在统一才具有其重要意义的。解释不是一种在理解之后的偶尔附加的行为，正相反，理解总是解释，因而解释是理解的表现形式。"参见汉斯－格奥尔格·加达默尔：《真理与方法》（上），洪汉鼎译，上海译文出版社，1999，第312~313页。

进行分析的过程，并具有更为普遍的诠释学意义。

从中国学人的角度对美狄亚母题进行探索，则是在久远的历史间隔之外，增添了地域、文化和语言的间隔。然而，也许正是这种双重间隔，使父母与子女、男人与女人、个体与社会、道德与选择等人类基本关系的延展得以特别的显现，使不同时代对这些关系的理解得以勾连，从而也使我们对特定母题及其意义的分析成为可能。

二　美狄亚母题的阐释史

"美狄亚"母题的传承，肇始于《荷马史诗》所代表的古希腊神话；至古希腊悲剧时代，则有欧里庇得斯的《美狄亚》、品达(Pindar)的诗作和亚里士多德（Aristotle）的评论；希腊化时期及古罗马时代，又有阿波罗尼乌斯（Apollonius）、奥维德（Ovid）、塞内加（Seneca）、克里斯普斯（Chrysippus）、加仑（Galon）等人的进一步阐释。中世纪与文艺复兴时期的达莱斯（Dares）、狄克提斯（Dictys）、薄迦丘(Bocaccio)、乔叟(Chaucer)、克利斯坦·德·皮桑(Christine de Pizan）等，也以不同方式改写过美狄亚的故事。近现代有关美狄亚的描述，不仅与理性主义的激情观、荣誉观紧密相连，而且与殖民主义的背景、女性主义的观念息息相关。德国女作家沃尔夫(Christa Wolf)发表于1996年的小说《美狄亚——声音》，则代表着美狄亚母题在"后现代"语境中的回响。不同时代对美狄亚母题的改写和重述，都在社会环境、时代观念的雕琢和打磨中留下了深刻的历史痕迹。

关于美狄亚母题的改写和重述，在西方文学史上形成了一条独特的互文性线索（inter-textual chain），而回顾本文可以发现，美狄亚的"身份"和"爱欲"（厄洛斯情结）始终凸显其间，成为后世阐释及其母题再现的焦点。

自古希腊以降，美狄亚形象的"身份"问题一直备受争议。无论她是外来者、弃妇、女巫、女人，还是愤世嫉俗的叛逆者，实际上都作为两种基本符号而不断激发后世的想象：第一种符号是她的"性别身份"，第二种则是她的"政治身份"。如果"性别"使西方历史上的主体、话语、权力等结构性关系联合起来，那么美狄亚的"性别身份"往往也是她的"政治身份"。反之，她的"政治身份"始终通过其性别和性格的独特折射，显示出一种根本意义上的挑战性、颠覆性，亦即"他异性"。

希腊人眼中的美狄亚，首先是一个来自蛮夷之地的科尔喀斯女子，这不仅与科林斯的文明格格不入，很难被转折中的社会形态所涵纳，也很难被视为任何一种社会观念的代表。她既可以因为情感的诱惑背弃自己的父亲、成全丈夫的功名，也可以由于情感的破灭牺牲自己的儿子、报复当年的情郎。因此无论对母系传统还是男权社会而言，这个外来的女子都只能是一个"异己"的"他者"。

而偏偏是这个既定秩序的"异己者"和希腊文明的"外来者"，又恰好具有"女神"的身份。在品达的颂歌中，美狄亚既是女人，又是缪斯；在欧里庇得斯的悲剧中，美狄亚既是弃妇，又是太阳神的后裔。因此，当美狄亚采取最残酷、极端的手段挑战人类情感和道德秩序时，她似乎只是在行使复仇女神的职能而已，仍然不失其"神"之逻辑和品格。也就是说，无论美狄亚是怎样的"外来者"和"异己者"，她的身份终究都带有某种先天的神圣性。这种神圣的身份相对于人类社会和文明的规范，注定是外来的、异己的。然而，在人类的集体想象中，这一"他者"也正因此而不可动摇，甚至成为永恒。

美狄亚从科尔喀斯的公主到科林斯的女奴，从希腊女神到受制于情欲的普通人，似乎是顺应了人们的普遍期待，但是人们逐渐意识到这一形象的"归顺"其实等同于"丧失"；甚至可以说她所归顺的未必是"从神到人"的文明演进，而可能是逻各斯－菲勒斯中心的惯性和秩序。因此，沃尔夫笔下的美狄亚通过新的颠覆而显示出独特的价值。

无论是神还是人，美狄亚都只能与一种古老的情感法则相联系，而与理性的秩序格格不入。美狄亚所体现的"厄洛斯"不仅是人类心灵深处最隐秘、阴暗的情感以及人性中最原始、嗜血的复仇本能，而且是迥异于男性权威和理性秩序的阴性气质。即使是决定着美狄亚的"爱情""杀子"等极端行为的"爱欲"，也同样可以通过"厄洛斯"而与神圣的、非理性的秩序相关。

因此无论是古希腊神话中的美狄亚、古希腊悲剧中的美狄亚、中世纪基督教作家笔下的美狄亚，还是后世种种出人意料又在情理之中的改写，"阴性气质"往往是"神圣"的一部分，或者正是人们对"神圣"的一种理解。于是，美狄亚的"爱情"时而以"情欲"的形式出现，时而又被改写为"博爱"（caritas）、"惠爱"（charity），甚至"圣爱"（agape）。如果说科林斯人所崇拜的女神美狄亚是"生"的神圣象征，那么美狄亚母题的变形与迁转，则可能反映了不同时代对"神圣"的追寻。

三　美狄亚母题阐释的意义

关于美狄亚母题的探寻，或许永远都难以穷尽。不过从品达的"外来者"到沃尔夫颠覆性的"声音"——以女性作家的读解对美狄亚母题的传承作结，至少可以实现一种相对的圆满。美狄亚母题的生成和延续，始终是通过"他异性"的特质而与不同时代的本质主义（essentialism）形成鲜明的对比，这当是其活力之所在、魅力之所在。也许作为逻各斯－菲勒斯中心的"永恒的他者"，其为"主体解体后寻找主体的陷阱"[1] 提供了一种解脱的可能。

---

① 李银河:《女性权力的崛起》，文化艺术出版社，2003，第189页。

第三节　塞壬的歌声——人类生存的困境

一　塞壬的传说

据说塞壬是河神阿刻罗俄斯的女儿，是从他的血液中诞生的美丽妖精。最早记录塞壬海妖的文献是荷马的《奥德赛》。喀耳刻教导奥德修斯经过墨西拿海峡时要用蜂蜡堵住其他同伴的耳朵，如果自己想听那美妙的歌声，就先叫同伴用绳索将他绑在桅杆上。然而，荷马关于塞壬的这些描述非常含糊，如奥德修斯遇到的是一个还是数个塞壬？塞壬长什么样子？从哪里诞生？居住何处？这些问题在荷马的史诗中并没有明确指出。实际上，在《荷马史诗》中，所有妖怪的形象都是模糊的，荷马对于妖怪的描写很简洁，留给后人无穷的想象空间。后来关于塞壬神话发生变化的所有文献，全部是以这个故事为出发点而不断予以变形和补充的。在后来的阐释中，塞壬神话的细节不断丰满，在填补空缺的时候，新的故事又有了新的含糊性和不确定性，神话也得以不断产生。

二　关于塞壬的各种阐释

从狭义上说，塞壬仅仅指古希腊神话中的海妖；从广义上说，塞壬则代表女海妖，但其内涵和形象在各个时代的发展中不断地发生变化。公元前 6 世纪的陶器上已出现如同幼鸽的海妖形象。公元前 490 年的希腊红陶器上所刻的塞壬形象是鸟身人面，它张着嘴，似乎正在歌唱。这一时期在另一幅描述奥德修斯和塞壬的图画上，塞壬却长有人的胳膊和胸脯，正在演奏齐特拉琴或笛子。到公元 3 世纪时，在亚历山大城流传的一部大众寓言《生理学》中，海妖被描述为恶毒的动物，从头部到肚脐眼是女人身，下半身则是鸟体。

塞壬为什么被认为是鸟身人面的妖怪？是因为水手的想象——在

海上旅行常能遇到声音悦耳的海鸟，还是因为后来的传说——塞壬的母亲乃是缪斯之一，而缪斯也有鸟身的形象，这些都不得而知。还有另一种传说，塞壬海妖是居住在冥国的，传说她们乃宙斯和得墨忒耳的女儿珀尔塞福涅的女伴。珀尔塞福涅被冥王掠为冥后，塞壬们化身为长翅膀的小鸟去寻找、陪伴珀尔塞福涅。这些温柔的塞壬们，以轻柔甜美的歌声安慰死去的亡灵，她们的形体是长着翅膀的精灵，所以往往被做成鸟身人面的陪葬品。但是根据《生理学》在7世纪的另一个版本，塞壬海妖的形象发生了变化——海妖被描述成女人、鸟和鱼尾的混合体。在8世纪的一个僧侣的著作中，海妖第一次被确定为这种形象——从头到肚脐眼为处女，长有一条布满鳞片的鱼尾。至于鱼尾的演变，恐怕来自人们的关联想象——海妖出没于海中，理所当然与鱼同类，所以当然有鱼尾。这一想象恐怕也与古希腊神话中其他海中仙女的形象有关——传说中涅柔斯的女儿们是海中仙女，因此塞壬的形象与海中仙女的形象被混淆了。在中世纪的艺术作品中，海妖的形象基本被定位为鱼尾女人，有双尾的海妖形象出现在当时的一些钱币甚至十字架上。但是，关于鸟身的记忆并没有彻底消失。在13世纪《动物志》的某些版本中，海妖是鸟身，有利爪，手里还抓着鱼；也有一些海妖的形象是两手抓鱼、有着鱼尾并赤裸着上身的女人。1250年的《动物爱情故事》是这样描绘的：海里有三种女妖，前两种上半身是女人，下半身是鱼；第三种上半身是女人，下半身是鸟。三个不同的海妖会同时唱歌奏乐，第一个吹号角，第二个弹拨竖琴，第三个则展现媚人的歌喉。这些描述混同了古希腊塞壬海妖鸟身人面和中世纪海妖人身鱼尾的形象，但保留了海妖美妙动人的音乐及歌唱以及善于魅惑人的特征。

海妖具有的魅惑人的特征，已经不仅仅限于歌声的甜美，她们被刻画成长发飘飘有着迷人的女人上身和丰满的乳房以及撩人心弦的本事，富有诱惑力，能让男子一见销魂。为了强调塞壬是妓女的代名词，各路艺术家还结合"巴比伦名妓"的形象，让塞壬海妖成为一个手持镜子、梳子，披散着金色长发的美女。同时，基督徒们重新解释了《奥德赛》中含混的关于海妖"迷惑""危险""白骨"的意义。《奥德赛》中并没有说明塞壬岛为何堆满白骨，也没有说明危险和死亡是如何发生的——"塞壬居住的海岛上尸骨累累，十分恐怖阴森"[①]。至于后世的阐释在塞壬身上堆加的种种意义，乃是作者有目的的创造，如 3 世纪的《生理学》乃是基督徒的创作，说塞壬以优美的歌声迷惑了男子，让他们昏昏欲睡，然后扑上去吞食了他们。塞壬在这里直接捕杀了男人，正所谓魔鬼最好的诱饵是女人。塞壬海妖象征着一切淫逸和享乐，塞壬的诱惑包括一切世俗的享乐——书信、戏剧、音乐、杂技，她是阻止基督徒接近上帝的障碍。在基督徒眼中，海妖几乎等同于撒旦。中世纪，《奥德赛》里的情节被传教士们重新解释了一遍：水手们用蜡塞住耳朵，不去听塞壬的歌声，表示基督徒宁可塞住耳朵，也不接受魔鬼的诱惑。奥德修斯好似基督，背负着十字架（桅杆）承受原罪，面对化身为海妖的撒旦的种种诱惑（包括甜美的歌声），以意志和对上帝的信念来克服欲念。这个时候，大船成了教会，大海里涌动着生活的波涛，而奥德修斯和船员们的航行意味着努力接近上帝的意旨。奥德修斯的海上之路是克服种种阻挠，通往天堂的路途，是另一出《天路历程》。中世纪对塞壬海妖的重新阐释是普遍现象，海妖在基督徒眼里，只保留了诱惑者的面目，即便薄伽丘、但丁的文学作品也不能避免这样的理解。

基督教禁欲主义的影响，使这一时期的海妖成为肉欲淫荡的象征。在这一时期，海妖的形象结合了"巴比伦名妓"的形象——金色长发、一手持镜、一手拿梳子。但是文艺复兴后，文学作品中的海妖形象，不再是中世纪被色情化的模样，虽然继承了美女上身、长

---

① 古斯塔夫·施瓦布：《希腊古典神话》，曹乃云译，译林出版社，1996，第 493 页。

发、鱼尾的形象，却往往被赋予了美好的性情，如安徒生童话《海的
女儿》，将美人鱼的美好形象定格在人们心中。到 15~16 世纪，一些
博物学家试图寻找现实中的海妖，将其形象与海牛联系起来，如此一
来，海妖就变得非常丑恶了。

三　有关塞壬各种阐释的原因

塞壬本来有多重形象，然而有些渐渐退隐到历史长河之中，被消
解、淡忘，甚至被变动和篡改。经过中世纪的筛选、歪曲，塞壬作为
肉欲的、淫荡的、诱惑人的色情海妖的形象被强化。是什么导致其他
几种关于塞壬的传说消失？是什么凸显了色情海妖的形象？是因为海
妖不被记录在《神谱》中，不是名门正派，还是因为中世纪的禁欲主
义者需要树立一个淫荡的反面形象作为清规戒律来说教世人？中世纪
的阐释将塞壬海妖定位为欲望与诱惑的象征。塞壬被认为是媚俗的、
放荡的、轻浮的女子，她们展现的是表面的美貌、动人的歌声，掩藏
的是居心叵测的邪恶，会给人带来灾难。过往的水手听了她们的歌
声，会被迷惑而昏然欲睡，以至触礁身亡。其实早在柏拉图的时代，
一些喜剧家就将如此定位的色情海妖搬上了舞台。公元前 4 世纪的希
腊作家帕拉埃法图斯索性明确地说："海妖就是妓女！优雅只是她们的
外表，下面掩藏的尽是邪恶、背信弃义和死亡。"按照这种定义，奥
德修斯就成了能抵御诱惑的道德典范。实际上，如果这样来解释塞壬
海妖的魅惑，《奥德赛》中的描述恰恰表明，对于欲望的诱惑，人性
是无法抵御的。因为奥德修斯的同伴们不得不用蜂蜡塞住耳朵，一旦
听到海妖的歌声，就必定会朝塞壬奔去，甚至面临死亡也毫不畏惧。
即便是机智、理性的奥德修斯也不能免除人性对欲望的好奇和渴望。
对奥德修斯来说，他要享受这样的欲望，所以他想听那歌声；因为知
道自己克服不了肉身的欲望，所以不得不用绳索绑住自己。桅杆象征
着正义与道德，绳索表示理性的力量。即使是道德典范，也仍然需要

绳索和桅杆，这说明了欲望的强大。将塞壬定义为肉欲、灾难的来源并不新鲜，宙斯为了惩罚人类使用普罗米修斯盗来的火种，就制造了一个女人潘多拉赠送给人类。潘多拉其实是宙斯的一个圈套，她携带装有各种灾难的瓶子来到人间。潘多拉的外表是"一位温柔可爱的少女，模样像永生女神"，[①]令人和神看了都惊叹，但赫耳墨斯"给她一颗不知羞耻的心和欺诈的天性"[②]。潘多拉将灾难从瓶子里放出，自身则有着强大的性欲和食欲。

对塞壬灾难性的肉欲的定位，与潘多拉如出一辙。淫荡的塞壬在中世纪禁欲主义者那里，被发挥到极致，以至人们都忘记了原初的塞壬还代表着多种可能的意义。其实，古希腊还有另外一种对塞壬的描述——海妖的歌声象征宇宙和谐的七重天，这个观点认为音乐是解放人的魂灵最理想的途径，竖琴的七弦象征宇宙的七重天。柏拉图以为，哲学家设计了宇宙八环，每一环都站有一个海妖，各发一个音，八音齐奏宇宙的和谐旋律。这里的塞壬接近于缪斯。文艺复兴时期，新柏拉图主义者重新推崇海妖的歌唱，将其等同于精神的感知。在彼特拉克的作品中，塞壬就是以缪斯的形象出现的。塞壬能知道过去、现在，并可以预知未来。西塞罗在《论目的》中说："勾摄海船水手魂魄的既不是她们的声音，也不是她们的歌，而是她们绝对知晓事理。"在拜占庭时期，学者们通常以"海妖塞壬"互相称呼，这种头衔相当于"博士"的称号。他们还说，荷马就是一个"塞壬"。但关于博学的海妖的说法，后来似乎没有更广泛地流传下去，而这一进程的中断，大概是中世纪色情海妖形象的广泛流传所致。

四 结论

回首塞壬海妖走过的路程，可以发现人类文明的足迹：历史是阐

---

① 赫西俄德:《工作与时日》，张竹明、蒋平译，商务印书馆，2006，第3页。
② 赫西俄德:《工作与时日》，张竹明、蒋平译，商务印书馆，2006，第3页。

释的历史。在文献典籍里，在口耳相传的故事中，在水手的想象里，在科学家所谓的发现里，在文学家的描绘中，在传教士的道德训诫下，我们看到的不是一个神话，也不是一种类型的塞壬海妖。塞壬以各种形式，裂变成各种形象，在塞壬形象的迷雾中，要想找到本真的塞壬，无疑是可笑的。塞壬神话的意义就在于这些"不同"：不同的塞壬，不同的叙事，不同的目的，不同的意义。在无尽的阐释中，我们试图发现"真正的塞壬"，而"真正的塞壬"之所以找不到或许就在于根本没有"塞壬"。塞壬就如同缪斯，她们知晓过去、现在，能够预知将来，因为她们跟随着人类文明一直前行，所以有着穿越时空的记忆和知晓一切的能力。

第四节　从纳西索斯神话看声音的现象学价值

一　声音的意义

克里斯蒂娃批评结构主义将语言设想为静态的同质结构，将语言简化到逻辑命题那样的层次，简化到能够为理性随时把握的层次。她的符号论揭示了语言基本的异质性，并且关乎话语以及话语的言说主体。

二　纳西索斯神话

古希腊神话中还有一则故事说明了女性被男性拒斥的悲哀。水仙神长得非常英俊，常常顾影自怜。回音神爱上了他，却发现除了模仿他讲话外，不能用其他任何方法表达自己的爱。有一回，纳西索斯（Narcissus）越过群山对她喊："让我们彼此融合！"艾蔻(Echo)满心欢喜地跑到他在的地方，正想伸出双臂拥抱他，他却大声说："拿开你的手！我宁愿死，也不愿让你占有我！""占有我，"女神说，可是没用。从那以后，她一直居住在山林中，直到香消玉殒，只剩下了声音。这声音在主流话语中不具有任何有效性，只能回荡在山谷崖壁之间。

声音只有在被听见时才具有意义，发声的主体通过声音获得认可，这种认可不仅是他者的认证，也是自我的认证。各种语音符号被主体听见，主体并不会越到自我之外直接被表达的活动所影响。"我的言语是活的，因为看来它们没有离开我：它们没有在我之外、在我的气息之外落入可见的远离之中，它们不间断地归属于我，并且无条件地归我所支配。因此，无论如何，声音的现象表现为现象学的声音。"[1] 通过声音，主体获得一种存在的确认，得知自己活着并且也让他者感觉到自己活着。

三 声音的现象学价值

声音的现象学价值即它相对于任何其他能指的实体之尊严的超验性。声音的"表面超验性"系于总是身为理想本质的所指，即被表达的意义直接指向表达活动在场的东西。这种直接的在场系于能指的现象学"身体"（corps）在它产生时就似乎消失的东西上，能指似乎已经属于理想性的因素。从现象学角度看，它自我还原，把自我身体的世俗不透明性改造为纯粹的半透明性。这种可感身体的消失与其外在性的消失，在意识看来就是所指直接在场的形式本身。

因素是符号中最理想的原因在于，它与主体之间具有同谋关系。当我说话时，它具有在我说话时期待的活动过程的现象学本质。被赋予活力的能指由于我的气息和意义的意向是与我绝对接近的。活生生的活动，就是给出生命，赋予能指身体以活力并把身体改造为"意谓"的表达的活力，就是语言的灵魂。它不与自身分离，也不与它的

---

① 德里达：《声音与现象》，杜小真译，商务印书馆，2002，第96页。

自我在场分离。它能指出理想的对象和理想的意义，这种理想的对象或意义并没有在理想性、自我在场生命的内在性之外被遭遇。

声音赋予主体生命力，在透明精神性中活跃着的自我在场对自身的生命内在性进行了设定：说话的主体在现在被听见。这就是言语的本质或正常状态，涉及说话者所期待的言语结构本身，同时发现现象的可感形式并了解其固有的表达意向。如果一些事故发生，似乎驳斥了这种目的论的必然性，那么它们或者被某种补充过程所超越，或者没有言语。缄默和耳聋双双而至。聋子只有把这些活动悄悄塞入词的形式中才能参加讨论会，这些词的最终目标意味着它们被那些使其发出声音的人听见。从纯粹现象学的角度看，在还原的内部，言语的进程就具有了已经表现为纯粹现象学的生命力，它已经把自然立场和世界存在的论题悬搁起来。"被听见—说话"的过程是一种独特类型的自我影响。一方面，在这个过程中显现的能指应该是一些理想性，人们应该理想地重复这些理想性或把它们作为同样的理想性来传递。另一方面，主体能够被听见或对自己说话，任凭自己被能指所影响，这是主体根据内在要求、世界或一般非本性的要求而毫无转折地制造的能指。

声音在世界上扩散时不会遇到任何障碍，这恰恰由于它是作为纯粹的自我影响在世界上产生的。这种自我影响可能是人们称作主体性或自为的东西的可能性；但是，若没有它，任何世界都不可能显现出来。这种普遍性从结构上讲有权利使任何意识只要离开声音就变得不可能。声音是在普遍形式下靠近自我的作为意识的存在，声音是意识。向某人说话，可能听见的是自己说话，被自我听见。但同时，如果人们被别人听见，也就是使别人在我造成了"被听见—说话"的形式下在自我中直接地重复。

亚里士多德把野蛮人和奴隶说成是"缺乏语言的存在物"。这当然不是说野蛮人和奴隶在生理上缺乏说话的能力，而是说他们被剥夺了使自己的发言具有意义的权利。女人们是扮演着和奴隶相同角色的群体,当然也失去了自己的声音,而这一过程被"法律"合理化了。本来"权力"之神和"暴力"之神乃是宙斯王座趋前附后的扈从,象征着神圣权力的暴虐和非理性的猖獗。德里达说过:"话语就是一切,文本已经死去。"(There is nothing outside the text)古代的女人没有文本也没有对文本的诠释——话语。"一种无书写的声音绝对是活生生的,而同时又是绝对死亡的",[1] 不论是赫尔墨斯为众神传送的信还是教会的释经(exegesis),在很多情况下,"经"之所以成为"经",都是阐释的结果。因此,对经典的阐释活动往往体现着某种权力意识。[2] 女性在漫长的历史进程中,只剩下一种无书写的声音,当这种声音也被淹没了,究竟是谁让她们既是活着的,又是死去的?

有种女性主义分析倾向于人体解释学,强调女性是用不同的主体或感性来体验世界,主张"话语是分性别的"的。男权社会的历史是有意识地淹没女性声音的历史,这种淹没使女性在失去主体性的同时也让男性感觉到深刻的无聊。无聊就是无话可说,无话可说的一个原因是没有人听你说,既然作为世界另一半的女性被物化,那么男性也相应地失去了能够理解自己的听众。

声音是主体性确认的一种方式,女性声音的缺失不仅使女性失去了存在的价值,也使男性存在的意义受到了质疑:意义在与他者的关系中凸显。失去了女性这个整体的"他者",男性的世界成为一种单向度的存在,一种得不到确认的自恋。沃尔夫对卡桑德拉和美狄亚神话的改写就是揭示女性声音被淹没的历史真相,是一种努力让女性重新说话的尝试。

---

① 德里达:《声音与现象》,杜小真译,商务印书馆,1999,第131页。
② 杨慧林:《移动的边界》,中国大百科全书出版社,2002,第176页。

第五节 自由、正义与死亡——安提戈涅的象征

一 引言

安提戈涅（Antigone，希腊语解释为怪物），一个令人震撼的名字，从《荷马史诗》开始，通过索福克勒斯的渲染，历经黑格尔、拉康、玛莎·纳斯鲍姆、朱迪斯·巴特勒等众多哲学家的分析，成了人类文明上空的达摩克利斯之剑，成了人类社会思想史上的北斗星，成了哲学、法学、文学、伦理学、精神分析学、女性主义等诸多学科争夺的对象。

文学家从安提戈涅身上看到了英雄牺牲的悲剧美；哲学家从安提戈涅身上看到了爱与正义的碰撞；法学家从安提戈涅身上看到了国家法、自然法、人法和神法的冲突；政治家从安提戈涅身上看到了人权与主权的对立；伦理学家从安提戈涅身上看到了乱伦与社会秩序的不相容；女性主义者则从安提戈涅身上看到了反叛与抗拒的可贵。

黑格尔在讲述苏格拉底命运的时候曾经引用"安提戈涅"的例子，并赞誉她是"在大地上出现过的最壮丽的形象"[1]。能成为众多学科争相研究的对象，能成为众多大家评说的话题，安提戈涅一定不凡。那么，她究竟有何魅力，受到人们几千年的阐释，并获得了中西方的共同关注？答案是象征，安提戈涅的象征——象征着自由、正义与死亡。她是一个符号，代表着反抗——反抗男权社会的秩序、理性、制度、法治；代表着思索——思索人类社会的法治、秩序、理性、制度。而无论是反抗的象征，还是思索的动物，安提戈涅都是一种超越现实的存在。

---

[1] 黑格尔：《哲学史讲演录》第2卷，贺麟、王太庆译，商务印书馆，1997，第102页。

二 故事情节

忒拜国王俄狄浦斯弑父娶母，并生有二子二女：一子波吕涅刻斯，另一子厄特俄科勒斯；一女安提戈涅，另一女伊斯墨涅。波吕涅刻斯与厄特俄科勒斯为争夺王位，兵戎相见。波吕涅刻斯率岳父城邦的军队攻打忒拜，厄特俄科勒斯率军抵抗，最后两人都战死沙场。克瑞翁——俄狄浦斯王之母（妻）的弟弟，俄狄浦斯的舅舅（小舅子）继任了城邦的王位。为惩罚叛徒，克瑞翁下令不许安葬波吕涅刻斯，违者处死。俄狄浦斯之女安提戈涅为死去的弟弟举行了象征性的葬礼——在波吕涅刻斯的尸体上偷偷地撒上了一层土（连续两次）。安提戈涅的这一行为挑战了克瑞翁的政令，也导致了自己的死亡。妹妹伊斯墨涅试图劝说安提戈涅，却遭到安提戈涅的斥责。在安提戈涅被关后，伊斯墨涅表示要陪姐姐一起赴死，但遭到安提戈涅的拒绝。

安提戈涅这样做的理由是，即使哥哥是叛徒，也应当得到安葬，因为人死后入土为安是天神制定的永恒不变的不成文法。克瑞翁也尝试宽恕安提戈涅，但是她宁愿死也不放弃自己的责任，克瑞翁在盛怒之下判安提戈涅死刑，即将其关进墓室，让其自然死亡。

安提戈涅的未婚夫、克瑞翁之子海蒙去找父亲，希望他能够倾听百姓的声音，收回成命，然而克瑞翁不仅一意孤行，而且斥责了自己的儿子。最后，海蒙为了爱情而自杀，而海蒙的母亲即克瑞翁的妻子也随之自杀。于是，克瑞翁成了"孤家寡人"而陷于极度的痛苦之中。

三 安提戈涅的"英雄主义情结"

对于源自古希腊神话的这一母题，后世进行了多次重述。最著名的当数黑格尔的阐释，而黑格尔的阐释又引发了现代、后现代的更多阐释，其中荷尔德林、海德格尔、德里达、拉康、伊瑞格瑞、齐泽克、朱迪斯·巴特勒、玛莎·纳斯鲍姆的阐释尤为引人瞩目。这些后世的阐释从伦理学、哲学、精神分析学、女性主义等不同角度展开，使这一母题所蕴含的意味得到了空前的挖掘，并在意义不断丰富的基础上进一步扩大了人类思想的维度。

虽然国内对安提戈涅的研究仍然集中于法学界，但是晚近十年对国外安提戈涅研究的介绍，逐渐拓宽了这一研究领域，尤其是对伯纳德特的古希腊文本细读的翻译整理以及对玛莎·纳斯鲍姆的古希腊伦理学（哲学）的文学研究的介绍，使国内学人对安提戈涅这一古希腊神话母题所承载的思想意义有了新的认识。

在对安提戈涅母题研究的梳理过程中，首先不能回避的应当是古希腊神话。在古希腊神话思维中，安提戈涅具有古希腊人所极力推崇的"英雄主义情结"。在古希腊的文化氛围中，"勇敢"与"对荣誉的追求"总是相伴而生，被古希腊人视为"美德"。安提戈涅之所以被载入史册并成为一种"经典"，就在于她所具备的这种"勇敢"的品质以及"对荣誉的追求"的美德。虽然在黑格尔的阐释中，安提戈涅的这种"勇敢"以及她"对荣誉的追求"有些固执、片面，但仍不失英雄所为。尤其是在女性主义的解读中，安提戈涅就是一个敢于反抗男权社会的典范，是所有女性都应该效仿的楷模。而后世所有对安提戈涅"英雄主义情结"的赞美、对其"苏格拉底式的殉道"的肯定，都来自古希腊神话的这种定位。然而，在古希腊神话的最初阐释中，安提戈涅并非如黑格尔阐释所定位的那样——是家庭伦理实体的代表，因为在故事发生的年代，还没有"伦理实体"这个概念。即使是女性主义的安提戈涅解读，也有"偏颇之嫌"，因为女性主义研究者认为，安提戈涅与克瑞翁的对立，是女性与男性的对立。也就是说，古希腊神话阐释中的安提戈涅，虽然"勇敢"，却不像黑格尔阐释的那样——"有意识的勇敢"。同样，古希腊神话阐释中的安提戈涅虽然是"英雄"，却非女性主义阐释中那种"有性别对抗意识的英雄"。换言之，古希腊神话阐释中安提戈涅的"英雄主义情结"，只是古希腊文化氛围中简单的"英雄主义情结"，而没有后世添加的种种"光环"。

将安提戈涅的"英雄主义情结"还原到"英雄时代"，我们会发现，安提戈涅与克瑞翁的对立既是两种最高伦理的对立，也是女性与男性的对立（虽然当事人并没有这种意识），而引发这种对立的因素，就是社会形态的更替、社会制度的健全以及社会观念的变迁。

一方面是家族伦理的衰落，另一方面是城邦政治的兴起，但这两者的关系无论是在制度上还是在普遍的社会意识形态上均未最终形成稳定的格局。安提戈涅和克瑞翁则在无意识中分别代表了这两种具有一定合理性的诉求。

安提戈涅的故事发生在英雄时代（古希腊神话记载）。"英雄"这个限定词表明，当时城邦还没有真正确立，人们还受限于自身的情感，即他们已经习惯的家庭伦理。即使是索福克勒斯笔下的"安提戈涅"，恐怕也很难接受亚里士多德的观点——这是一种城邦确立之后的社会政治意识形态：人是城邦的动物，城邦有别于而且在本性上先于包括家庭在内的任何其他社会团体。英雄时代的政治权威往往来自那些勇武高尚的人及其家族，政治权威和行使政治权威的人是混在一起的。但是在城邦，形成了一种政治性的权威体系，这一体系往往借助一些重大的政治事件、军事冲突或其他意外事件而形成。其中，最著名的事件就是与安提戈涅的故事几乎同时发生的特洛伊战争。

在特洛伊战争中，阿喀琉斯身上体现了不可遏制的"英雄主义情结"，即使为此牺牲生命也在所不惜，安提戈涅同样如此。在阿喀琉斯和安提戈涅生活的英雄时代，格外强调个人的荣誉。虽然这种对荣誉的追求有时显得鲁莽（如安提戈涅），有时甚至显得凶残（如阿喀琉斯），但这就是古希腊人真实的生存状态。对阿喀琉斯来说，只有"荣誉"能够配得上他的高贵出身——海洋女神忒提斯的儿子；对安提戈涅来说，只有反抗克瑞翁的命令埋葬波吕涅刻斯，才配得上她王室成员的高贵身份。在那个英雄时代，只有勇敢的人才是高贵的人，只有高贵的人才能成为统治者。安提戈涅对这一点深信不疑，所以她拒绝了伊斯墨涅的请求并报之以嘲笑。在这一点上，安提戈涅与阿喀琉斯有所不同：安提戈涅是王室成员而阿喀琉斯不是，所以阿喀琉斯追求的只是"荣誉"，而安提戈涅除了追求"荣誉"还注重行为的高贵性。也就是说，安提戈涅认为自己的行为是高贵的，只有她才配得上王室成员的称号，而伊斯墨涅不配。

在古代缺乏强有力且普遍有效的政治法律秩序的情况下，这种高度个体化的人格是可以替代政治制度的。一方面，这种"英雄的个人魅力"是进行统治的保障；另一方面，这种"英雄主义"或"个人主义"却成为成熟社会的政治制度的障碍，因为它可能与国家法律发生强烈冲突。首先，有强烈的个人荣誉感或者英雄主义情结的个人，是排斥政治秩序和科层化制度的。在崇拜英雄的时代，人们更多支持的是血缘的神圣以及个人的勇武和魅力，这是古代一种建立在家族之上的个人主义。如果政治法律秩序已经初步形成，那么，这种个人英雄主义的品格也会抵制、排斥和妨碍制度的有效运作。安提戈涅的英雄主义就印证了这一点。

安提戈涅的英雄主义不仅是个人主义的，也是贵族式的。一个普通人不可能具有这种心态，也只有在她先前的生活环境中才可能培养出这种无视行为后果、目中无人的贵族心态。这是一种大无畏的精神，虽然激动人心，但未必是明智的，尤其是对于成长中的城邦来说，这或许是具有毁灭性的。

安提戈涅和克瑞翁的冲突就发生在这种社会变迁的宏大背景下。故事一开始，安提戈涅的家庭就已经瓦解了。在一定意义上，俄狄浦斯王弑父娶母，意味着血缘社会已经"礼崩乐坏"。两兄弟刀兵相见，意味着血缘关系已无法解决政治冲突。在这种社会背景下，克瑞翁代表的是正在形成、尚不稳固的城邦政治制度，而安提戈涅代表的是正在衰落，但影响仍然巨大且永远不会完全消失的作为一种制度的血缘家族伦理。在这个意义上，克瑞翁代表的是一种变革的力量，而安提戈涅代表的是一种保守的力量。尽管"激进"与"保守"在此都不具有褒贬之义。

虽说是"代表"，但事实上克瑞翁与安提戈涅都没有清醒的意识。也就是说，克瑞翁并没有意识到他代表的是新兴的政治制度，而安提戈涅也没有意识到她代表的是正在退出历史舞台的血缘政治制度。克瑞翁能够肯定的是，他这样做是为了巩固城邦的发展、巩固自己的统治。安提戈涅能够肯定的是，她所做的是为了维护古老的神律。如果克瑞翁更审慎一些或者安提戈涅更理智一些，如果他们两个人都不固执于自己的价值观或不过于坚持自己的原则，那么新旧制度的这种惨烈碰撞就可以避免。

安提戈涅是悲剧性的，因为她过去生活的时代已经过去了，永远不会再回来；她现在生活的时代不再需要英雄了，也不允许贵族的心态存在了（这并不是说贵族不存在，只是说贵族精神不再存在了）。可是，她自己却未能意识到这一点。克瑞翁也是悲剧性的，他在社会变革压力的推动下，要对城邦和未来负责，尽管这种负责对他自己也是有利的，但是他遭到了来自旧势力的、保守派的抵触。从这个角度来说，克瑞翁是弱者，因为挑战已经长久确立的家族伦理体制和意识形态意味着失败甚至牺牲。因此，尽管克瑞翁拥有政治权力，似乎还很强大，但这种权力在转型时期是不稳定的。他只是一位僭主。

四 结论

正义同样是一个亘古不变的话题。在古希腊神话中，就有代表正义的雅典娜；至古典理性主义时期，又有苏格拉底对正义美德的认定。正义不仅是哲学的诉求、法的目标，也是政治的手段。对正义的追求，在人类文明史上从来就没有停止过。也因此，有了关于俄瑞斯忒斯弑母案的审判，有了苏格拉底的审判，也有了安提戈涅的死亡。正义是一面旗帜，它始终引导着人类社会的前进——哲学的正义、法的正义、政治的正义、道德的正义，人类不断地修正自己的思想和行为，向着完美迈进；然而，正义又是一面幌子，它始终诱导着人类社会前进——战争的正义、专制的正义、迫害的正义，人类不断为自己的错误找寻着冠冕堂皇的借口、为自己的贪欲找寻着正当的理由。也因此，才有了克瑞翁认为的正义、安提戈涅认为的正义、苏格拉底认为的正义。正义究竟是什么？什么样的正义是具有公共性的、是普遍性的、是不被利用的？

　　死亡，与自由和正义一样，也是亘古不变的话题。没有谁能够摆脱它的纠缠，也没有谁能够逃离它的掌控。To be or not to be——莎士比亚笔下那个忧郁的丹麦王子一直思索、困惑的问题，至今仍然让我们思索和困惑。五百年了，这个问题一直困扰着我们。或者说，从人类开始思考的时候，这个问题就在困扰着我们。对于这个问题，各种各样的人用不同的方式思索并得出了各种各样的答案，可是，这些答案并不能解决我们的困惑。为什么？这是一个吊诡（paradox），是斯芬克斯之谜——这个谜并没有因为斯芬克斯的坠崖、俄狄浦斯的智慧而被破解，反而因为斯芬克斯之死和俄狄浦斯的命运而更加匪夷所思。我们可以为了正义选择死亡、可以为了自由选择死亡，也可以选择死亡来放弃自由与正义，但是，关于正义、自由与死亡的勾连，我们仍不能作答。

　　安提戈涅就是这样一个巨大的隐喻。在这个隐喻中，自由、正义、死亡紧密交叉在一起——你无从分清自由与死亡、正义与死亡、自由与正义的关系，但是，你又非常清楚它们都在安提戈涅的身上体现。这就是永恒的吊诡，也是永恒的安提戈涅。

第三章　古希腊城邦与政治

第一节　古希腊城邦制度的兴起

一　迈锡尼文明

《荷马史诗》描绘了迈锡尼人的文明，近代考古发现了迈锡尼人的陶器、雕塑、工具、墓葬、建筑等，并发掘出《荷马史诗》中描绘的特洛伊城。考古证据显示，迈锡尼人在富庶的东方和西北方蛮荒的欧洲大陆之间从事掮客、海盗、小规模的制造业，并经营一点农业。他们掠夺弱小落后的邻居，与不易掠夺的强大国家进行商品贸易，贩卖武器、奴隶、木材、原料、金属工具、首饰、香料及皮革。其贸易网东至小亚细亚半岛，西到南意大利和西西里岛、法国沿海地区、西班牙，甚至英伦三岛。如同他们的后辈，迈锡尼人未能克服地理障碍而建成统一的帝国，仅在希腊本土和爱琴海岛屿上建立了许多小型王国，而这些小国的社会管理水平达到了相当高的水准。在希腊本土发现的皮罗斯国（Pylos）的政府档案显示，其王室的集中统治是经由组织完善而且机构复杂的官僚体系实现的，这个体系分区管理税收征集、货物分配和宗教生活等事务，而且建有监督机构来控制腐败和纠正行政错误，这种专业化的机构显然不属于农业社会。这些小国政治上互不隶属，在语言文化上却保持高度一致，说明他们之间的商业和文化交流非常密切。一位西方文明史专家就迈锡尼人获得的成就评论道："其高峰时期的文明比公元前 6 世纪的希腊文明更发达。"公元前 6 世纪的上半期是雅典的梭伦时代，下半期是雅典比西特拉图父子的僭主时期。

二　多利亚人的入侵和"英雄时代"

在公元前 1200 年左右，即我国商朝末期，迈锡尼文明持续了二百年的繁荣发展被突然打断，一些讲另一种希腊方言的野蛮部落从北部侵入，他们大约是进入希腊地区的最后一个讲希腊语的部落。这些被称为多利亚人（Dorians）的部落摧毁了迈锡尼文明。一些迈锡尼人向东逃亡到未被铁蹄践踏的阿提卡平原（Attica，即雅典地区），以及爱琴海上的岛屿和小亚细亚沿岸，如后来的复兴基地爱奥尼亚地区。公元前 1190 年左右（即我国西周开始的前夕），在小亚细亚的爱琴海沿岸爆发了特洛伊战争，那大概是迈锡尼人逃亡过程的一段插曲。自此到公元前 8 世纪，希腊和爱琴海地区陷入了史学家所称的"黑暗时代"，作为多利亚人和迈锡尼人后裔的古希腊人则据《荷马史诗》称其为"英雄时代"，是"巨人在大地上行走，留下无数奇迹"的时代。考古发现，那时希腊各部落王国间的联系中断了，各地形成了不同的方言和不同的陶艺风格。由于邻近的两大帝国也处于被侵略的混乱状态中，希腊与东方的联系中断了。写作的技艺失传了，雄伟的宫殿坍塌了，地中海上的希腊商船没有了，商业财富消失了，墓葬里不再出现大量的金银制品，整个地区倒退回简单的农业社会。然而，讲不同方言的希腊人仍然能彼此交流，迈锡尼文明并未被彻底摧毁，后来古希腊文明中的一些重要部分是迈锡尼文明的翻版。

代表多利亚文明的斯巴达人把迈锡尼人的后裔变成了奴隶。

三　迈锡尼文明的意义

迈锡尼文明的兴起和衰落与世界其他文明史有相通之处：无论先进还是落后，也不管奉行哪种政治制度，（军事上的）安全是最终的保障。没有能力维持自身安全的文明是虚弱的文明。换言之，民族的兴衰不仅与文明的政治制度相关，还与能否持续地拥有强盛的军事力量相关。不能维系强大军事力量的政治制度是有重大缺陷的制度。

虽然那不是一个完美的时代，却是人类历史上少有的世人能够追求自由、张扬个性的时代。人们活着，不是为了崇拜，而是为了探求、感知、思考与自我实现。所以，这个时代的苏格拉底才会说：未经审视的人生，不值得一过。这个时代虽没有现代科技，但其明亮、纯真、充满神性的自由之风却在其后几千年的人类史上很少见到。为何今天的爱琴海仍然如此美丽？因为这浩瀚的海面之上，那永不停息的海风一直在讲述着史诗般的英雄故事与诸神传说。

四　古希腊的社会结构与城邦政体

希腊城邦政体的历史是英雄创造的历史，也是一部关于阶级力量对比的社会结构史。换言之，是英雄和人民共同创造的历史。在我国进入春秋时代（公元前 722 年）时，即公元前 8 世纪晚期，希腊的自由小农力量突然增强，阻碍了贵族阶层扩大耕地面积、变自由小农为农奴等。阶级力量对比的突然变化在当时的古希腊引发了普遍的政治危机。

中国传统社会的发展条件比较优越，既是以自由小农为主体的社会，又有大一统的帝国结构来支撑文明的发展。由于地理条件造成的交通困难，古希腊难以形成大型帝国。然而，由于黑暗时期留下的农民简朴的生活习惯，体量庞大的小农经济在希腊的"黑暗时代"一直存在，并像近东地区发达的帝国那样演变成贵族世家的附属。古希腊自由小农人数和势力的突然增长与普遍使用铁器有关，也同殖民扩张中的军事发明有关。

城邦起初不是城市，而是以部落血缘关系为基础的居民点。一些居民点逐渐发展成商业和议事中心，随后出现了庙宇、其他公共建筑和议事广场。以不同的宗教团体为核心，不同的城邦形成了自己特殊的认同，部落血缘意识逐渐淡化。紧接着在对外战争中出现了类似于今天的爱国主义精神，替代宗教和个人主义成为古希腊各城邦内聚力的支柱。城邦的第一个政治结果是王的消失和贵族统治的确立。古希腊地区的"王"大约相当于酋长一类，作战英勇和家庭财富是这种职位的基础。但这种"王"无力迫使整个地区定期定量缴纳税收，以致财政地位虚弱，组织能力有限。重甲步兵时代到来后，"王"的统治地位逐渐被贵族集团取代。城邦的第二个政治后果是贵族寡头统治受到自身派系和重甲步兵阶层的挑战，个人专制是最简单也最普遍的解决方式，而且专制者经常反对贵族，也最能吸引平民。城邦的第三个政治后果是公民们不间断地寻求理想的政府形式，以便建成稳定、中立的公共权威，获得当时公认的社会正义，初级法治或寡头法治是他们探寻的结果。城邦的第四个政治后果是各社会和经济集团都要求政府对自身利益负责，占人口多数的平民导致了直接民主制的出现。

五 民主制与城邦的兴衰

与前述两百年一样，古希腊后来的两百年既不是民主与专制斗争的历史，也不是民主发展史。一些意识形态斗争的行家会把 20 世纪描绘成民主与专制斗争的历史，或者是民主战胜专制的历史。他们有意遗忘了第一次世界大战是帝国主义瓜分世界的战争。战前的法国并不比德国民主，战后的德国则比法国民主得多。十月革命不是民主对专制的斗争，中国推翻清朝封建统治的革命也不是以民主反对专制，而是怒其不争，怒其无力将四万万散漫的小农组织起来，抵抗帝国主义对中国的瓜分，因此有了国民党人的"军政"和共产党人的奋起。他们把第二次世界大战也描绘成民主与专制的斗争，而那场战争分明是第一次世界大战的结果，或者说是继续。德国不是因为痛恨民主制度而入侵捷克、波兰、法国和苏联，日本也不是因为痛恨民主制度才侵略中国、夏威夷和东南亚。苏美同盟和中美同盟的目标是保卫祖国、战胜侵略者，而不是扩散民主制。这些人还对第二次世界大战之后风起云涌的民族解放运动持虚无态度，因为这数十个新兴国家浴血奋战的对象恰恰是西方民主国家。回顾冷战的历史，美苏各自在第三世界寻找盟友，中国在其间纵横捭阖，到底谁在为民主而奋斗？冷战后美国针对前苏联和中国的政策更为冷战的目的做了注脚。冷战无论如何也不是民主与专制之争，反而与雅典和斯巴达之间的伯罗奔尼撒战争有些相似。

六　结语

古希腊的政治制度是多样化的，这与那个时代剧烈的社会变迁相关，也与各城邦、各地区不同的社会条件和历史传统相关。人们可以评论制度的优劣，但所有现实必有其原因。对社会科学家而言，不是所有的原因都可以归纳为主观意志和价值观念，社会构成就是不以主观意志为转移的原因。所以，对某种政治制度的偏好可能导致这种制度的出现甚至确立，但同样的制度不可能在不同的地方导致同样的结果。

第二节　雅典与斯巴达的不同

一　引言

雅典和斯巴达是古希腊两个最大且最具代表性的奴隶制城邦国

家。将雅典和斯巴达加以比较，一方面可以看出两者所具有的相同之处。首先，二者都是古希腊地区当之无愧的最强大的城邦。其次，二者均是小国寡民的城邦。因为受地理环境的影响，雅典与斯巴达的发展受限。再次，二者都是奴隶制国家，内部出现了贵族奴隶主阶级，并且这一阶级在古希腊政治体制中产生了很大影响。另一方面，也可以发现两者的不同之处。若想了解雅典和斯巴达的不同，则要具体了解这两个城邦是如何发展起来的。本节通过分析雅典和斯巴达的发展历程来分析它们之间的差异究竟有哪些，对于我们有哪些启示。

二　雅典和斯巴达的形成

以雅典和斯巴达为代表的希腊城邦，在公元前 5 世纪繁荣发展，从公元前 4 世纪起逐渐衰落。由于贫富分化加剧，公民权与土地的关系日趋松弛，公民集体内部矛盾激化，公民兵制开始瓦解。公元前 338 年马其顿国王亚历山大大帝的讨伐以及公元前 323 年至公元前 30 年的希腊化时代许多国王对希腊的奴役，瓦解了希腊绝大多数城邦的政治独立和原有的公民集体，使这些城邦演变成庞大的中央集权管辖下的地方自治单位。

1. 雅典

雅典位于希腊东南部的阿提卡半岛。公元前 1600 年左右，爱奥尼亚人进入阿提卡与当地居民皮拉斯基人混居，过着氏族部落制的生活。到了荷马时代，杂居现象日益普遍，阶级矛盾和社会分化不断加剧。为了适应这一变化，改变这一现状，传说中的英雄忒修斯进行了改革，把阿提卡半岛各个分裂部落统一起来，以雅典的中央议事会和政府代替各地方议事会和政府，并制定了雅典第一部宪法。忒修斯改革的另一重要内容是把国内公民分为贵族、农民和手工业者三个等级，规定贵族担任官职、执行法律，农民和手工业者只在公民大会中有一席之地，不能当官掌权。这样一来，公民中贵族和平民（农民和手工业者）的划分便很明显，为日后雅典的贵族政治奠定了基础。这场改革实际上反映了雅典在阶级分化的基础上从部落走向国家的历史性转变，忒修斯也被视为国家的奠基者。通常认为，这是雅典国家形态的萌芽。至公元前 700 年左右，阿提卡全境已经形成了以雅典为中心的统一奴隶制国家。公元前 8 世纪，王权衰落，政权由氏族贵族执掌。自公元前 682 年起，执政官一年一选。公元前 7 世纪形成了由 9 名执政官分别掌管国家行政、军事、司法和宗教事务的局面。

2. 斯巴达

斯巴达位于伯罗奔尼撒半岛东南部的拉哥尼亚平原，居民原为多利亚人，非本地人。在迈锡尼文明时期（公元前 16 世纪上半叶至公元前 12 世纪），拉哥尼亚境内出现了国家。公元前 1100 年左右，多利亚人开始入侵拉哥尼亚，经过长期斗争消灭了原有国家。斯巴达人掠夺了当地的土地和财富后把当地居民贬低为"庇里阿西人"（自由民，在本地有自治权，但是没有斯巴达城邦的公民权），对不满于斯巴达统治的反抗者予以镇压，并将其贬低为"希洛人"，也被称为"黑劳士"（属于斯巴达集体所有的农业奴隶）。约公元前 10 世纪，多利亚人建立了斯巴达城。该城由五个村落组合成一个新的政治中心，虽名之为城，但实际上既没有城墙，也没有像样的街道。公元前 8 世纪中叶，随着社会分化的加剧和人口的增加，为了解决土地不足的问题，斯巴达人一方面向外殖民，另一方面入侵美塞尼亚，史称第一次美塞尼亚战争（公元前 740 年至公元前 720 年）。结果，斯巴达人占领了整个美塞尼亚，并将其居民变成了希洛人，将侵占的土地分配给斯巴达人与庇里阿西人：前者分得平原，后者分得山区。公元前 640 年至公元前 620 年，美塞尼亚人不堪奴役与压迫进行起义，史称第二次美塞尼亚战争，虽然给斯巴达人以沉重打击，但最后还是失败了。

三 雅典与斯巴达的差异

作为伯罗奔尼撒半岛的两个城邦巨头，雅典和斯巴达是古希腊两个著名的城邦。它们军事力量强大，各自建立军事同盟称霸希腊，是典型的奴隶制城邦，在经济上和政治上具有代表性。它们都重视体育，女子与男子一样参加体育锻炼。但是，由于地理环境和历史条件等差异，雅典和斯巴达又存在诸多不同之处。本节就雅典与斯巴达的不同问题进行论述。

1. 经济状况

希腊奴隶制经济的发展可分为两大类型，即斯巴达型和雅典型。斯巴达地处拉哥尼亚平原，南部临海且三面环山，中部有犹罗达河灌溉，气候温和，土壤肥沃，这种自然地理特点决定了斯巴达是一个以农业为主的城邦。斯巴达国内还实行土地国有制及国有奴隶制，奴隶多是掳掠来的被征服地的居民。雅典虽以农业为基础，但工商业比较发达，农业中经济作物占有很大比重，如葡萄、橄榄等作物。雅典山区有着丰富的矿产资源，如大理石、银矿、陶土资源等，对雅典的手工业发展提供了极大的便利。奴隶的来源也和斯巴达不同，多是通过市场买来的，用于社会生活的各个方面。

就整个希腊而言，当时用于农业生产的奴隶可以分三种情况。其一，斯巴达式的国有奴隶制，农业劳动全部由国有奴隶希洛人负责。这种奴隶制度往往通过征服来确立。其二，贵族田产中使用奴隶，是农业生产中使用私人奴隶的普遍方式，但规模不大，也不普遍。其三，自耕农或小农私有或使用的奴隶，是这一时期最为发达的农业奴隶经济形式。此外，奴隶还被广泛应用在手工业、商业、矿山开采和家务劳动等各个方面，这种情况在工商业比较发达的雅典等城邦比较普遍，反映了当时希腊社会的私有化比较彻底，市场交换原则在社会生活中起了很大的作用。

2. 政治状况

雅典民主制度的发展，共经历了以下三个主要阶段。

（1）打破血缘门第，首开先河。公元前594年的"梭伦改革"废除了雅典公民以人身为抵押的一切债务，禁止以人身为抵押借债，禁止把欠债的平民变为奴隶。由国家出钱把因无力还债而被卖到异邦为奴的人赎回，并废除了"六一汉"制度（平民无力还债，不得不为债主耕种土地；关于税率，国内外学术界有不同的说法，按亚里士多德的记述，税率为5/6，自己只能保留1/6，所以被叫作"六一汉"）。这一措施史称"解负令"。废除世袭贵族的垄断权利，不再以出身而是以财产的数量来划分公民等级。设立四百人议事会作为公民大会的常设机构和最高行政机关。设立陪审法庭（也译为民众法庭，相当于最高法院）作为最高司法机关，任何公民都有权上诉。同时，制定新法典取代了德拉古的严酷法律。

（2）消除财产限制，最终确立。公元前508年的"克里斯提尼改革"重新划分雅典区划，重组雅典的部落制度；建立"五百人议事会"，取代"四百人议事会"，并对所有等级公民开放；规范公民大会和民众法庭的活动，制定"陶片放逐法"；成立"十将军委员会"。

（3）全盛时期。公元前5世纪以后，尤其是希波战争之后，雅典的民主政治迎来了全盛时期。公元前443年至公元前429年，伯里克利连续当选为雅典十将军委员会的首席将军，自此开创了"伯里克利时代"。具体有以下措施：所有成年男性公民可以担任一切官职；确立"公民大会"、"五百人议事会"和"陪审法庭"的地位；解除取得"雅典公民"身份的限制。以伯里克利时代为代表的雅典民主政治，是古希腊城邦社会中先进的政治制度：它有利于调动城邦公民的积极性和创造性，有利于推动社会经济和文化的发展进步。

斯巴达国家的政体属贵族共和政体。城邦的主要政治机构如下。

第一，国王 2 人，分别由两个王室世袭。主要权力在宗教和军事方面，平时主持国家祭祀和处理家庭案件，战时一个国王领兵出战，另一个留守。由于两个国王拥有平等的权力，往往互相牵制，使王权受到限制。第二，长老会议。除两个国王外，另有成员 28 人。长老终身任职，出缺时从年逾 60 岁的公民中挑选补足。长老会议为公民大会准备决议案，主持刑事审判，并处理国家行政事务。第三，公民大会。由年满 30 岁的全体斯巴达男性公民组成，公民可以在大会上参加议案的表决和官员的选举，但不能提出议案。公民大会表决的方式，一般以与会者呼声的高低为准，因此未必能真正表达公民意愿。第四，监察官 5 人。每年改选一次，原则上每个斯巴达男性公民均有被选举权。据说，监察官原是国王手下处理司法事务的官员。在征服美塞尼亚之后，他们的权力逐渐扩大，不仅可以监督斯巴达城邦的一切官员，而且有权审判甚至处死国王。每次国王出征都有两名监察官随行，进行实地监督。为了镇压人数众多而反抗性很强的奴隶，斯巴达城邦规定了严格的公民军事训练制度。公民的孩子出生后，经体格检查合格才许收养。男孩 7 岁就要离开家庭，编入儿童连队，受初步的组织纪律训练；12 岁以后要受严格的军事和体育训练。成年男子结婚以后，平时必须生活在军营中，参加聚餐和操练，直到 60 岁才可退伍。

3. 女性地位

雅典妇女的权利地位相比其他城邦偏低。其中，雅典妇女权利的丧失从名字的变化中可见一斑。"雅典人"这一称谓指代取得了雅典公民资格的成年男性，而完全将女性排除在外。雅典的官方文件表述——"雅典人及其妻子和孩子"——就体现了雅典法律表述中把雅典女性划分到成年男性的"依附者"这一行列。此外，在实行民主政治的雅典，男人被鼓励学习如何读写，但由于妇女不参加政治事务，所以雅典人认为没有理由让妇女成为有文化的人。虽然雅典妇女中的一些人是有文化的，但是人数非常少。在雅典有文化的人群中，男女性别比例悬殊。家庭是雅典社会中经济活动的基本单位，也是雅典妇女主要的活动场所。雅典妇女没有经济自主权，不能管理或者控制她们的嫁妆，也不能继承任何财产。雅典法律规定："法律特别禁止一个未成年人缔结任何契约，或一个妇女签定价值为一麦斗以上的契约。"而雅典妻子的另一个职责，也即最重要的职责是为丈夫生育合法的子嗣，确保家庭的延续。这是妻子不同于其他妇女的根本之处。

相比雅典，斯巴达的女性教育稍显进步。在斯巴达，男孩接受教育是为了将其训练为公民兵，因此男性的文化教育时间很少。而女孩大部分时间是和母亲及其他年长女性在一起，且不用参加生产劳动，因此她们有很多时间用于文化教育。另外，斯巴达还出现了两位女诗人：梅加洛斯特拉塔（Megalostrata）和克利塔戈拉（Cleitagora）。此外，斯巴达与毕达哥拉斯的家乡萨摩斯（Samos）有文化上的交集。埃姆布里克斯（Iamblichus）提及的毕达哥拉斯的 235 位学生当中有十七八位是女性，其中 1/3 是斯巴达女性。值得一提的是，斯巴达人之所以信仰毕达哥拉斯学说，主要是因为毕达哥拉斯为人们每天的生活制定了相应的制度，其中包括饮食的禁忌及适合性交的季节等。对于整体社会生活甚至生活细节的戒律和阻止，是斯巴达人最熟悉的。在斯巴达，所有公民的主体任务只有一项，即保卫国家。儿童公育和男子终生过集体生活，消解了女人在家庭中的作用。她们的功能是为国家提供兵源，通过语言和性刺激使男子为国捐躯。斯巴达的妇女决不会因为丈夫战死而悲伤，因为她们本就没有固定的丈夫。该国立法者莱克格斯认为：一夫一妻是非常荒唐的，人们想方设法给自己的宠物挑选强壮美丽的交配对象改良品种，却想把女人垄断在家里为自己生儿育女，哪怕这位男子有各种缺陷和疾病，这是非常荒唐的。因此，在斯巴达，只有强者才有生育后代的权利。在性关系方面，女人不仅占有主动权，其临时性的丈夫也经常将妻子送于强者，这就是所谓的"共妻制"。

就妇女的社会地位而言，在古希腊城邦，虽然以民主标榜的雅典城邦内妇女地位低下是普遍现象，但是在斯巴达，妇女的社会地位相比其他城邦要高。主要体现为：①斯巴达妇女享有继承权，她们可以支配财产；②斯巴达妇女享有受教育权；③斯巴达家庭作用的削弱，消解了男性对女性的绝对束缚；④开放的性思想解放了妇女。

4. 教育状况

雅典的教育强调通过身体、道德、智力和审美等方面的训练，把受教育者培养成具有健美体格、高尚情操、较高的文化素养以及智力发展水平，兴趣广泛、能言善辩，即"身心既美且善"的公民。7 岁前的男女幼儿在家中接受身体和精神方面的教育，男孩满 7 岁即进入私立的雅典文法学校和音乐学校，但住在家中，上学有教仆陪伴。文法学校为启蒙教育，学习读、写、算的初步知识。音乐学校教孩子演奏乐器，还教《荷马史诗》的选段和抒情诗，并配以乐曲让孩子们边弹边唱，以培养学生的美感、节奏感和旋律感。重视音乐教育，强调通过音乐陶冶情操、涵养德性。12~13 岁的少年在音乐学校学习的同时，还被送入体操学校学习。教育内容除赛跑、跳远、角力、掷铁饼、投标枪五项竞技外，还有游泳、舞蹈和拳击，使青年人身体健壮、肢体匀称，并养成坚韧、勇敢、克制等道德品质。15~16 岁的青年从音乐学校和体操学校毕业后即结束了基本教育，大多数人就业谋生，少数富家子弟可进入国立体育馆，接受身心和谐发展教育。身体教育仍以五项竞技为主，但更重视赛跑和角力，还学习骑马、射箭、驾车等军事技术。心灵教育除教授与演讲有密切关系的文法、修辞、哲学等，还通过演奏、唱歌、舞蹈实施美育，组织学生参加宗教祭祀、社会庆典、公共集会、法庭审判等实际活动，进行政治道德教育。青年到了 18 岁，经审查确认为正式公民后裔者，可升入埃弗比，接受 2 年的正规军事训练。此后先在城市部队服役 1 年，学习重装步兵操练和武器使用，第二年从国家领取一矛一盾，戍守边疆或学习航海技术。等到年满20岁，通过一定仪式取得正式的公民资格，即可参与国家政事。

斯巴达的教育以军事化教育为主，主要是由斯巴达社会的等级制度所致。一等级公民要统治二、三等级，为数不多的斯巴达人要想统治多数的奴隶和自由民，就不得不实行全民皆兵的责任军事化管理，进行军事化训练。这也决定了斯巴达的教育性质属于军农一体教育，即以培养骁勇善战的军人为目的的教育。斯巴达人在婴儿时就要接受生命的考验，父母用烈酒为他擦洗，还要让长老检查他们的体质是否健康，凡是经受不住考验或被长老认为是虚弱的就被抛在弃婴场。男孩7岁时进入国家教练所，从此开始接受心魄和筋骨的磨炼，以形成坚韧、勇猛、凶顽、残暴、机警和服从的品质。训练的主要形式是格斗，训练所里的生活制度非常严酷，孩子们一年四季光头赤足，只穿一件单衣，白天吃的是不足以饱腹的饭菜，晚上睡的是粗糙的芦席垫，能忍受或能采取抢盗方式谋生者都会受到奖励。除了军事体育训练之外，音乐和舞蹈也是斯巴达人的教育方式。他们认为音乐可以陶冶情操使人敬神尚武，舞蹈可以协调身体活动的节奏。此外，孩子们还要经常接受奴隶主的道德教育，文化知识则不被重视。18岁的青年将接受正规的军事训练。青年军训团至少要组织一次军事"演习"，即在夜间采取突然袭击的方式包围、殴打和肆意残杀奴隶，以塑造性格、培养本领。20岁以后的青年要常年戍边习武，30岁时才能结束教育和训练，成为一名真正的军人和公民。斯巴达对女子也采取同样的军事和体育训练方式，如竞走、掷铁饼、投标枪、格斗等。对女子来说，这样的训练还有另外一种意义，因为身体强壮的女子结婚后才能生育出健壮的孩子。

根据斯巴达和雅典的教育情况，可以对比得出以下结论。①受教育者不同：雅典的民主政治规定受教育者为全体雅典公民，而斯巴达的受教育者仅为斯巴达人，庇里阿西人和希洛人没有受教育的权利。②教育内容不同：雅典注重公民德智体方面的教育，斯巴达关注军事训练和体育锻炼。③教育目的不同：斯巴达式军事教育主要是为了对外扩张领土，对内镇压奴隶，而雅典的教育是为了更好地发展邦国，培养具有素养、品质良好、多才善辩、身体强健的公民。

四　结论

通过了解分析雅典和斯巴达两大城邦，我们可以看出：雅典是一个开放式外向型的城邦，自由、进步、民主思想深入人心，并最终发展成一个在政治、经济、文化等方面都相对比较发达的大城邦；斯巴达的贵族寡头政治虽然不像雅典的民主政治那样开放、包容、进步，但同样被西方宪政思想家作为考察古希腊宪政体制的经典案例。

第三节　宙斯神统的确立对西方政治的影响

一　引言

希腊神话诞生于原始时代，因其有较为完整的神话体系和独特的文学魅力，所以流传至今已有数千年。我们接触西方文化，必然会遇到希腊神话中的典故，而为人熟知的西方经典文学作品几乎都涉及希腊神话，有些作品甚至直接取材于希腊神话。因此，希腊神话对整个西方乃至人类的宗教、哲学、思想、风俗习惯、自然科学、文学艺术所产生的影响是毋庸置疑的。同时，从古希腊神话中第一位神的权力转移可以看到希腊人政治权力思想的变化，其思想观念的变化也充分表现在古希腊的政治现实之中。这不仅仅是万物有灵观念的直接表现，更是古希腊人对自然万物以及社会制度的思考。

二 宙斯神统确立

1. 第一世代神

作为起源神的第一批后代，天空之神乌拉诺斯相比其他神要更加强大，他垄断了和盖亚的交配生育权。他的孩子们见了他也经常发抖，乌拉诺斯就称他们为"泰坦"，意思是"紧张者"。

一共有 12 位泰坦神，他们是俄刻阿诺斯（环绕世界的大洋，古希腊哲学家泰勒斯认为水是万物的本原，土地是漂浮在水上的，大洋生动体现了这个观念）、泰西斯（海之女神，俄刻阿诺斯之妻）、许珀里翁（高空）、忒亚（光明女神，许珀里翁之妻）、福柏（神谕女神）、科俄斯（天体运行，福柏之夫）、伊阿帕托斯（灵魂，克吕墨涅之夫）、谟涅摩叙涅（记忆，宙斯之妻，九位缪斯之母）、忒弥斯（规律，宙斯之妻，时序三女神和命运三女神之母）、克利俄斯（天体）、瑞亚（空间，克洛诺斯之妻）、克洛诺斯（时间，瑞亚之夫）。狭义的泰坦神就是这 12 位，广义的泰坦神还包括所有的远古神祇。

2. 第二世代神

由于乌拉诺斯迷恋权力，独享和地母盖亚的交配生育权，把孩子们（12 位泰坦神、3 个独眼巨人、3 个百臂巨人）全部推进盖亚的肚子里。盖亚很伤心，并鼓动孩子们反抗他们的父亲。泰坦们都被这个念头吓坏了，只有最小的泰坦克洛诺斯勇敢地答应了母亲。盖亚交给克洛诺斯一把镰刀，在乌拉诺斯准备和盖亚交配的时候，克洛诺斯用镰刀割掉了乌拉诺斯的生殖器，乌拉诺斯痛苦地飘到世界最高处，并诅咒克洛诺斯会被自己的孩子推翻。乌拉诺斯的生殖器掉入了大海，随后在浪花中诞生了爱与美之神阿佛洛狄忒；乌拉诺斯的血则形成了复仇女神和巨灵。

克洛诺斯上位，成为第二任神王。由于独眼巨人和百手兄弟们力量强大，克洛诺斯认为他们的存在是对自己王位的潜在威胁。因此，克洛诺斯设计将他们抓住并囚禁于塔耳塔罗斯（地狱的创造者）的地狱。但是乌拉诺斯的诅咒依然让他不能安心："你也将像我一样被自己的儿子推翻。"为了避免诅咒成真，克洛诺斯做了一个残忍的决定：把生下来的孩子全部吃掉。

瑞亚为克洛诺斯生了五个孩子，全都在刚出生时被克洛诺斯一口吞下。因此，瑞亚在生下第六个孩子后，决心要保全此子，并给这个男婴取名为宙斯。她用布裹住一块石头谎称这是新生的婴儿，克洛诺斯毫不犹豫地将石头一口吞下。于是，宙斯躲过一劫，被送到自己的叔辈——大洋神俄刻阿诺斯和海之女神泰西斯夫妻那里抚养。

宙斯长大成人后知道了自己的身世，决心救出自己的同胞兄弟。他先娶俄刻阿诺斯和泰西斯夫妇的女儿墨提斯为妻，并听从妻子的计谋，给父亲克洛诺斯下药以致他把吞入腹中的子女们都吐了出来。他们是赫斯提亚 (Εστα, Hestia)、德墨忒尔 (Δμητρα, Demeter)、赫拉 (ρα, Hera)、哈迪斯 (δη, Hades) 和波塞冬 (Ποσειδν, Poseidon)，随后孩子们都被俄刻阿诺斯和泰西斯夫妇及时带走并收养。最终宙斯联合众神，开始正式反击克洛诺斯。

后来宙斯听从表兄弟普罗米修斯的建议，解救了被克洛诺斯囚禁的独眼巨人一族——库克罗普斯，以及百臂巨人一族——赫卡同克瑞斯。库克罗普斯是整个宇宙中最伟大的锻造师，而赫卡同克瑞斯可以一次投掷 100 块巨大的石头，巨大的力量令泰坦诸神无法抵抗。独眼巨人在火神赫菲斯托斯（宙斯与赫拉之子）的帮助下，为宙斯打造了闪电长矛，为波塞冬打造了三叉戟，为哈迪斯打造了双股叉。在巨人们的帮助下，最终宙斯赢得了胜利。

3. 宙斯神统确立

在取得了泰坦战争的伟大胜利之后，宙斯和他的兄弟们又因为如何分配世界的统治权而互不相让，矛盾重重。眼看又要因此开战，这时充满智慧的普罗米修斯提出用抓阄的方式来决定世界的统治权。而按照抓阄的结果，宙斯分到了天空，成为天神。波塞冬分到了大海，成为海神，而哈迪斯分到了冥界，成为冥神。至于大地，通过协商后由三兄弟共有。随后，宙斯履行承诺封赫拉为天后，两人共享权力，掌管奥林匹斯与天空。

之后宙斯将克洛诺斯和那些战败的泰坦族囚禁在地下监狱中。为了避免他们逃走，宙斯命令波塞冬在监狱四周建造了青铜门窗以及墙壁，再令百臂巨人与三头犬负责看守。

至此，古希腊神话第三世代神上位，建立起以宙斯为首，宙斯、波塞冬、哈迪斯三兄弟并立的十二主神体系：宙斯（众神之王、雷霆之神）、赫拉（天后、婚姻和生育女神）、赫斯提亚（炉灶和家庭女神）、波塞冬（海神）、德墨忒尔（农业和丰收女神）、雅典娜（战争和智慧女神）、阿波罗（光明、音乐、预言与医药之神）、阿尔忒弥斯（狩猎女神）、阿瑞斯（战争和暴力之神）、阿佛洛狄忒（爱情和美丽女神）、赫菲斯托斯（火焰和工匠之神），以及赫尔墨斯（神使、小偷、旅者和商人之神）。形成了由他们共同掌管奥林匹斯山的新局面。

值得一提的是，关于宙斯的态度，荷马与赫西俄德有着不同的描述。《荷马史诗》中的《伊利亚特》在开篇有着如下描述：

> 这毁灭性的愤怒带给阿卡亚人多少苦痛，
> 把多少勇士的英魂送给冥神，
> 使他们的尸体成为野狗和各种飞禽的食物：
> 宙斯的意愿得以实现。[①]

荷马将英雄的愤怒、暴力屠杀乃至尸身不得安葬的命数称为"宙斯的意愿"，显然是在强调英雄们所代表的贵族荣誉。在古希腊人眼

---

① 荷马:《伊利亚特》，罗念生、王焕生译，上海人民出版社，2012。

里，"宙斯的意愿"无疑是至高无上的法则，但是字里行间表现出荷马对宙斯行径的批判。

赫西俄德在《神谱》中则是另外一种态度：

> 伟大宙斯的意愿如此。
> 克洛诺斯之子的意愿如此。
> 宙斯的意志难以蒙骗，也无法逃避。[①]

从赫西俄德的话语中不难看出，《神谱》作为诗歌，主题虽然是神的世代繁衍，却把对宙斯的信仰置于一切之上，并对宙斯竭诚赞美。

三　宙斯神统确立对西方政治思想的影响

对古希腊的研究并不仅仅局限于宗教和神话，它在一开始就被指引到政治层面，并试图通过一系列的社会与思想革新，来把握政治的发展脉络。随着作为集体生活形式的城邦制度的诞生，政治的出现跟那些条件联系在一起，古代的历史学家便勾勒出一种"神话—宗教—政治"的思想体系，并立即将之运用到城邦建设中。亲族内部的权力递交系统、统治者的道德威严、武装力量、与神沟通的权力独占和财富本身的独占，使城邦得以快速成长，并不断发展完善。而神话在城邦权力建构中的作用不容小觑，正是神话赋予建构体系以神性，并通过这种神圣性来强化城邦政治权力。

1. 权力过渡

从第一世代神王乌拉诺斯统治一直到第三世代神王宙斯即位，其权力过渡的方式充满了血腥与暴力。上文提及，乌拉诺斯被自己的儿

---

① 赫西俄德:《神谱》，王绍辉译，上海人民出版社，2010。

子克洛诺斯用暴力推翻，而克洛诺斯也被自己的儿子宙斯推翻。这是一种通过暴力反抗来进行权力交替的方式，简单来说，这是一种"压迫—反抗—更迭—驱逐"的运作方式。以第三世代神宙斯即位为例，克洛诺斯害怕乌拉诺斯的诅咒，将自己的孩子全部吞进肚子，对新神进行极度打压；地母瑞亚保全了宙斯，为后期反抗做了准备；宙斯解放了众兄弟姐妹，推翻了克洛诺斯的压迫，并建立了以自己为首的神统；新神统确立后，宙斯等神又对泰坦神进行了驱逐与打压。

这种权力过渡方式，与古希腊城邦中出现的"僭主制"异曲同工，或者可以说是"神话版僭主制"。与克洛诺斯的僭主式夺权不同，克洛诺斯是根据地母盖亚的建议，用暴力取代了乌拉诺斯；而宙斯选择的是暴力革命路线，他先是团结了其他诸神，然后联合前代泰坦神共同进行反抗。这也体现了王者执政官巴塞勒斯在雅典社会发挥的作用。

宙斯推翻了父亲的统治，建立了新的统治秩序：奥林匹斯十二主神。古希腊神话中，十二位主神构建了一种"一核心，三元，十二并立"的权力架构，即以宙斯为十二主神之首、众神之王；宙斯、波塞冬、哈迪斯三兄弟分管世界上三个最主要的部分——天空、海洋、冥界；宙斯等奥林匹斯十二主神共同管理世界。此外，奥林匹斯山众神商讨事件或者讨论某一事情时，都是十二主神共同参与讨论，表明自己的看法，这或多或少地影响了西方议会制度的形成。正是这种集会制度，经过漫长的历史演变发展成如今西方国家政治制度中的议会制。以英国君主立宪制为例，英国的宪政制度是让君主处于统而不治的地位，以议会为国家权力中心，按照"三权分立"的理念将立法、行政、司法三权分开并使其相互制约，国家各职能机关在内阁的领导下处理国家事务。这是古希腊神话发展到第三世代神统以来第一次将政治理想融入神话体系之中。

在宙斯统治时期，权力的否定是不可或缺的。在很大程度上，宙斯统治的基础便是其强大的武力。在神话中，宙斯从未被推翻，即便是普罗米修斯所掌握的推翻宙斯的秘密也被宙斯巧妙化解。自古以来，虽然在新的统治力量奠基期间潜藏着危险，但是古希腊人并没有让以武力为统治基础的宙斯彻底垮台，而是形成了更美好的设想，这便是象征着民主和智慧的雅典娜。古希腊人把强大的武力与无人能及的智慧赋予了她。雅典娜的设定体现了古希腊社会对女性以及权力归属等问题进行了思考。值得一提的是，随着民主改革的推进，雅典城邦女性的地位相比以往有了新的提升。

2. 民主思想

在古希腊神话中，雅典娜是第一个以强大的武力出现的女性形象，古希腊人还赋予了雅典娜民主策略。在古希腊人的观念里，民主若能实现则必定以智慧与强大的武力支持为保障，而雅典娜兼具了这两点。尤其是到了希腊全盛时期，雅典商业的繁荣与雅典娜崇拜是分不开的，雅典娜是掌管艺术、工艺、妇女手工的女神。对雅典娜的崇拜，在一定程度上推动了伯里克利当政时期的雅典手工业达到鼎盛，且极大地推动了雅典商业的发展，而雅典经济的繁荣在神话思想上的反映便是雅典娜的神性。所以，雅典娜作为完美的统治者设定时，便已经有很大的民主成分包含其中，这是一种智慧地运用武力的方式；而且，现实延续了这种想象，使雅典成为古代世界民主的先驱。

3. 契约观念

在古希腊神话中，神界所有机构都是依据规则运行的，而这些规则是在众神都同意和认可的条件下得到遵守和实施的。普罗米修斯违反神界公约将火种送给人类，被宙斯困在高加索山脉的一块岩石上，并且遭受着恶鹰的啄食。这映射到当时古希腊的现实生活中就是古希腊人对共同制度承认与遵守的一种契约意识，如果有人违反这种制度，就会受到惩罚。西方政治制度中的议会制度在很大程度上就是基于这种契约意识形成的。当奥林匹斯山众神遇到需要解决和应对的事情或状况时，都会聚集在一起商量对策，各神都有权表达自己的意见和看法。而在雅典城邦和斯巴达城邦中，都有公共集会的场所，这些场所也是古希腊城邦议会召开的场所，后来经过不断的发展和演变而最终形成了西方国家政治制度中的议会制。

结合上述神话系统，古希腊人对制度的整体认同感与内部否定性，在很大程度上造就了西方政治中常见的议会内部的两党分歧和全体公民共同遵守社会契约的局面。以后者为例，社会契约强调社会各阶层的人对契约的继承。这种社会契约是对古希腊神话所蕴含的制度的肯定，是对古希腊神话中政治表现的实体化。

4. 女性地位

在古希腊人的神话观念中，女性神相比男性神而言，更多地代表着理性与智慧。大地之母盖亚，作为创世神之一，从混沌中诞生后就代表着创造与毁灭、秩序与混乱；缪斯女神主司艺术与科学；雅典娜主司智慧、绘画、园艺、法庭等，而且同时掌管军事和武力。与之对应，古希腊的社会生活中，普遍都是由女性祭司掌管神谕。由此看来，在古希腊人眼中，智慧属于女性。但是随着文明的发展，女性的地位开始衰落。雅典的文明程度高于斯巴达，因此雅典妇女的地位要低于斯巴达妇女，当然这是后话。

四　结论

古希腊是西方民主政治的发源地，这也是古希腊文明对世界文明做出的最重要的贡献。英国诗人雪莱说过："我们全都是希腊人。我们的法律、我们的文学、我们的宗教，根源皆在希腊。"我们一直讲的"民主"（democracy）一词便源于古希腊语。尽管雅典的民主政治是奴隶制基础上的民主，带有局限性和狭隘性，但是，雅典民主政治的理论和实践在经过西欧中世纪神学政治的阻碍和中断之后，为文艺复兴以来西方国家的民主政治提供了思想和灵感的源泉，为近现代西方政治制度的形成和确立奠定了基础。

　　古希腊人通过对古希腊神话的创造与发展，对西方政治文化和西方人文主义思想产生了重要影响。由上文可知，早在公元前 9 世纪至公元前 8 世纪，便已经有了政治权力思想意识。这种早期的希腊神话思想，不仅反映了古希腊人对政治权力的看法，而且与近代政治思想所描述的近乎一致。古希腊神话与雅典民主政治一起为近现代西方的政治制度奠定了理论基础，对其他现代民族国家的建立与发展也做出不可磨灭的贡献。

第四章　古希腊戏剧

第一节　阿里斯托芬的《云》与智者学派

一　引言

苏格拉底无疑是古希腊最伟大的思想家之一，也是对西方文化影响最为深远的道德圣贤。在大众的眼中，他总是一个充满了智慧、正义、理性以及道德的光辉形象，然而其好友——古希腊伟大的戏剧家阿里斯托芬却以一种诙谐的语言、幽默的表达对苏格拉底的形象进行了颠覆性描写，塑造出一个在大众看来完全"不可思议"的苏格拉底形象。

二　故事情节

1. 苏格拉底的崇拜者

斯瑞西阿得斯的儿子过着奢侈的生活而不知节俭，只知赛马玩乐，由此欠下了大量债务。为了逃避债务，斯瑞西阿得斯让儿子去学修辞术，地点就在苏格拉底的思想所，因为只要学会此术就能让人在任何辩论中获胜，所以到时候斯瑞西阿得斯因儿子欠下的债务也就不用还了。为了让儿子去学习这样的"不义之辞"，斯瑞西阿得斯也是极力讨好自己的儿子，由此映射出的无疑是民主政治对社会伦理的毒害。尽管苦口婆心，儿子却怎么也不愿意去，因为他认为那是"下流的东西"。可见他虽然玩物丧志，具有不好的生活习惯，但尚具有道德感，知道什么是对什么是错。在这里，阿里斯托芬首先对苏格拉底进行了一次颠覆性描写，他借斯瑞西阿得斯父子之言讽刺苏格拉底其实是在教人如何诡辩，如何不道德，而这些都是"下流的东西"。

2. 苏格拉底的思想所

劝不动儿子的斯瑞西阿得斯最终自己叩响了思想所的大门，门徒甲给他开了门，并且介绍了思想所的情况。此外，门徒甲还给他介绍了苏格拉底最近的成就，而这些成就都是一些尽显荒唐的举动。思想所里，苏格拉底的门徒们都弯着腰，低头"研究地下事物"，就像四足动物一样。阿里斯托芬说："如果一个人对世界的观察仅仅局限在自然界，那么他就丧失了作为直立行走的人的尊严。"斯瑞西阿得斯发现，当他们在研究地下事物时，他们的屁股是朝向天空的，现在是人体中的低俗部分得见天日了。在这里，思想所成了一个荒诞而无用的存在，苏格拉底以往的智慧形象也被作者一并抹杀。

3. 苏格拉底的出场

苏格拉底登场了，他坐在一个悬挂在半空的吊篮里。阿里斯托芬在这里将哲学家苏格拉底安排在吊篮中出场的确是别有用心。刚出场的哲学家苏格拉底衣衫褴褛，打着赤脚，滑稽可笑。苏格拉底认为他在思索高深的问题，所以有必要把自己提升到空中。苏格拉底说他在空中行走，在逼视太阳，这岂不危险，太阳怎么能被逼视？而苏格拉底又怎敢逼视太阳？苏格拉底抛弃了他的神，甚至逼视着他的神。苏格拉底悬在空中，映射的是哲学越来越远离生活和人间，而这样的哲学没有也罢。这无疑是阿里斯托芬对苏格拉底的一个警告。

三 苏格拉底与智者学派

整部戏剧中，阿里斯托芬都在以一种强烈的措辞来讽刺和批评苏格拉底，当然这是一种善意的批评。他同时也在隐秘地提醒和警告着苏格拉底，他的思想终会给自己带来一场灾难。前期的苏格拉底行走于空中，远离大地，不关心政治，但后期的苏格拉底回归人间，将哲学拉回大地，开始密切关注政治。

古希腊颇有影响的智者包括普罗塔哥拉、高尔吉亚和安提丰等人。在这些智者中，普罗塔哥拉被认为是"智者中最有才华、最具有创造性的"，而且是"智者学派理论上的领袖"。

柏拉图以智者为敌，但青年苏格拉底和青年柏拉图曾经也是典型的智者。另外，归功于苏格拉底的"辩证法""美德是否可教""把哲学从天上拉回人间"等重要的哲学命题或教育问题，都在普罗塔哥拉等智者那里得到了讨论和发展。

四 智者学派的实践哲学

智者哲学与泰勒斯等人的自然哲学不同，泰勒斯等人的自然哲学只研究自然本体，对人间事务并不关心，而智者是第一批把哲学从天上拉回人间的人。过去，人们认为"苏格拉底是把哲学从天上拉回人间"的第一人。这个说法大体是对的，因为青年苏格拉底是一个典型的智者。阿里斯托芬的《云》叙述了作为智者的青年苏格拉底的形象。阿里斯托芬笔下的苏格拉底与柏拉图笔下的苏格拉底完全不同。前者笔下的苏格拉底过着典型的智者生活，与普罗塔哥拉等智者一样，向青年人传授"雄辩术"，不以追求真理为目的而以在辩论中击败他人为目的。与普罗塔哥拉等智者不同的是，成年苏格拉底开始追求正义和真理并以直言不讳的反讽的方式反对世俗道德和民主政治。苏格拉底后来因此被处以极刑。

柏拉图之所以反感和贬低智者，是因为其年少时也做过智者，对智者哲学有深切的体验和理解。随着年岁的增长，柏拉图走上了另外一条道路（绝对主义哲学），并对过去的做法进行清算和自我批判。柏拉图之所以反感和反对智者，主要是因为智者哲学顺应了当时的民主政治生活，而民主制恰恰是柏拉图所反对的。

专制社会因崇尚暴力而压制言论，民主社会因崇尚法律而重视辩论。古希腊智者学派之所以产生，正是因为智者提供的辩论与雄辩术教育顺应了当时民主社会的需要。伯里克利所创立的公众的、经常性的陪审法庭，恰恰为雅典人的才智开辟了一条最能满足其自然倾向的发展途径。这种新的司法制度促使雅典人的天赋向雄辩术方面发展。这时，不仅那些想在政治上崭露头角的人必须具备一定的演说能力，而且那些普通公民也必须如此，以便在法庭上维护自己的权利或驳斥他人的控告。姑且不论它能否用于实现一个人的雄心壮志，雄辩术总是一种最有实用价值的才艺，其重要性绝不亚于武术或体育训练。于是，那些讲授文法和修辞学的教师，以及为他人撰写演说稿的文人墨客，在这时开始多了起来，并且受到前所未有的重视。不仅如此，智者还从事某种游说或外交活动。早期智者是高尚的、备受尊敬的人，他们常常被所在城邦委以外交使命。

智者哲学也正因为顺应了民主社会的需要而受到伯里克利等人的支持和赞助。伯里克利执政时，奉普罗塔哥拉等智者为座上宾，并多次与他们谈话。后来民主政治的失势，使智者受到打压。"三十僭主"所实行的第一个重要措施，就是明令禁止讲授雄辩术。阿里斯托芬曾讥刺雅典人爱好议论和争辩，因为他觉得那种风气削弱了雅典人的军事力量。柏拉图对智者的攻击，也可以视为对伯里克利等民主派的批评。

苏格拉底和柏拉图师徒二人也曾热衷于智者式的辩论和雄辩术教育。不过，苏格拉底和柏拉图后来发生转向，开始追求"哲人王"的政治哲学和绝对主义、客观主义的知识哲学。柏拉图由此对智者的相对主义和主观主义哲学进行了批判。柏拉图对智者的批判首先是因为他们在知识哲学（客观主义与主观主义）和政治哲学上的分歧（关于民主政治与哲人王政治的分歧），但也有嫉妒和嫉恨的原因。智者说服优秀青年放弃向他人学习而转投自己门下，从一开始就不是一件安全的事情。他们赢得了仰慕，也招来了憎恨。不少智者遭受了"焚书"之灾，虽不至"坑儒"，但因"不敬神""败坏青年"等指控而被驱逐（后来苏格拉底也因受同样的指控而被处以极刑）。普罗塔哥拉曾被逐出雅典，他的书也被付之一炬。

由于柏拉图对智者学派"有敌意的描述"，智者在西方哲学史上一直名声不佳。柏拉图在《普罗塔哥拉》（也译为《智者》或《智术师》）、《高尔吉亚》和《泰阿泰德》等作品中以文学的夸张方式诋毁智者哲学，这不仅使后人普遍鄙视智者，而且使智者的著作未能完整地保存和传播，只剩下支离破碎的片段和模糊的摘要。受柏拉图的影响，智者被视为"江湖骗子"：利用公众的轻信挣得大量钱财；以教德行为名，教给人一种虚伪的演说术，同时鼓吹不道德地使用等观点。

不过，智者尤其是当时的普罗塔哥拉能够成为柏拉图的"大敌"，本身就说明智者学派有足够的实力以至于令柏拉图感到不安和恐惧。柏拉图之后，黑格尔在《哲学史讲演录》中对智者学派有较多的肯定，但他只是把智者哲学作为反对泰勒斯等人的自然哲学的"反题"，把柏拉图哲学视为自然哲学（正题）和智者哲学（反题）之后的"合题"，这就默认了柏拉图哲学高于和优于智者哲学。不过，黑格尔将智者纳入哲人之列，本身就是对智者的肯定。黑格尔之后，不断有人对智者做出新的评价。比如，英国史学家格罗特（G. Grote，1794~1871 年）所著的《希腊史》和德国学者策勒尔（E. Zeller，1814~1908 年）所著的《古希腊哲学史纲》对智者提出了完全不同于柏拉图的评价。罗素（B. Russell，1872~1970 年）在《西方哲学史》中也站在智者的立场上对柏拉图的敌视和诋毁表示不满。

五 智者学派的学说

智者哲学的核心精神主要为经验主义（以及怀疑主义、相对主义）。也正因为选择了经验主义和相对主义哲学，智者在"自然"与"习俗"之间做出不同于柏拉图哲学的选择：柏拉图站在"自然"那边，而智者更关注"习俗"（世俗的道德法律和政治）。智者哲学的第一个特征是立足于经验观察而对一切独断论表示怀疑和不信任。"它的方法是经验—归纳法。"

泰勒斯等人的自然哲学虽然在很多方面不同于柏拉图哲学，但当时的自然哲学与柏拉图哲学有一点是一致的：二者都强调超经验的沉思并追求客观真理，都一致地显示为独断论、客观主义和绝对主义哲学。与之相反，智者哲学坚持经验观察并由此选择了怀疑论、主观主义和相对主义哲学的道路。柏拉图开启的理性主义哲学相信"事物是我们的理智可以理解的"，而智者哲学坚持"事物是我们的理智不能理解的"。所谓"不可理解"，既隐含了某种"怀疑主义"的哲学态度，也意味着人们只能获得"相对"的真理或"有限"的真理。"普罗塔哥拉把一切道德和法律都看作只是相对有效，这种有效性只是与产生这些道德和法律的人类社会紧密联系着，并且，只有在那个社会认为这些道德和法律是良好的，才有效。……没有绝对的宗教，没有绝对的道德，也没有绝对的正义。"他认为，"每个问题都包含着相互对立的两个方面"，并在《真理或根据》的开头指出："人是万物的尺度，既是存在者存在的尺度，也是不存在者不存在的尺度。"黑格尔认为这是一个"伟大的命题"，"从现在开始，一切都是围绕着这个命题旋转。……一切客观的东西，只是在与意识的关联中存在；因此，思维在一切真理中被宣布为基本环节；因此绝对采取了思维着的主观性的形式"。普罗塔哥拉由此进一步认为，任何真理都依赖于意识，没有任何自在自为的客观的存在，"一切都只是相对的"，"事物对于我就是它向我呈现的样子，对于你就是它向你呈现的样子"。

普罗塔哥拉的相对论本身就是对一切独断论的怀疑和不信任。这种怀疑论在高尔吉亚那里获得了"更大的深度"的发展。高尔吉亚在《论自然》的三个部分中分别提出了他的三个论点：第一，无物存在；第二，即便有物存在，也不能被认识；第三，即便能被认识，也不能被言说。高尔吉亚的这三个命题在后来的哲学研究中不断被人回忆和引用。

智者哲学的第二个特征是引入了自然（physis）与习俗（nomos，包括道德法律规范和现实政治）的评价标准。普罗塔哥拉的同龄人索福克勒斯的戏剧《安提戈涅》之所以引起关注，是因为自然与习俗的冲突在其中获得了严肃的讨论。这部戏剧一开始就将安提戈涅置于两难情境之中：若遵从不成文法（自然法或神法）去埋葬自己的弟弟，就会因忤逆国法被处死；若依从国法不埋葬自己的弟弟，则会因忤逆神法而遭天谴。紧接着，戏剧开始了"人类颂"："奇异的事情虽然多，却没有一件比人更奇异。他要在狂暴的南风下渡过灰色的海，在汹涌的波浪间冒险航行；那不朽不倦的大地，最高的女神，他要去搅扰，用马的女儿（指骡子）耕地，犁头年年来回地犁地。他用多网的网兜儿捕那快乐飞鸟、凶猛的走兽和海里的游鱼。人真是聪明无比；他用技巧制服了居住在旷野的猛兽，驯服了鬃毛蓬松的马，使它们引颈受轭。他还把不知疲倦的山牛也养驯了。"[1] 索福克勒斯的这段"人类颂"既是对人类文明、理性的赞美，也是对人类文明、理性的警惕和反讽。

在自然与习俗之间，柏拉图哲学站在自然那边，而智者更关注习

---

[1] 索福克勒斯:《安提戈涅》，载《古希腊悲剧经典》，罗念生译，人民文学出版社，2014，第137页。

俗。智者虽然总体上坚持类似"人是万物的尺度"的相对主义标准，但这并不意味着他们没有任何标准。正因为智者认为一切人为的或世俗的道德和政制都没有绝对的正当性而只有相对的正当性，他们才提醒人们要有临时约法。即便这种约法是临时的、可修改的，但在制定之后和修改之前，人们必须尊重和遵守现成的道德和律法，否则，社会就会趋向混乱。智者讨论了法的三种来源：第一，来自神的律令，这是神法；第二，来自强权和统治者的指令，这是强权意志，体现统治者（强者）的利益；第三，来自多数人的约定，这是"社会契约"，体现弱者的利益。三者之中，智者往往站在社会契约这边，同时提醒人们对强权意志保持警惕。例如，安提丰就坚持人与人之间的的平等以及社会契约论。他"利用自然与习俗之间的对比，把国家归之为一种社会契约，并把道德和习俗看成是对本性的束缚。他以毫不含糊的词语断言，所有的人都是平等的，并谴责贵贱之分和希腊人野蛮人之分，这种区分本身就是野蛮的说法"。高尔吉亚认为："道德和法律是大多数弱者所制定的，他们以此驯化像食肉猛兽一样的强者的本性，并向年幼者指点那貌似真正正义的正义观。但自然和历史却背道而驰，当强者识破这一骗局，就将冲破这些束缚而使自己成为弱者的主人。"色拉叙马霍斯则提醒人们，所谓法律或正义，可能只是体现强者的利益。人们往往由此认为色拉叙马霍斯坚持强权正义观而受到了苏格拉底和柏拉图的反对。苏格拉底和柏拉图站在自然法那边反对强权正义观是理所当然的事，不过作为智者，色拉叙马霍斯只是在学理上指出强权正义观的可能性而他本人并不信奉强权正义观。智者的责任是在法庭辩论中获胜，如果色拉叙马霍斯在法庭上面对公众时坚持强权正义观，就不可能获胜。

从总体上看，智者哲学是经验论哲学的古典形态。后来的经验主义哲学家如贝克莱、休谟、杜威，几乎都可以视为现代智者。贝克莱的"存在就是被感知"，休谟否认一切因果关系，杜威的"从绝对主义到实验主义"等都是智者哲学的现代回声。甚至被休谟唤醒的康德提出"物自体"时，也有智者哲学的元素。据说，普罗塔哥拉被驱逐的原因是他不敬神。他在《论神》的开头写道："关于神灵，我不能够知道他们究竟存在还是不存在；因为有许多东西阻碍我们得到这种知识。"康德的"物自体"与普罗塔哥拉的这一说法如出一辙。

六　结论

经过以上分析，我们会对阿里斯托芬为何在《云》中对苏格拉底进行批判有一个大致的了解。不管是阿里斯托芬对作为哲学家整体代表的苏格拉底的严肃批判，还是在希腊之后不断参与诗与哲学之争的众多思想家，他们最终都是为了探索真理，找到一条正确的道路，确定一个正确的引导者。而诗与哲学之争的反复进行，也表明了在探索真理的过程中，要经历很多的矛盾与曲折。正是这种对真理的执着追求成为人类不断前进的动力，而这其中的任何思想家，都理应得到后人的尊敬。

第二节　苏格拉底的面具与《酒神的伴侣》

一　引言

在《悲剧的诞生》中，欧里庇得斯被称为"苏格拉底的面具"，而尼采一向不喜欢有着"世界教师形象"的苏格拉底。虽然，欧里庇得斯与处于同一时代的苏格拉底颇多相似之处，然而其诗化哲学毕竟与理性哲学不尽相同。《酒神的伴侣》充分展示了欧里庇得斯对"理性"与"非理性"的思考。

二　欧里庇得斯的悲剧

欧里庇得斯出身于拥有土地的贵族阶级，但在伯罗奔尼撒战争后沦平民，这使他的悲剧含有一种亲切的平民意识和民主思想。欧里庇得斯是一个和平主义者，因为揭露不义战争背后的财富和权力之争而惹恼了政治当局。同时，欧里庇得斯是一个人道主义者，是民主政治的坚决拥护者，他严厉谴责了当时存在的性别压迫问题，为饱受欺凌的妇女申冤。

欧里庇得斯的悲剧在他的时代并没有获得像索福克勒斯那样的好评，在其五十年的写作生涯中，只获得四次头奖，而同时代的索福克勒斯获奖二十次。具有讽刺意味的是，《酒神的伴侣》是诗人被逐出雅典后在马其顿写的，而且是在他死后，他的儿子拿出来上演才获奖的。欧里庇得斯何以如此失败又如此成功呢？

三　欧里庇得斯的哲学

欧里庇得斯居心叵测：他要人们理解他们不愿理解的真理，并将哲学思考强加在他的悲剧中；他亵渎神明，因为他在宗教精神上给人提出了更高的要求——这些要求是如此有力，以致即使达不到也不能等闲视之。

欧里庇得斯很早就醉心于哲学，曾在阿那克萨哥拉斯门下听过自然哲学的演讲。阿那克萨哥拉斯提出了月食原理，这种学说显然破坏了当时宙斯神统的宗教信仰，因此诗人被指控不敬神，并被逐出雅典。欧里庇得斯在《美狄亚》中为阿那克萨哥拉斯做辩护："一个有头脑的人切不可把他的子女教养成'太聪明的人'，因为太聪明的人除了得到无用的骂名外，还会惹本地人忌妒：假如你献出什么新学说，那些愚蠢的人就会觉得你的话太不实用，你这人太不聪明。"[①] 智

---

① 《罗念生全集》第3卷，上海人民出版社，2004，第98页。

者学派的普罗塔哥拉和普洛狄科斯作为诗人的朋友也对其有深刻的影响。据说，前者曾在诗人家里诵读他关于神的论文："我不能断言是否真的有神存在。这点认识有许多障碍：一是对象本身不明确；二是人类寿命的短促。"① 这篇论文后来被公开烧毁，普罗塔哥拉因此被判有罪。欧里庇得斯在剧场经常传播这些新学说，因此政治煽动家克勒翁曾控告他不敬神。

欧里庇得斯深受苏格拉底的影响。苏格拉底的知识，特别是道德知识，他的神（demon，δαιμων），亦即充满神圣感的至上神，在那个社会道德处在崩溃的边缘的时代，显得尤其重要。尼采在《悲剧的诞生》中说："欧里庇得斯仅是一个面具：通过这个面具而说话的神祇，既非狄奥尼索斯，又非阿波罗，而是一个完全新生的异教之神。那就是苏格拉底。"② 然而，与其说是苏格拉底影响了欧里庇得斯，倒不如说是相同的历史条件使他们走到了一起。但是，作为诗人的欧里庇得斯与作为哲人的苏格拉底毕竟不同：欧里庇得斯的悲剧充分体现了哲学肇始的年代，诗怎样以其特有的方式表达哲学的思考。

尼采崇拜狄奥尼索斯，崇拜生命的神秘与率性，所以他不喜欢主张认识世界的教师形象苏格拉底。尼采指出，苏格拉底提出的理论型文化，根植于一种乐观主义而企图消解悲剧，"他相信世界可以用知识来纠正,生命可用科学来领导"③。虽然尼采认为悲剧的实质是日神精神与酒神精神的对立与和解，是两种精神的复合，但他实际上更倾向于后者。尼采对希腊狂欢文化的极度推崇和偏激的理解说明他并未充分理解酒神精神的实质。而这一精神的实质早在公元前5 世纪就已经被欧里庇得斯充分认识到了，可惜的是，他的认识始终

① 《罗念生全集》第 3 卷，上海人民出版社，2004，第 98 页。
② 尼采:《悲剧的诞生》，李长俊译，湖南人民出版社，1986，第 172 页。
③ 尼采:《悲剧的诞生》，李长俊译，湖南人民出版社，1986，第 175 页。

被尘封在历史的记忆中。

四　古希腊与古罗马的酒神崇拜

酒神，狄奥尼索斯（Dionysus，Διονυσος）或巴克科斯（Bacchus，Βακχος），是葡萄种植业和葡萄酿酒业的保护神。传说他走遍了希腊、叙利亚、亚细亚，直至印度，一路上他向人们传授葡萄酿酒技术。正因为他具有丰产神的特点，而且能使人们从生命的烦恼和悲伤中解脱出来，因而使人们对他的崇拜近乎狂热，这种崇拜还伴随着狂欢仪式。在仪式中，信徒们通过酒、舞蹈和歌曲达到一种迷醉状态。特别是那些女信徒，被称作"酒神的狂女"。当时民间还流行对狄奥尼索斯的秘密祭祀：春天播种季节，人们身披羊皮，头戴羊角，化妆成半人半羊的萨提洛斯（酒神的随从），组成合唱队，绕着神坛歌唱酒神在尘世的苦难和再生。这种叫作"山羊之歌"的原始艺术形式就是悲剧的前身，而"悲剧"一词的希腊语即"山羊之歌"。

《酒神的伴侣》就是欧里庇得斯以酒神神话为基础创作的。欧里庇得斯在《酒神的伴侣》中曾经这样赞美酒神："他酿造液体葡萄酒送给人类，弥补营养的不足，减轻那些可怜人的忧愁，在他们喝足了葡萄酒的时候；他还奉送睡眠，使他们忘却每天的痛苦，此外再没有什么解除痛苦的良药了。他自己是一位天神，却被奠在地上敬奉，使人们获得幸福。"[1]

罗素比较了古希腊人与古罗马人不同的酒神祭。他肯定了前者而否定了后者：在希腊，这种狂欢活动由于与庄严的宗教仪式和宗教情感的宣泄结合在一起，所以显得既野蛮又美丽，既疯狂又神圣，具有神秘色彩和净化灵魂的意味。罗素认为，酒神侍女们在山坡上的纵情歌舞虽然狂野，但也是"从文明的负担和烦忧里逃向非人间的美丽世

---

[1]　欧里庇得斯：《酒神的伴侣》，载《罗念生全集》第3卷，上海人民出版社，2004，第357~393页。

界和清风与星月的自由里面去"的一种超越性冲动。[1] 但是罗马人的酒神祭却为人不齿:"意大利人酒神庆典是在十字路口进行的,狂热而又放荡。人们以利伯尔(罗马酒神)的名义对男性生殖器顶礼膜拜,这种仪式是一种极度的公开堕落行为。"[2] 李维在《罗马史》中也以厌恶的口吻描述了罗马酒神祭的狂乱景象。

狄奥尼索斯崇拜是原始而粗野的,它所导致的精神迷狂是在肉体迷狂中实现的,正如尼采所说:"这些庆典之中心观点乃是一种纯粹的性之乱婚,蹂躏了每一种业已建立的部落宗法。所有这些心中之野性的冲动,在这些机会里都得到解放,一直到他们达于一种欲望与暴戾之感情激发的顶峰。"[3] 因此,这种迷狂一开始就遭到了坚持审慎原则的贵族阶层的反对。

五 欧里庇得斯的《酒神的伴侣》

诗化哲学未必不"理性",而理性哲学未必排斥"非理性"。《酒神的伴侣》(公元前407年)充分体现了欧里庇得斯对理性与非理性辩证关系的思考。欧里庇得斯的哲学深受二元论的影响,这从对理性与非理性的划分就可以看出:母亲阿高厄(Agaue,Αγαυη)显然是非理性的代表,是狄奥尼索斯的狂热信徒;儿子彭透斯(Pentheus,Πενθευς)是理性的代表,是阿波罗的忠实拥护者;祖父卡德摩斯(Cadmus,καδμος)兼有二者的特点。

彭透斯对酒神祭充满厌恶并将其称为"祸事":"我们的妇女都出了家门,去参加巴克科斯的虚伪仪式,在山林中到处游荡……她们一个个溜到僻静地方,去满足男人的欲望,假装献祭的狂女,其实是把

---

① 罗素:《西方哲学史》(上),何兆武、李约瑟译,商务印书馆,1963,第44~45页。
② 伯高·帕特里奇:《狂欢史》,刘心勇、杨东霞译,上海人民出版社,1992,第40页。
③ 尼采:《悲剧的诞生》,李长俊译,湖南人民出版社,1986,第28页。

阿佛洛狄忒放在巴克科斯之上。"①彭透斯认为酒神崇拜是以阿佛洛狄忒的情欲败坏了妇女的道德。彭透斯最终死于非理性之手，这是理性对非理性蔑视的结果。

狄奥尼索斯来希腊的目的是惩戒理性的狂妄："只恨我母亲的姐妹们——她们真是不该——说我狄奥尼索斯不是宙斯 (Zeus，Ζευς) 所生，她们诽谤说塞墨勒 (Semele，Σεμελη) 同凡人结了私情，却把失身的罪过推在宙斯身上，又说这是卡德摩斯说诳，她们还狂妄地说，宙斯因此把她杀死，都只怪她隐瞒私情，说了假话。"狄奥尼索斯因为人们不相信他的神族血统而心生报复，这里暗含的意味是：狄奥尼索斯代表着非理性，他的存在是人的理性无法遏制的存在，如果否定他、蔑视他，就会招致他的报复。狄奥尼索斯心胸狭隘，报复欲极强，手段也极其残忍，"因此我才使她们姐妹发了狂，她们现在精神错乱，住在山上；我叫她们穿上我这宗教的服装"。

作为理性内部滋生的抗衡力量，非理性虽然对理性的张狂有所制约，然而非理性自有其偏执。阿高厄提着狩猎的成果——儿子的头颅频频呼唤胜利的赏赐者，"在他的帮助下，她赢得的只是眼泪"②。

作为一种非理性的象征，克利特岛的弥诺陶洛斯永远虎视眈眈地注视着人类社会的理性文明：理性永远无法逃出它的迷宫。而阿里阿德涅的线团才是走出迷宫的唯一希望：对待非理性决不能靠单纯的压抑，疏导才是正确的途径。

彭透斯与狄奥尼索斯的对话堪称经典，反映了理性与非理性刚愎自用、自以为是的可笑："（狄奥尼索斯）向傻子说聪明话的人往往被当作傻子。""（彭透斯）是你引导这个神首先到这里来的吗？""首先

---

① 欧里庇得斯:《酒神的伴侣》，载《罗念生全集》第 3 卷，上海人民出版社，2004，第 357~393 页。

② 欧里庇得斯:《酒神的伴侣》，载《罗念生全集》第 3 卷，上海人民出版社，2004，第 357~393 页。

到外地，所有的外国人都举行这教仪。""只因为他们远不及希腊人聪明。""在这方面他们更聪明，尽管他们的习惯不同。"当彭透斯要把狄奥尼索斯关进马房，把同他一起"做坏事"的妇女拉去做奴隶的时候，狄奥尼索斯说道："就是你所谓不存在的神，要向你报复，惩罚你的暴行。""神的力量来得慢，但一定会来，让时间的漫长脚步前进，但是他们终于会捕获那不敬神的人……承认神圣的事物有力量，承认不变的习惯和自然在长时间所树立的信仰并不难。"此处的弦外之音是，理性蔑视非理性的存在，它的偏执和狂妄终将招致非理性的报复：狄奥尼索斯给彭透斯"注进迷乱的疯狂，使他精神失常；因为他若是神志清明，就不肯穿女人衣服，他穿上了，就会死在他母亲手中。那样一来，他就会知道宙斯的儿子是有权威的神，对人类最和善而又最凶狠"[1]。

六 结语

欧里庇得斯笔下的酒神是哲学化了的神，这个神讨厌理性的自以为是，也讨厌非理性的放纵和疯狂。尽管是非理性的代表，狄奥尼索斯却很理性，他精心策划了一出戏，不仅让专制的理性受到了惩罚，也让疯狂的非理性自食恶果。卡德摩斯对女儿说："他（彭透斯）和你一样，不尊敬这位神，神因此把你们全体，把你们和他一起卷进了同一件灾祸。"祖父之所以如是说，是因为他清醒地意识到一个新兴的神出现了，这个真正的神与古希腊神话里的狄奥尼索斯不同，他虽然与日神的理性精神对立，但同样反感非理性的盲目和愚昧。这个新神集日神精神和酒神精神于一身，并以一种奇特的方式证明，理性与非理性并无界限，而是彼此蕴含在对方的机体内，在特定的情境下会相互转化，任何一方的放纵都只会导致人的毁灭。彭透斯"想用武力

---

[1] 欧里庇得斯:《酒神的伴侣》，载《罗念生全集》第3卷，上海人民出版社，2004，第357~393页。

征服这不可征服的力量，他的意志招来的惩罚便是死亡，惟有诚心按照人的本分信仰神的人，才能无忧无虑地生活"[1]。

苏格拉底似乎没有很好地实践他的座右铭——"毋过"（Μηδεν αγαν）法则，而这句镌刻在德尔菲神庙的箴言倒在欧里庇得斯的悲剧中得到了体现。然而，欧里庇得斯对理性的暴力与非理性的暴力的辩证思考，并没有引起广泛关注，这一点由其后古罗马的肉欲狂欢和基督教的禁欲主义两个极端得到了证明。

第三节　悲剧精神——古希腊与后现代

一　引言

被称为一种最高的文学形式，悲剧是当之无愧的，就像钢琴是乐器之王一样。悲剧涉及美学、文学批评、心理学，也与宗教和哲学密切相关。在两千五百年的悠悠岁月中，悲剧作品不断涌现，研究悲剧的各种论述也比比皆是。

二　悲剧作品

自古希腊始，便有以三大悲剧家的创作为代表的大量悲剧作品——虽然现今这些作品大部分已经失传或散佚。至古罗马时代，又有塞涅卡对古希腊悲剧的改写与重述。中世纪虽然不是悲剧的舞台，但是宗教戏剧也一直活跃在基督徒的生活中。文艺复兴时期自然是古希腊文明重见天日之时，其间以莎士比亚的悲剧为典型代表。至古典主义时期，高乃依、拉辛更是百般推崇古希腊悲剧，并在其基础上进行了符合自己目的的再加工。浪漫主义时期，德国的浪漫派将目

---

[1] 欧里庇得斯:《酒神的伴侣》，载《罗念生全集》第3卷，上海人民出版社，2004，第357~393页。

光聚焦于古希腊，其间的诗歌创作是古希腊光芒的再现，如席勒、歌德、雪莱的作品，应该是古希腊文明的现代回响——只可惜，浪漫派的古希腊之梦实则是自我膨胀的一种表现，与古希腊精神相去甚远。之后西方的戏剧舞台上又出现了社会悲剧，以易卜生为代表，随后尤金·奥尼尔的作品，更是社会悲剧和心理悲剧的紧密结合。20世纪是一个风云变幻的世纪，其诡异、迅速的变化，使生活光怪陆离、魅影纷呈，也因此，荒诞剧掌握了文学、艺术乃至哲学、历史的话语权。

三　悲剧精神

使悲剧成为悲剧的是一种内在的悲剧感、悲剧精神，悲剧感源于人类生命的痛感及对痛感的反省。在很多悲剧作品中，它往往表现为人在社会实践中因外在的社会、历史局限而遭受的痛苦和磨难，但仅有外在的痛苦和磨难还不足以产生悲剧，只有悲剧感、悲剧精神，即人对悲剧产生的沉重的生命体验，以及人自觉的、内在的悲剧性情绪，才能成就悲剧。纵观悲剧发展的历史，我们可以发现，蕴含在古希腊悲剧中并真正使其成为永恒的悲剧精神，在历史的演进中不断蜕变、消解直至消亡——虽然这一点还不能为悲剧评论家普遍接受，而更多的是一种自我见解，然而谁又能说这一见解完全荒谬呢？毕竟，"一千个读者眼中有一千个哈姆雷特"。

朱光潜先生在他的《悲剧心理学》中，谦逊地指明了他的立场："我们将依次讨论在说明悲剧快感的原因时，可以在多大程度上考虑审美观照、恶意、同情心、道德感、乐观的人生观和悲观的人生观、情绪缓和作用、活力感、智力好奇心的满足以及其他一些因素。如果可能，我们将把这些因素归纳成一些共同标准。但既然承认'原因的多样性'，我们也就用不着拘泥于某一抽象教条而歪曲具体经验。我们无意于为建立理论而削足适履。我们将主要在具体事实的基础上展开讨论，既不想用任何玄学的大前提来作我们关于悲剧的结论的理论依据，也不想用任何悲剧理论来支持某种预定的哲学学说。我们的方法将是批判的和综合的，说坏一点，就是'折衷的'。"[1] 在《悲剧心理学》中，朱光潜先生的工作是梳理性质的，他的主要目的是呈现各家各派的观点，并将其集中于"悲剧快感"问题上来。

我们必须认识到，这种梳理工作本身就是一种价值，虽然这种为了避免受到同行们的攻击而"折中"的办法听起来有些取巧，但"折中"的立场本身就是一种立场。不过本文的立场并非"折中"的：出于对古希腊的偏爱，出于对现实生活环境的无奈，本文执意选择一种立场，意图表达一种观点，即悲剧属于古希腊。

古希腊之后，古罗马的塞涅卡也有悲剧作品留世，然而其悲剧夸张的恐怖气氛，使悲剧已然不具古希腊悲剧独有的悲剧精神；中世纪的宗教戏剧，只不过是戴着"悲"的面具来表现"喜"的本质；文艺复兴时期的悲剧，充斥着戏谑的市侩气息；古典主义时期的悲剧，更像是一种政治说教；现代的荒诞剧，在荒诞不经中流露出刻骨的无聊和悲哀。因此不论后世的努力如何，古希腊悲剧那种独有的悲剧精神已经一去不复返了，随之而去的是那种独有的美、独有的高贵、独有的悲壮。

悲剧与"美"有关。作为一种美的形态，悲剧是美学的一个重要范畴。悲剧有一种美，一种冷峻而又壮丽的美。但是，悲剧的审美特征究竟是什么？这是一个既古老又现实的问题。自亚里士多德至今，已过去了两千多年，不知有多少哲人和美学大师对之进行了孜孜不倦的研究和探索，并提出了各种各样的观点，但是，这一问题的答案仍然模糊不清。

总体来说，关于悲剧的研究资料可以分为以下四种。第一，悲剧

---

[1]　朱光潜:《悲剧心理学》，生活·读书·新知三联书店，2000，第20页。

诗人们发表的言论，如高乃依的《论文》《序言》、拉辛的《序言》、席勒的《审美教育书简》、雨果的《克伦威尔序言》，以及其他类似的著作。这些文章一般是为作者的创作实践做辩护的。第二，哲学家们关于悲剧作品的论述，如亚里士多德的《诗学》、休谟的《论悲剧》、卢梭的《论戏剧》、黑格尔的《美学》、叔本华的《作为意志与表象的世界》、尼采的《悲剧的诞生》。第三，观众、读者、编辑、评论者的言论，如约翰逊的《莎士比亚全集序言》、狄德罗的《谈演员的矛盾》、莱辛的《汉堡剧评》、施莱格尔的《戏剧艺术和文学演讲集》、布拉德雷的《莎士比亚悲剧的实质》、詹姆斯·阿格茨的《英国戏剧家批评文集》。第四，演员们的言论，这类著述十分有限，因为演员们一般很少撰写关于自己表演艺术的书籍。不过有时候，一些传记作家在撰写演员的生平经历、表演艺术的时候会间接提到他们演绎的作品，如珀西·菲茨杰拉德的《大卫·伽立克传》就是典型。

这些不同的观点和解释，突出反映了悲剧产生的时代特点，悲剧在每一个时期的不同表现形式及主题内容，反映了人类文明发展的足迹，反映了人类每前进一步的思考和困惑。然而，这些思考有的是片段式的，如悲剧作家"序言式的"感想以及席勒的《审美教育书简》；有的是哲学家一整套理论中的一个点缀，如黑格尔的《美学》；还有的偏重于某一学科和领域，如亚里士多德的《诗学》，唯独没有一部完整的分析作品。朱光潜先生的《悲剧心理学》做了有益的尝试，他梳理了不同的理论派别的观点，然后加以整理，偶尔加入自己独特的观点。不过这部作品侧重于"心理学"，即悲剧的审美心理。

固然，与"悲剧精神"相关的"崇高"脱离不了美学范畴，与"悲剧精神"相关的"感受""体会"也脱离不了心理学范畴，然而，根本问题在于：悲剧精神的实质是什么？悲剧精神何以消解？为什么悲剧属于古希腊？为什么后现代没有伟大而崇高的悲剧？为什么印度、希伯来、日本、中国、古罗马没有所谓的"伟大而崇高的悲剧"？所有这些为什么，不仅与不同民族、时代的宗教、哲学有关，也与宗教的伦理道德、哲学的思维方式有关。

托马斯·库恩在《科学革命的结构》中提出了范式（Paradigm）的概念。作为一位科学哲学家，托马斯·库恩认为结构决定本质，即所有的解释、陈述、理论都必须在假设的有秩序的框架内操作，这个框架就是范式。科学上的重大突破，不仅仅是新的发明与发现，更是推翻一个旧的范式，建立一个新的范式。至于文学批评和文艺理论，就是不断地推出新的范式和解释理论。以悲剧研究为例，亚里士多德提出了过失说的范式，黑格尔提出了伦理实体自我分裂与和解的范式，布拉德雷（英国哲学家、逻辑学家，新黑格尔主义的代表）提出了最终道德秩序的范式，尼采提出了日神精神与酒神精神融合的范式，弗洛伊德提出了"俄狄浦斯情结"的范式，荣格以及诺斯洛普·弗莱（加拿大多伦多大学神学家和文学批评家）则提出了原型范式。

从亚里士多德的"过失说"到黑格尔的"伦理实体说"，从尼采的"日神精神与酒神精神说"到弗洛伊德的"俄狄浦斯情结"，从荣格的"集体无意识"到弗莱的"原型"，其实只有"命运说"是阐释古希腊悲剧最好的范式。以"命运说"解释古希腊悲剧的兴起与消亡，可以清晰地展示悲剧精神的实质。

四 古希腊的悲剧精神

悲剧源于人的生存困境。人对于生存处境的畏惧、对于命运无常的恐惧，不仅催生了原始的宗教、巫术、祭祀仪式，也催生了悲剧。实际上，悲剧产生于祭祀仪式。美国戏剧评论家弗兰西斯·弗格森说："古典人类学者中的剑桥学派已经十分详细地说明，希腊悲剧的形式追随的是一种古老仪式的形式，即草木动物之神，或生长季节之神的仪式的形式。"①欧里庇得斯的《酒神的伴侣》清楚地显示了这一点。英国著名古典学者吉尔伯特·默雷详细研究了宗教仪式向悲剧转变的过程。雷纳·弗里德里希也说："模仿与宗教的结合产生了仪式，进而仪式产生了戏剧。在仪式中，戏剧性的模仿与宗教礼仪形成一种无差别的结合；正是这种结合使模仿能够发展到一个精炼的阶段，正是这个阶段使戏剧这种复杂的艺术形式成为可能。"②可以说，无论是仪式、宗教、巫术还是悲剧，都产生于人的生存困境。

对自然环境的敬畏，渐渐演变为对神的敬畏，而对神的敬畏，不仅催生了宗教，也催生了悲剧。别林斯基在谈及悲剧的性质时说，悲剧的结局"永远是人心中最珍贵希望的破灭，毕生幸福的丧失。由此就产生了它的阴森庄严，它的巨大宏伟，悲剧中笼罩着劫运，劫运是悲剧的基础实质"③。

然而与宗教不同的是，悲剧不仅反映人的畏惧，也反映人的反抗。同样是对人神关系进行探索，悲剧与宗教却走上了不同的道路。在宗教中，人被要求无条件地敬畏神；而在悲剧中，除了宗教要求的对神的敬畏，还有人类英勇的反抗——虽然这种反抗大有僭越的意味，然而这种僭越是神圣的。悲剧就是在对神的敬畏与神圣的僭越之张力中发生、发展的。命运的范式，展现的正是这种张力。因此，贯穿本文的论点之范式，是命运。命运是悬在古希腊人头上的达摩克利斯之剑，是游移在古希腊悲剧中的魅影，是成就古希腊悲剧特有的悲剧精神的落脚点。

---

① F.Fergusson, *The Idea of a Theatre*, New Jersey: Princeton University Press, 1972, p.26.

② James Redmond, *Drama and Religion*, London: Cambridge University Press, 1983, p.159.

③ 别林斯基:《诗的分类》，转引自《西方文论选》(下)，上海译文出版社，1979，第381~384页。

五 后现代悲剧精神的复兴

至于后世的悲剧，如文艺复兴时期的悲剧，虽然继承了古希腊悲剧的某些精神特质，也反映了人的生存困境，但是命运的色彩已经淡化。再至古典主义时期的悲剧，命运的色彩已经荡然无存，悲剧所反映的人的生存困境，不再是人神的冲突，而完全是人类社会、人与人之间、人与社会之间的冲突；更确切地说，是理智与情感的冲突、利益与利益的冲突。

至于 19 世纪的社会剧，乃是此种悲剧的进一步延伸，更加深刻地反映了人与社会的冲突、人与人之间的冲突。如果说古希腊特有的悲剧精神在后现代有重现的迹象，那大概是因为人类理智走到了某个尽头，科学精神走到了某种界限，正如尼采所说："如果说古老悲剧被辩证的知识冲动和科学乐观主义冲动挤出了它的轨道，那么，从这一事实可以推知，在理论世界观与悲剧世界观之间存在着永恒的斗争。只有当科学精神被引导到了它的界限，它所自命的普遍有效性被这界限证明业已破产，然后才能指望悲剧的再生。"[①]

经历了两次世界大战之后，黑格尔的人类道德乐观主义遭到了质疑——纳粹德国的犹太人集中营与日本人的南京大屠杀是鲜明例证；经历了科学进步带来的种种成果与危机——日本人的化学武器与美国人的原子弹是鲜明的例证，坚持理性至上的人们开始重新反思科学的乐观主义。在这个时候，悲剧精神似乎才得以复苏。

20 世纪的荒诞剧便是这一反思的产物。然而，20 世纪的荒诞剧仍然缺了些什么。以《等待戈多》为例，这一戏剧除了滑稽、无聊的"等待"这一动作，没有其他的戏剧情节，如果按照亚里士多德的理论，这部戏剧则称不上是悲剧。只是，这部戏剧的主题——等待"上帝"，似乎是古希腊悲剧精神的现代回响。如果说形式决定了内容，

---

① 尼采:《悲剧的诞生》，周国平译，生活·读书·新知三联书店，1986，第 49 页。

或者说形式本身就是一种内容，那么后现代则没有悲剧，尽管后现代荒诞剧所蕴含的悲剧精神似乎回应了尼采那种乐观的期待。

关于西方现代有无悲剧的争论，一直到现在也没有定论。以约瑟夫·伍德·克鲁契和乔治·斯坦纳为代表的学者认为，不存在现代悲剧；而以加缪为代表的文学家则认为，现代也存在悲剧。1992 年，美国著名学者沃尔特·考夫曼的学生理查德·H. 帕尔默在专著《悲剧与悲剧的理论》中再次提出西方现代是否存在悲剧的问题："在一个失去共同接受的哲学标准或者宗教标准的现代社会中，悲剧是否能够存在。"①

本文倾向于前者，尽管以加缪为代表的剧作家的确借荒诞戏剧表达了某种悲剧精神的回归，然而就形式来说，后现代没有严格意义上的悲剧；其表达的悲剧精神就实质来说，与古希腊悲剧独有的悲剧精神相去甚远。同样是对于"神"的渴望与期待，古希腊悲剧家心中的"神"与后现代的悲剧家显然不同；同样是对于人神关系的思索，古希腊悲剧家思索的重点与后现代的剧作家显然不同。因此，纵然 20 世纪的荒诞剧在某种层面上体现了悲剧精神的回归，但这充其量只是一种努力而已。

六　结语

可以说，悲剧正是在近代走向衰亡的。虽然近代西方仍然有高乃依、拉辛和歌德，但那些支撑近代悲剧的关于理性与情感的冲突、情感与责任的冲突，都已经不是支撑古希腊悲剧的悲剧精神了。近代没有滋生悲剧的土壤有两点原因：其一，滋养悲剧精神的异教精神已经被基督教驱逐；其二，科学的发达所造成的怀疑主义，已经把信仰的机能耗尽了——上帝已死，还有什么值得纠结呢？再之后，无论人类

---

① Richard H. Palmer，*Tragedy and Tragic Theory*，*An Analytical Guide*，New York：Greenwood Press，1992，p.1.

的生活有多么荒谬、悲惨，也无论现代的荒诞剧是多么深刻，悲剧作为一种最高形式的文学作品，都已不复存在了。我们有的只是对生活的冷漠，所以不可能再产生以"激情"为底色的"悲剧"。欧里庇得斯的悲剧之所以缺乏像索福克勒斯悲剧那样的"激情效果"，原因就在于欧里庇得斯比索福克勒斯更怀疑神的存在。因此，现代人被认为达不到悲剧的境界，或者说悲剧的境界是在我们之上的。

从大众文化的角度来看，传统的悲剧理论中保留着根深蒂固的贵族化偏见，而且对现代性和普通生活有着官僚式的轻蔑——蝼蚁之生，何足挂齿？可是按照精英文化的观点，既有的悲剧观念始终是具有超越性的——一种超越于现实之上的理念，一种形而上的关注，并非指涉不幸的现实本身。或如朱光潜所说，"悲剧表现的是一种理想化的生活"[①]。

总之，古希腊悲剧反映的是一种理想，是高于现实生活的，对于过分注重现实的中国人和罗马人来说，悲剧不是最好的文学形式；古希腊悲剧具有一种后世无法比拟的悲剧精神，这种在困惑中不断思索的品质，不是佛教徒、希伯来人所能理解的。因此，印度和希伯来人也没有悲剧。在科学主义、理性主义主导的近现代，悲剧更不可能存在，因为哲学从根本上毁灭了诗的精神——无论黑格尔、尼采、叔本华的悲剧观点多么精辟，他们始终只是评论家而不是悲剧家！因此，悲剧只能属于古希腊。

---

① 朱光潜:《悲剧心理学》，安徽教育出版社，1996，第18页。

第五章　古希腊哲学

第一节　厄洛斯神话的重述与柏拉图的诗哲之争

一　古希腊神话中的爱神厄洛斯

厄洛斯是爱神，他的拉丁名称丘比特更为人们熟知。他是阿瑞斯和阿佛洛狄忒的儿子，是一位小奥林匹斯山神。他的形象是一个裸体的小男孩，有一对闪闪发光的翅膀。他带着弓箭漫游，会恶作剧地射出令人震撼的神箭，唤起爱的激情。他给自然界带来了生机，授予万物繁衍的能力。这位可爱而淘气的小精灵有两种神箭：加快爱情产生的金头神箭和终止爱情的铅头神箭。另外，他还有一束照亮心灵的火炬。尽管有时他被蒙着眼睛，但没有任何人或神（包括宙斯在内）能逃避他的恶作剧。有一次这位淘气的精灵被自己的箭射中，对人间少女普赛克炽热的爱在心中复苏，以至于他不顾母亲的干预，鼓起勇气让宙斯给予公正评判。厄洛斯起了重大作用的另一个著名故事是阿耳戈英雄的远征。美狄亚——国王埃厄忒斯的女儿，被厄洛斯的神箭射中后，和伊阿宋一起寻觅金毛羊，最后成为这位英雄的妻子。

厄洛斯的母亲是阿佛洛狄忒，也即罗马神话里的维纳斯。维纳斯是从海里升起来的。据说世界之初，统管大地的盖亚女神与统管天空的乌拉诺斯结合生下了一批巨人。后来夫妻反目，盖亚盛怒之下命小儿子克洛诺斯用镰刀割伤其父。乌拉诺斯的生殖器落入大海，海上升起了泡沫，阿佛洛狄忒就这样诞生了。希腊语中阿佛洛狄忒的意思就是"泡沫"。

在希腊神话中，阿佛洛狄忒虽是赫拉的儿子赫菲斯托斯的妻子，但她多次与别人相好：与战神阿瑞斯私通，生下 5 个子女；与赫耳墨斯交欢；与英雄安基塞斯生下埃涅阿斯。在荷马时代，她常有时序女神、美惠女神及儿子丘比特相随。在罗马，她与当地的丰产植物女神维纳斯合并，成为丰收和爱情女神。由于她是埃涅阿斯之母，故被视为尤利西斯家族的女始祖。她的早期形象风华正茂，容光焕发，后来常被描绘成裸体女性。

二　柏拉图对厄洛斯神话的改写

柏拉图的诗与哲学之争，并非诗与哲学之间的永恒斗争，而是古希腊在公元前 5 世纪前后新崛起的哲学家与以荷马为代表的诗人之间谁能够言说真理的斗争，是哲学家的理性思维以及用确定的理念规定的世界对此前神话—巫术思维盛行的传统世界的清算和批判。这一争论不仅意味着古希腊文化从神话—巫术世界向理性世界的转换，也意味着一场古代的文化政治革命的来临。在这一转换的话语机制下，柏拉图的灵魂"回忆"理论对神话—巫术的灵魂概念进行了扭转，在人的灵魂中发掘出能够与非感性的理念进行沟通的先验理智直观；柏拉图的"爱欲"理论对神话爱欲进行了批判性改造，形成了去肉身化的哲学爱欲，使爱欲趋向于理念知识。因此，柏拉图的诗哲之争显示了柏拉图试图用哲学所依赖的先验理智直观，对隐含于神话—巫术中的诗性直观进行清理和转换，以便使先验理智直观对感性直观进行规范并与之契合。

《理想国》一书总结了柏拉图思考过的所有重大问题——人的德

性与政治、诗歌与教育、精确的科学、哲学以及神话，并且展示了每一主题在柏拉图整个思想体系中所处的地位。而正是在《理想国》中，柏拉图为了维护心中理想城邦的"正义"，多次抨击、贬低诗歌，对诗人下达了严厉的驱逐令，还提到了"古已有之"的"诗哲之争"，并认为这种"重大的斗争"是决定一个人善恶的关键。

柏拉图在书中所说的诗哲之争古已有之实际上提高了哲学的地位，因为哲学产生的年代远远晚于诗歌。早在荷马描述的时代，诗歌就已经被看作祭祀和表达情感的手段，评判是非与记录功过的工具。诗人作为最早的知识分子，既是历史的记述者又是宇宙观的阐释者，既是原始神学的奠基人又是各种知识和记忆的传授者。诗体现的是城邦的"习俗"，只是这习俗如今在哲学视野中成了"意见"。

在柏拉图的对话中，哲人对诗的攻击也毫不留情。《理想国》中，柏拉图站在"爱智者"的立场上对诗及诗人发起了猛烈攻击。他认为诗是"发高烧的城邦"的产物，诗人作为非必需人口之一，是引起非正义和战争的原因。他讽刺诗人荷马不懂真理，被自己的学生鄙视，不受人爱戴，颠沛流离；认为自荷马以来的所有诗人都"只是美德或自己制造的其他东西的影像的模仿者，他们完全不知道真实"[1]。同时认为诗人除了模仿其他一无所知，如果去掉了诗的音乐色彩，诗人的语言就将变得平淡无奇。他把诗人看作单纯的模仿者，模仿是与真理隔着两层的影子。诗人养肥，放纵不良的情感，并提出把这种只会模仿的诗人驱逐出他口头建立的理想国。他把诗与哲学放在一起做比较，认为诗歌不是包含着真理的正经事物，而哲学追求的正是真理；认为诗歌会对人的心灵产生不良影响，而哲学本身就是真理与秩序。

柏拉图对诗的严肃批判使人们不敢相信其在拜苏格拉底为师之前曾是一名热爱写诗，尤其擅长写悲剧诗的青年。然而菲利普·锡德尼

---

[1] 柏拉图:《理想国》，郭斌和、张竹明译，商务印书馆，2002，第406页。

在他的作品《诗辩》中称柏拉图是他最尊敬的老师，因为在所有的哲学家中，柏拉图是最富有诗意的一位。柏拉图还是一位诗评专家——西方文评史上现存第一篇广泛论及诗和诗人的著述《伊安篇》就出自柏拉图。另外，从柏拉图哲学论著的文本来看，他对神话的大量引用、生动的对话说理形式、流畅丰富的语言，以及字里行间流露出的诗性都真切地反映了柏拉图对诗的热爱。

这种对"诗哲之争"的矛盾态度在《理想国》中有所体现：第二卷和第三卷仅仅是对诗人及诗人的模仿提出要求，但在最后一卷却提出把诗人驱逐出理想国。对于悲剧诗人的鼻祖——荷马，柏拉图虽然发起了猛烈攻击，但仍然不否认荷马在整个城邦中的地位及其作品中那些精彩绝伦的描写和包含的丰富知识。柏拉图甚至一边说要把诗人逐出理想国，一边又允许诗人辩护：我们大概也要许可诗的拥护者——他们自己不是诗人，只是诗的爱好者——用无韵的散文申述理由，说明诗歌不仅是令人愉快的，而且对秩序的管理是有益的。我们也要善意地倾听他们的辩护，因为如果他们能够说明诗歌不仅能令人愉快而且有益，我们就可以清楚地知道诗对我们是有利的。

可见柏拉图并不是完全否定诗的存在价值，也并非真的要把诗和诗人彻底驱逐出"理想国"，他从不认为人的生活可以没有诗的参与和点缀。诗是神赐的"愉悦"，是技巧的"产儿"，是哲学的对手（由此可见诗的能耐），也是寻求真理的有效手段。柏拉图之所以要在《理想国》中对诗和诗人进行驱逐，是因为文本中体现的看法及其诗学观、哲学观都建立在"理想国"的政治基础之上，旨在构建一种适合真理与哲学发展的环境。模仿诗的存在使城邦的"正义"受到不良影响，出于对他内心的正义和城邦正义的维护，他驱逐了诗和诗人。

三　神话—诗性思维向先验理智思维的转换

柏拉图的形而上学话语机制，使他把理念看作比现实的东西更为真实，而理念规范着现实中所有现象最后的确定性。因此，哲学作为"爱智慧"，就是要去追寻比现实更为真实的理念的知识，包括美的最高理念。理念的世界是一个摆脱了杂多性和现象性的永恒确定的世界，但重要的是，当这样一种纯粹的作为理念存在的正义、善和美等概念被确立之后，人这个必死者如何与在永恒世界中存在的理念本身发生关系就被凸显出来。柏拉图对这个问题的解决，正显示了蕴含在诗与哲学之争中的另外一种变革：理智直观（intellectual intuition）对蕴含在神话诗和巫术中的诗性直观（poetic）的转移。

柏拉图对知识的诉求以及由此导致的对神话—巫术所营造的世界的清算，首先反映在其对话中的是不断向他的辩论对手提出这样的要求：不要举例子，而要下定义，以及对可靠的经过论证的知识的追求。在这种情况下，一方面，神话、诗、巫术等古希腊传统以及人们的习惯和经验，都被纳入了怀疑的范畴；另一方面，知识、论证、定义等都被置于习俗、经验、意见和神话巫术之上。在此意义上，从苏格拉底到柏拉图的哲学是具有启蒙的政治革命含义的。

在古希腊苏格拉底那里，人类的智慧是有限的。同样，在把握柏拉图式的教义方面也是如此。没有什么知识是坚不可摧的，除非我们完成了成为像神一样的命令。据此，"爱智慧"的哲学就是灵魂中的神性理念的直观，它需要通过"死亡练习"来远离肉身，以实现灵魂中理性直观与理念世界的一致和沟通。

在这个意义上，诗哲之争就是要摆脱流变的、虚幻的现象世界，而归于可以用理念的最高知识来规定的确定的世界；就是用理念知识取代诗和神话的感性描述，用理性思维取代诗性模仿或想象。这也使柏拉图看不到诗和艺术中感性美的价值，因为它们是感性的、挑动情感的、涉及模仿的。重要的是，这一话语逻辑也使柏拉图改变了"poiesis"的传统含义。"poiesis"的原初含义是"带出或绽出"（bringing forth）、"带入显现"（brings to appearance）或"敞开"。但在柏拉图这里出现了颠倒和扭转，"poiesis"变成了"poetry"，后者主要是一种模仿，与真实的生产（produce）相对立。这样，"poiesis"原初所具有的性质就隐而不彰，而变成了模仿性制作。诗被置于制造欺骗谎言的位置上，诗的美也只能是一种满足感性快乐的东西而遭到排斥。

　　但要注意的是，正是这种话语机制使柏拉图能够最清晰地把握美的理念，即一种纯粹的、不与现实需要纠缠在一起的美。这对此后的美学发展是至关重要的，因为它奠定了美学所要讨论的问题的概念基础。当一种真正的概念被提炼出来后，与该概念相关的现象就会围绕着该概念聚集并丰富其内涵与外延。在此意义上，一个核心概念的形成意味着一种去蔽的显露。而柏拉图通过其形而上学对美的概念的铸造，将纠缠于神话巫术中的感受性的但缺乏定性的美，转变为一种独立的、具有自身定性的美本体。在柏拉图的阐述中，这种美本身就是一种存在的真理，是一种共相。也就是说，柏拉图通过形而上学的架构，不仅呈现了一个清晰的、独立的美的概念，还将美与真理融合在一起。尽管有学者称，柏拉图对话中对美的讨论不能看作柏拉图的美学。但我们认为，柏拉图对美的讨论，固然是其形而上学的一部分，但不能把这种讨论看成是非美学的，因为在柏拉图所建立的美的理念与诗和艺术的感性美的对立中，也隐含了一条从前者思考后者的道路，即如果美的理念是正当的，那么诗和艺术中的感性美如何才能具有这样的内涵？如果美本身是一种真理，是本真知识的显示，那么，艺术如何才能与这样的真理相关？也就是说，柏拉图的哲学显示了一条通过先验理智直观校正隐含于神话巫术中的诗性直观直接通向理念知识的路径。这种先验理智直观对隐含于神话巫术中的诗性直观的校正，在柏拉图的爱欲理论中得到了另一种展示。

四　结论

柏拉图的诗与哲学之争，并非要完全取消诗和艺术，而是要对只提供感性幻象和感性快乐的传统的神话诗与模仿的艺术进行清算，并转变为一种与本真知识兼容的生命的理智直观奠基的诗和艺术。从这个层面来看，我们才能理解柏拉图排斥的是什么样的诗，希望造就的又是什么样的诗和艺术。也就是说，诗哲之争体现了一种用先验理智直观剥离出遮蔽在神话巫术中真正的诗性直观的探索。

综合看来，柏拉图的理想即在于诗与哲学的融合。当然，他心目中诗与哲学的融合不仅仅是形式上的联合，他真正关心的是二者内容上的互补。一方面，哲学可以采用诗的表达方式，使哲学言论更能被理解和接受；另一方面，诗人能从哲学中吸取自己所需要的知识，增强思想中理智的力量。理想境界就是诗和哲学在某种程度上的"配合"给柏拉图关心的语言艺术带来蓬勃的生机。语言可以"升华"，可以讲述含义深刻的道理。富有诗意的"哲学论谈"将最大限度地发挥语言揭示真理的潜力。

客观看来，柏拉图实现诗与哲学融合的理想在西方美学史上是具有开创性意义的，不仅拓宽了人们的学术视野，在诸多问题的理解上也都颇为独特。但是，这种"跨学科"思想是在没有严格定义诗和哲学的前提下产生的，无疑会造成概念的模糊和内涵的混乱。更重要的是，柏拉图评价文艺的标准是政治标准而从根本上否定了艺术标准。因此，在肯定它的同时，也应认识其局限性。

第二节 古希腊悲剧时代的哲学

一 上帝之死

形而上学的上帝死了，标志着哲学的终结；道成肉身的上帝死了，象征着宗教的开始。"上帝死了"意味着真正的宗教：不是一个权威在我们之上，而是一个精神在我们之中。[①]

尼采的"上帝之死"是继启蒙运动之后对西方形而上学最彻底的批判，是对逻各斯中心主义的彻底瓦解，是对柏拉图传统的彻底颠覆。尼采要将作为"体系"的哲学传统置换为"哲学家"的哲学传统，呼唤用"酒神精神"来对抗"日神精神"，要将哲学的目光投向柏拉图之前的古希腊。然而，尽管尼采的哲学回归有着重要价值，其寻找真理的努力值得赞赏，但是他的路径仍然是哲学式的，亦即柏拉图式的。他寻找真理的目的值得肯定，但寻找真理的手段仍然是哲学式的，这里的问题是：哲学是唯一的寻找真理的手段吗？哲学的手段是否真的可以找到真理？尼采坚持在这一持续了两千余年的柏拉图传统的基础上批判这种传统。如此，他的批判是彻底和有效的吗？

二 古希腊悲剧时代的哲学

尼采的"上帝之死"让我们不得不重新思考古希腊悲剧时代的哲学。古希腊悲剧时代不独有苏格拉底、柏拉图，还有悲剧家如埃斯库罗斯、索福克勒斯和欧里庇得斯。除了柏拉图笔下的苏格拉底，以及在舞台上谈论哲学的欧里庇得斯，我们还有在大街上拉着人谈论哲学的苏格拉底，还有不谈论哲学的索福克勒斯。那么，这其中的差别何在？假如哲学肇始于亚里士多德，我们或许永远无法理解柏拉图，更

[①] Kevin J. Vanhoozer, *Biblical Narrative in the Philosophy of Paul Ricoeur: A Study in Hermeneutics and Theology*, Cambridge: Cambridge University Press, 1990, p.131.

无从理解苏格拉底以及前苏格拉底的古希腊文明。"哲学首先意味着一种生活或生活方式，一种以沉思和言谈为行动的特殊生活方式。"[①]哲学不是一个体系，而是哲学家的"个性"。哲学家的"个性"，应该指哲学家对人生的独特理解和态度。哲学家对生活的理解关乎生命的意义，哲学家对于生活的态度体现了人性的伟大，因此哲学启迪着民族和人类。假如哲学史变成体系更替的历史，"势必会埋没那些个性的东西"[②]。纵然体系会遭到摒弃，哲学家的个性却永远散发着光芒。与体系相比，个性不但更有价值，也更接近本原。哲学不是知识，而是一种生活方式。哲学不以求知为目的，因为那是科学的思维。"哲学就是从给'伟大'立法开始的。"[③]哲学所寻求的是神圣而无用的东西，利益和有用是科学的动机。哲学关乎生命——不是肉体的存在，而是精神的价值。哲学对生命的关切乃是对生命意义的关切。

假如哲学也是一种生活方式，那么，哲学与作为生活方式的诗有何区别？既然哲学也是一种生活方式，那么柏拉图何以要将诗人逐出理想国？诗是一种生活方式，这是毋庸置疑的。苏格拉底曾视荷马为全希腊的教育者。早在柏拉图之前，希罗多德就说过："荷马和赫西俄德……把诸神的家世教给希腊人，把它们的一些名字、尊荣和技艺教给所有的人，并且说出了它们的外形。"[④]荷马和赫西俄德通过对神的谱系的描绘，为希腊的民族、城邦政治共同体制定了一种生活方式——一种由诸神参与、保证的生活方式。荷马的史诗将英雄的德性如勇敢确立为最高的生活伦理，而将诸神保证或体现的生活确立为"最好的和最高尚的生活"。也就是说，"诗"对于立法和建立政治制度还有进一步的意义。[⑤]与哲学相比，诗这种方式更能提供或容纳整

① 戈登等：《戏剧诗人柏拉图》，刘麒麟、黄莎等译，华东师范大学出版社，导言第19页。
② 尼采：《希腊悲剧时代的哲学》，周国平译，译林出版社，2011，第8页。
③ 尼采：《希腊悲剧时代的哲学》，周国平译，译林出版社，2011，第62页。
④ 希罗多德：《历史》（上），王以铸译，商务印书馆，1959，第135页。
⑤ 戈登等：《戏剧诗人柏拉图》，刘麒麟、黄莎等译，华东师范大学出版社，导言第19页。

全的知识——荷马的两部史诗《伊利亚特》和《奥德赛》可谓涵盖了人的全部生活。因此，哲学要追求关于人的生活的整全知识，就要向诗学习。也因此，柏拉图一方面将诗人逐出"理想国"，另一方面却以"诗"为城邦重新立言。

柏拉图以"诗"为批判对象，并借助"诗"为城邦重新立言，意义何在？既然荷马的史诗是政治性的，那么作为竞争者的柏拉图的"诗"也一定是政治性的。荷马的史诗描述的是城邦人必需的生活方式，柏拉图则用哲学诗替换这种生活方式。柏拉图自己就是诗人，而他也决意以"诗"的方式驱逐荷马。究其原因，一是理性的限度问题，二是以彼之矛攻彼之盾。哲学家要求整全的智慧或者绝对的知识，但只有神才拥有绝对的知识和整全的智慧，哲学家无法依靠理性做到这一点。诗的语言对哲学来说是必需的，理性言辞无法达到终极言说的目的。就算哲人穷尽一生追问理性，理性的根本限度也依然无法克服。因此在《理想国》中，苏格拉底接二连三地运用太阳、洞穴等比喻说明形而上的道理。[①] 就政治而言，政治生活的秩序不能仅仅依靠论证——论证可以无限制地拖延，但是政治问题刻不容缓。因此，立法者的立法行动不能完全听命于理性，而必须借助神话、故事、寓言，也即借助诗。所以对政治来说，重要的不是知识、论证、哲学和真理，而是意见、神话、诗和谎言。也因此，哲学家必然与城邦政治共同体发生冲突。柏拉图所谓的"高贵的谎言"，是针对大多数人而言的。既然理性是有限度的，既然大多数人不可能依靠理性想明白哲人立法的理据和基础，那么最有效的方式就是利用"故事"来对多数人进行说服和教育。"故事"（诗）因此成了城邦政治教育最好的方式。当故事一代一代地流传下去，当子孙后代最终相信了故事，一种崭新的习俗或宗法制度就被确立了。这种"故事"就是"高

① 参见 J.Howland, *The Republic: The Odyssey of Philosophy*, Philadelphia: Paul Dry Books, 1993, p.120。

贵的谎言"。"高贵的谎言"并非完全与真理背道而驰，而是"正确的意见"，即使不是"正确的意见"，也是大多数人乐于接受的意见，柏拉图的新诗就是这样一种"高贵的谎言"。然而，并非所有的"谎言"和"故事"都是高贵的。假如编撰故事者刻意污蔑他人、篡改历史，这种"恶意的谎言"就会遗祸万年。

哲学在离开物理、数理探究之后重新起航，这是柏拉图在《斐多》里借苏格拉底之口说的"第二次起航"。哲学的"第二次起航"离不开诗，因此柏拉图以"诗"为手段为城邦重新立言。如果说荷马的史诗是旧体诗，那么柏拉图的哲学诗就是新体诗。荷马的史诗代表的是民众的习俗生活，是城邦中多数人过的那种宗法生活；柏拉图的哲学代表的是一种新兴的生活，是少数人过的那种追求智慧的生活。荷马的史诗规定的是一种神学—政治的生活方式，而柏拉图的哲学诗规定的是一种哲学—政治的生活方式，这或许可被视为雅典内部的"雅典与耶路撒冷之争"[1]。虽然同为政治性的，但前一种是宗教的、感性的，后一种是哲学的、理性的。柏拉图反对荷马，是因为荷马的史诗拥抱的是"意见"，依赖的是"爱欲"，所处的位置是"洞穴里"，目的是"在每个人的灵魂里确立一种恶的政治制度"。柏拉图写戏剧，运用神话、比喻、寓言等文学手段和修辞手法，目的是以新的诗体对抗荷马的旧诗。荷马的笔下有阿喀琉斯，柏拉图则塑造了新的英雄形象苏格拉底：阿喀琉斯为荣誉而生，苏格拉底为正义而死；阿喀琉斯是勇敢的化身，苏格拉底是道德的楷模；阿喀琉斯为爱欲驱使，苏格拉底受理性制约。总之，柏拉图用自己的诗驱逐了荷马的诗。

古希腊悲剧时代的哲学，是"诗哲之争"的开始，也是"诗哲之争"的结束。旷日持久的诗哲之争导致了西方两千年逻各斯中心主义的危机，而重回诗哲之争是解决这一危机的路径。"解铃还须系铃

---

[1] Thomas Pangle, "Introduction", in *Studies in Political Philosophy*, Chicago: The University of Chicago Press, 1983, p.20.

人"，柏拉图被视为西方理性哲学的奠基人，那么重回柏拉图，便是破解逻各斯中心主义危机的关键。

尼采批判柏拉图以降的西方理性哲学传统，因为在这个传统中"诗"已经没有任何地位。在两千余年为柏拉图注解的传统中，柏拉图的"诗哲之争"被单纯理解为"诗"与"哲学"的冲突。然而，"诗""哲"的彻底对立不仅是对柏拉图的曲解，也无法解决现代人的精神危机。哲学对生命意义的关切不可避免地把人类引向形而上学，然而问题在于，形而上学是直观的、神秘的而非科学的、逻辑的——"这个形而上信念的根源深藏在某种神秘直觉之中"[①]。尼采重回悲剧时代的哲学，目的是推翻西方两千余年来对柏拉图注解、误解的传统。

尼采重回古希腊，将矛头指向悲剧时代的哲学，但落脚在更久远的传统上。尼采更推崇赫拉克利特，尽管毕达哥拉斯和恩培多克勒也是无比骄傲的，但是赫拉克利特更为孤绝：他超越了人类，与宇宙融合，成为世界的本体，成为不朽的真理和神灵。"世界永远需要真理，因而永远需要赫拉克利特，尽管赫拉克利特并不需要世界。"[②]尼采之所以推崇赫拉克利特，是因为他坚决反对靠逻辑来把握世界的本质，这一点显然深受康德的影响。尼采认为哲学对世界本质的认识首先是一种直觉，而它达到这种认识的真正手段是想象而非逻辑。从一开始，尼采就把形而上学看作一种信念、直觉、想象，而非科学和逻辑。为此，尼采尤其推崇泰勒斯、赫拉克利特等古代哲学家。他说："当泰勒斯说'一切是水'的时候，人类就突破了单门科学的蠕虫式的触摸和原地爬行，预感到了事物的最终答案，并借助这种预感克服了较低认识水平的一般限制。"[③]在尼采看来，用科学的、逻辑的手段来表达任何一种深刻的哲学直觉，虽然是描述所观看到的东西的唯一

---

① 尼采：《希腊悲剧时代的哲学》，周国平译，译林出版社，2011，第 59 页。

② 尼采：《希腊悲剧时代的哲学》，周国平译，译林出版社，2011，第 84 页。

③ 尼采：《希腊悲剧时代的哲学》，周国平译，译林出版社，2011，第 62 页。

手段，但也是一种可怜的手段，从本质上来说，这只是"向一种不同领域和不同语言的隐喻式的、完全不可靠的转译"①。泰勒斯看到了存在物的统一，但是如何描述、如何传达他的发现呢？这里涉及的不仅是理性的限度问题，还有语言的限度问题。于是他想到了"水"，选择用"水"这一意象来表达最深奥的哲学思想。这一意象无疑是诗性的，这一语言也是诗性的，它唤醒的不仅仅是诗的感觉，还有诗的想象。其实无论是泰勒斯的"水"、赫拉克利特的"火"，还是德谟克里特的"原子"，事情并无本质不同。在科学的构筑崩塌的时候，也终归还剩下一些东西，正是这些剩下的东西，包含着一种动力，甚至包含着将来开花结果的希望——"这剩下的东西实际上就是对于'存在物的统一'的直觉，就是使人类能够超越于经验世界的形而上信念"②。如果舍弃这种直觉，哲学就失去了其存在的动力。

三 结语

古希腊人是典型的哲学民族，他们的"爱智传统"闻名于世。"其他民族出圣徒，希腊出哲人……在别的时代、别的地方，哲学家是在最敌对环境中偶然的、孤独的漫游者，他们不是隐姓埋名，就是孤军奋战。只有在希腊人那里，哲学家才不是偶然的。"③古希腊人不是为了求知而从事哲学，他们"凭借对生命的关切，凭借一种理想上的生命需要，约束了他们原本贪得无厌的求知欲"，从而创造了"典型的哲学头脑"。④对生命意义的关切，使古希腊人变得有"文化"。我们的时代之所以在尼采看来没文化，是因为我们失去了对生命意义的关切，在没有文化的时代里，哲学注定只是"孤独的散步者的学术

---

① 尼采：《希腊悲剧时代的哲学》，周国平译，译林出版社，2011，第62页。
② 尼采：《希腊悲剧时代的哲学》，周国平译，译林出版社，2011，第15页。
③ 尼采：《希腊悲剧时代的哲学》，周国平译，译林出版社，2011，第51页。
④ 尼采：《希腊悲剧时代的哲学》，周国平译，译林出版社，2011，第49页。

自白，是个别人的侥幸的战利品，是隐居的密室，或者是老态龙钟的学者与稚子之间无害的唠叨"①。古希腊人是有文化的,因为他们健康，一个民族唯有健康才能赋予哲学以充分的权力。古罗马人也健康，但他们无需哲学而生活。文化使古希腊人具有了敏锐的辨别能力，这是一种极高的趣味。"要给一个民族定性，与其看它有些什么伟大人物，不如看它以什么方式认定和推崇这些伟大人物。"②古希腊盛产哲学家，古希腊人以他们为荣。哲学家傲视一切，视利益为过眼云烟。哲学家的伟大不取决于人类对他的态度，而人类的伟大却取决于其对哲学家的态度。哲学家的骄傲莫过于此，古希腊的骄傲也莫过于此。古希腊哲学是古希腊人的骄傲，也是全人类的宝贵财富。

---

① 尼采:《希腊悲剧时代的哲学》，周国平译，译林出版社，2011，第51页。
② 尼采:《希腊悲剧时代的哲学》，周国平译，译林出版社，2011，第51页。

第二部分

希伯来传统

第一章 《旧约》传统之历史篇

第一节 《耶利米哀歌》与希伯来人的苦难史

一 引言

希伯来文明诞生在迦南，即今巴勒斯坦地区。公元前 1200 年至公元前 400 年，希伯来人创立了犹太教，他们信仰上帝耶和华，宣称希伯来人是上帝的选民，与上帝签订有契约。近千年的历史中，希伯来人饱受战火蹂躏、流离失所，犹太教成为维系希伯来人民族意识的精神组带。《耶利米哀歌》深切地反映了希伯来人命途多舛的苦难史，以及在灾难面前的无能为力，他们希望依托信仰获得救赎、重建家园。

二 希伯来人的历史

希伯来人原本是闪米特族的一个分支，本意为"渡河而来的人"。公元前 3000 年左右，在犹太族长亚伯拉罕的带领下，犹太人从乌尔城渡过幼发拉底河和约旦河迁往迦南，史称希伯来人。公元前 935 年，希伯来王国分裂成北方的以色列国和南方的犹大国，以色列国在公元前 722 年被亚述人所灭。公元前 972 年，犹大国国王大卫之子所罗门执政，并在都城耶路撒冷建造了圣殿，从此圣殿成为犹太人权力的中心和信仰的象征，但犹太人并未从此过上安稳的生活。此后的几百年，犹大国纷争不断，先后被多个国家攻占，圣殿一度被毁。

公元前586年，犹大国被巴比伦王国消灭，尼布甲尼撒大帝占领了犹大国首都耶路撒冷，摧毁了所罗门圣殿，并俘虏了大量上层民众到巴比伦做苦役。公元前538年，波斯帝国征服巴比伦王国后将囚禁在巴比伦的犹太人遣返，犹太人返回耶路撒冷后又重建圣殿（第二圣殿）。波斯帝国允许犹太人在服从波斯统治的前提下进行神权统治，此时的犹大国虽然享有自治权，却早已不是一个独立的主权国家。公元前331年，亚历山大攻克迦南，犹大国被希腊帝国统治。希腊统治前期，犹太人依然享有宗教自由。安条克四世即位后，为了稳固政权，开始对犹太人实行高压统治，镇压犹太教。公元前168年，安条克四世颁布了人类历史上第一个毁灭宗教的命令。他公然宣布犹太教为非法宗教，下令废止一切犹太教的节期，焚烧全部圣书，禁止犹太人行割礼、过安息日，废除犹太人的所有宗教禁忌，命令犹太人必须改信希腊宗教，并在耶路撒冷圣殿拜祭奥林匹亚宙斯祭坛。违者一律当场处死。为了羞辱犹太人，就用犹太人视为不洁的猪进行献祭，并强令犹太人食猪肉。在安条克四世的残暴统治下，犹太人揭竿而起，爆发了玛喀比起义。经过25年漫长而艰难的斗争，英勇顽强的犹太民族终于在公元前143年解放了巴勒斯坦全境，取得了民族独立。后来的罗马帝国将犹太地区变成罗马的一个行省。罗马攻占巴勒斯坦后，犹太人爆发起义反抗罗马占领者，但都遭到了罗马统治者的血腥镇压。公元135年，犹太人再次起义，最终惨败。在这一个多世纪的时间里，罗马统治者屠杀了150万犹太人，最后将剩余的犹太人全部遣散，耶路撒冷被彻底夷为平地，犹太政权不复存在，犹太人长达两千年的流浪从此开始。

三　《耶利米哀歌》

《耶利米哀歌》属于智慧书，共有 5 章，记载了犹太人在耶路撒冷和圣殿被毁（公元前 586 年）之后所作的哀歌。一般认为《耶利米哀歌》是先知耶利米所作，创作于公元前 586 年巴比伦王国攻克耶路撒冷时期。此次战争是希伯来人苦难史的开始，其间圣殿被摧毁，大批希伯来居民被俘往巴比伦为奴长达半个世纪，史称"巴比伦之囚"。曾经的犹大国在大卫—所罗门时代达到鼎盛，百姓安居乐业。如今城陷国殇，犹太人只能在敌人的践踏下悲惨地唱着亡国哀歌。

这首哀歌表达的并非"个人之悲"，而是国破家亡的"民族之悲"，其哀伤程度远比任何伤感作品都要深切沉重。没有任何一种情感比国破家亡、飘无所依更为灰暗和震撼人心。而在希伯来人的民族记忆里，亡国之痛将他们内心的痛感放大到极致。然而，对于这种亡国之痛、丧权之辱，当时的犹太民族却无力改变。在《耶利米哀歌》中，犹太人将战争的源头指向了现世的罪恶——"耶路撒冷大大犯罪，所以成为不洁之物。素来尊敬他的、见他赤露就都藐视他。他自己也叹息退后"[1]。他们认为"耶和华是公义的，他这样待我是因我违背他的命令"[2]。耶和华发怒降罪于人世，唯有虔诚忏悔，才能依靠"信仰得救"，这是一种对悲惨现世的无力呼告。希伯来人一直宣称自己是上帝的选民，而在现实中，犹太地区却始终饱受战乱之苦。希伯来人信仰的最高象征——所罗门圣殿已被敌人的铁蹄无情踏碎，希伯来精神已被摧毁。这种信仰与现实的矛盾将他们引向了一种解释人间一切苦难的基本观念，即"人罪"与"神罚"。

以"神的意旨"作为一切行为的绝对价值标准，信靠耶和华，彻底悔罪才能改变悲惨的命运，这一解释很好地连接了绝望的现实和希

---

[1] 《圣经·耶利米哀歌》第 1 章第 8 节。
[2] 《圣经·耶利米哀歌》第 1 章第 18 节。

望的未来，这是在肉体折磨的基础上实现精神解脱的必然要求。所以《耶利米哀歌》整体来说是乐观主义的，符合一般信仰的基本特点。其前几章描述了耶路撒冷的悲惨状况和上帝的判罚，而后几章转而呼告上帝惩罚侵略者，"耶和华啊，你要按着他们手所作的，向他们施行报应。你要使他们心里刚硬，使你的咒诅临到他们。你要发怒追赶他们，从耶和华的天下除灭他们"[1]。他们祈求重得上帝的悦纳，庇佑信徒脱离困境，重回家园。

四 结语

希伯来民族是一个命途多舛的民族，饱受战乱之痛，倍受流离之苦。然而希伯来人凭借顽强的信念和坚定的信仰一直英勇抗争，最终创作出一部部不朽的名篇经典，同时在世界文明史上留下了不可磨灭的精神印记。

第二节 《旧约》中的民族主义

一 一神论的信仰

希伯来人自亚伯拉罕以来就确立了一神教信仰，这在亚伯拉罕献祭以撒的故事中表现得淋漓尽致：《创世记》讲述了亚伯拉罕献祭以撒的故事。神要考验亚伯拉罕，要求亚伯拉罕带着他最爱的独生子以撒前往摩利亚地，在神指示的山上，把以撒献为燔祭。而这个儿子是亚伯拉罕晚年才生育的，所以对他来说十分重要。在独生子与神的命令之间，亚伯拉罕该做怎样的选择呢？虽然心痛万分，亚伯拉罕还是决定服从神的命令。于是清早起来，备上驴，带着两个仆人和儿子

---

[1] 《圣经·耶利米哀歌》第 3 章第 64 节。

以撒，并劈好了燔祭的柴，起身前往神指示的地方。亚伯拉罕把燔祭的柴放在他儿子以撒身上，自己拿着火与刀。以撒问父亲亚伯拉罕："请看，火与柴都有了，但燔祭的羊羔在哪里呢？"亚伯拉罕说："我儿，神必自己预备作燔祭的羊羔。"于是二人同行前往，等到了神指示的地方，亚伯拉罕开始筑坛，把柴摆好后捆绑起他的儿子以撒，并将其放在神坛的木柴上。之后亚伯拉罕伸手拿刀，准备杀他的儿子。耶和华的使者从天上呼叫他不要杀以撒，天使知道亚伯拉罕是真的敬畏神灵。这时正有一只公羊，两角扣在稠密的小树中，亚伯拉罕就将那只公羊献为燔祭，来代替他的儿子。

二　信仰与民族身份

在雅各与天使角力后，神让雅各更名为"以色列"，从此雅各的子孙就被称为以色列人。虽然以色列人仍然保留着一神教信仰，然而在迦南多神教的氛围中、在埃及人的统治下、在亚述人的征服中，以色列人渐渐受到多神教的影响并逐渐偏离了自己的信仰传统，或者说他们的信仰不那么纯正了。而北以色列亡国以后，南犹大国在被掳巴比伦和波斯的危难中意识到信仰的纯正对于维系民族的重要性，因此开始以各种方式加强信仰的力量；然而这一努力也逃不过后来希腊化的侵袭，犹太人要么在希腊化的环境中被希腊化，要么在外邦人的逼迫中开始走向民族主义的极端。纵观这一发展历程可以发现，犹太人的信仰与其民族意识的关联相当紧密，无论是对第二圣殿犹太教还是对拉比犹太教来说都是如此。

"巴比伦之囚"后的亡国历史，使犹太人对民族身份更加敏感。虽然波斯人的短暂统治和亚历山大大帝、托勒密王朝的宽松政策在一定程度上缓解了这种敏感，但是塞琉古王朝的苛刻政策进一步强化了这种敏感；虽然希腊化的环境让一部分犹太人的民族意识逐渐淡化，尤其是犹太人中的贵族阶层、祭司阶层、既得利益者，但是犹太教内部的改革却让一部分犹太人（尤其是法利赛人）的神经更加敏感。这里颇有意思的是法利赛人对亲罗马的希律家族和犹太人祭司阶层的仇恨，还不及对耶稣的仇恨。由此可见，所谓的民族主义，有时只不过是一种借口：法利赛人是之后拉比犹太教的主力，因为第二圣殿被毁后，犹太人的其他支派如撒都该人、拿撒勒派和奋锐党人都消失了；法利赛人由此形成了一种更加敏感的民族主义。那为什么在耶稣的时代，法利赛人的民族主义情结不如奋锐党人呢？他们把矛头指向改革者耶稣而非罗马的傀儡政府，是因为耶稣对他们的指责吗？可见，民族主义有时候只是出于某种目的而被某一群人利用的工具。再以马卡比家族为例。马卡比家族起义最初是具有民族解放的积极意义的，但是当哈斯蒙尼王朝建立后，它也与异族进行了极大的利益交换，这足以说明所谓的民族主义在利益面前的虚伪性。

历史上北以色列与南犹大的争执，似乎是犹太人狭隘的民族主义的最好例证。自家兄弟尚且不断争斗、互相残杀、水火不容，更谈不上对外邦人的宽容！从重建圣殿开始，犹太人激进的民族主义不断强化：从尼西米、以斯拉禁止犹太人与外族人通婚开始，到后来的马卡比革命，这种倾向性愈演愈烈。遭受了亡国之痛的犹太人，开始反思自己的历史：一些先知勇敢地抨击希伯来人的偏激、固执，抨击上层统治者的腐败、堕落，呼吁宗教宽容，但是另一部分先知却强化了希伯来人的民族意识与排外情绪。例如，大祭司以斯拉就是一个狭隘的民族主义者。在重返耶路撒冷后，以斯拉最重要的工作除了重建圣殿，就是重整民风，认为那些"没有离绝迦南人、赫人、比利洗人、耶布斯人、亚扪人、摩押人、埃及人、亚摩利人"的希伯来人是罪恶的。而他的反应也异常强烈："撕裂衣服和外袍，拔了头发和胡须，惊惧忧闷而坐。他们便应许必休他们的妻。他们因有罪，就献群中的一只公绵羊赎罪。"这一时期祭司们与犹太人重新订立了公约，让剩下的民众发誓："并不将我们的女儿嫁给这地（外邦）的居民，也不为我们的儿子娶他们的女儿。"这种与外邦人划清界限的做法，虽然保持了犹太人的血统，但加深了不同民族间的隔阂。

犹太人不仅与外邦人、外族人断绝往来，甚至与同族也不能和平共处。例如，先知俄巴底亚就自称得到耶和华的启示，诅咒以东人，因为在耶路撒冷遭到破坏时，以东人幸灾乐祸，甚至助纣为虐、抢劫灾民，把难民出卖给侵略者。然而实际上，以东人是雅各的哥哥以扫的后代，他们住在以东，因为以东是山国，所以人们住在山上。但是犹太人认为以东人是宿敌，并要求耶和华惩罚以东。《玛拉基书》的开头也是骂以东人，传达的宗教思想极为狭隘，缺乏宽广的胸襟。《哈该书》也表现出狭隘的民族主义：哈该盼望犹大省长做国王，把财宝都集中到耶路撒冷，让万国之民都来此崇拜耶和华。

先知们诅咒巴比伦、亚述等侵略者，等待着他们的灭亡。如《那鸿书》就控诉了亚述王，并寄希望于尼尼微的毁灭："万军之耶和华说：'我与你为敌，必将你的车辆焚烧成烟，刀剑也必吞没你的少壮狮子。我必从地上除灭你所撕碎的，你使者的声音必不再听见。"经历了国破家亡的先知，不但将愤怒倾泻于侵略者亚述，也波及其他所谓的"仇敌"："耶和华是忌邪施报的神。耶和华施报大有忿怒；向他的敌人施报，向他的仇敌怀怒……巴珊和迦密的树林衰残；黎巴嫩的花草也衰残了。"使以色列与犹大灭亡的强权帝国固然可恨，但那些经济实力不如犹太人的邻国、不信仰耶和华的人在希伯来人看来也很可恶："迦萨必致见弃；亚实基伦必然荒凉。人在正午必赶出亚实突的民，以革伦也被拔出根来。住沿海之地的基利提族有祸了！迦南、非利士人之地啊，耶和华的话与你反对，说：我必毁灭你，以致无人居住。"北以色列在亚述帝国的统治下与南犹大在巴比伦的统治下都没有爆发激烈的起义，而在塞琉古王朝统治下却爆发了著名的马卡比革命。原因大概在于：亚述与巴比伦都属于亚洲国家，其文化、宗教和希伯来的相似，外来统治者不太干预文化；而希腊文化跟希伯来文化有着根本区别，统治者干预希伯来人的宗教文化，甚至用强制手段改变希伯来人的宗教文化。如公元前 2 世纪，塞琉古王安条克四世埃庇芬（公元前 175 年至公元前 164 年）大力提倡希腊文化。他在耶路撒冷旁边建竞技场，在耶和华的圣殿中立起宙斯神像叫人膜拜，在耶和华的祭坛上献猪，并禁止犹太人行割礼。这些文化上的压迫比政治上的压迫更令人不能忍受，于是引发了公元前 165 年的马卡比革命。

对于某些犹太人的极端民族主义，基督徒是持反对态度的，尤其是初期的基督徒，因为他们不仅仅是犹太人，更多的是外邦人。如果说初期的基督徒还包括犹太人（尤其是散居地的犹太人、混居在外邦人中的犹太人）的话，那么后来的基督教就慢慢被外邦人占据了（尤其是基督教变成罗马国教之后）。虽然大部分的犹太人坚持民族主义，尤其是狭隘的、极端的民族主义的态度，但是更多的表现在文化领域，奋锐党人则将这种极端民族主义变成了政治行动。而这种狭隘、极端的民族主义，又成为初期基督教内部争论的焦点（保罗、约翰派与彼得、雅各派），也成为之后基督教与拉比犹太教的重要区别（甚至可以说是主要区别）。

三 选民意识

那么，是什么造就了希伯来人（以色列人或犹太人）如此狭隘的民族心理呢？答案是"选民身份"和"选民意识"。在以色列人的自我理解中，有一点是基本的：他们确信自己是耶和华拣选的。神拣选了以色列，而以色列通过特殊的契约（covenant）回应了神的拣选。这一点比"一神论信仰"更深地植根于放逐前的时代，在远古的故事和信经的教义中，这一点被不断地强调：从亚伯拉罕被神拣选到神应允亚伯拉罕土地。《创世记》第 12 章第 1~3 节和第 15 章第 1~6 节叙述了最初的选择和神对亚伯拉罕的应允，而这一点在第 15 章第 17~21 节以及第 17 章第 1~8 节中以契约的形式得到了明确的规定。

在《申命记》中，我们能够看到这种强势的陈述："要从应许之地上清除其他民族，不要与他们纠缠在一起。"中心部分则叙述了耶和华帮助以色列出埃及，并把土地赐予以色列先祖的神圣动机。

这一选民意识在第二圣殿犹太教中扮演了极为重要的角色，也就是说，北以色列灭亡的教训与南犹大国被掳的命运强化了这一选民意识。于是，选民意识与圣殿、妥拉一起，成为第二圣殿犹太教的主要支柱。对于选民身份和圣殿意义的强调（波斯人允许犹太人重建圣殿、先知以斯拉带领族人重建圣殿，这对犹太人来说有着不同寻常的意义：第二圣殿对于犹太人民族身份的意义更甚于所罗门圣殿）、对于妥拉的整理（第一圣殿被毁后被掳的犹太人失去了敬拜的场所，因此对于书面的妥拉传统更加重视），成为第二圣殿犹太教的主要支柱，这些支撑重建了犹太人后放逐时代的信仰。民族主义在第二圣殿犹太教时期被加强了，因为北以色列的亡国（不是客观意义上的，而是精神意义上的）给予犹太人一个沉重的经验教训，使其意识到信仰身份与民族身份对建立国家的重要性。以斯拉坚决反对异族通婚（虽然这一传统在以色列人的历史上一直存在），并借此清除这种纠缠中的人民与土地。先知们以严厉的话语警告犹太人：以色列是神拣选的与他族隔离的人民。虽然先知们的这种做法是可以理解的：遭受了亡国之痛的犹太人，如果不能采取极端方式维护自己的信仰身份和民族身份，那么他们就会像撒玛利亚人一样消失于历史的尘埃中。但是这种选民意识和选民身份很容易造成一种族裔的优越感和极端的排他性，而这也成为后来犹太人被西方世界排斥的重要原因。

以斯拉的改革再一次使妥拉占据了以色列人生活的核心位置。与第二圣殿犹太教的其他基本特点一起，契约律法主义的模式在马卡比革命时期被大大加强了。在马卡比时期，契约子民、律法子民的以色列身份危如累卵；而部分犹太人对这一危机的回应通过"对律法的热心"表现出来，并将此作为民族反抗的口号。马卡比反抗异族文化与民族同化的力量出自这样一种信念：以色列的土地和民众，不仅仅是众多中的一个，而是那个独一神的特殊拣选。在马卡比革命后，拣选、契约与律法的交错仍然是犹太人自我理解的基本主题。便·西拉（Ben Sira）呼应了《申命记》的假设：耶和华的王权与对以色列的特殊拣选。便·西拉把宇宙神圣智慧称为"至高无上神的契约书、摩西命令我们遵守的作为雅各遗产的律法"。《禧年书》也对犹太人的选民身份与契约身份进行了强化。通过不断重复耶和华订立的契约、与之相关的律法义务、耶和华对以色列人的特殊拣选，这些作品不断强化着犹太人的选民意识。昆兰社团的情形也是如此。

以色列人（犹太人）对律法的坚守会让人产生一种很自然的、或多或少都无法避免的看法：这一独特性意味着特权，即被独一神拣选和赐予契约律法的民族拥有一种特权。在那些忽视、否定外邦人并将其视为罪人的叙述中，这一点显而易见。这种特权意识不仅引起了希腊化时期外邦人的反感，也引发了后来基督教世界对犹太人的普遍仇恨。即使在今天巴以激烈的对抗中，我们也无法以绝对的同情站在以色列一边。对于外部世界的这种敌视，犹太人要么闭关自守、视而不见，要么试图美化自身的这一传统（特权意识）。面对越来越强大的外邦人世界，犹太人不得不试图对以色列的这种宣言（独一神拣选的子民）、叙述（将外邦人视为罪人）进行道歉。

犹太教所坚持的以色列的独特性及特权意识造就了犹太民族狭隘的、极端的民族主义。这种特权意识让以色列人（犹太人）产生了一种优越感，这种优越感在得势的时候，会成为压迫外邦人的工具；而在外邦人得势时，这种特权意识作为犹太人自我理解的一部分，在其对社会、世界的看法中处于重要位置。从社会学的视野来看，特殊的拣选与契约律法主义不可避免地成为犹太人独特的表达方式——尤其是律法，还有仪式上的实践，都强化了犹太人独特的身份意识。在犹太人的律法中，除了不与外族（主要指亚扪人、摩押人）通婚的律法，还有三点将犹太人与外邦人明显区分开来：割礼、安息日、食物律例。无论从犹太人内部，还是从希腊—罗马世界外部来看，这三点都是犹太人的身份标记。

四　结语

从最初的拣选开始，"犹太教"这个词的含义就不断被强化："犹太教"将犹太人的信仰与民族意识越来越紧密地结合在一起，而这种强化也带来了极大的负面影响。以色列人的这种选民意识所造成的族裔优越感和排他性成了自己被排斥的原因。由此可见，这种族裔身份就是一把双刃剑：它可以保全犹太民族，也可以毁灭犹太民族。然而可惜的是，犹太人的这种信念一直延续到我们这个时代，巴以冲突就是一个见证。更可悲的是，这种极端的民族主义不仅仅体现在阿拉伯人与以色列人的冲突中。综观全球局势，从爱尔兰人与英格兰人的矛盾到俄罗斯人与其他民族如乌克兰人的冲突，全世界范围内的极端民族主义倾向愈演愈烈。可见，二战时纳粹德国的屠杀只不过是一个缩影，而其带来的教训也没有为人类真正接受。恰恰相反，狭隘的民族主义还在被一些学者鼓吹、被一些政客利用，世界和平仍然面临着巨大威胁。从这个角度来说，犹太人就是全人类的缩影，因此反思犹太人的历史，就是反思整个人类的历史；而正视犹太人的现在，就是正视全人类的现在。

第三节　《旧约》中的世界主义

一　《旧约》中的耶和华

在《旧约》中，上帝被称为"耶和华"（也译作"雅赫维"）：希伯来语 Jahweh 中间的 h 本来不发音，后来为了方便起见，把无声的

h 读成 ho，成了 Jehoweh 。耶和华原是迦南地区以南米甸人的神，被希伯来人南方的犹大族人吸收。从这里可以看出摩西娶外族女子为妻并接受妻子一族宗教信仰的踪迹。但是，北方的以色列人起初并不信奉耶和华，他们的神为伊洛欣（Elohim），原是迦南和北边叙利亚的神。叙利亚人和希伯来人是兄弟民族，语言、信仰、思维、民族和风俗有诸多相同之处。摩西在带领以色列人出埃及以及在旷野的 40 年中，逐渐确立了自己的权威与统治地位。摩西的统治不仅是政治上的，也是宗教上的。为了便于思想控制，摩西利用强制手段使"耶和华"成为全民族统一的神。

与《新约》中的耶稣相比，《旧约》中的耶和华似乎有更多的戾气。同是"耶氏父子"，何以如此不同？学界总是有这样一种偏见：《新约》代表了一种世界主义思想，而《旧约》代表了一种狭隘的民族意识。此种观点虽然反映了基督教脱身于犹太教并形成自己独特个性的发展趋向，却忽略了作为基督教源头的犹太教本身也为基督教的世界主义开辟了道路。

实际上，犹太教在分裂为拉比犹太教与基督教之前，一直存在多元因素，并没有一个统一的、标准的犹太教。尤其是在第二圣殿犹太教时期，许多不同的利益群体有自己的宗教观点，而这些宗教教派或不同的思想团体——法利赛人、撒都该人、爱色尼派、奋锐党人——都有各自的文献，如《死海古卷》里有许多爱色尼派的文献。在放逐后的犹太教思想中，有一种思想最值得关注，那就是"第二以赛亚"思潮。与排外的民族主义不同，"第二以赛亚"思潮有着宽容的民族精神与宗教意识。

经历了亡国之痛与被囚之辱的希伯来人，发展出两种截然相反的民族观念：一种是将原有的狭隘的民族意识强化，形成极端的民族主义；另一种强调与外邦人和平共处，在"上帝"的庇佑下共同追求世界大同的理想。在《旧约》的先知书中，这两种思想并存，互相对抗，互为补充，竟形成了一道独特的风景线。

二 《旧约》中的暴力倾向

摩西是伟大的开国英雄、军事战略家、政治家、宗教家和立法者，又是诗人和演说家。在埃及法老宫中生活的 40 年间，他学会了文、史、军、政等各方面的知识；在米甸岳父家的 40 年间，他学会了畜牧业知识和宗教知识；在旷野的 40 年里，他实现了自己的政治统治、军事统治和宗教统治。任何一个国家的建立都带有暴力——"合法的暴力"，摩西的统治同样建立在血腥之上。60 万人在沙漠中行军，又饥又渴，还有敌人阻拦，因此，并不是每个人都愿意追随摩西。摩西要应对的不仅是百姓在宗教上的抱怨（如有人拜金牛犊——埃及多神教的象征），还有生活上的抱怨（"不如不离开埃及"，在埃及至少有肉吃）；更甚者，摩西面临着反叛：利未族中有个人叫可拉，联合了亚比兰、安等 250 个有名望的领袖，组织了一个新集团，反对亚伦做祭司长。

摩西对待叛徒的手段是残忍的。把金牛犊融化了，磨成粉末让以色列人喝，以此对付宗教上的反叛；对生活有怨言的，则不允许他们进入"应许之地"；指使百姓抱怨的，都将遭受瘟疫。对于政治上的反叛，摩西的手段更是毒辣，指派利未人的子孙杀害自己族人中的叛徒："凡属于亚卫的都到我这边来。"利未的子孙都聚集在他那里。"亚卫上帝说，你们把刀挎在腰间，巡行营中，从这门到那门，各人杀自己的兄弟、朋友和邻居中的叛徒。"利未人照办了，结果那天被杀的有 3000 人。摩西让可拉第二天带着香炉到圣幕门口，然后宣告了他们的罪行，叛徒们脚下的地裂开后，吞没了可拉和其同谋者的家。接着，亚卫又降火烧焚同党的 250 人，还降下瘟疫，导致 14700 人死亡。

无论是约西亚的宗教改革，还是《旧约》正典的编纂，都为犹太教的统一和发展奠定了坚实的基础。在以色列南北宗教的统一中，政治扮演了主要角色：北以色列比南犹大先亡国；北以色列在亚述民族融合的政策下与外族通婚，南犹大在巴比伦的统治下得以保存自己的宗教与文化；南犹大比北以色列先复国，并负责圣殿的重建；南犹大的祭司们负责《旧约》正典的编纂工作。基于这些客观原因，"耶和华"理所当然地代替了"伊洛欣"成为希伯来人唯一的神，而北以色列也从此失去了话语主导权。

从希伯来人的历史中，从约瑟、摩西等以色列人祖先的婚姻中，从约书亚所谓的"征服迦南"的故事中，从南犹大与北以色列的关系中，尤其是从耶和华与伊洛欣两位神的命运中，我们清楚地看到了犹太人所谓的"一神教"信仰、"民族主义"、血统纯正和信仰纯正等特点。既然血统的纯正、信仰的纯正、民族的团结都是"所谓的"，那么犹太人极端民族主义的情结就是有问题的，他们本不该如此极端。而这些所谓的"纯正"，反倒让我们更容易理解犹太人的和平主义思想产生的原因。既然极端民族主义只是一种刻意的宣传，那么与它同时存在的另一种思想，即和平主义思想，就是被刻意压制的。

先知是时代的产物，因此先知们的思想受时代思潮的影响。晚期先知受到希腊文化对希伯来文化的干扰，群情激愤，因此先知文学思潮也趋于民族主义。如《撒迦利亚书》前后两部的风格完全不同，完全是两部截然不同的作品：前者是先知文学，后者是启示文学；前者的时代写得很清楚（公元前 520 年至公元前 518 年），后者写得很模糊，根据考证，是马卡比时代初期的作品（公元前 2 世纪 60 年代）。[1]《撒迦利亚书》前后两部的最大差异，是前者抱有世界大同的思想，而后者有着狭隘的民族主义思想。因为当时正值希伯来人抗击外族统治，这种对异邦人憎恨的态度，以及狭隘的民族主义思潮的泛滥也就

---

[1] 朱维之：《圣经文学十二讲》，人民文学出版社，2008，第 262 页。

不难理解了。但是理解不等于认同，更不等于抹杀真实的历史。也就是说，我们可以理解犹太人极端民族主义产生的原因，但不能认同这种极端的民族主义，更不能忽视与极端民族主义同时代的犹太人的和平主义思想。

三 《旧约》中的世界主义

历史是被阐释的历史。从《旧约》正典的编纂过程中就可以看出"史料"是如何服务于"政治""宗教""文化"的。首先是"申命记派"将自己的宗教观点加入"史料"，其次是"祭司派"的看法变为"史料"，再到后期将先知们的观点融入"史料"，希伯来人的"历史"就此被确定下来。在撒母耳和扫罗时代，甚至是大卫时代，历史的描述是纯粹的故事叙述，没有宗教偏见和神学倾向。这些史书后来由一些好教训的、重功利的历史学家加以编撰，最后成为我们现在读的经典史书。[①]然而有趣的是，《旧约》经典与《新约》经典相比，还是有太多异质的声音：如果仔细研读人们被囚之后编纂的那些史书，尤其是那些先知书，就会发现迥然不同的观点。在被囚末期，人们经过内省和悔改，希望"愤怒的神"变成"慈悲的神"。于是，希伯来的神的固有名字"耶和华"也变成了世界性的名称"神""上帝"。下面再以"第二以赛亚"运动为例来看看犹太人的和平主义思想。

"第二以赛亚"运动是以《第二以赛亚书》等先知书中的观点为指导思想的。《第二以赛亚书》是附在《以赛亚书》后面的一段文字，风格与阿摩司的儿子"以赛亚"的书完全不同。据推测，该书是在波斯消灭巴比伦后到重建圣殿之前的这段时间里完成的。《第二以赛亚书》的思想境界在先知中达到了顶峰，由狭隘的民族主义升格为天下

---

① 朱维之：《圣经文学十二讲》，人民文学出版社，2008，第170页。

大同的思想。"第二以赛亚"中的世界大同思想受《撒迦利亚书》的影响，而《撒迦利亚书》的写作年代在公元前 520 年到公元前 518 年，所以《第二以赛亚书》的成书时间大约在公元前 5 世纪初期。

基督教之所以发展为一个普世性的宗教，与犹太教中已经发展起来的世界大同思想有直接关联。如果切断了基督教与犹太教的渊源，也就切断了基督教的来龙去脉。但是"第二以赛亚"思想鼓吹希伯来民族有让全世界脱离罪恶的天职，这也影响了后世的基督教，成为基督教普世思想中压迫性的来源。所以，基督教（尤其是新教）热衷于在世界范围内宣教，希望充当整个世界的救世主。这种世界大同的思想在"普世""博爱"的意义上有它的价值，但不可否认的是，这种"大同"本身也具有某种强迫性。因此，认真体会"第二以赛亚"思想，并一分为二地分析、借鉴，对于当今社会的民族问题与宗教问题具有重大意义。

从犹太教中发展起来的"第二以赛亚"思想，对犹太教本身以及从犹太教中发展出来的两大宗教——基督教与伊斯兰教——均有着重要意义。假如基督教与伊斯兰教真的都发源于犹太教，假如基督教与犹太教都以《圣经》（犹太教的《圣经》与基督教的《圣经》不同，犹太教的《圣经》只包括《旧约》部分；伊斯兰教的《古兰经》与《旧约》有诸多相似之处）为信仰的核心，那他们不应该忽略犹太教以及《圣经》中的世界大同思想而一味片面地强调其中狭隘的民族主义意识。如果这三大宗教能够检点自己、反省自己，那么历史上的种种宗教战争，以及由宗教冲突引起的民族战争，甚至目前世界范围内仍然持续着的宗教冲突与民族冲突，都将消失殆尽。然而事实恰恰相反，这些由宗教信仰引起的民族主义的偏执与狂热，似乎有越来越流行的趋势。在"人类学"的鼓励、自由民族主义思想与"多元文化"的鼓吹下，激进的民族主义大行其道，弃"人权"与"人道"而不顾。"地域性""民族性""少数性"竟成为肆意妄为的幌子，成为倒行逆施的掩护，这不得不让我们对"多元"进行更深层次的思考。

众先知中，阿摩司是使"耶和华"走出犹太人群，走向外邦的重要人物。阿摩司是犹大国人，却跑到以色列国说教，打破了南犹大与北以色列经久的族裔界限。不仅如此，他还打破了国界，在叙利亚、非利士、以东、苏丹等国说教，削弱了狭隘的民族主义思想。

在先知书中，《约拿书》是最具有普世思想的一部。《约拿书》是"十二小先知书"的第五卷，与其他十一卷有很大的差异，因为它并非有关先知的说辞，而是有关先知的故事。有人认为《约拿书》不是先知书，而是一篇小说。作者的目的是"非难"当时希伯来人对外国、外民族的仇视，鼓吹"第二以赛亚"开通豁达的思想，认为希伯来人的使命是以自己的信仰去照亮异邦人，与《路得记》同为初期小说的精品。[1] 作为"狭隘的民族主义"的代表，"约拿"这个先知与其他先知不同，是一个反面形象。上帝让他去尼尼微传神的讯息，他不愿去并逃到了与尼尼微相反方向的他施（Tarshish），因为他不愿意看到外邦人得到拯救。上帝见尼尼微的人有悔改之意，就发善心不再毁灭这座城，约拿就发怒了。《约拿书》中的"上帝"是慈悲的，与约拿的狭隘、任性、暴戾形成了鲜明的对照。《约拿书》的作者继承了"第二以赛亚"先知的传统，认为上帝不仅关心犹太人，而且关心他所创造的世界上的所有人。这卷书所阐释的主题是，以色列人作为上帝的子民，其真正的使命是在外邦人中传扬上帝之爱的好消息，打破以往偏狭的民族界限、国家界限。从《约拿书》中三种平行的比照（耶和华与约拿、水手和约拿、约拿和尼尼微人）可以清楚地看到普世主义思想，它"突破了以色列先前将雅威的救赎和创造之工局限于以色列一族范围之内的观点"[2]。首先，信仰异教的水手为了解救约拿

---

[1] 朱维之：《圣经文学十二讲》，人民文学出版社，2008，第396页。
[2] 黎新农：《简探先知及其神学》，《金陵神学志》2002年第2期，第46页。

的性命，都愿意向约拿的神"耶和华"求告，[1]但是约拿却不愿救尼尼微人的性命，这形成了鲜明的对比。其次，当约拿向尼尼微人宣布了"尼尼微必将倾覆"的消息后，尼尼微王就"脱下朝服，披上麻布，坐在灰中"，又命令全城百姓披上麻布，虔诚求告。神见他们离开了恶道就后悔了，也没有把之前说的灾祸降临到他们身上。这里的对比在约拿与尼尼微人之间展开：尼尼微人的真心悔改与约拿的气急败坏对比鲜明，约拿自以为是神的选民，就可以任情任性、不知悔改；而尼尼微人却勇于承认错误，努力向善。孰对孰错，一目了然。最后，耶和华的悲悯与约拿的残忍形成了强烈的对比：约拿不愿去尼尼微宣布神的消息，耶和华虽然生气，却原谅了他；约拿不愿神向尼尼微发慈悲，竟发怒以至于求死，而耶和华也没有降罪于他，反而用蓖麻树的例子耐心解释道："这蓖麻不是你栽种的，也不是你培养的；一夜发生，一夜干死，你尚且爱惜；何况这尼尼微大城，其中不能分辨左手右手的有 12 多万人，并有许多牲畜，我岂能不爱惜呢？"[2]

《路得记》不属于先知书，而更像一篇小说，但与《约拿书》一样，传达了"第二以赛亚"的思想。路得本是摩押人，竟然做了大卫王的曾祖母，而且她的贤德比希伯来人更值得赞赏。通过摩押女子与希伯来人的两次婚姻，作者批判了狭隘的民族主义。在《尼西米记》

---

[1] 约拿的逃亡旅途是充满危险的，因为耶和华对约拿的行为感到愤怒并要惩罚他。当船在海上遇到风暴时，有一群异教的水手，他们尽力去了解到底发生了什么事，而约拿却不关心风暴，在船舱底睡觉。当水手们确认约拿是这件事的起因，意识到上帝的能力蕴藏在风暴中时，就尽可能地解救约拿，当然这一切努力都是徒劳的。当约拿要求水手们将他投入大海中时，水手们却不愿意这样做，因为"流无辜人的血"是罪，这罪也会使水手们遭受惩罚，所以他们求告耶和华。

[2] 约拿出了尼尼微城，坐在城边为自己搭了一个棚，要看城究竟如何。神使一棵蓖麻高过约拿，影子遮盖了他的头，并救他脱离苦楚。次日黎明，神却安排一条虫子咬这蓖麻，以致其枯槁。日头出来的时候，神安排炎热的东风、日头暴晒约拿的头，使他发昏而向神求死。神于是借约拿"因蓖麻发怒"的事与自己"怜悯尼尼微"的事进行类比，希望约拿明白自己的心意。然而这个比喻的问题在于：约拿也许不是因为"怜悯蓖麻树"而发怒，是因为"自己得不到蓖麻树的遮蔽而被日头暴晒而发怒"，所以神的心意他未必能够理解，因为他的本性是自私的。

和《以斯拉记》中，犹太祭司们为了维持血统和宗教信仰的"纯洁"，不许犹太人与外族通婚，这一政策遭到很多人的反对，而《路得记》的作者大概是为了反对这一政策而为路得立传。由此可见，被囚之后的以色列人的思想有了很大的改变。此外，《诗篇》中也有一些反映世界大同的思想：如第46篇，其思想境界超越了狭隘的民族主义，把耶和华看成是统治世界的力量；又如第19篇，诗人通过对宏观宇宙的赞扬，使耶和华成为天下万民的耶和华。走出原始的迷信的宗教、走出狭隘的民族的宗教，这一境界正是当时"第二以赛亚"的境界。

四 结语

《圣经》之所以成为一部"永远的书"，恰恰在于它包含了不同的思想，甚至互相冲突的思想。作为"源头活水"，《圣经》本身的这种包容性和异质性，为思想的自由、宗教的宽容，提供了绝佳的范式。

第四节 从潘多拉与夏娃的神话看西方"厌女症"传统

一 引言

西方社会的"厌女症"传统由来已久，从古希腊到后现代，"厌女症"传统始终贯穿着西方社会的历史发展。母系社会时期，女性处于支配地位，恩格斯曾说："在一切蒙昧人中，在一切处于野蛮时代低级阶段、中级阶段、部分地还有处于高级阶段的野蛮人中，妇女不仅居于自由的地位，而且居于受到高度尊敬的地位。"[1] 原始社会末期，

---

[1] 恩格斯：《家庭、私有制和国家的起源》，载《马克思恩格斯选集》第4卷，人民出版社，1995，第45页。

母系社会开始瓦解，社会生产力发展，随之而来的是男女经济地位的变化，父权制逐渐取代了母权制。正如恩格斯所说："在这个时代中，任何进步同时也是相对的退步，因为在这种进步中一些人的幸福和发展是通过另一些人的痛苦和受压抑而实现的。"[1]女性地位的下降标志着私有制社会的形成，而在男权社会中，被压抑的正是女性群体。社会形态的转变必然体现在意识形态领域，而意识形态也必然以特定的形式巩固和维系社会形态的转变。因此，男权社会通过编纂、制造"故事"来达到维系社会形态转变的目的。

二 古希腊社会中的潘多拉神话及其引申

马尔库塞曾说："文明社会以压抑性为基础。"而对于女性的"性"之压抑，更是重中之重。于是，潘多拉神话应运而生。赫西俄德生活的时代，古希腊土地贫瘠、人口渐多，人们食不果腹、生活艰苦，加之与兄弟的财产之争，赫西俄德对女人怀有深刻的仇恨就不难理解了，他将女人视为邪恶、贪婪的象征。宙斯为了惩罚盗取天火的普罗米修斯，创造了满足男人一切幻想的潘多拉并将其送往人间。厄庇米修斯不顾哥哥普罗米修斯的警告，欣然接受了来自诸神的礼物。潘多拉是美与诱惑的象征，也是男人欲望与权力的象征。人间从此有了灾难，而希望被永远地留在了潘多拉的盒子里。人们习惯于将错误归结为潘多拉对男人的魅惑力以及对魔盒不该有好奇心，认为女人是"红颜祸水"。其实，"厌女症"来自对女性的恐惧，对人类自身缺陷的恐惧。男人从心底感到害怕，害怕女人，害怕茫然未知的世界，于是将一切过错归结于女人，将女人进行负面定义，认为是女人对男人的影响和诱惑使男人犯错。男人对女人的否定其实是男人对自身缺陷的一种逃避。

---

① 恩格斯：《家庭、私有制和国家的起源》，载《马克思恩格斯选集》第4卷，人民出版社，1995，第63页。

　　这一"厌女症"传统深刻影响了之后的古希腊文明。在古希腊的城邦制中，女人的地位极其低下（当然斯巴达的情况和雅典有所不同——古希腊社会由众多城邦构成，在不同的历史阶段、不同的城邦，妇女地位有很大差异。而妇女地位的表现以雅典和斯巴达的城邦最为典型。斯巴达实行奴隶主贵族专制政治，雅典则是奴隶主民主政治，雅典和斯巴达相比文明程度更高，因此女性地位更低）。亚里士多德在论述城邦制度时曾指出，城邦的半数人口是妇女，如果妇女的地位没有规定好，半个公民团体就会欠缺法度。他认为："男人生来优越，女人则卑贱，男人是统治者，女人则是被统治者。"古希腊时期，地理环境恶劣，土地贫瘠，而希腊人将"土地"比作"女人的肚子"，女性地位的卑微由此可见一斑。

　　古希腊所有城邦中，妇女均不享有政治权利。在雅典，妇女被排除于公民团体之外，被称为"雅典人的妻子"，仅属于家庭成员，并不享有公民权。号称古希腊民主之最的雅典，妇女地位甚至不及其实行民主制之前。梭伦对雅典女人的行为举止、饮食、出行、婚嫁等进行了一系列规定，还设立"妇女监察委员会"以监督雅典妇女在公共场合的行为规范。而女性的婚姻不过是从父权到夫权的一种关系转让，女人作为男人的一种私有财产而存在，只是所有权的象征。监护权转让后虽然新娘父亲会得到新郎的一笔聘金，但新娘父亲也要准备一份十分丰厚的嫁妆，通常要送其家产的 1/10 以上。因为这是一笔"不划算的买卖"，所以一个家庭如果经济条件不足以支付嫁妆时，便不会再生养女儿，甚至有些地方会出现溺杀女婴的现象。妇女生下孩子之后，孩子无论男女七岁前均可在母亲身边抚养，而七岁时男孩可以上学，女孩则只能留在家聆听母亲关于妇德的教诲。母亲会教育女孩将来作为母亲和主妇所应具备的知识，而最理想的教育是教育女性足不出户，谨言慎行，循规蹈矩，默默无闻地过完一生。亚里士多德曾借用索福克勒斯的诗句定义妇女的优良品德，即"娴静就是妇德"。

对此，恩格斯曾指出："在雅典人看来，妻子除生育子女以外，不过是一个婢女的头领而已。"[1]

在斯巴达，由于男人长年征战在外，妇女便有了更多参与城邦事务的机会。亚里士多德说："在斯巴达人力国力的鼎盛时期，很多事务都是由妇女管理的。"斯巴达妇女所拥有的自由曾经也不被统治者所允许，但面对统治者的约束，斯巴达妇女极力反抗，最终争取到一定范围内的自由。但斯巴达妇女最重要的责任仍然是生孩子。古希腊时期，雅典的女性被禁止参加体育运动，甚至连观看都不被允许，偷看男性体育运动会被处死。但在同时期的斯巴达，女性却被允许参加体育运动。因为斯巴达人认为参加体育运动可以使女性身体健壮，只有健康的母亲才能生出健康的孩子，所以女性参与体育运动在于其生育价值。因生产而丧生的妇女，荣誉等同于战争中牺牲的战士，可以在其墓前立下有铭文的墓碑。与妇女有关的法律几乎都涉及生儿育女，而那些保持单身、晚婚或婚配不当的人则要受到相应处罚。斯巴达女孩可以和男孩接受一样的培养，而公有制下的斯巴达妇女一般不用从事生产劳动，生活用品也由统治阶级提供，所以日常生活中她们有更多的时间和机会接受文化教育。

虽然古希腊时期的城邦社会都很重视生育和家庭，但城邦中的女性并未得到应有的尊重。古希腊时期，城邦社会普遍认为孩子的本源是父亲，而母亲不过是一个生育的工具而已。在希腊神话中，甚至女人的生育权利也被剥夺，雅典娜从宙斯的头颅中诞生，酒神狄俄尼索斯从宙斯的大腿中诞生，生育也可以由男人完成，侧面体现出古希腊对女人的生育能力并不认可。无论在雅典还是斯巴达，妇女主要扮演的是贤妻良母的角色，尽管她们的标准有所差别，但实质是一样的，始终被男人所支配。从宗教地位来看，无论是雅典还是斯巴达，妇女

---

① 恩格斯:《家庭、私有制和国家的起源》，载《马克思恩格斯选集》第4卷，人民出版社，1995，第62页。

的宗教地位都比男人高。而事实上，宗教事务中的高级权力仍掌握在男人手中。

三 圣经世界中的女性

从《旧约》中上帝创造亚当和夏娃，就能看出其对女人的定位——夏娃是从亚当身上取出的一根肋骨，是男人的附庸。上帝创造夏娃的初衷不过是看到亚当孑然一身，说："那人独居不好，我要为他造一个配偶帮助他。"创造了亚当夏娃后，上帝又对他们说："要生养众多，遍满地面，治理这地，也要管理海里的鱼、空中的鸟和地上各样行动的活物。"上帝创造夏娃不过是为了与亚当做伴，繁衍后代，帮助亚当一起管理伊甸园。而在伊甸园中，是夏娃禁不住蛇的诱惑，第一个偷尝禁果，接着又让亚当一起吃下。原罪的始作俑者是女人，而男人是无辜的受牵连者。上帝发现后降咒于人：蛇与女人生生世世对立；女人将倍受怀胎生产的苦楚，且必将恋慕自己的丈夫，受丈夫的管辖；男人则因听从女人将终身劳苦，必汗流满面才得糊口，直到归于尘土。女人因罪受罚，男人则因听从女人而受罚。女人总被赋予一种能左右男人想法、引诱男人犯罪的能力，一切错误都源于女人，是女人总是无法抵抗诱惑，是夏娃的堕落导致了人类的原罪。实际上女人的影响只是直接原因，男人本身的欲望才是堕落的根本原因。

夏娃是亚当的"骨中骨，肉中肉"，她从来就不是一个独立的存在，而是亚当的一部分。夏娃的存在是为了完善亚当的生命，这是女人的悲哀——从夏娃被创造的初衷到对女人的诅咒，女人只是男人的附属品：被创造仅仅因为亚当孤独，被赶出伊甸园后除了要受怀孕生子的痛苦，除了必须恋慕丈夫外，还要受到丈夫的管辖。无论是希腊神话中的潘多拉，还是《旧约》中的夏娃，女人始终都是负面形象——外表美丽，内心却贪婪，充满了谎言，最终为男人招致祸害。从《旧约》与《新约》中也可以看到女人地位的下降。《旧约》中曾出现了五位女先知（米利暗、底波拉、户勒大、挪亚底、以赛亚的妻子），而《新约》中仅有一位女先知（亚拿），女人在宗教中的地位大大下降。

四　西方社会中的"厌女症"传统

康德在《论优美感和崇高感》的后记里说："女人会使男人眼光狭窄。在一个朋友结婚时，便是你失去这个朋友的时候。"为此，康德提出了"一个人可以不结婚"，并且终身践行了这个原则。《论优美感和崇高感》中，康德认为男人和女人各自的特性不同，女人是"优美"，而男人是"崇高"；男人善于理性思辨，而女人善于感性体察。"女性美只是相对的，男性美才是绝对的。这就是所有雄性动物在我们眼里都是美的原因，因为他们对我们感官的诱惑相对很少。"[1] 正因为女人和男人本质上的特性差异，女人从来都不被哲学世界所接受，他甚至嘲讽说："一个有学问的女人理论上也应可蓄胡须。"[2] 在康德眼里，女人只适合艺术感官领域，一旦女人涉足哲学，那么她将失去对男人的魅力。在他生活的时代里，女人是第二性的，他将女人等同于物质，遂选择了孤独而未涉足婚姻，"当我需要女人的时候，我却无力供养她，而当我能供养她时，我却再不需要她了"。[3]

"是去找女人吗？别忘了带上你的鞭子。"尼采的《查拉图斯特拉如是说》深刻地表达了他对女人的嗤之以鼻。尼采早年生活凄惨，父亲早逝，童年时期一直和外婆、母亲和姐姐居住在一起。面对女性时，他敏感而又自卑。尼采曾经对女人怀有美好的幻想，也曾经对爱情有无限的渴望，但在感情面前他谦卑羞涩，一次次示爱被拒后，他彻底从甘心挨女人的鞭子变为向所有女人扬起鞭子。此后，尼采的

---

① 康德：《论优美感和崇高感》，何兆武译，商务印书馆，2001，第33页。
② 康德：《论优美感和崇高感》，何兆武译，商务印书馆，2001，第30页。
③ 刘士林：《情人节让哲人走开》，《出版广角》2004年第3期，第64~65页。

作品中对女性的诋毁和抨击层出不穷。罗素在他的《西方哲学史》中一语道破真谛："十个女人有九个会让尼采丢掉鞭子。他是明知如此，所以才要避开女人呀！"而罗素是一个不折不扣的花花公子，他对待感情轻浮，女人不过是他眼中的玩物。卢梭、叔本华同样有厌女症倾向。纵观西方社会传统，哲学的大门从来不为女人敞开，"哲学"仿佛成为男人的特权，不欢迎也不允许女人涉足。而在生活中，女人仍然沦为男人的附庸，仅仅被看作一种"需要"，是"第二性"的存在。

五 结语

马克思认为，女性解放是全人类解放的标志。妇女地位的不断变化见证着文明社会的进步与变迁。解构男权主义的限制，倡导女性解放和女性权利的获得；重构女性主义，纠正女权主义过分强调女权的问题，弱化男权思想，进而实现真正的男女公平是女性主义的最终走向，也是文明社会的必经之途。

第二章 《旧约》传统之文学篇

第一节 希伯来人没有悲剧——《约伯记》解读

一 《约伯记》是悲剧吗?

对来世有所期许的宗教、对赏善惩恶有所允诺的宗教,很难培养出悲剧精神。悲剧精神不仅来自敬畏和恐惧,也来自迷惘、困惑、诘问与抗争。仅仅有敬畏和恐惧,只能产生宗教的虔敬。只有在敬畏和恐惧中的诘问和反抗,才能造就伟大而崇高的悲剧精神。从此意义上看,《约伯记》勉强可以算作希伯来人的悲剧,因为它包含了一种诘问和反抗的精神。在《约伯记》中,我们看到的不再是希伯来人对耶和华的敬畏和恐惧,而是约伯对神的种种质疑和诘问。只不过,约伯的质疑和诘问仅限于思想层面而没有付诸任何行动。因此,他的质疑和诘问是不彻底的。而且,《约伯记》最终以约伯和上帝的和解为结局——约伯认识到自己的错误,仍然虔敬地皈依神而神也原谅了约伯的悖逆,这显然不符合悲剧精神。

悲剧精神是一种对混乱的恐惧之情、对暴力的憎恶之情、对压制的反抗之情,然而希伯来人的民族特质与悲剧精神格格不入。在希伯来人的宗教信仰中,世界是井然有序的,上帝是全知全能的。纵然有大洪水灾难，但也有挪亚方舟予以拯救；纵然有所多玛和蛾摩拉的毁灭，但也是上帝有目的的安排。一切均服从于正义原则，一切邪恶必将受到惩罚。人无须有自由意志，无须反抗，只须服从上帝的旨意。在希伯来人的世界里，没有对命运的恐惧，没有对恶的反抗，因为上帝安排好了一切。也因为如此，希伯来人没有悲剧，因为悲剧源于对命运的思考、对恶的反抗。

在整部《圣经》中（严格地说是《旧约》），《约伯记》可以算作最具有悲剧精神的——约伯悲愤地质疑上帝的正义，痛苦地思索自己的命运，为此和朋友们辩论，并提出了一系列问题——关于善与恶的问题。假如《约伯记》不是以约伯的悔改结束，假如《约伯记》不是以上帝的赏赐结束，假如《约伯记》有一个悲壮的结尾，那么《约伯记》或可称为希伯来人的悲剧。然而，《约伯记》就在即将达到悲剧观念的标准时笔锋突转，用宗教信仰回避了悲剧精神。上帝重新赐予约伯牛羊满圈，比以前的还多；上帝原谅了约伯的悖逆，并决定再也不试探人的信仰。对此，约伯也报之以真心悔改，不再苦苦追问那些困惑着索福克勒斯和欧里庇得斯的问题。从此，约伯更加虔诚，给上帝献更多的燔祭。上帝与约伯就此和解，《约伯记》也就此结束。一切都很圆满，哪里来的悲剧呢？

二 希伯来人为什么没有悲剧？

《约伯记》是《旧约》智慧书的一篇，也是最难读懂的一篇。《约伯记》中提出的主要问题相当尖锐：为什么信徒会经历苦难？经过漫长的辩论，约伯聪明的朋友们也不能回答这个问题。他们甚至犯了严重的错误——认为苦难来临仅仅因为人们犯罪，以致被神责备。对于约伯的问题，实际上耶和华并没有做正面的回答——因为这是极难回答的问题：假如神是正义的，他为什么要让恶人逍遥法外、让好人受苦？假如神不是正义的，我们为什么要信仰他？假如神是全能的，为什么他容忍世上有如此多的罪恶而无动于衷？假如神不是全能的，我们为什么要信仰他？

实际上，关于神义论的问题，神学家们已争论了两千多年，仍然没有一个满意的答案——或许永远都不可能有一个满意的答案。因此，耶和华的策略是迂回的：他没有正面回答约伯的问题，而是提出了另外一些穷尽人的智力也无法解答的问题，譬如宇宙形成的问题、动物们神奇的特性、自然界无法解释的奥秘，于是约伯屈服于神的大能，并以缄口作为信仰的标志。然而，这一屈服并不能满足所有人的智力需求，就像启蒙主义思想家们、科学家们后来所做的那样：他们试图回答耶和华提出的问题。

对于同样的问题，约伯不能回答，于是走向了信仰，而对索福克勒斯和欧里庇得斯来说，信仰并不能完全解决这些问题。虽然他们也有信仰，但是在其生活的年代，传统的信仰已经瓦解，尤其是欧里庇得斯，深受智者学派、无神论者和苏格拉底的影响，无法用信仰来解释自己的困惑。他们甚至将各种各样的罪恶归咎于神的意志，如欧里庇得斯的《希波吕托斯》责备了美神阿佛洛狄忒、《伊翁》责备了阿波罗、《特洛伊妇女》责备了三女神以及宙斯，于是悲剧诞生了，但这并不是尼采所认为的悲剧诞生的理由。实际上，尼采的日神精神与酒神精神的对立，仍然是启蒙的结果，他对于悲剧起源的解释是哲学式的，并不能完全解释古希腊悲剧诞生的特点。

通过《约伯记》，我们可以清楚地看到希伯来人思维的特质：希伯来人绝不允许像索福克勒斯写俄狄浦斯那样写人，更不允许像埃斯库罗斯写宙斯、欧里庇得斯写阿波罗那样写神。在《约伯记》中，耶和华是至高无上的，是全知全能的，我们找不到三大悲剧家笔下的神——贪婪、残暴、荒淫好色、嫉妒成性。对希伯来人而言，耶和华是宇宙的创始者，是万物的主宰，是正义的源泉。他不容置疑、不容反抗，即使约伯提出了连耶和华也回答不了的问题，最终的结局还是约伯在尘土和炉火中懊悔，谦卑地把自己奉献给神。因此，就算《约伯记》中充满了崇高的观念、绚丽的想象，充满了激烈的感情、智慧的思考，也绝不是一部悲剧。

希伯来民族没有悲剧，因为悲剧所独有的质疑精神和反抗精神在希伯来人的宗教信仰中被消解了。即使约伯提了那么多问题，即使约伯想以死来抗争，但最终的结果是约伯懊悔自己的诘问，谦卑地俯向耶和华神。《约伯记》中充满了激情和想象，充满了智慧和启蒙，这一点与索福克勒斯和欧里庇得斯的悲剧相比毫不逊色，甚至略高一筹。但是，约伯那些尖锐的问题、激烈的反抗最终还是被消解了，上帝解答了约伯的疑问，而约伯却懊悔自己的诘问。最后，一切尘埃落定：上帝赐予了约伯更多的物质财富，而约伯谦卑地俯向了耶和华神。

此外，希伯来人信仰的神是其终极价值，这种价值观消解了不同价值观之间的激烈冲突，而不同价值观之间的激烈冲突正是悲剧形成的关键。对此，黑格尔有充分的论述，而保罗·蒂利希的《文化神学》有更深入的阐释。

古希腊之所以有惨烈的悲剧，是因为古希腊人的多神教信仰。不同的信仰导致了不同的价值观，而不同的价值观之间必定有剧烈的冲突。此外，新旧信仰之间、不同政治体制的交替，也会导致冲突的发生。有冲突才会有悲剧，悲剧诞生于冲突。

首先，多神教信仰导致了悲剧的发生，以欧里庇得斯的《希波吕托斯》为例。希波吕托斯因为蔑视美神阿佛洛狄忒而招致了美神的报复。希波吕托斯信仰的是贞洁女神（月亮女神、狩猎女神）阿尔忒弥斯，他十分讨厌阿佛洛狄忒流连于床第的轻浮与放纵。在古希腊人的信仰体系中，美神占有重要位置，尽管阿佛洛狄忒是舶来的神，来自小亚细亚，然而这个舶来品渐渐成了古希腊人的十二主神之一。有人崇尚爱情，有人信奉贞洁；有人信仰阿佛洛狄忒，有人则膜拜阿尔忒弥斯，所以冲突是不可避免的，希波吕托斯就是一个例子。

其次，新旧信仰交替造成的价值观冲突也是悲剧得以形成的原因，以埃斯库罗斯的《被缚的普罗米修斯》和《俄瑞斯忒斯》为例。在《被缚的普罗米修斯》中，普罗米修斯是古老的神灵，宙斯是新的神灵，在新与旧的更迭与交替中，冲突是不可避免的。普罗米修斯激烈地反抗宙斯的统治，并因此成为悲剧英雄，而受到世世代代的传颂。在《俄瑞斯忒斯》中，俄瑞斯忒斯为报父仇杀害母亲，代表的是父系制度的观念，而复仇女神追杀俄瑞斯忒斯，则反映了母系制度残留的痕迹。最后，太阳神阿波罗委托雅典娜审判这一案件。在案件的审判中，雅典娜代表的是新一代神灵，而复仇女神代表的是旧的神灵；雅典娜代表的是父系社会的利益，而复仇女神代表的是母系社会的利益；雅典娜代表的是依法治国的社会制度，而复仇女神代表的是血亲复仇的社会制度。新与旧的交替必然引起冲突，而冲突的发生就是悲剧最好的素材。

最后，不同政治制度的更迭引发的价值观冲突，也是悲剧发生的原因，以索福克勒斯的《安提戈涅》为例。安提戈涅持有的价值观是古老的家庭制度的价值观，而克瑞翁持有的价值观是新兴的国家（城邦）制度的价值观。安提戈涅埋葬兄弟是血亲制度的要求，而克瑞翁惩罚叛徒的做法是城邦政治制度的要求。公说公有理，婆说婆有理，两种不同的价值观必然引发激烈冲突，而冲突也造就了安提戈涅这一英雄形象。

总之，古希腊悲剧之剧烈冲突，是人将各自持有的价值绝对化、终极化而导致的。因为人类是渺小的、有限的，所以总是在追求绝对的、永恒的价值。属于人的任何价值都是相对的、有限的，不能妄称终极之名，而人的智力总是希望追求永恒与无限。因此，有着爱智传统的古希腊人总喜欢将自己的价值认同奉为绝对的，而绝对、终极只有一个，当每种价值的崇奉者一起来争抢"绝对"时，结局便一定是悲剧，既毁灭他人，又毁灭自己。

"真理是什么"的问题在希伯来人那里并不是问题，因为"真理"意味着上帝以及对上帝的信仰。然而在希腊—罗马乃至整个西方哲学史中，"真理是什么"的问题却是一个问题，这个问题被反复提出、探讨、争论，持续了两千余年，最后成为一个永恒的问题。可以说，"真理是什么"的问题是一个阐释学问题，你可以不断地言说，却找不到终极答案。

戏剧是具有娱乐性质的，尽管它同时具有教育功能。在古希腊，无论是悲剧还是喜剧，都有极强的政治意味，尤其是悲剧，是统治阶级实行统治的一种手段。然而，政治上的统治毕竟是外化的。尽管伯里克利时代观看悲剧具有政治强迫性，但这只是一种外在的形式。与希伯来人的宗教信仰和道德规则相比，古希腊人因为观看悲剧所受的这种政治上的"强迫"实在不能算是强迫。与古希腊人相比，希伯来人所受的强迫是无以复加的——这种强迫不仅是外在的，也是内在的，不仅是有形的，也是无形的，希伯来人早已将这种强迫内化为一种驱力。

此外，戏剧是由游戏的冲动产生的，是闲暇生活的产物。希腊人（当然指希腊公民，奴隶哪有闲暇可言呢？）生活安逸（希波战争和伯罗奔尼撒战争等特殊时期除外），因此有时间和心情来创造多种娱乐形式，而希伯来人生活颠沛流离、辗转迁徙、常年征战、屡次被异族统治，哪有心情去体验快乐呢？在他们的文学里，除了哀歌还是哀歌，至于《雅歌》，那只是遥远的回忆罢了——回忆所罗门时代曾有的辉煌，回忆历史上未被占领时期的安逸生活。

三 结语

于是，在苦难的经历中，希伯来人形成了虔诚的宗教信仰，也形成了强烈的道德主义。这种虔诚的宗教信仰和强烈的道德主义不允许悲剧存在，因为悲剧是具有娱乐性质的。希伯来人的宗教情感和道德情感不允许他们把痛苦和灾难转化为悲剧这种文学形式，因此希伯来人创造了特殊的艺术形式——哀歌，其中最著名的当然是先知耶利米写下的《耶利米哀歌》。

第二节 《雅歌》的解读与禁欲主义

一 《雅歌》简介

《雅歌》的希伯来原名是 Sir has-sirim，意为"最美之歌""歌中之歌"。《雅歌》是智慧书中的一卷，作者据说是国王所罗门，描写的是所罗门与书拉密女之间的爱情以及男女双方短聚的欢愉和暂别的相思之情。

《雅歌》是圣经文学中最特殊的一部经典，因为它并未像其他作品那样热情讴歌"神的福祉"。从全文来看，只有一处提及上帝之名："求你将我放在你心上如印记，带在你臂上如戳记。因为爱情如死之坚强。嫉恨如阴间之残忍。所发的电光，是火焰的电光，是耶和华的烈焰。"

《雅歌》是一部民间爱情诗歌总集，与中国的《诗经》极为相像，但相比《诗经》，语言更凝练，抒情更直接，风格更粗犷质朴，笔锋直指尘世间的男女之恋。据传所罗门一生曾作诗一千零五首，《雅歌》是其所有作品中最为珍贵的一首，诗的第一句就是"所罗门的歌，是歌中的雅歌"。不过，也有人认为《雅歌》是有人假托所罗门之名而作。关于《雅歌》里的爱情，传统意义上认为是所罗门王和书拉密女之间的爱情。乔装成牧羊人的所罗门王在葡萄园中，与看管葡萄园的书拉密女相遇。两人彼此吸引，一见倾心。牧羊人许诺一定会回来求娶书拉密女便与她依依惜别，此后，两人相互思慕，饱受相思之苦。

最终，所罗门兑现诺言，前来迎娶书拉密女，二人在皇宫举行了盛大的婚礼，他们的爱情终于修成正果，也由此成就了一段千古佳话。还有另外一种说法是，书拉密女所爱之人并非所罗门，而是另一位牧羊青年。所罗门想要迎娶书拉密女，便开展各种攻势想引诱她。但书拉密女深爱牧羊人，忠于自己的爱情，矢志不渝，最终拒绝了所罗门王，等到了自己心仪的牧羊人，二人终成眷属。但不管是哪一种说法，《雅歌》的主旨不变，都是歌颂爱情的纯洁欢愉和对爱情的忠贞不渝。

《雅歌》具有其他经卷所没有的特殊性。无论是其内容主题、语言风格还是行文结构，都显示出与其他经卷不同的地方。

首先，《雅歌》的内容极其丰富，不仅描写爱情，也描写自然风景，而且寓情于景、情景交融。诗中提及各种植物："没药""水仙花""玫瑰花""百合花""苹果树""香柏树""松树""无花果""葡萄""巴嫩木"等。同时，诗中还出现了"葡萄园""田野""山岗""王城""婚宴"等一系列意象，描绘了春华秋实的生机，画面活泼生动，情景转换流畅，营造出一种随性自在、无羁无绊的氛围。在主题上，《雅歌》题材奇特，是唯一一部围绕尘世情爱创作的诗歌集。相比传统意义上的圣经经典，《雅歌》抛开了基督教的沉重主题和严肃格调，用一种轻快、缠绵的语调热烈赞颂世俗的爱恋。

其次，《雅歌》的文笔优雅生动、感情热烈奔放。作者描述男女之情，极尽柔情蜜意，使用的语言文笔极其细腻。"我的良人在男子中，如同苹果树在树林中。我欢欢喜喜坐在他的荫下，尝他果子的滋味，觉得甘甜……我的良人好像羚羊，或像小鹿。他站在我们墙壁后，从窗户往里观看，从窗棂往里窥探。"牧羊女与良人相聚时的欣喜、愉悦之情尽显其中。"我的佳偶，你甚美丽，你甚美丽。你的眼在帕子内好像鸽子的眼。你的头发如同山羊群卧在基列山旁。你的牙齿如刚洗完澡爬上岸的母羊群，个个都是双生，没有一只丧子。你的唇好像一条朱红线，你的嘴也是迷人的。你隐藏在面纱后的双颊，如同石榴的两半。你的颈好像大卫建造的收藏兵器的高台，其上悬挂着一千块盾牌，都是勇士的藤牌。"诗人对感官世界的描绘细致入微，生动呈现了人体之美，牧羊女之形态在诗人笔下惟妙惟肖，入木三分。

最后，《雅歌》的行文结构极其复杂——人称多变，人物多变，场景转换复杂。全诗很短，共有117节，却是最难解释、最具吸引力的。全诗中出现的人物有"所罗门""王""耶路撒冷的众女子""勇士""书拉密女"等；而称呼也由"我的佳偶""我的良人"，变为"我妹子""我新妇""我的完全人""王女"等。人物及人称变换极其复杂，但总体而言是所罗门与书拉密女的男女二重唱，同时伴随着耶路撒冷所有女性的和声。

二 《雅歌》与禁欲主义

《雅歌》是希伯来人的经典传奇，但它最后才被认同为基督教正典，整部《圣经》是希伯来人集历史、地理、文学、文化、宗教信仰于一体的经典著作。《雅歌》描写了世俗之爱的主题，是氤氲着人间爱欲之烟火气息的至善至美之作。如果不将《雅歌》列为基督教的正典，那么这将是希伯来传统的缺失，也将是希伯来文化书写史上最遗憾的事情。然而自古以来，宗教传统的主线都是"禁欲主义"，无论是基督教还是佛教，都历来如此。而如果将《雅歌》纳入基督教正典体系之中，则意味着《雅歌》所歌颂的"俗世爱欲"与基督教传统的"禁欲主义"相背离。尤其诗中曾多次出现的句子，如"你的两乳好像百合花中吃草的一对小鹿，就是母鹿双生的"，这种对人体露骨的刻画，足以使基督徒脸色大变。因此，几个世纪以来如何消解这种悖论一直困惑着释经者们。如何解释《雅歌》，将世俗之情升华为宗教之情，成为基督教神学史乃至《圣经》阐释史上的永恒悖论。最终释经者们找到一种完美的方案，即将所罗门和牧羊女的关系比喻成凡人和教会的关系。他们将教会看作上帝在尘世中的代理人，教会是新郎，信众是新妇，以纯洁神圣的婚姻誓约做比喻，从而引导信徒热爱教会。其实在《圣经》中出现过很多次对上帝和凡人关系的描述，比如"基督是头，我们是身体""基督是真葡萄树，我们是枝子"，又比如"上帝说：'我的羊听我的声音，我也认识他们，他们也跟着我。'""信众说：'耶和华是我的牧者，我必不至缺乏。'"而将上帝和凡人的关系表述为圣洁的婚姻关系则是最崇高的说法。在基督教传统中，婚姻关系是尘世所有关系中最神圣的一种，对《雅歌》的阐释，实际上是在用基督教的宗教逻辑阐述世俗化的伦理事物。

其实从基督教的传统来看，早期的宗教伦理中，"灵魂"和"肉体"之间并没有差别。上帝创造亚当和夏娃时，他们二人本为一体，都是泥身塑人，只因得上帝的"灵气"才有了精魂成为人类。而"灵"与"肉"本就是不可分割的，若是将"肉体"视为污浊，那它也会玷污上帝的"灵气"。如此一来，基督教的教义阐释史出现了分歧：如何在世俗生活与宗教禁欲之间达成妥协，成了基督教教义阐释的一大难题。至于解决的办法，释经者们以《雅歌》为切入点进行了尝试。尽管这一悖论无法从根本上得到解决，但至少缓解了尖锐的冲突——基督教并非完全倡导"断情绝欲"，而是教育信众不可过于放纵情欲。本能的压抑只会导致另一个极端，即欧洲"搜巫浪潮"中对"女巫"的迫害。所以《雅歌》的主题内涵在被赋予"宗教精神"之后，与原本的基督教教义融为一体，即"神圣化"的纯澈之爱。其实质是原本"不食人间烟火的"宗教精神向世俗生活的渗透。

三　结语

《雅歌》对纯洁质朴的男女爱情的热情赞颂，深刻体现了希伯来文明的世俗精神，只是这一维度在基督教信仰中被刻意抹去了。《雅歌》经历了《圣经》体系的"正典化"，这种俗世之爱被加上了"神圣的光环"。因此，意识到《雅歌》的特殊性即意识到基督教对希伯来文明的继承与改造。

第三节 《传道书》中的悲观厌世思想

与《耶利米哀歌》不同，《传道书》中没有哭号、没有祈求，只是深切地表达了一种悲观、绝望之情，道出了人生之虚幻、万事皆虚空的真理。信仰的底色是乐观的、充满希望的，因为信仰者被允诺在死后进入另一个世界。但是《传道书》不同，《传道书》与《雅歌》一样，都属于"另类"。其整体思想与希伯来人的信仰传统格格不入，甚至是相反的。《传道书》的开篇"虚空的虚空，虚空的虚空，一切皆是虚空"传达出强烈的悲观厌世的情绪。如果将《传道书》的"虚空"与中国道家思想的"虚空"做一比较，就会发现二者之间有趣的相似之处，但也有很大的不同。

如果说《耶利米哀歌》是在苦难中寻找希望，那么《传道书》就是在虚无中寻求智慧。《传道书》创作于公元前 930 年，作者据说是犹太国王所罗门。所罗门在诗中自称"传道者"，《传道书》之名便由此而来。相对于《耶利米哀歌》，《传道书》要更为悲观，即使哀歌是在整个国家遭受灭顶之灾的绝境中所作，犹太人也依然在绝境中坚信信仰的力量，祈求上帝耶和华惩罚敌人，对脱离苦海、民族振兴抱有希望。所以总体而言，《耶利米哀歌》仍旧是乐观主义的，但是《传道书》却完全不同，其对现世所有的一切都持否定态度，认为"我见日光之下所做的一切事，都是虚空、都是捕风"[1]，一切都是幻境，而

---

① 《圣经·传道书》第 1 章第 14 节。

所有的一切，无论是新的还是旧的，都将遵循一个原则——"回归"的智慧。"一代过去，一代又来，地却永远长存。日头出来，日头落下，急归所出之地。风往南刮又向北转，不住地旋转，而且返回转行原道。江河都往海里流，海却不满。江河从何处流，仍归还何处……已有的事，后必再有。已行的事，后必再行。日光之下并无新事。岂有一件事人能指着说这是新的，那知，在我们以前的世代早已有了。"[①]遵循自然的回归，人同兽"所遭遇的都是一样"，所以死后也无区别，"这个怎样死，那个也怎样死，气息都是一样。人不能强于兽。都是虚空"。所以传道者发出疑问："都归一处，都是出于尘土，也都归于尘土。谁知道人的灵是往上升、兽的魂是下入地呢。"人与兽都将归于虚无，死后灵魂也不知所踪，所以"莫强如在他经营的事上喜乐，因为这是他的分，他身后的事，谁能使他回来得见呢"。

这种"虚无主义"深刻影响了西方近现代的哲学思想，尤其在叔本华和尼采那里发扬光大。自叔本华的悲观厌世至尼采的"上帝之死"，西方的"虚无主义"之根终于开花结果。

《传道书》中呈现的"虚无主义"与中国传统道家的"虚无主义"极为相似，但道家追求的是恬淡寡欲、超然脱俗，而《传道书》更为务实，强调在现实中及时享乐。以道家为底色的《红楼梦》是曹雪芹写下的末世哀歌，其开篇第一章有一首《好了歌》："世人都晓神仙好，惟有功名忘不了。古今将相在何方？荒冢一堆草没了。世人都晓神仙好，只有金银忘不了。终朝只恨聚无多，及到多时眼闭了……"在道家眼中，世间万物不过一场虚空，一切浮华终将烟消云散化为乌有，道的本源才是永恒且唯一的。

"我又见日光之下，在审判之处有奸恶，在公义之处也有奸恶……我又转念，见日光之下所行的一切欺压，看哪，受欺压的流

---

① 《圣经·传道书》第 1 章第 4 节。

泪，且无人安慰，欺压他们的有势力，也无人安慰他们。"①与《红楼梦》相似的是，《传道书》同样看透人生万象，打破了人生的幻景，两者都对丑恶的社会现象进行了无情的批判和讽刺。而不同之处在于，《红楼梦》看到了绝望，却找不到出口。最终贾府家败没落，黛玉泣血而终，宝玉看破凡尘远走他乡，曾经显赫一时的名门望族终究湮没在浩瀚的历史烟云之中。"满纸荒唐言，一把辛酸泪。"《红楼梦》以贾、史、王、薛四大家族的兴衰史生动呈现了众生百态，或明争暗斗，或明哲保身，或痴情迷途，或舍情遁世，芸芸众生各自奔走追逐，最终只留下一声"花落人亡两不知"的叹息。《传道书》则寻觅到与现实世界和解的方式，即及时享乐，寻找生命之光。而这种享乐并非宣扬纵情纵欲，而是主张"劳作即所得"："凡我眼所求的，我没有留下不给他的。我心所乐的，我没有禁止不享受的。因我的心为我一切所劳碌的快乐，这就是我从劳碌中所得的分……你只管去欢欢喜喜吃你的饭，心中快乐喝你的酒，因为神已经悦纳你的作为。你的衣服当时常洁白，你头上也不要缺少膏油。在你一生虚空的年日，就是神赐你在日光之下虚空的年日，当同你所爱的妻快活度日。因为那是你生前、在日光之下劳碌的事上所得的分。"②这种享乐是原则范围内的享受，并非"放纵"。况且，用"劳碌的快乐"换取"从劳碌中所得的分"，是一种最朴素的社会分配方式，在善恶不公的社会现实中，这也是一种最为平衡的社会发展模式。

与《雅歌》相似，《传道书》体现了深切的世俗关怀。尽管与《旧约》的风格差异很大，但仍然被收录进来成为经典，反映了信仰对世俗生活的介入和妥协。

---

① 《圣经·传道书》第 3 章第 16 节。
② 《圣经·传道书》第 2 章第 10 节。

第三章 《新约》传统

第一节 耶稣的激情——承载神圣的脆弱

一 引言

基督教信仰是对希腊理性哲学传统与希伯来信仰传统的整合。理性哲学成就了基督教神学形而上的思考，而真正触动基督徒乃至人类灵魂的却非抽象的证明，而是耶稣的激情——充满爱与苦难的激情。假如一种宗教只停留在思考的层面，它就会沦为哲学的奴隶。正是耶稣的激情拯救了基督教，或者说，基督教始于耶稣的激情。耶稣的激情点燃了基督徒的激情、成就了福音书的叙事，使基督教在理论建构之外，没有忽略对实践的履行。耶稣的激情是耶稣神性的形而上构建，还是耶稣人性的历史性记录？又或许是历史与想象兼有的叙事？无论是历史还是故事，耶稣的激情对于人类的终极关怀都是必要的，而这种激情触动人心之关键，就在于其承载神圣的脆弱。

二 客西马尼（橄榄山）的祷告与耶稣之死

倾向于历史叙事的《共观福音》与倾向于哲学证明的《约翰福音》，在客西马尼事件与耶稣之死的叙述上，有着发人深省的差异。

《共观福音》的历史之见证与《约翰福音》的哲学之证明在叙事形式上的差异，或可作为基督教神学中信仰与理性之争的例证，也可作为弥合这一裂缝的手段。因此，四部福音书既可视为"系铃人"，又可视为"解铃人"，它们互为证明、互相补充的叙事特点，可视为信仰与理性之争的调和。

比较四部福音书对耶稣被捕前以及耶稣之死的叙述，是颇有意思的事。《共观福音》关于客西马尼（橄榄山）的祷告之叙述大同小异，而《约翰福音》中没有这一情节的叙述。另外，对于耶稣之死的叙述，四部福音书也有不同。如果耶稣事件是真实的历史，那为何有四部福音书来叙述？如果关于耶稣事件的叙述是虚构的，那为何又有惊人的相似之处？历史与启示之表述的差异背后，是否有相同之处？

三 四部福音书：差异与互补

没有一部经典文本纯粹或自主地与我们相遇。每一部经典都有被矛盾地接受和理解的历史。[1] 文本的理解与接受之多样性令人困惑。《马太福音》吸引着基督徒群体中追求团契生活的听众，如宗教改革运动中激进的门诺派（Mennonites）、阿曼派（Amish）和兄弟会教会（Church of the Brethren）。《路加福音》和《使徒行传》在不同的基督徒群体中有不同的解释：灵恩派诉诸圣灵的作用；政治和解放神学家坚持对穷人的偏爱；自由派基督徒喜欢路加对耶稣完整的描述；巴特派则将其视为19世纪的现实主义小说；《约翰福音》始终吸引着基督教传统中的沉思派、神秘主义者、形而上学家和神学家。

这种理解的多样性虽然源自接受者不同的理解，然而更显而易见的原因是文本自身的复杂性。四部福音书的叙述是历史还是虚构？是带有历史成分的现实主义小说，还是虚构性质的隐喻故事？四部福音

---

① 特雷西：《诠释学·宗教·希望——多元性与含混性》，冯川译，上海三联书店，1998，第23页。

书之间的差异，是对历史见证的互相补充，还是对叙事结构的互相补充？或者，两者兼而有之。作为公元 1 世纪耶稣事件的见证人，马太、马可、路加与约翰的叙述大同小异，这足以证明耶稣的历史性，而四部福音书叙述的侧重点和风格之不同，似乎又是对历史事件的互相补充。

四部福音书呈现的互文性（inter-textuality）与他异性（otherness），或许正是走近《圣经》的途径：它避免了同一性这张普洛克鲁斯特之床（Procrustean bed）。[①] 基督教之危机并非只在当代有明显的迹象，虽然当代的世俗化背景确实是信仰危机的根源之一，但实际上，基督教从诞生的那一刻起，就没有脱离过它由之脱胎的犹太教与新生儿——基督教的冲突、上帝的选民与外邦人的冲突、正典与异端的冲突。"宗教的最佳形式乃在其作为一种抗争的力量。"[②] 这种抗争不仅仅存在于宗教与政治、意识形态之间以及宗教与宗教之间，更为重要的是，存在于宗教内部不同的观点之间。正是这种抗争，使宗教保持了它最鲜活的力量并防止了话语霸权或极权的出现。基督教颠覆性的反叛力量，或许并非来自自然科学、进化论或启蒙运动，而是来自内部。克尔凯郭尔认为基督教包含的他性，是"在神学家的游乐场中扔的炸弹"[③]。

四部福音书的"敞开"（disclosure），是专门用来挑战充分领悟、确定性，及最终的控制与驾驭的主张。[④] 这种敞开提供了对话的可能性—文本间的对话以及读者与文本的对话。如果我们不能容忍有异于

---

① 源自古希腊神话：强盗普洛克鲁斯特强迫被抓住的过路人躺在一张特别的床上，如果躺的人身体比床短，他就把人拉长；如果比床长，他就把人砍短，即削足适履。

② 特雷西：《诠释学·宗教·希望——多元性与含混性》，冯川译，上海三联书店，1998，序言第 12 页。

③ 特雷西：《诠释学·宗教·希望——多元性与含混性》，冯川译，上海三联书店，1998，第 25 页。

④ 特雷西：《诠释学·宗教·希望——多元性与含混性》，冯川译，上海三联书店，1998，第 36 页。

我们的问题，对话就不可能发生。四部福音书之间存在对话，因为对话是对差异性和他性的容忍，而差异性和他性是真正的"可能性"。这种理解的可能性使我们最终找到"差异中的相似"—耶稣由一个宣讲者变成被宣讲的内容之原因。耶稣之所以能成为"楷模"，不仅仅因为他与我们道德上的"差异"，更因为他与我们肉体上的"相似"。

四 "自有永有者"与"爱的上帝"

从《旧约》中的"自有永有者"到《新约》中的"神离弃的儿子"，神的形象几经演化，尤其是拿撒勒的耶稣形象，在过去的两千年中成为每个时代被持续讨论的"基本命题"，成为人类追寻意义的可贵尝试。怀特海认为，一个时代的哲学与该时代的耶稣形象之间的关系，如果颠倒过来也是成立的：每一个时代描绘耶稣的方式常常就是理解那个时代特质的一把钥匙。[1] 耶稣形象的变化使信仰史变得复杂深奥，但对于文化史却是不可多得的宝藏。

耶稣不是耶和华——那个具有大能、给埃及人降了九大灾祸[2]，又将"头生的"宰杀的神，那个"自有永有者"。[3] 耶稣之所以不是那个神，是因为他虽然也行神迹，但行的是治病救人的神迹。[4] 耶稣不是那个神——那个令雅各和摩西惧怕的神：雅各在伯特利梦见天梯，睡醒后就惧怕地说："这地方何等可畏！这不是别的，乃是神的殿，也

---

① 帕利坎：《历代耶稣形象及其在文化史上的地位》，杨德友译，香港：汉语基督教文化研究所，1995，第6页。

② 《旧约·出埃及记》第7~11章。

③ 《旧约·出埃及记》第3章第13~14节。摩西对神说："我到以色列人那里，对他们说：'你们祖宗的神打发我到你们这里来。'他们若问我说：'他叫什么名字？'我要对他们说什么呢？"神对摩西说："我是自有永有者。"

④ 《马可福音》第1章第21~32节，赶逐污鬼、治好彼得岳母和许多病人；《马可福音》第1章第40节（《马太福音》第8章第1节、《路加福音》第5章第12~16节），治好麻风病人；《马可福音》第2章第1~12节（《马太福音》第9章第1~8节、《路加福音》第5章第17~26节），治好瘫痪病人；《马可福音》第3章第1~6节（《马太福音》第12章第9~14节、《路加福音》第6章第6~11节），治好萎缩的手。

是天的门。"① 摩西在被神召唤的时候，表现出同样的惧怕：他蒙上脸，因为怕看见神。②"服从是人类灵魂必不可少的一种需求。"③ 尽管薇依认为，服从是生命的营养，然而，它毕竟源于畏惧。同样是信仰，"恐惧与战栗中的信仰"和"爱中的信仰"差别何在？④

希伯来预言是与上帝的震怒和谴责、子民的恐惧和服从分不开的。摩西在何烈山、以赛亚在圣殿、以西结见到上帝的光轮，都以恐惧打动人心：他们以整个民族的名义体验上帝与人的不相容。⑤ 在从"罪的畏惧"到"爱的信仰"的转化过程中，耶稣扮演了至关重要的角色，而让这种"爱"生效的，正是耶稣作为人子的脆弱性。假如上帝只是一个全然的他者，他听不见人的祈求；假如罪人只是先知谴责的对象，则他不再有理由去祈求。爱能在爱中生长：人子的爱唤醒了世人的爱，"爱"的信仰也唤醒了信仰中的"爱"。

哲学家保罗·利科认为，"上帝死了"意味着真正的宗教：不是一个权威在我们之上，而是一种精神在我们心中。利科说："一旦克服了偶像的存在，父亲的形象就恢复成象征。"⑥ 上帝为父意味着上帝为了人的目的而走出了自己。保罗·利科的哲学神学凸显了信仰中的爱和爱中的信仰：上帝是绝对的爱，而不是绝对的权威。耶和华允诺亚伯兰："为你祝福的，我必赐福于他；那咒诅你的，我必咒诅他。"⑦ 然而耶稣却为所有的人祷告："你们的仇敌，要爱他；恨你们的，要

---

① 《旧约·创世记》第 28 章第 17 节。

② 《旧约·出埃及记》第 3 章第 6 节。

③ 西蒙娜·薇依：《扎根——人类责任宣言绪论》，徐卫翔译，生活·读书·新知三联书店，2003，第 10 页。

④ 克尔凯郭尔：《颤栗与不安》，阎嘉等译，天津人民出版社，2007，前言。

⑤ 迪巴勒：《圣经中的原罪》，转引自保罗·里克尔《恶的象征》，公车译，上海人民出版社，2005，第 56 页。

⑥ Kevin J. Vanhoozer, *Biblical Narrative in the Philosophy of Paul Ricoeur: A Study in Hermeneutics and Theology*, Cambridge: Cambridge University Press, 1990, p.130.

⑦ 《旧约·创世记》第 12 章第 3 节。

待他好；咒诅你们的，要为他祝福；凌辱你们的，要为他祷告。"① 德尔图良的神学不仅形成了作为上帝之子的耶稣在神学和教义上的意义，而且澄清了耶稣的文化意义，因为耶稣是历史转折的终决者，因而也是解释历史的新方法和新史学的基础。②

五 "神遗弃的儿子"：脆弱与激情

在一种世俗化的语境中，基督教思想史与哲学、基督教教会史和教义神学的关联性渐趋微弱，而作为个体的耶稣之重要性却日益凸显。在作为个体的耶稣身上，我们看到的不仅是形而上的思考、道德的高尚，还有一个真实的人对信仰的执着追求。从"自有永有者"到"爱的上帝"，基督教发生了转变，然而，这并不意味着其间没有传承。耶稣虽不是耶和华，但他是先知，是一个真实的人。既然耶稣是先知，他就避免不了苦难：耶利米毫不怀疑真正的先知是不幸的。③ 既然耶稣是真实的，那么他就应该接受人自身的脆弱性——各种爱欲情愁的纠缠。

神学家坦尼黑尔认为：耶稣的激情是必要的，因为苦难是先知不可避免的命运。苦难的必要性"源于上帝的目的必须在盲目的、顽抗的世界中被实现的事实"④。先知命运的这一事实是重要的，因为它也赋予耶稣的追随者同样的特征，《使徒行传》中耶稣的见证者符合同一模式。

根据康德的观点，福音书展示了理念以及道德完美的理想，这是我们应该拥有的典范。这种人类至善和自由的理念并非仅仅是字面上的真实，对康德来说，理念在实践中是有效的。也就是说，它鼓励我

① 《路加福音》第 6 章第 27 节。
② 帕利坎：《历代耶稣形象及其在文化史上的地位》，杨德友译，香港：汉语基督教文化研究所，1995，第 34 页。
③ 保罗·里克尔：《恶的象征》，公车译，上海人民出版社，2005，第 59 页。
④ Kevin J. Vanhoozer, *Biblical Narrative in the Philosophy of Paul Ricoeur: A Study in Hermeneutics and Theology*, Cambridge: Cambridge University Press, 1990, p.243.

们在理性和道德层面进行实践。康德明确指出，基督的理念是价值上的而非事实上的。康德的论断是，基督的象征而非耶稣的历史对人类的自由更为重要。康德的道德宗教引发了诸多神学家的不满和争论，然而有一点是值得肯定的：耶稣是道德的楷模。然而，如果耶稣不具备人性，那么这种道德的楷模如何履行道德实践？

在《善的脆弱性》开篇，美国著名学者纳斯鲍姆引用了品达有关"葡萄藤"的比喻以及柏拉图的《会饮篇》。作为现代斯多葛主义者，纳斯鲍姆对于情欲的肯定耐人寻味：在这位女学者的心目中，爱欲正是人这种脆弱的美的力量所在。人，唯其脆弱，才有力量，才有美，才有卓越和高贵。尽管对灵魂来说，这沉重的肉身让我们感觉疲惫，但谁又能否定这肉身帮我们承担了灵魂所有的苦痛和欢乐。在《会饮篇》中，当阿尔西比亚德斯陈述完他对于人之美德的看法后，苏格拉底以不无揶揄的口气问道："那么，何谓一个人呢？"基于此，纳斯鲍姆开始了她的哲学、伦理学反思："对斯多葛派伦理学的日益投入已经让我在一个新的视野下来看待这部早期著作的许多主题——尤其是情感的本质和人的概念。"[1]

耶稣不是传统意义上的"英雄"，他没有通过战斗而获胜，也没有屠杀火龙："与官方的历史相比，他不是战绩累累的统治者和征服者，他的故事将是苦难的故事。"[2] "激情"叙事是关于脆弱、受苦、自我牺牲的叙事。与其他的英雄不同，耶稣并没有做什么使他的存在更安全，使他的生命有意义，而是把这些托付给了上帝。福音一定是叙事，因为它涉及存在的方式，而这种方式导致了苦难史。宣讲内部本身，也需要叙事形式。因为宣讲者的宣讲以及生活方式被卷入了苦难

---

[1] 玛莎·纳斯鲍姆：《善的脆弱性——古希腊悲剧和哲学中的运气与伦理》，徐向东、陆萌译，译林出版社，2007，第5页。

[2] Kevin J. Vanhoozer, *Biblical Narrative in the Philosophy of Paul Ricoeur: A Study in Hermeneutics and Theology*, Cambridge: Cambridge University Press, 1990, p.133.

史中，所以宣讲者变成了被宣讲的内容。

奥古斯丁虽然推崇《约翰福音》，但也对耶稣的人性大加肯定，因为他是我们应该变成的样子："基督耶稣是上帝与人之间的调解者，不是因为他有神性，而是因为他有人性，不仅因为他是一切完美的源泉，而且也是一切完美的目的。"① 在奥古斯丁去世的大约一千二百年之后，法国科学家、基督教哲学家帕斯卡尔继承了奥古斯丁的衣钵："如果不理解人类的苦难，关于上帝的知识就会造成骄傲。没有关于上帝的知识，而只了解人类的苦难，我们就会感到绝望。而关于耶稣的知识则构成了中庸之道，因为我们可以从神的身上找到神的痛苦和我们的痛苦。"

另外一个现象更生动地体现了耶稣之人性在文化史上的地位：对圣母马利亚的崇拜。尽管聂斯托利派因为否认马利亚的神性（当然它的"两位两性说"也违反了"三位一体"的正统教义）而被列为"异端"，然而天主教（包括其艺术成就）兴盛的原因之一，不正是圣母崇拜吗？"在崇敬或思辨歌颂基督为主、为王而失去了与这位拿撒勒人的联系之时，马利亚就取代了他；她是人性的、充满同情心和平易近人的。因此，对她的崇敬和对她的思考也不再是依据'出自对主的尊崇'而展开了。"②

在耶稣基督事件中证明了自己存在的上帝，是爱的上帝。这个"爱的上帝"的现实，也是人类爱和被爱之意义的中心线索。对于耶稣的询问——"你问我是谁？"特雷西可能回答："你是基督，一种在世的爱之模式的象征。"③ 尽管耶鲁学派抱怨这里的"耶稣"转变成了

---

① 帕利坎：《历代耶稣形象及其在文化史上的地位》，杨德友译，香港：汉语基督教文化研究所，1995，第104页。

② 帕利坎：《历代耶稣形象及其在文化史上的地位》，杨德友译，香港：汉语基督教文化研究所，1995，第114页。

③ Kevin J. Vanhoozer, *Biblical Narrative in the Philosophy of Paul Ricoeur: A Study in Hermeneutics and Theology*, Cambridge: Cambridge University Press, 1990, p.164.

"普遍的意义"的寓言，^①然而这种人性之普遍的真理，不正是耶稣以及关于他的叙事（福音书）在人类历史上的独特价值所在？

尽管耶稣"坚决地期待着"死亡的时刻，也从未动摇过他的信仰，但是这并不意味着死亡的终结时间没有痛楚。福音书呈现了我们在世的罪恶及受苦的体验：在快乐重新到来之前，那里充满了对痛苦的恐惧。对特雷西来说，这种看法更加坚定地揭示了人类存在的真理：正如梵高的受难画比拉斐尔艺术所呈现的无纷扰的、轻灵的世界对当代经验来说更加真实。^②

耶稣如何能够肯定并且爱着这个让他受苦的世界？客西马尼的祷告显示了作为个体的人的耶稣之脆弱性，然而这种脆弱性的高贵之处在于：尽管死亡是痛苦的，但这并没有动摇耶稣信仰的决心。以脆弱的肉体来承担俗世的痛苦、以爱的勇气面对罪恶的世界，正是耶稣作为一个人的价值所在。耶稣对造物的"肯定"比他对苦难的否定的影响要大得多。意义比荒谬更为根本。^③

六　福音书的激情叙事：爱的体会与实践

诗的可能性引诱着诗的情感。按照过程诠释学的观点，文本看起来似乎是邀请读者根据文本传达的象征重新检验自己的生活。耶稣的问题"你说我是谁"的切入点在于，它提出了一个基本的问题并且向读者提出了挑战：这就是生活的方式吗？如果读者进入了耶稣激情的故事并发现，它存在的十字架方式照亮了读者的世界，那么读者就遭遇了作为启示的福音。

---

① Kevin J. Vanhoozer, *Biblical Narrative in the Philosophy of Paul Ricoeur: A Study in Hermeneutics and Theology*, Cambridge: Cambridge University Press, 1990, p.164.

② Kevin J. Vanhoozer, *Biblical Narrative in the Philosophy of Paul Ricoeur: A Study in Hermeneutics and Theology*, Cambridge: Cambridge University Press, 1990, p.162.

③ Kevin J. Vanhoozer, *Biblical Narrative in the Philosophy of Paul Ricoeur: A Study in Hermeneutics and Theology*, Cambridge: Cambridge University Press, 1990, p.203.

如果命题的基本功能是引诱情感，那么对于耶稣的故事，读者更多地关注它的情感价值而非现实性。文本的世界被赋予了读者的想象。圣经文本即使看起来是现实主义的，也可以被看作为了读者的想象性情感而加以陈述的真实可能性。阐释是理解的途径。因此，当读者遵循诱惑并占有文本的意义时，他们获得了主体性的新形式。对利科而言，重要的耶稣，不是潘恩伯格的历史的耶稣，也不是巴特的上帝之启示的耶稣，而是由福音书邀请读者分享的历史性耶稣。也就是说，福音书是关于人类历史的故事。行动要屈从于情感。主体性的改变比灵魂外部的波动更重要。[1]

福音书的功能不仅在于表现新的上帝，而是为这个新的上帝创造机会。[2] 很多故事对读者有强大的影响力，即使它们所叙述的事件从未发生过。耶稣基督的形象不仅呈现了最初的启示事件，也为随后的启示事件提供了机会。因此对蒂利希和利科而言，福音叙事具有证明和改变生活之功能。对特雷西与利科来说，耶稣故事的关键在于，它能使读者以新的方式看待生活。特雷西希望读者在福音书中发现强化信仰和希望的表述。然而，并非是耶稣改变了世界之结构或人类的本质，而是我们通过耶稣的故事能以不同的方式看待世界。

第二节　耶稣事件——历史抑或想象

一　引言

作为"芝加哥学派"的代表，保罗·利科的诠释学具有显而易见

---

[1] Kevin J. Vanhoozer, *Biblical Narrative in the Philosophy of Paul Ricoeur: A Study in Hermeneutics and Theology*, Cambridge: Cambridge University Press, 1990, pp.209−211.

[2] Kevin J. Vanhoozer, *Biblical Narrative in the Philosophy of Paul Ricoeur: A Study in Hermeneutics and Theology*, Cambridge: Cambridge University Press, 1990, p.218.

的调和性。他试图调和的不仅是哲学与神学的裂隙、信仰与理解的矛盾，也是历史与想象的分歧。如果说利科的诠释学是哲学性质的，那么圣经叙事只是其哲学诠释学的一个局部例证；如果说利科的诠释学是神学性质的，那么圣经叙事就成了其神学诠释学的整体框架。然而无论如何，圣经叙事在利科的哲学—神学思考及叙事理论中都占有不可忽视的独特地位。利科哲学中对圣经叙事的凸显，使他的哲学框定在神学的构架内，而他对圣经叙事中历史与想象的分析，又使其神学在诠释哲学的维度中得以提升。而无论是神学还是哲学，诠释总是思考最本质的特征。历史与想象是诠释面临的困惑，而它们之间的纠缠由两个向度、三个因素构成。两个向度指历史本身和历史的书写；三个因素指文本、书写者与阅读者。文本是连接书写者与阅读者的媒介，而书写与阅读本身也是一种阐释。

二 圣经叙事：普遍真理的象征？

特雷西与利科对福音叙事的分析，使耶稣的故事本身成为普遍真理的象征。特雷西把福音叙事包含在诠释学的类型"经典"中，这使福音叙事不仅与神学有牵连，也与诠释学关系密切。这种把宗教世俗化、神学化的做法，使"芝加哥学派"受到了"耶鲁学派"的猛烈攻击。假如福音揭示了关于人类总体经验的普遍真理，那么耶稣基督的特殊意义又是什么？

带着这个问题，我们来看看弗雷对利科诠释学的基本批评。众所周知，利科相信诗歌和文学的特殊功能是揭示新的可能性。利科与特雷西跟随布特曼的指引，认为《新约》为读者的自我理解提供了新的可能性。然而，此种诠释学策略需要付出代价。弗雷指控利科和特雷西没有保留福音书"字面的"阅读，从而也没有为基督教神学保留耶稣及其行为的必要性。这是如何发生的？

假如福音真的是关于人类的普遍经验和可能性的，那么利科和特雷西的诠释学立场将把耶稣视为"以意识形式存在的主体，也就是说，他的自我是作为'理解'存在的"①。故事中耶稣到底发生了什么？这仅仅是允许他进行自我理解的一个衬托。弗雷认为这种阅读没有对福音书做出公允的评价，没有把它看作一个有关人的行为、性格和这个世界上所发生的重大事件的故事，而这样的阅读失去了福音书特有的"神学"因素，即上帝的行为在基督教中的历史见证。

难道耶稣不能继续扮演自我理解的送信人的角色吗？弗雷认为不能，因为在这种计划中呈现的福音叙事，不是第一位的个体自我，不是他们的谓语主体，而是"'在世存在的模式'(the mode-of-being-in-the-world)，这种模式是自我的例子，是'被揭示'(disclosed)给'理解'的'再现'(re-presented)"。②基于这一叙述，耶稣的角色"就仅仅是特定的一套态度之现世的个体化的加强"③。"耶稣"不再作为故事中主要角色的名字存在，而是作为意识的特定模式的标签，作为自我理解的可能性而存在。弗雷认为此种福音叙事的阅读不能保留耶稣故事的中心位置："最多，从这个观点来看，意义—证明与故事内个体主体的归属之联系是微弱的。最糟糕的是，这种联系已经被消除。"④个人主体的"耶稣"发生了什么不再重要。

在利科的"圣经诠释学"中，"寓言的最终参照物……不是上帝之国，而是人类的全体现实"⑤。弗雷指出，利科的意图是把耶稣关于上帝之国的教导包含于更全面的证明之中，而这一做法的错误在于，

---

① Kevin J. Vanhoozer, *Biblical Narrative in the Philosophy of Paul Ricoeur: A Study in Hermeneutics and Theology*, Cambridge: Cambridge University Press, 1990, p.159.

② Kevin J. Vanhoozer, *Biblical Narrative in the Philosophy of Paul Ricoeur: A Study in Hermeneutics and Theology*, Cambridge: Cambridge University Press, 1990, p.159.

③ Kevin J. Vanhoozer, *Biblical Narrative in the Philosophy of Paul Ricoeur: A Study in Hermeneutics and Theology*, Cambridge: Cambridge University Press, 1990, p.159.

④ Kevin J. Vanhoozer, *Biblical Narrative in the Philosophy of Paul Ricoeur: A Study in Hermeneutics and Theology*, Cambridge: Cambridge University Press, 1990, p.160.

⑤ Kevin J. Vanhoozer, *Biblical Narrative in the Philosophy of Paul Ricoeur: A Study in Hermeneutics and Theology*, Cambridge: Cambridge University Press, 1990, p.160.

由于把圣经叙事的字面意义和理想的参照物分离开来而使圣经叙事逐渐衰落。

三 历史与想象：叙事的两种模式

如果哲学是对人类存在的思考，那么这种思考一定是被最能表达人类存在的语言的各种形式（包括人类行为和历史本身）所推动的。叙事被利科推崇，因为这种语言形式最能表现人类的现世性。叙事体现了行为的可能性，体现了做事的可能方式，也体现了可能的"世界"。叙事或许可以看作利科学术思考的顶峰，因为叙事不仅把语言、诠释学和哲学人类学的思考联结起来，而且是利科对可能性、现世性、创造性三个想象性主题进行讨论的汇合点。

历史与想象，作为叙事的两种模式，是人类的历史性被重新描述的方式。因此，历史与想象一起为人类的可能性建构了叙事的"系统性计划"。叙事创造并呈现了我们活着的无数种方式。此外，叙事呈现的可能性不仅仅是为个体提供的可能性，更是为整个社会和团体提供的可能性。通过叙事的历史和想象，我们对希望的对象发出声音，这个对象是人类生命的形式，是我们渴望的但还未实现的形式。通过呈现可能的世界或者在时间中存在的方式，并恳求读者把这个可能的世界变成自己的，叙事达成了利科渴望已久的"意志诗学"的目的。

历史与想象的争执，是西方思想家们难以避免的尴尬，是历史哲学和诠释学无法逾越的沟壑。从克罗齐的"一切历史都是当代史"[①]到柯林武德的"一切历史都是思想史"[②]，再到海登·怀特的"历史叙事的本质就是虚构"[③]，历史与想象的界限已经彻底模糊。思想者在历

[①] 克罗齐:《历史学的理论和实际》，傅任敢译，商务印书馆，1982，第 2 页。

[②] 柯林武德:《历史的观念》，何兆武、张文杰译，中国社会科学出版社，1986，第 244 页。

[③] Hayden White, *Metahistory: The Historical Imagination in Nineteenth—Century Europe*, Baltimore: The Johns Hopkins University Press, 1990, p.ix.

史叙事中发现了充斥在字里行间的想象的身影。历史为想象留下了空间，想象背负着历史翱翔。那么，文学虚构与历史想象的边界又在哪里？

最高妙者亦最危险者，而"危险所在，必是有更多拯救之处"①。历史抑或想象的尴尬，或许恰好成全了利科的哲学—神学—文学之旅，也如彼得手中之钥，为利科的信仰诉求开启了天国之门。因此，《时间与叙事》的任务是双重的：一方面，利科需要展示历史在依赖想象的力量构建情节方面与虚构非常相似；另一方面，他需要展示虚构在关于人类行为的真实世界的证明方面与历史也非常相似。在利科看来，历史与虚构构成了可能的激情的两种类型：历史提醒我们什么是可能的，虚构提醒我们什么将是可能的。

四 耶稣事件的历史与虚构

利科是一个解决纠纷的思想家。利科在选择立场时独具天分，本来看似相互排斥的立场，在他的调停中会变得相容而又相互独立。根据利科的观点，福音书最显著的特点是叙事与福音传道的结合。② 福音书是宣布耶稣其人及其历史的精彩叙事。作为叙事与福音传道的结合，福音书保留了历史的耶稣和信仰的基督的整体性和永续性。利科对圣经叙事中历史与想象的调和，实际上在信仰的基督和历史的耶稣之间建立了一种理性。

尽管历史学家参与建构虚构的可能性实验室，但历史还存在一个客观性问题。历史学家的认识论与其他人类科学不同，它要求对批判

---

① 基阿尼·瓦蒂莫:《踪迹的踪迹》，载雅克·德里达、基阿尼·瓦蒂莫主编《宗教》，杜小真译，商务印书馆，2006，第 94 页。

② Kevin J. Vanhoozer, *Biblical Narrative in the Philosophy of Paul Ricoeur: A Study in Hermeneutics and Theology*, Cambridge: Cambridge University Press, 1990, p.204.

（历史的研究）和想象（叙事的使用）的双重忠诚。[1] 历史之客观性意味着一个历史学家的结论应该与另一个历史学家的结论互补，也就是说两种叙述是关于同一个世界的，而福音书正是以这样的方式表现了耶稣事件的历史性。

历史实际上讲述的是已经发生的事件，而历史学家被审判过去的欲望所激励。历史学家只有过去的"踪迹"(traces)，而在目前是缺席的。一方面，这些"踪迹"是思想的枷锁，提醒我们过去是不能被拥有的，是不可接近的存在；另一方面，这些"踪迹"是历史研究的导向。审判过去的"踪迹"的义务，以及对实际上发生事情的回应，使历史仍旧保留了与虚构的界限。

历史学家不是描述，而只是重述。对利科来说，历史就像隐喻，是想象的结构：历史学家发明了再现过去的图像。像隐喻的主人一样，历史学家不是在复制，而是在发明，为了发现而发明。历史的叙事是创造性的模仿。

对很多哲学家来说，虚构并不涉及缺席的某物，而是涉及非真实的某物，利科认为，这才是真正的诽谤。利科开拓了虚构的独特认知功能：通过发明来发现。虚构要求我们悬置对现实世界的关注，并去留意另一个世界："在这种没有约定的状态下，我们尝试新观点、新价值、新的在世方式。想象就是可能性的自由竞争。"[2] 历史学家打开了通向可能的真实的大门："过去的'真实的'故事揭示了现在的潜力。"[3]

虚构的真理在阅读中得以体现。当文本的世界与读者的世界相

---

[1] Kevin J. Vanhoozer, *Biblical Narrative in the Philosophy of Paul Ricoeur: A Study in Hermeneutics and Theology*, Cambridge: Cambridge University Press, 1990, p.95.

[2] Kevin J. Vanhoozer, *Biblical Narrative in the Philosophy of Paul Ricoeur: A Study in Hermeneutics and Theology*, Cambridge: Cambridge University Press, 1990, p.98.

[3] Kevin J. Vanhoozer, *Biblical Narrative in the Philosophy of Paul Ricoeur: A Study in Hermeneutics and Theology*, Cambridge: Cambridge University Press, 1990, p.102.

遇时，虚构变成一种真实，因此，读者对文本之虚构世界的"占有"(appropriation)，是虚构转化为真实的必要条件。阅读调和了文本的虚构世界和读者的现实世界正是在这个特殊的地方，文本的可能性世界才与现实的世界交会。无论文本的世界具有怎样的本体论地位，它始终处于悬置状态，直到被阅读、被"占有"。虚构通过其影响，即生命、道德的转化来到真实的世界。[①] 因此，利科不是以证明的理论，而是以影响的理论来探索虚构的真理。虚构具有启示和转型的力量，它使读者从日常生活中解放出来，并对现实、对自己有了新的评价。换句话说，即虚构与现实的关系是应用、占用而非证明。紧随伽达默尔，利科发现历史在很大程度上通过阅读来影响我们。历史开放的可能性必然会被想象所占有。

五 结语

如果一个民族既没有故事又没有历史，那么它就既没有过去也没有将来。叙事给予我们一种历史的意识，并赋予我们一种身份。利科说，事实上，个人的身份在本质上是叙事性的，这种特征是与生俱来的。要理解我们是谁，就要了解我们的故事。叙事还为我们提供了自我的持续性和断裂性之间的重要联系。叙事身份的暗示在于，我们必须是自己生命的"读者"。使"我们是谁"这个问题具有意义的一种途径就是，通过其他的故事和历史中的角色来辨认自己。如果这样的话，这些叙事就"重塑"了我们的生活。在其哲学事业的开端，利科就否定了笛卡儿直接审视的特权。人这个主体既不是自我透明的，也不是虚幻的，而是留下一些需要被阐释以及有关它存在的"踪迹"的

---

① Kevin J. Vanhoozer, *Biblical Narrative in the Philosophy of Paul Ricoeur: A Study in Hermeneutics and Theology*, Cambridge: Cambridge University Press, 1990, p.99.

时间中的存在:"这个主体因此也是自己生活的读者和作者。"[①] 叙事身份也在社会层面上发生作用。无论是个体还是群体,都由一定的叙事来决定他们的身份,这些叙事就成为他们的故事或历史。利科说,正是通过讲述某些基本事件的故事,圣经中的以色列人才成为一个历史性群体。

第三节 《新约》中的世界主义

一 引言

纪元之初的基督教,实际上是对希腊和希伯来两大文化传统的融合。基督教通过犹太人的经典承袭了希伯来文化,又由于历史和地域的规定性,受到了希腊文化的渗透和冲击。早期的教父们为了使基督教得到统治阶层和罗马民众的认同,大体采用了两种有效的策略:其一是论证基督教与罗马政体的共同点,以便求得国家机器的保护;其二是寻找基督教与希腊哲学的相通之处,借助更为严谨的哲学观念来丰富和传播自己的信仰。但是就其实质而言,基督教对两大古代传统的融合首先体现为对旧有信仰的反叛和更新,所以耶稣和保罗的"超越尘世""因信称义"命题,是它真正的起点。

二 《新约》中的世界主义

《新约》中的世界主义有两个来源:其一是希腊哲学中的世界主义思想,尤其是罗马时代斯多葛学派晚期的世界主义思想;其二是希伯来文化中固有的民族融合、文化交流的传统,尤其是被掳被囚时期犹太人已经产生的和平主义思想。对耶稣来说,后者的影响可能更大

[①] Kevin J. Vanhoozer, *Biblical Narrative in the Philosophy of Paul Ricoeur: A Study in Hermeneutics and Theology*, Cambridge: Cambridge University Press, 1990, p.104.

一些，而对保罗来说，前者的影响可能更大。实际上，在被掳被囚时期，狭隘的民族主义思想与和平主义思想同时产生，《旧约》中的先知书有大量证据证明了这一点。如果说希伯来人最大的努力是试图颠覆希腊文化的价值系统或者是使希腊文化成为希伯来文化的附属，那么基督教则试图融合两种传统，而在这种融合中，实际上希腊文化已经从附属地位变为主导地位。

其实在《新约》形成之前，亚历山大的斐洛（Philo）就曾在《政治家》等著作中论及上帝的"大城邦"（megapolis）和人类之城。斐洛试图将《旧约》中的世界主义与希腊—罗马世界中的世界主义融合在一起的努力，强烈地激励了《新约》的作者们。而真正将两种传统融合起来的是以约翰和保罗为代表的初期基督教的创始人。他们将《旧约》世界主义神学与希腊—罗马世界主义哲学融为一体，希望将此作为基督教信仰的哲学支撑。值得赞许的是，《新约》的作者们是在批判《旧约》狭隘的民族主义基础上汲取了希伯来传统和希腊传统的精华而形成基督教普世主义神学的。

福音书中对两希传统的融合最为突出的是《约翰福音》，而《约翰福音》的开篇不仅是对世界主义的最好阐释，也是两希融合的最好见证："太初有道，道与上帝同在，道就是上帝……万物没有一样不是借着他造的……生命在他里头，这生命就是人的光……那光是真光，照亮一切生在世上的人。"在这段话中，我们首先感觉到的是"普世主义的光"，它照亮了所有生在世上的人，而不是只照亮"选民"，于是《旧约》中"以色列"的独特性不复存在了，上帝的光照亮了所有的人，上帝的慈爱、救赎赐给所有的人，于是犹太人的优越感不复存在。

《约翰福音》将有着犹太面孔的耶和华变为"道""光""逻各斯"，变为宇宙理性和生命之光，这就使基督教神学进入了世界主义范畴。

耶稣的宗教改革承继了"第二以赛亚运动"的宝贵传统，他挑战了神的子民的界限，重新定义了"义人"与"罪人"，并将那些被排斥的群体纳入自己的拯救范围，这一切都展示了和平主义与世界主义的希望。"登山训众"被认为是基督教伦理思想的基石，其中不少言论关乎耶稣对犹太人狭隘的民族主义的批判。针对犹太人狭隘的复仇心理——"以眼还眼、以牙还牙""当爱你的邻居、恨你的仇敌"，耶稣教导说："不要与恶人作对，有人打你的右脸，连左脸也转过来由他打……要爱你们的仇敌，为那逼迫你们的祷告。"耶稣的世界主义思想充分体现在这句话中："日头照好人，也照歹人；降雨给义人，也给不义的人。"耶稣对以色列人心中上帝形象的改变，为基督教的普世主义奠定了坚实的基础：在《旧约》中，耶和华经常被描绘成威严可怖、脾气暴躁、心胸狭隘的军事统帅，他不仅对以色列人的仇敌埃及人、非利士人施加惩罚，而且对悖逆的犹太人也毫不留情。然而在耶稣的改变下，上帝从一个民族神变为全人类的共同天父；而且这个天父的脾气也变好了，变得和蔼可亲、宽容大度。在耶稣的心里，犹太人没有任何特权，以前备受歧视的妇女、罪人、撒玛利亚人，都是他救赎的对象。因此，在耶稣的信仰体系中，救赎的对象由群体变成了单个的人，这与希腊哲学的世界主义对个体的强调如出一辙。耶稣的诫命中最重要的两条就是"爱上帝"和"爱人如己"，这充分显示了耶稣的世界主义思想与犹太人狭隘的民族主义思想的不同。耶稣复活后对门徒们的最后嘱咐也有着世界主义的意味："天上地下所有的权柄都赐给我了，所以你们要去，使万民做我的门徒。"

保罗进一步拓展了耶稣福音的逻辑——耶稣的好消息不仅带给"义人"，也带给"罪人"，而保罗的好消息不仅带给"罪人"，还带给"外邦的罪人"。在《罗马书》第2章第10~11节，保罗明确地说："神将一切荣耀、尊贵、平安加给一切行善的人，先是犹太人，后是希腊人。因为神不偏待人。"又如《罗马书》第4章：亚伯拉罕作为信仰的表率，其对信仰的虔诚并不是借着割礼的特殊记号来表现的。

再如在《罗马书》第 9 章第 6 ～ 12 节中，保罗重申了神召或神圣拣选的特点——不分种族或是身体的记号。在《罗马书》第 11 章中，保罗声称，末世的希望不仅临到犹太人身上，也临到外邦人身上，要临到所有人身上。

如果说福音书更多地记载了基督教创始人的世界主义思想，那么《使徒行传》更多地记载了基督徒初期的世界主义实践。《使徒行传》生动地记录了第一代使徒全面推行耶稣的世界主义思想的传教活动，描绘了第一代使徒以不屈不挠的意志向世界各地尤其是地中海周边地区传播基督教（其时基督教与犹太教还未正式分裂，属于犹太教的异端）的图景。这卷书的主要线索是使徒们如何把福音从耶路撒冷传到"犹太全地和撒玛利亚，直到地极"的故事，其间充满了艰辛、困苦，甚至付出了生命。如司提反，他为了传扬耶稣的世界主义思想，与犹太人据理力争，将所有人驳斥得无言以对，这一切使犹太人恼羞成怒，收买坏人做伪证控告他，最后被拉出城外用乱石砸死。再如彼得，他两次被犹太官府拘捕，后来又被希律王捉拿，行将于逾越节后被处决，后因奇迹般的保护才逃出监牢化险为夷。

至于保罗，其所经受的苦难更是令人难以置信，他不仅 3 次远征海外，屡屡遇险，足迹遍及巴勒斯坦、小亚细亚、地中海诸岛、希腊、罗马，而且著作颇丰，对基督教的世界主义思想做了系统的阐释。针对犹太人"因律法称义"的观点，保罗提出了"因信称义"的观点，使基督救赎涵盖了所有信仰基督的人——这就废除了犹太人以律法界定民族身份、信仰身份的做法，打破了犹太人与外邦人之间难以逾越的界限，将犹太人狭隘的民族主义发展为博爱的世界主义。为了搬走摩西律法这个拦路石，保罗机智地绕过摩西回到了亚伯拉罕。亚伯拉罕并未受割礼，也不知道摩西律法，但这并不能妨碍他称义。这说明所有的人都可以如此，称义并不局限于遵行律法的犹太人。

在保罗的书信中，处处可见世界主义思想，如《哥林多前书》第

12 章第 12 ~ 27 节说:"就如身子是一个,却有许多肢体;而且肢体虽多,仍是一个身子。基督也是这样。我们不拘是犹太人,是希腊人,是为奴的,是自主的,都从一位圣灵受洗,成了一个身体,饮于一位圣灵。"再如《以弗所书》第 2 章第 11 ~ 15 节说:"所以你们应当纪念,你们从前按肉体是外邦人,是称为'没受割礼的',这名原是那些凭人手在肉身上称为受割礼之人所起的。那时,你们与基督无关,在以色列国民以外,在所应许的诸约上是局外人,并且活在世上没有指望,没有神。你们从前远离神的人,如今却在基督耶稣里,靠着他的血,已经变得亲近了。"

在保罗的普世思想中,耶稣关于爱的教导成为基督教神学的基本特征:"爱是恒久忍耐,又有恩慈;爱是不嫉妒;爱是不自夸,不张狂,不做害羞的事,不求自己的益处,不轻易发怒,不计算人的恶,不喜欢不义,只喜欢真理;凡事包容,凡事相信,凡事盼望,凡事忍耐。爱是永不止息。"这是一种不分国界、不分种族、不分社会地位、不分贫贱的爱,是一种无条件的爱。这种爱与犹太教狭隘的同胞之爱截然不同,与中国儒家思想中"由近及远"的爱也不相同,这是一种普世性的爱,是超越了一切界限的爱。

相比之下,《启示录》中则充满了狭隘的民族主义情绪,处处是血淋淋的仇杀场面,处处是上帝的审判;上帝仍然是那个动辄发怒并施以惩罚的万军之神。也因此,《启示录》是最后被收录于《新约》的,其正典地位曾长期遭受质疑。

第四节 《新约》中的排他性

一 奥古斯丁的"上帝之城"

虽然初期基督教吸收了斯多葛学派的世界主义观念,但是在随后的发展中渐渐背离了这一观念所倡导的世界精神，而这在最初的教义中就埋下了伏笔。对世俗的国度与神的国度的区分——"恺撒的归恺撒，神的归神"，使不信神的人群被排斥在了神圣之外，这与其前身犹太教以宗教信仰和割礼等习俗来界定身份的做法虽然貌似不同，实则异曲同工——不信神的与信神的成为两种截然不同的身份，这种身份界定造成的极端主义情绪，并不比极端民族主义造成的危害小。奥古斯丁对"上帝之城"的阐释，使世界城邦再次成为只包含特定人群的共同体。通过把神之城的公民资格限定为那些热爱神的人，奥古斯丁明确地表达了这个观点。

二 反闪族主义

事实上，基督教的排他性最先体现在对"犹太人"的排斥上，而反闪族主义，成为基督教后来近两千年发展过程中隐含的特点。对基督徒来说，"谁是神的子民"这个问题关系到基督教的自我理解与自我定位。如果基督教和犹太教还没有分裂，还在同一个框架内，那么这个问题就不是问题。然而公元 1 世纪基督徒的几项宣言与犹太教形成激烈的竞争，于是"以色列"的概念开始更新、扩张。[1] 随着道路的最终分裂，这一问题愈发尖锐而让人不能回避。谁是神的子民？所有的犹太人吗？还是那些加入了基督教（末世论的犹太教）的犹太人？也包括外邦人吗？那么大多数不相信耶稣为弥赛亚而且似乎没有转变的犹太人又将如何？[2] 基督教是否接管了以色列？"新的以色列"是否超越了旧的以色列？在公元 2 世纪，这一问题更加复杂：基督徒感觉到自己是第三个种族[3]——犹太人和外邦人成了"他

---

[1] 这一问题在《新约》中很突出，参见《罗马书》第 9 章第 6 节、《加拉太书》第 6 章第 16 节、《雅各书》第 1 章第 1 节、《彼得前书》第 1 章第 1~2 节。

[2] M. Barth 使这一问题成为谈论的焦点，参见 *The People of God*, Sheffield: Sheffield Academic Press, 1983.

[3] 参见 Simon, "Verus Israel," *Journal of Jewish Studtes* 37 (1986).

们"，而只有基督徒是"自己人"，只有基督教是真正的以色列。基督徒这种日益强化的身份意识催生了反闪族主义。一个长久以来令人烦恼的事实是，天主教一直努力地将自己与犹太教区别开来，一直排斥犹太人。在最初的几个世纪，这一倾向明显地表现在克里索斯托姆（Chrysostom）的《反犹太人训诫》里（*Homily Against the Jews*）。极具反讽意味的是，基督教开始反对犹太教和犹太基督教的种族中心主义，但又认为自己是独立的"种族"，并开创了一种不同类型的种族主义。在基督教的种族主义中，基督徒极力将自己与"犹太人"区别开来，而这是保罗曾极力反对的。

基督教若想意识到自己的这种排他性、狭隘性，并且能够克服这种排他性和狭隘性，恐怕要重新回到耶稣。耶稣挑战了神的子民的边界，这是他传道的一个中心思想。这对基督教内部的所有宗派而言都是一种暗示和挑战。不仅仅是宗派之间，就连宗派之中的支派也都面临着这样一种挑战——这些支派总是以"义人"自居，借此与"罪人"相区别。这种打着"神的意志"的旗号排斥其他宗派的做法，如今在基督教内部很盛行，不论是罗马教廷还是新教的基要主义者都是如此。因此，耶稣对这种态度的批判无论从前还是现在，都一样有效。

三 教会的权力

长期以来，基督教神哲学的争论围绕着"神学"与"哲学"的地位展开，而基督教会只关注"世俗政治权威"与"普遍教会"（universal Church）的权力，对教会的世界主义的强调却日渐衰退，尽管它理想中的宗教共同体是包含所有人的。简单地说，争论的焦点是在世俗与宗教之间，而非地方与世界主义之间。如此一来，初期基督教思想中进步的世界主义倾向逐渐被遗忘了，取而代之的是狭隘的身份界限，即属灵的与不信神的区分，这使基督教重新陷入了其前身犹太教的偏狭之中。这种偏狭在基督教后来的发展中愈演愈烈，直至宗教改革时期的宗教战争、宗教迫害发展到令人惊心的地步。

早期基督教会惨遭迫害，尤其是在尼禄与图拉真皇帝的治下，很多殉道者为了他们的"信仰"而献身。这些殉道者的"护教"精神可歌可泣，然而这段被压迫的历史却更值得反思——因为1000年后，这一曾经备受迫害的宗教，却成了欧洲历史上最大的迫害者。313年，君士坦丁大帝承认基督教的合法地位；392年，狄奥多西皇帝将其定为国教。在漫长的中世纪，基督教在思想文化的传承与社会制度的建立及巩固方面无疑起了巨大的作用，然而其对思想的禁锢和对社会权力的滥用也不容忽视。

476年，西罗马帝国的灭亡与日耳曼民族的入侵，使社会陷入一片混乱。两千年的希罗文明陷入绝境。而基督教的教士们，担起了启蒙教师的重任，因为在那个时候，只有教士们才能掌握拉丁文和希腊文这一代表希罗文明的工具。基督教的教士们被要求学习蛮族的语言，去未开化的地方传教，也因此奠定了西欧封建制度的基础。与此同时，基督教会成了西欧最大的封建主，占有大量的土地，不但实行权力控制，也实行思想控制。"黑暗的中世纪"，固然指我们对这个时代有许多未知，然而更多的时候，"黑暗"是指思想的钳制造成的蒙昧；更甚者，是这种极端的钳制造成的迫害。

历史总是容易被遗忘，或者说，是我们有意识地选择了遗忘，而且是"选择性的"遗忘。基督教从犹太教中分离出来，表面上看，"因信称义"的教义已经使基督徒消除了"犹太人族裔身份"的意识，然而新一轮的"身份意识"却在不断地强化。"身份"的英文identity，本有"同一"的意思，因此，基督徒的"身份"仍然摆脱不了 to identify，即追求"同一"的阴影。"身份"为什么一定需要一种"同一"？是否因为"异己"的存在会威胁到"同一"？可是"异己"始终存在，这是不可避免的，即使"异端裁判所"也不能将其驱逐殆尽。也因此，战争不间断，冲突不止歇。

四 基督教的排他性

基督教的"排他性"，集中表现在四个方面：第一，对不同于"正统"的"异端"的排斥（这里包括两个方面，一是对不同于"正统思想"的"异端思想"的排斥；二是对不同于"正统教会"的"异端派别"的排斥）；第二，对不同于"正典"的经卷（包括次经、伪经、《死海古卷》）的排斥；第三，对反驳"正典"描述的"创世思想""神迹"等的达尔文主义、科学主义、历史主义的排斥；第四，对其他宗教信仰的排斥（如伊斯兰教、佛教、中国的儒家思想）。如果说前两个方面是基督教针对内部的"坚壁清野"，后两种则是针对外部的"闭关自守"。

五 结语

《新约》所持有的世界主义当然是历史的进步，在希腊化的背景下，基督教能够反思犹太教的局限性、能够积极进行改革来应对希腊化的环境，能够以宽容、开放的态度对待外邦人，无疑是一种进步。然而，这种进步也是有限的，因为基督教（尤其是在后来的发展中）对其他的宗教信仰（如伊斯兰教、佛教、中国的儒家思想）是排斥的（至少在宗教教义方面、宗教礼仪方面）。举例来说，在教义方面，基督教关于"拯救"的观点就与佛教、儒家思想有着强烈的冲突。对基督徒来说，"拯救"是神施行的，因此不是基督徒就得不到拯救；对基督教会来说，"教会之外无救恩"，而无论是基督徒还是基督教会的这种思想，都对非基督徒和教会外人士造成了一种心理压迫：对热衷于"立地成佛"的佛教徒来说，人不能依靠自身的"冥思苦想""行善积德"达到佛的境界，这就被剥夺了"希望"；而对相信依靠自己的理性和道德能够"成德成圣"的儒家学者来说，"因信称义"之外无所作为是一种"被动"而非基督徒所认为的"主动"。再以礼仪方面的冲突为例。明朝末年、清朝初年，天主教的在华传播是顺利的，也是成功的，这种中西文化的交流对双方都助益良多。然而在康熙年间，双方终于因为"礼仪之争"而分道扬镳：对中国人来说，"天地、祖先、君师"这三大崇拜是不能废除的，而对基督徒来说，跪拜"神"之外的任何"偶像"都是不被允许的。基督教的这种"一神"传统与中国传统的"多神"信仰和儒家道德最终发生了悲剧性冲突。由此可见基督教的世界主义的另一面：假如世界主义以基督教的标准为标准，那么这种世界主义就失去了其原本的意义而变成了一种新的压迫。从犹太教的民族性中走出来的基督教，因为其普世性价值而成为一种世界性的宗教，然而在后来基督教神学的不断完善中，这种世界性渐渐变质，并滋生出一种与其本源犹太教异曲同工的狭隘性，这不能不说是一种遗憾。

Contents

Part 1

Greek Traditions

Chapter 1　Zeus System

01　The Euro-centrism in the Love Stories of Zeus

Ⅰ　The Origin of Europe

Europe means " the west where the sun sets". About the name, there was a widely circulated Greek legend. Zeus, the king of gods, took a fancy to Ευρώπης, the beautiful daughter of Phoenician king. He wanted to marry her, but was afraid that she wouldn't agree. One day, Ευρώπης was accompanied by a group of girls at the seaside. Zeus saw it and immediately turned into a powerful and docile bull. When he came to her, she saw the lovely bull crouching beside her and mounted on its back. Zeus saw that she had been tricked and stood up and went ahead, jumped into the sea. He took Ευρώπης to live on a distant land. Soon after the word "Europe" was born, there appeared the idea of "Euro-centrism". The myth of Ευρώπης reflects the traces that westerners holify their history. The Oxford English Dictionary interprets Euro-centrism as :Regarding Europe as the center of the world, believing that European culture is supreme in the world culture.

Ⅱ　The Detailed Embodiment of Euro-centrism Thought in Zeus' Love Myths

As one of Zeus' lovers, Leto gave birth to Apollo and Artemis for Zeus. Apollo was the god of sun, while Artemis was the god of moon. Her two children later became the gods of Olympus. On one occasion, Niobe,wife of Thebes king, once said that her children were more than Leto's. Leto became furious after hearing that. She asked Apollo to shoot all Niobe's sons and Artemis to shoot all her daughters. At last, Niobe committed suicide, Zeus turned all the residents of Thebes into stones, and this cruel revenge came to an end. From this story, we can see that in ancient Greek mythology, the status of god is incomparable to ordinary people, and the majesty of god cannot be violated, even by unintentional fault. On the other hand, it shows a kind of contempt that God civilization represented by Zeus to human civilization. To some extent ,Leto's son and daughter were the branch of the God civilization. Niobe was different. Specifically, one was in heaven and the other was on earth, one was divine and the other was common.

This is actually the belittling and despising of other cultures by Greek culture at that time, which is exactly the expression of Euro-centrism thought. With time flying and the development of the society, this idea has been given a deeper meaning. The geographical scope it represents is expanding and the cultural ideology is also increasing. Europe began to appear as a cultural entity, and its connotation and self-identity were realized in comparison with non-Europe. From the very beginning, the understanding of the European and non-European civilization were linked to the European prejudice against non-Europe.

The Greeks originally lived in Peloponnese, Aegean Islands and the northern Greek continent . They established Athens, Sparta, Thebes and other city-states. In their conflicts and struggles with the outside world, the Greeks seemed to have confirmed their superiority over other races. This superiority became more obvious after defeating the invasion of the Persian Empire in the 5th century B.C. The ancient Greeks divided the world into Europa, Asia and Libya. Europa was Greek home and the superior one. This idea was reflected in many works at that time. Herodotus (484B.C.-430/420B.C.) pointed out this idea that the world was divided into three parts, including Europa,Asia and Libya, and also referred to Greece many times with the name of "Europa" in wars. Hippocrates agreed with the division of the mainland and tried to explain European superiority with climate and natural environment. He pointed out that the stable climate in Asia was the reason why Asians lacked courage and spirit, while the changeable climate in Europe was the reason why Europeans made positive progress. In the Greek ideology of self-superiority, they unconsciously formed a world centered on Greece. Anaksiman's map showed Greece in the center of the map and parts of Europe and Asia around Greece. Although Herodotus was from Asia Minor, he was deeply influenced by Greek culture. In his works, Greece was regarded as the center, and countries around it were all vassals. Although his *History* recorded the known world at that time including Greece, West Asia and North Africa, and was called a "little encyclopaedia", in fact, its background introduction was to set off the superiority of Geography of Greek environment.

Ⅲ　"East" from the West

In the 18th century British Industrial Revolution further strengthened the modern Euro-centrism theory. The industrial revolution set western countries on the road of capitalism, and a large-scale overseas colonization was launched. In the 19th century, Europe had established its hegemonic position with its strong economic and military strength. Their plunder of colonial resources has gradually turned into a comprehensive occupation. Europe, which trampled the world under its feet at that time, believed that the expansion was due to its superiority in civilization. Based on this understanding, a European-centered view of history had gradually taken shape. The view of history mainly discussed the historical process of Western Europe as a benchmark.And it also supposed that the different nations and countries must follow this stereotype in the process of the modernization. Although this view was later criticized strongly in that era, the idea did have a profound impact on human society, economy, politics and other fields. Hegelian, one of unknown scholars holding Euro-centrism, believed that although world history started from the east, the end of history would finish in Europe, especially in Prussian Constitutional Monarchy. In his philosophy of history, he announces that although the world history begins from Asia, the centre and ultimate of the old world is in Europe; while the European "centre" is France,Germany and England. He described China and India as lifeless and stagnant countries with no internal motivation. "China has something fixed that will last forever to replace something real of history. China and India are still outside history, and both of them need to wait for the combination of several factors before they can make vivid progress." Leopold Von Ranke ignored the existence of regions outside Europe and simply regarded the historical development of Europe as the main body of global historical development. He believed that the development of the world was dominated by Europe. Latin and Teuton nationalities (Germanic people and their generations) were the two main characters of the subject; the process of human history development was basically the process of mutual struggles and integration between the two nations. He even said, "India and China have nothing but natural history. So world history is just western history."

There are still many scholars who are critical of Eurocentrism. Gondar said, "Whether conscious or not, we are all followers of this completely European-centered social science and history." He criticized some Western scholars and said, "In some key historical, economic, social, political, ideological or cultural fields, the rest of the world is deficient compared with the West. They claim that it is precisely because the west owns the so-called lacking in 'other regions' that 'we' have an endogenous development advantage." And then "we" expand this strength as 'the mission of Civilization and Enlightenment' shouldered by the white race to the other regions of the world.Adeno Joseph Toynbee thought that the unit of historical research should be society, not country. He strongly criticized the "Eurocentrism" advocated by the "racist propagandists" in the West. Toynbee said in his book *Historical Research* that since our western society has expanded to the whole world in the past 400 years, the modern westerners have also emphasized the ethnic factors in history. The expansion brought the West into contact (often unfriendly) with people who were culturally and physically different from them. As a result of the contact, the concepts of superior and inferior biological types naturally emerged. However, the "Orientalism" , written by Edward. W. Said in his book *Orientalism* is centered on the discovery and construction of the East by the West, and the cultural construction of the colonized East by the West according to the western ideology and value calibration. In other words, the West deconstructs, reproduces and reconstructs the East on the cultural level. The book*, Post-colonial Cultural Criticism and Post-modern Context and Identity Orientation of Chinese Intellectuals* gives a more detailed description of Said's Orientalism: The book reveals how the West embarks on its own political, economic and cultural interests. He thinks that the "East" is not the east, but the text constructed by imperialist ideology. Said emphasized that during the process of western colonial expansion, the strong western culture penetrated into the colonized Eastern countries, dismembered the local traditional culture and national cultural system, derogated the values and ideology of the local cultural system of the eastern countries in accordance with the western consciousness and values. Polly said, "Orientalists divide the world into backward, uncivilized 'others' and the opposite highly developed us." It is an opposing relationship, and this hostile attitude towards the East and West stems from people's authenticity of their own culture and national identity and simple belief, that is the emotion of simple patriotism and nationalism. Said's original intention was not to intensify the hostility between the East and the West, but to make the West better understand the East and break the prejudice of people who hold the thought of Euro-centrism. However, his critical attitude towards the West has won the support of many "non-European" people who have long suffered from western hostility.

（苗博译）

02 Exploration on the "Civilization and Wisdom" of Ancient Greek from the Variation of Athena Myth

I Athena

We often see the statue of the owl standing on the shoulder of Athena. There is also a goddess with a snake around her waist—it may also be Athena; The goddess holding the shield with the head of the snake-haired banshee "Medusa" was Athena. (it is recorded that from 447 B.C. to 438 B.C., the famous ancient Greek sculptor Phidias and his assistants dedicated themselves to carving statues and reliefs for Athena's temple. They sculpted three goddess statues for the Acropolis of Athens. One of them is the goddess of protection of Lemnos Island in the northwest Aegean Sea. This statue is made of bronze, slightly larger than a real person and very delicate. The other is a huge bronze statue of the "Guardian of Athens", which stands between the main gate of the Acropolis and the temple is in the form of an armed protector of Athens, with its base 70 feet above the ground. It is not only a symbol for mariners, but also a fortress to make the enemies scared. Of the three statues, the most famous is the "Athena Statue". The statue stands in the temple of Athena, 38 feet high, symbolizing wisdom and chastity.

Athena is one of the twelve major gods of Olympus and the daughter of Zeus. Her status is naturally noble. She is both a protector of war (armed with spear and shield) and a lover of peace (olive tree is also one of her symbols); She is not only the protector of navigation, but also the inventor of weaving technology. She taught people to domesticate horses and cattle and to make cars and boats. She also gives the world plows and rakes, spindles and looms. According to the legend Athena invented weaving and helped Hera and Hercules weave robes. In *Illiad*, Hera wore a robe knitted by Athena and a gold pin on her chest to date Zeus. Athena also gave the hero Hercules robes; It is said that the Argo ship on which the heroes sought golden fleece was built under Athena's instructions.

Athena is a symbol of wisdom (for Greeks with a tradition of "love of wisdom", the goddess of wisdom naturally holds an important position) and an art lover (it was said that Athena's musical instrument was laughed at by the gods because its cheeks bulged when playing, and was abandoned, only to be picked up by Malexus, who thought Athena's musical instrument must be able to compete with Apollo, thus challenging the sun god. Apollo stipulated, however, that the instrument must be played upside down, but only the front end of the flute can produce sound, so Malexus lost).

What is the story of this goddess who was worshiped by the Greeks and fully enjoyed the grand ceremonies of the Athenians? We followed the path which the goddess came from, trying to find the real "girl" and to break through the fog shrouded in myth.

Ⅱ Historical Changes of Athena Myth

1. The Origin of Athena's Name

Athena's name is abbreviated from Ἀθῆναα or Ἀθῆναια in ancient Greek. It is written as Ἀθήνη or Ἀθηναίη in Ionia dialect (the name can be seen in the name marked on *the Relief Drawing of the Besieged City of Troya*) and Ἀθάνα or Ἀθαναία in Dorian dialect.According to Ionia's dialect Ἀθήνη, we can speculate that Athena is named after Athens—because in ancient Greek place names, there are many city names ending in-ήνη, such as Μυκήνη (Mycenae), that is to say, -ήνη is a typical place name suffix.

However, Athena is usually called Pallas Athena (Παλλάς Ἀθήνη). Pallas—some people have interpreted it as "Maiden" and others as "The Weapon-Brandish", but these statements are not based on sufficient grounds and cannot be generally agreed with by people. In Greek mythology, there are several statements about the relationship between pallas and Athena. First, Athena was born by Zeus and raised by Triton, the river god. Pallas was Triton's daughter and Athena's playmate, but she was killed by Athena. In order to express her condolences, she put pallas's name before her own. Second, Pallas is one of djinn. In the battle between the gods and djinn, she was killed by Athena. In order to show her exploits, Athena put pallas's name before her own. Third, in *Ancient Cities-Studies on Religion, Law and Institution in Greece and Rome*(1885), Fistel Glase once said that Pallas was a sea god. Unfortunately, the real meaning of this word has not been clearly understood so far.

2. Athena and the "Snake Goddess" of Crete

In *Iliad*, Homer called Athena "owl's eye (γλαυκῶπιν)". Virgil said in *Aeneas* that she was "the protector of snakes". Herodotus described this in volume 8 of *History*: In the temple of Athens, there was a python guarding the acropolis of Athens.

These characteristics of Athena as an animal god originated from Crete's "snake goddess". In Crete mythology, owls and snakes guarded the palaces of Minotaur. The goddess with Mycenaean shield was the prototype of Athena of Olympus. One of Athena's symbols was a shield made of sheepskin decorated with Medusa's snakelike hair (Aegis).

In the 13th century B.C., a pottery statue of "snake goddess" was found in the small shrine of Gournilhat's family residence: a snake was wrapped around the goddess. In the ancient Greek concept, snakes lived underground and were the incarnations of underground gods and ghosts. "Snake Goddess" was the patron saint of the house, but Mino's seal and murals had never seen the shape of "Snake Goddess". In 1903, three pottery statues of "snake goddess" were found in the secret room of the temple area on the west wing of Crete maze. They were dressed in fashionable and open clothes, just like ladies of the court, but the snakes wrapped around them revealed their identities. One of the statues had a milky white background, and three green snakes with purple-brown spots wrapped around her body.

From the points of Minoans, snakes are not terrible, but friendly and protective. Minoans' families provide for snakes and worship the "snake goddess" in the ancestral hall of their homes. Even in modern times, the worship of house snakes has not disappeared. The custom of taking snakes as pets and feeding them has been recorded in Europe, Slavic countries, Albania and Indo-European countries. The snake is Athena's sacred object, and the spotted snake is her nickname. Herodotus tells a story: during the Hippocratic War, the Persian army was under siege and Athens was in danger. The generals decided to evacuate the entire city to the island. The Athenians were unwilling to retreat. So the priestess of Athena temple declared: they witnessed a "spotted snake" fly away from the temple with their own eyes. The Athenians heard that the goddess of protection had flown away and knew that the city was in danger, so they retreated to a safe island.

Sculptor Pheidias once made a colossus of Athena inlaid with gold and ivory for the Parthenon. The holy snake stood beside her. There was a myth circulating in Athens that Hephaestus (Vulcan in Roman myth), the god of fire, coveted Athena and attempted rape. Athena threw the semen left behind by Vulcan on the ground, fertilizing Mother Earth and giving birth to a boy, Orik Tonios. Athena gave the baby to the three Athenian princesses and told them not to watch. Curiously, the princess uncovered the cloth of the basket and found a snake (there is also a saying that she saw a child with snake legs). She was scared out of her mind. The information revealed in this story is that Athena is a "goddess of snakes". Her predecessor may be a mother rather than a virgin. She was the ancient Greek goddess of reproduction and the snake was her own son. Perhaps, in order to maintain the dignity of the goddess of chastity, the myth makers changed the word "snake" to the son of the mother Earth.

There is also a myth about the "snake goddess": Medusa, a female demon with full head of snake hair, was a stunning beauty and a priestess of Athena. Poseidon coveted the beauty of Medusa and raped her in Athena's temple. Athena was angry and turned Medusa into a monster. Later, at Athena's instigation, hero Perseus killed Medusa and dedicated the banshee's head to Athena. Athena set Medusa's head on her shield. The message revealed by this myth was that Medusa was the prototype of Athena. Athena has become a beautiful virgin and killed her prototype, the gorgon.

There is another story about Athena's association with snakes: in the tenth year of the Trojan War, Odysseus came up with a wooden horse to attack the city with Athena's help. Laocoon, the Trojan priest, saw through the plan and tried his best to prevent the Trojan horse from entering the city. Athena sent two poisonous snakes to entangle Laocoon and his son to death, which may also be used as evidence of Athena's "snake goddess". In addition to the identity of "snake goddess", Athena still retained other characteristics of Minoan religion: owl and olive tree are her sacred symbols.

3. Athena of Pirasky

Athena has been an important deity since ancient times. Her name has appeared on the line B. The mycenaean tablets also used to call her "mistress" and she was often called "queen (πότνιαν)" in later epics and prayers.

According to the Pelasgians, the goddess Athena was born on the shores of Lake Triton in Libya. Therefore, Athena was also called Tritochania (Τριτογένεια, which meant she was born in "Triton"). Three Libyan goddess Shuize discovered her, dressed her in goatskin and nurtured her to grow up. She later came to Athens via Crete. For this legend, please refer to *Apollonius*. But according to Crete legend, Athena's hometown was in Crete, and she was born near the creek named Triton near Knossos. Since this piece of material was recorded according to the legend of the ancient Pelasgians , it has led many scholars to associate the origin of Athena with the Libyan goddess. This view has several circumstantial evidence.

According to Herodotus's *History*, the clothes worn by Athena's idol were learned by Greeks from Libyan women—except for two things: Libyan women's clothes were made of leather; The tassel of their goatskin Aegis jacket were not snakes but grass. In addition, in all other places, their clothes were the same. Herodotus also recorded Athena's worship in *History*: the Osaeans were next to the Mercurian Egyptians; They lived on the bank of Loch Ness in Tritto, separated from the Marcoule Estes by a Triton River. They hold a memorial ceremony for Athena once a year. During the ceremony, the young girls were divided into two groups and fought each other with stones and sticks. It was said that this was done in accordance with the way of ancestors to worship Athena.

The findings of Greek archaeology showed that Libyan immigrants entered Crete as early as 4000 B.C., and the historical records are basically consistent with the archaeological findings. Therefore, it was said that Athena's worship originated from Libyans and finally entered the Greek myth system through Crete civilization.

4. The Patron Saint of the Royal Family

The goddess of war and wisdom of Zeus, formerly known as the "snake goddess" worshiped by Minoans in Crete. "Snake Goddess" was originally the patron saint of the family home, but it spreaded to Greece and was turned into the patron saint of the royal family by the martial Mycenaean. The royal family bore the important responsibility of defending the country. Therefore, the patron saint of the royal family naturally became the god of war, and Athena had the function of defending the country.

In *Iliad*, Athena helped the Greek hero win the war: she helped the hero Perseus kill Medusa, and helped Bellerophon ride the Pegasus to defeat the banshee Camera. In *Odyssey*, Athena helped Odysseus end his ten-year wanderings and return home. Most importantly, Athena left Odysseus and returned to her residence in Athens, the palace of Athens' king Erectus, implying the identity of the goddess "the patron saint of the royal family".

5. The Patron Saint of Athens

Athena became the patron saint of Athens, a legend related to the battle between Athena and Poseidon. Poseidon, Zeus's brother, was in charge of the sea. Hades, another brother of Zeus, was in charge of the underworld. It was said that when Athens was built, Poseidon and Athena competed for the honor of naming it. At last they reached an agreement that the man who could provide the most useful things for mankind would become the patron saint of the city. Poseidon struck the ground with his trident and turned into a horse—representing war and grief, while Athena turned into an olive tree—symbolizing peace and wealth. Therefore Athens was named after the goddess (we do not know whether the goddess is named after the city or the city is named after the goddess, but the degree of connection between the two is unquestionable). Athens has built a typical symbol of Greek religious art, the Parthenon (Παρθενών, meaning virgin), which is the largest temple dedicated to Athena. The temple is located at the highest point in the center of the Acropolis. There is also a statue of Athena inlaid with gold and ivory made by Pheidias.

6. Athena From the Head of Zeus

Hesiod's *Psalm* described the birth of Athena as follows: Zeus, king of the gods, first married Metis, who was the wisest of gods and mortals. However, Gaia and Uranus predicted that the son born by Metis would overthrow Zeus, because Metis was destined to give birth to several extremely clever children. The first was the bright-eyed young girl, Athena, who was equal to her father in strength and wisdom. But after that, Metis will have a son to be king of gods and men. Fearing that the prophecy would come true, Zeus swallowed up Metis. Since then, Zeus had a severe headache and had to ask Vulcan to open his head. Vulcan did that. To the surprise of the Olympus gods, a beautiful goddess with great strength jumped out of her split head. This was Athena.

Ⅲ The Trial of Orestes

The Greek commander-in-chief Agamemnon angered his wife Clytemnestra by sacrificing her daughter Iphigenia and bringing back Cassandra, a female prisoner of war, after defeating Troy. Clytemnestra conspired with her lover to kill Agamemnon while bathing. Apollo, who represents patriarchy, was very angry with Clytemnestra's behavior, so he told the truth of the matter to Agamemnon's son, Orestes, and ordered him to take revenge and kill his mother. At the time of dying, Clytemnestra cursed Orestes because the act of killing the mother would be punished by the Furies, who represents the matriarchal status. The curse came true after her death. The voice of Megaera made Orestes mad. He left his palace and kingdom and searched everywhere for Apollo's protection to avoid the vengeful goddess's pursuit.Apollo knew that protection alone was not enough, because

Orestes had killed his mother after all. So Apollo told Orestes to go to Athens and pray for Athena's just judgment. Athena called together judges to hear the case, cast a white stone under the condition that the number of black and white stones was exactly equal, and declared Orestes innocent according to the majority vote.

Ⅳ Greek Civilization Process Reflected by Historical Changes of Athena Myth

1. From "Asia" to "Great Greece"

From "snake goddess" to "war goddess", we can see a certain track of the fusion of different religious beliefs in ancient Greece. Comparing the legend of Pirasky people with Herodotus' textual research, and looking at the description of Athena's birth in Hesiod's *Psalm*, we can find that Athena's identity and status are constantly changing—Athena and Metis were both Greek indigenous gods more than 2000 years (about 4000 B.C.) before the Thracian civilization of Arcaya represented by Zeus entered the Greek mainland. Perhaps Athena's existence predates that of her mother Metis—her earliest prototype may be the huge snake that bound Laocoon to death. This worship of "snake goddess" exists in the form of a primitive totem. Athena was later coined as the daughter of Zeus, which can be said to be the submission of the weak civilization to the strong civilization, but also can be said to be the recognition of the weak civilization to the strong civilization.

Zeus represents the religious belief of Akaya, who created Mycenaean civilization and later Crete civilization and moved to Greece around 2000 B.C. Metis is a symbol of the original Greek indigenous people's spiritual beliefs. Regard Metis as the goddess of wisdom, which may mean that the Greek civilization at that time was superior to that of the later settlers. Zeus swallowed Metis into his belly, which meant the fusion of different religions and civilizations among the aborigines, Akayans and West Asian immigrants, thus forming a new Greek classical civilization system. The symbol of Greek orthodox religion is still Zeus rather than Athena, because she is not the "son" in the "prophecy", so she did not really replace Zeus in the end, which somewhat represents the submission of the conquered nation at that time. However, Metis remained in Zeus's belly, which symbolizes that these nations have somewhat retained their own traditions.From the evolution history of Athena worship, we can see that the Greek spiritual world has a long process of formation, which is the result of merging the spiritual concepts of many nationalities.

2. From "Mars" to "Goddess of Wisdom"

In *Iliad*, Athena is a Sivir equal to Ares. On the Trojan battlefield, Athena supported the Greek allied forces headed by Agamemnon. She eagerly provoked the discord between the Greek allied forces and the Trojans, promoted the development of the war, and constantly encouraged people to fight on the battlefield to help the heroes kill the enemy. The goddess even put on her own clothes and took part in the fight. She helped Achilles kill Hector. Athena, the image of the female god of war, has won the admiration of the Greeks, because Athena can bring death to the enemy and win trophies or wealth for the Greeks. According to Hesiod's *Psalm*, Athena is a terrible, screaming general, an invincible queen who longs for tumult and war.

Compared with the savage belligerence in *Iliad*, Athena in *Odyssey* gradually faded from the image of a female god of war, although she still carried weapons (once she held a bronze spear in front of Odysseus's house; She once appeared dressed as a shepherd boy with a gun in her hand), but the goddess no longer appeared in a fully armed combat posture. Athena is a guardian accompanying Odysseus and his son in the *Odyssey*, and is a symbol of wisdom. The quality of Mars is almost submerged by these images.

3. From Matriarchal Society to Patriarchal Society

Athena's new myth emerged from Zeus' head is the result of patriarchy's overall victory over matriarchy: when Athena was Hellenized and became an object of worship for many city-states, the work of describing an orthodox and sacred origin for the goddess began, which was also the need for patriarchy to establish and consolidate its rule. Zeus gave birth to Athena from his own head. Only in this way can Zeus determine his eternal power. In other words, Zeus must put an end to the reproductive rules inherited from father and son in the divine world and take possession of the reproductive ability of women both physically and mentally, so as to consolidate his patriarchy or, more precisely, to establish his dominant position in the gods.

This myth describes the birth of Athena from the perspective of patriarchy, so

Athena seems to be the continuation of Zeus and the executor of Zeus' will. She is Zeus in action. Metis' mother status gradually blurred, it seems that Athena was born by Zeus alone. Zeus received wisdom from Athena just as he did from Metis in the past.

The story of Athena's "birth" from Zeus' head reveals Athena's identity—she is the representative of patriarchy. Her position was determined by her birth. She cast a vote for Orestes, which reflected that she would safeguard the rule of the male-dominated society.

4. From "Girl" to "Asexual"

The Parthenon designed by Perikles for Athena is the main building of Athens Acropolis. "Parthenon" means "virgin daughter" and "virgin bedroom", highlighting Athena's loftiness and chastity as a virgin god. Athena, as one of the three virgins, also attached great importance to her virginity. There is a story that proves this: the mother of Tiresias, the prophet of Thebes, was Kariko, the goddess of water, and Athena's good friend. Tiresias once accidentally saw Athena naked. Athena covered Tiresias's eyes with her hands, and Tiresias became blind. Kariko asked the goddess to help her son restore his eyesight, but the goddess could not. However, she washed Tiresias's ears so that he could hear bird language and gave him a crutch instead of his eyes. However, this is only one of the legends about the origin of Tiresias's blindness.

The message revealed by this myth is that Athena's gender characteristics have gradually blurred from the original "snake goddess" to "wisdom goddess". Especially, the new myth popped up from Zeus' head has even obliterated the position of her mother Metis. It seems that Athena was not born by her mother and is asexual. This new myth maintains the rule of the male-dominated society by giving Athena a pure and noble birth—without her mother Metis, without reproduction and without threats from women, the male-dominated society can be stabilized. On the surface, Athena's birth is pure (asexual), in fact Athena has become one of the male gods; On the surface, Athena's birth was noble, but in fact she was just an ornament of Zeus' divine system and the last place left for women by male domination.

5. Seeing Ancient Greek "Wisdom" from Athena Myth

(1) Male Wisdom and Female Wisdom

Athena was a female god of war in the image of a young girl when she was introduced to Crete and the Greek mainland. She has a title of Areia, which means "militant", another title of Promachus, which means "warrior", and another title of Sthenias, which means "powerful". This is suitable for those nationalities in nomadic times. However, with the evolution of Greek social civilization, Athena became the patron saint of the city-states and then had the title of the goddess of deliberation. As a result, the "female god of war" became the "goddess of wisdom". This change marks that Greek civilization has developed to a higher level after absorbing many factors.

Jumping out of the head of her father Zeus gave Athena the wisdom of a man. Compilation of a new birth for Athena not only meets the needs of conquering women in a male-dominated society, but also meets the needs of women actively adapting to a male-dominated society. The new myth of Athena's birth is a derivative of the patriarchal society, and her wisdom is naturally the wisdom of the patriarchal society, which is used to maintain the continuation of patriarchy.The trial of Orestes once again demonstrated Athena's position: in order to safeguard the rule of patriarchal society, Athena must vote for Orestes.

As a protector of textiles and navigation, Athena, who invented the flute, seems to see the "wisdom" of her mother Metis. However, as for Athena, daughter of Zeus, we can no longer see the "wisdom" of her mother Metis, but only the "wisdom" of Zeus.

(2) "Plot" and "Wisdom"

From *Iliad* to *Odyssey*, from the original female god of war to the later inventor of skills and standards, Athena's nature as a goddess of peace seems to obscure her nature as Sivir. It can be said that Athena embodies the progress of Greek civilization.

In the contest with Poseidon, Athena won. It was her wisdom that won the victory. Poseidon used brute force to subdue horses,while Athena used complete sets of harness to deal with wild horses. Poseidon was making waves in the sea, while Athena helped people build ships. Poseidon used his trident to make the earth salty, while Athena planted olive trees around it. Here, we see the wisdom of women, as if it were the continuation of the wisdom of her mother Metis.

Athena also used wisdom in Orestes' trial, but what we see here is rational wisdom, male wisdom, which seems to be a continuation of the wisdom of his father Zeus. Although as Sivir, Athena is not as belligerent as Ares, and prefers to settle disputes by legal means. Ares and Athena respectively represent the two sides of the war: Ares represents the cruel side of the war—untold sufferings; Athena, on the other hand, represents the rationality in the war—winning the war by means of ingenuity and strength. For example, in the final stage of the Trojan War, Athena taught Odysseus to use a wooden horse, which also enabled the Akayans to finally win the war.

Athena's wisdom also lies in her nurturing and helping many heroes. In *Introduction to Greek Religious Studies* (1903), the famous British classicist Jane Ellen Harrison described Athena's deeds: although Gaia gave birth to Orik Tonios, it was Athena who brought him up. She has a similar relationship with Hercules. She is Hercules' adoptive mother. She helped Jason build the Argo ship and completed the voyage to find golden fleece. She also helped Odysseus return to his hometown.

Athena's help to the son of Odysseus, Telemachus, fully demonstrated her "wisdom". Athena suggested that Telemachus go to Pylos and Sparta to find his father Odysseus. Athena obviously knew that Odysseus's return journey had been arranged by the gods, but instead of telling Telemachus directly, she arranged for him to leave his comfortable home and embark on a perilous sea journey, visiting powerful nobles to find traces of his father. In fact, for Odysseus's return, Telemachus' trip did not help. But why did Athena make such an arrangement? Because Athena knew that Telemachus needed capital—the capital to become an aristocrat in line with the epic era, to become Odysseus's real son, and to become a figure equivalent to Orestes. After that, Telemachus learned to make his own decisions, think for himself, understand his father Odysseus, and understand how to become a Homeric aristocrat. Of course, all this was done according to the will of the goddess. Athena, who is "known among all the gods for her sagacity and resourcefulness", planned Telemachus' growth journey with her extraordinary wisdom, with the aim of inspiring his wisdom—a kind of wisdom that can adapt to changes at random.

Athena's love for Odysseus and his son reflects the ancient Greeks' love of wisdom. Athena, as wisdom itself, was also widely worshipped among the ancient Greeks. People's respect for Odysseus and the blessing of the gods on him show the Greek attitude towards wisdom. Philosophy comes from Greek "Philo-sophia", meaning "wisdom-loving", which is exactly the embodiment of ancient Greek "wisdom-loving tradition".

However, what we need to pay attention to is that there are "two kinds of wisdom" in ancient Greece: Socrates' "wisdom"—wise man's "wisdom"; The "wisdom" of gods such as Zeus, Athena and Muse—the "stratagem" of Prometheus and Odysseus (or even "trick"—the intelligence used to achieve a certain purpose); The "Wisdom" of Goddess Gaia and Metis—The "Wisdom" of Male Gods such as Zeus. In Athena, we see the coexistence of two kinds of wisdom—here "wisdom" does not refer to knowledge alone.

We should also pay attention to the fact that the Greek people's "love of wisdom" stems from their recognition of "ignorance". Socrates' "self-knowledge of my ignorance" is a common understanding of ancient Greeks. Perhaps, only faith can give mankind a limit. Line 649 of Hesiod's *Works and Days* has the same meaning as line 202 of Homer's *Odyssey* volume I: I am not a prophet, nor do I know the secret of bird flying.

V Conclusion

From the "snake goddess" in Crete to one of the twelve major gods of Olympus, from the "Sivir" in *Iliad* to the "goddess of wisdom" in *Odyssey*, from the founder of various skills to the patron saint of Athens, Athena has too many identities.

In fact, in ancient Greek religion, it is common for a deity to have multiple images. Due to the migration of population, the alternation of new and old religions and the integration of various religions, Greek local religions mixed with many foreign gods, which made Athena have different functions and properties, and made her have different attributes and different images. Moreover, due to the change of Greek gods and the change of Greek god-human experience, the image of Athena carries more religious and cultural factors. In fact, the changes of Athena's image, identity, role and status exactly reflect the process of ancient Greek civilization.

All sorts of myths and legends about Athena make us see clearly the footprints of ancient Greek civilization. By analyzing all kinds of "wisdom" contained in Athena, we seem to have a new understanding of ancient Greece's "wisdom-loving tradition"—we exhaust our "wisdom" and are "ignorant", and our recognition of "ignorance" paves the way for us to get "wisdom". Athena's myth also reveals such a message: there are many kinds of wisdom—good wisdom and cunning tricks; Non-utilitarian wisdom, quick success and quick profit calculation. The question is: What kind of wisdom do we need?

（茆博译）

03 The Concept of Fate in Greek Mythology

I Greek Myths Knocking on the Doors of Destiny

The ancient Greek gods were the same as human beings except that they were immortal and powerful. They were not different from human beings in other aspects, such as desire, sorrows and joys, etc. The form of fate was vividly displayed in Greek mythology: Zeus carried a small balance with him as a symbol of fate and dominated his own judgment. Even Zeus himself sometimes had to obey fate. In *Classical Thought*: However, it is not always clear that Zeus' own will is carried out. A person's "fate" or "share" determines the time of his death. When two heroes fight, Zeus will weigh the fate of both of them to see which hero must die. Sometimes Zeus considered whether to save the fate of a particular hero, but he never violated the fate. His final decision always coincides with his fate.

Besides Zeus, the god who closely related to fate is Moirae. As for Moirae, the name of them means part, quota, and extensive meaning is life and destiny. In Greek mythology, the three gods of fate were all solemn and busy. In Hesiod's *Theogony*, there is a record about the goddess of fate: Night has three daughters who manage fate and punishment. They are Croso, Lachesis and Atropos. Croso spun the thread of life, and Atropos was the goddess of revenge with terrible scissors. The three goddesses gave people good or bad fates when they were born and monitored all the crimes of God and human beings.They would never stop their terrible anger until the criminals are punished.

The Greeks attributed everything to fate, which seemed to represent their innate understanding of life. Myths and legends about gods and heroes profoundly reflect that. Prometheus, the god of wisdom, was punished for deceiving the gods with butter at a meeting held by the gods to determine human rights and obligations in order to reduce the burden on mankind. Therefore, Zeus refused to give mankind the fire to build civilization. But Prometheus ignored Zeus' anger and sent the stolen fire to the world. Zeus was furious and ordered Hephaestus, Athena, Hermes, the messenger of the gods, and Aphrodite, the goddess of love, to jointly create the beautiful woman Pandora. She had concentrated the evil in the world and brought untold disasters to mankind. Prometheus, on the other hand, was punished and suffered the pain of hawks pecking at his liver every day. Prometheus, though capable of predicting the future, could not break the mercy of fate. He said, " No matter who, as long as he learns to recognize the unshakable power of fate, he would need to bear the pain given by the goddess Fortuna." In *Iliad*, Achilles pursued Hector crazily at the gates of Illion. Zeus sympathized with Hector and tried to encourage the gods to save his life, but Athena refuted it.

Father who throws lightning, God who can gather clouds, what are you talking about!
The fate of this mortal has long been limited.
Do you want him to be saved from terrible death?
Zeus has to give up.
When the two sides of the fight were at loggerheads,
The Lord of gods took out his gold balance,
And put two tragic death sentences into the two plates.
One for Achilles and the other for Hector.
He lifted the center of the scale, Hector's side down.
Apollo immediately abandons him.

Achilles killed Hector mercilessly. Even though Zeus felt pity for Hector, he could not avoid his death. Achilles, the son of god, could not escape the fate of death too. Paris shot his ankle and killed him. In front of fate, we cannot fight against it, no matter god or human beings. However, Prometheus and Achilles knew that they were doomed, but they did not choose to escape. Prometheus, knowing that he would be punished by violating Zeus, insisted on his choice and gave the kindling to the world. Achilles knew before the war that he would die in Troy, but he did not hesitate to choose the battlefield instead of staying at home.Because though the latter was a kind of way for life, it was not worth mentioning. That was the view of destiny for ancient Greeks:facing the unchangeable fate, the ancient Greeks would make their life more colorful and glorious, even they scarified themselves.

Ⅱ The Ancient Greeks' Questioning of "Man"

Marx said, " Any myth uses imagination to conquer, dominate and visualize natural forces; Therefore, as these natural forces are dominated, myths disappear." The ancient Greeks used myths to explain their world and to seek the answers to "who am I?" "where do I come from?" and "where do I go?" The thinking and attention to "human" is the most precious spiritual wealth the ancient Greeks gave to mankind. Oedipus cracked Riddle of Sphinx, but could not explain "what is man". It is a research topic that ancients could not finish at the present time. The Apollo altar in Delphi Temple was inscribed with the epigram "know yourself" to alert the world, reflecting the ancient Greek thinking on human nature. Take Sophocles as example. He believed in the power of god and fate. Everything was destined for a long time, he gradually shifted his attention to ordinary people and began to require people to have the spirit of independence and autonomy. This is vividly reflected in *Oedipus*. Although Oedipus finally suffered the fate of killing his father and marrying his mother, he tried, fought and struggled before the doomed fate, which is a major characteristic of "human" to some degree. Oedipus, king of Thebes, tried to find the killer of the old king in order to eliminate the disaster in Thebes. However, when he was looking for the killer everywhere, the chorus sang of the terrible force of fate that could not be avoided.

Oedipus' tragedy is all human beings'. Oedipus' tragedy lies in the fact that the more he wants to get rid of the shackles of fate, the more he falls into the trap. The more sincerely he gets rid of an evil for the people, the closer he is to disaster and destruction. It is not difficult to find that the glory of human nature shines in this tragedy. The ancient Greeks have begun to look at the world with rational eyes. Due to the continuous development of democracy in Athens, the status and role of citizens in the city have been continuously recognized. Protagoras, a representative of the Wise School, put forward that "Man is the meassure of all things" and became the symbol of the rational thoughts in ancient Greece.

Ⅲ   The Modern Evolution of the Concept of Fate

The 14th century can be regarded as the beginning of the era of humanism. After more than 1000 years of religious theocracy, people began to break the shackles and oppression of spirit. The classical culture that has been locked up for many years has once again attracted people's attention. With the deepening of the Renaissance movement, people began to establish their own value in life and cherish the beauty of real life. People do not want to silently bear the fate gods have arranged for them. They hope to gain happiness by fighting.

Although humanism revived the ancient Greek culture, it did not inherit the concept of fate. People more often associate fate with worldly life and achievements. Influenced by Christian thought, although God is supreme, he does not play a decisive role in the fate of human beings.

Salutati advocated Stoic philosophy and active life in the early Renaissance. In *On Fate, Fortune and Contingency*, he emphasized that people can overcome fate by using free will to treat life positively. Alberti explained the question of "what is fate" in his article *On Fate and the Goddess of Fate*: Fate is the movement of human life which happens in turn. Fate is disturbed and influenced by the goddess of fate. What is the goddess of fate? He explained it by implication: when a person falls into the water, there is a board or a boat beside him. The goddess of fate is more generous to him. On the contrary, it is cruel to those who have to swim to the riverbank on their own. From his analogy, we can see that he regarded the goddess of fate as contingency, but with certain regularity: the hope of being rescued near the planks and boats is more, and the danger is more. He wants people to succeed through subjective efforts rather than by chance. Alberti believed in man's ability to fight against the goddess of fate by means of the power endowed by nature. Since then, humanism has entered a new stage. It's evident in Shakespeare's *Hamlet*. Unlike Oedipus, Hamlet's fate is his own fate, which is no longer defined by the divine realm that overrides others and is fighting against himself. "To be or not to be". Hamlet persisted in pursuing the meaning of human existence at the cost of life. Although it can not get rid of the tragic results, this question essentially shows that "human" can seek for the eternal value of living in the real life, which is very precious.

Whether the ancient Greek tragedy or Shakespeare's tragedy, the tragic heroes are full of the spirit of struggle, which is also reflected in the subsequent liberal tragedies. Such as Ibsen's *Doll Family* and *An Enemy of the People* and other dramas.They challenge the existing order with life to realize self-meaning.

At the end of the nineteenth century, Schopenhauer's Pessimistic Philosophy, Nietzsche's Strong Will, Sartre's Existentialism and Freud's Psychoanalysis, as the representatives of cultural thought, disintegrated the myth of infinity and eternity: God is dead. When human beings lose their spiritual home, they become at a loss, and the so-called "outlook of fate" begins to blur. It is against this background that the absurd drama was born after the twentieth century, and its creation was mainly based on Sartre's Existentialism: To deny the significance of human existence is to live in a meaningless universe. Beckett's absurd play *Waiting for Godot*, which premiered in 1953, presents an overall human condition. The polar opposition between tramps and travelers greatly limits any important human action. The questions "Who is Godot"and "Why should we wait for him" have no reason and no answer, everything seems to have not been carried out, but it seems to be happening again.

The illusion and absurdity of modern drama show more disorder and meaninglessness. The fatalistic attitude and the Utopia of idealism have never had practical significance. Even so, the understanding of the meaning and the destiny of human existence continues.

（茚博译）

04   The Oedipus Complex and Patricide Complex in Greek Mythology

Ⅰ   Oedipus Mythology

"Oedipus Complex" is first used by Freud as a psychoanalytic term. What it refers to is that children before the age of six are unintentionally attached to the opposite sex of their parents but hostile to the same sex. What greatly inspired him was the tragedy *Oedipus King* created by the famous ancient Greek tragedian Sophocles. The story is about King Laius of Thebes who, in order to avoid the realization of oracle, threw his son into the barren hills and inside of Catalonia after his birth. However, the baby was rescued by a shepherd and named Oedipus for his swollen feet. Later Oedipus became the adopted son of Thebes's neighboring country. Since the king of the country had no children, Oedipus was identified as heir to the throne. When he grew up, Oedipus, who did not know that Corinth king and queen were not his biological parents, fled to avoid the oracle coming true. He accidentally killed his own father on his way to the temple of Delphi. Later he became king of Thebes and married his mother Jocasta because he cracked Riddle of Sphinx. Finally, Oedipus, who knew the truth, blinded himself and chose self-exile.

The most obvious manifestation of patricide complex happened to the god of time, Cronus. He castrated his father Uranus with a sickle, then became the lord of gods. There was a prediction that he would be overthrown by one of his sons, so he devoured every child to avoid that happening. When Zeus was born, his mother Rhea replaced him with a big stone. Later he defeated his father and rescued his brothers and sisters.

As a poet, Hesiod praised Greek mythology. We may find it difficult to understand Hesiod's own feelings about Cronus and Zeus' "patricide", which in most people's view violates ethical common sense. But the feelings he expressed in *Theogony* were full of piety and praise. "*Having said this, the eloquent daughters of Zeus took a wonderful branch from a thick olive branch and blew a holy voice into my heart to let me sing about the future and the past.*" Both Cronus and Zeus overthrew their father. why not their mothers? Because in the period of creating the corresponding myth, the mother's power system had disappeared and was replaced by the patriarchy.

On the other hand, in the process of Cronus and Zeus killing their father, it is not difficult to find the figure of their mother. They all overthrew their fathers' rule at the behest or with the help of their mothers. Why do not mothers overthrow their husbands' rule by themselves? Because they no longer have the ability to compete with their husband, which further reflects the decline of matriarchy. However, judging from the results after the overthrow, the male gods still occupied the dominant position and were the representative of patriarchy, which is also the reappearance of the real life at that time. This is because the gods in Greek mythology are the same as human beings both in physical beauty and desires. They have joys and sorrows and participate in people's activities. The only difference between god and man is that the former has eternal life while the latter has not.

II Patriarchy in Ancient Greek Society

Engels said: "The overthrow of the matriarchy is a historic failure for women. Husband has the power at home, while the wife is belittled and enslaved, becoming a slave to her husband's lust and a simple tool to bear children. The belittled position of women is particularly explicit among the Greeks in Age of Heroes...In patriarchal society inside, property, children and wives all belong to the father, as was the case in ancient Greek society. Greek mythology is a true portrayal of the real life of ancient Greece. The whole Greek myth is full of extremely strong male chauvinism. It is in this context that Oedipus Complex and Patricide Complex are enlarged. Facing the harsh patriarchal imperium, children and mothers who are also in a weak position are more likely to form an alliance to resist the oppression of their fathers and husbands.

In Lacan's Phallus Centrism, men are the main part, while women are regarded as the others existing who prove the value of men, which makes Phallus Centrism what people commonly call male chauvinism. In Greek rank order, the binary opposition between men and women means that men present the positive values and "Phallus" represent males was a transcendental signifier. The ancient Greek society, as depicted in the myth, is full of the oppression of women. In other word, "Women are only a place to construct male , which exists as a thing without subjectivity."According to Greek history, the ancient Greeks gradually established a more perfect democratic system through continuous efforts, from barbarism to civilization, but the status of women is getting worse and worse.

In Homeric Age (B.C.1100-B.C.900), city-states are the main activity places for male citizens. Women are not only separated from men in activity space, but also have a great gap with men in education level. But at this time, they are not completely excluded from social life. By the 4th B.C., although politics had improved, the situation of women had deteriorated. Although ancient Greece practiced monogamy, the so-called monogamy was a restriction on women. Athenian women are required to strictly observe chastity and can not participate in public activities for any reason. At this time, they can only be oppressed and bullied by men, which is clearly shown in Greek mythology.

Iliad unfolds the story with Achilles's anger. Achilles was angry because a woman, a female prisoner belonging to him after the victory of the war, was taken away by Agamemnon. The two men competed for the woman not because they loved Briseis, but the prisoner was a symbol of honor at that time.The Greeks treated the female prisoners casually during the war as objects and gave them away like weapons and livestock even killed them. Of course, they were also used as "bedmates" at home.

Socrates also believed that his wife was only a good spouse, caring for the family and giving birth to legal heirs. In Greek mythology, Agamemnon, the Greek commander in chief, personally killed his daughter in order to appease Artemis's anger and made the trip to Troy which was being blocked. This is a tragic portrayal of women in ancient Greek society and a powerful demonstration of patriarchy.

Ⅲ   Silent "Lambs"

As Foucault said, "There is no need for weapons, physical violence or material restraint, only one gaze, one supervised gaze, and everyone will become humble under the weight of this gaze, and will make him become his own monitor. Thus, the gaze that seems to be directed at everyone from top to bottom is actually implemented by everyone himself."In ancient Greek society, most women were on the edge of society, and they were neglected by patriarchy. However, they seldom rebelled. The reason is that the central culture, ideology under patriarchy ruled and suppressed women, which made women internalize man's ideology and made them not aware of the injustice they suffered.

（茆博译）

Chapter 2   The Myth and Interpretation

01   Imagination and Truth—The Hermeneutic Meaning of Helen

I   Helen in Historical Interpretation

Since ancient times, beautiful girls have terrible fates. The sorrow of the beauty has long been untested, no trace can be found, but the name of the beauty has been tumbling with the history of the dust, never stop. Helen was just a name and the story circulated by this name was not only innumerable, but also very different. Was the goddess of light in Peloponnese, or the chief culprit of the Trojan War? Was she the daughter of Zeus and Leda, or the faithful woman who was waiting for her husband to return? Who was Helen? The veil and the curtains were heavy and the true face of this woman who has fallen into the history was not seen.

1. Goddess Helen in Ancient Myth

The questions about Helen's "death" and "eternal life", like Jesus' "humanity" and "divinity", were discussed heatedly. In the original legend, Helen was a goddess whose life was as repeated as a plant. Later she became the daughter of God and the human woman, but she was still eternal: the queen of Sparta. Leda and Zeus, gave birth to four children, Helen and Polydeuces, who were immortal; Clytemnestra and Castor, they were mortal. But in the literary imagination of later generations, Helen appeared more as a mortal woman.

Whether she was a goddess or a woman, it was indisputable that she had amazing beauty and lost the country and destroyed the city. How Helen was idealized into an eternal object of worship, slander, praise, envy, deconstruction and reconstruction was a topic worth pondering. All of her metamorphoses have accumulated as fossils of the evolution of female identity in Western culture, accumulating into the collective imagination of human history. Therefore, Helen's story was the story of the entire Western woman, the story of the entire human race.

Helen was once the goddess of fertility in ancient Minos and goddess of Peloponnese. It had the same function as Aphrodite, but its influence was less than that of the latter, and its status has declined. As a plant goddess, its encounter was a fate pattern of death and catastrophe and return after robbing. Like Adonis, Helen and the plant were periodically resurrected in the four seasons, so possessing her means holding a good harvest, which means affirmation and guarantee of life (reproduction). Therefore, "the significance of the Greek expedition to Troy, the recapture of Helen, means that the fortune will return to the predicament of Mycenae. As a symbol, this is the connotation of Helen's myth."

2. Homer and Hesiod's Helen

Whether it was the Gaia, Pandora, or Aphrodite, Helen, they shared the same motif of human founding mythology in different names. Whether it was the triangular symbol on the rock wall of the Paleolithic Age or the totem of the Neolithic Age, women were connected to "reproduction" and "death". Women can breed life and destroy life: "The womb is tomb." "Demonization" and "Angelization" of women make the narrative about Helen a confrontational situation: she was the giver of joy and the maker of disaster, and the "official" narrative was always in the "negative tradition" (misogyny) under the cover. This tradition was not only man's dislike of women, but also woman's dislike of women.

In Hesiod's *Theogony*, Helen was the daughter of the Oceanus and later evolved into the daughter of Aphrodite. Later legends found her father, Zeus. Zeus raped the Nemesis and her daughter, Helen, as the seed of revenge and the "girl of the night" became a permanent threat to the patriarchal society. The vengeful goddess of vengeance was constantly changing and was worshiped as an animal, plant and marine fairy (nymph). Later, she turned into a goose, and Zeus, who was incarnate as a swan, once again raped her and this was the predecessor of Leda. Keats's retelling of Helen's life in *Leda and the Swan* gave Helen's beauty a reasonable explanation.

Helen came out of the egg. One legend said that the moon-fallen egg fell from the moon and was transported by the fish to the shore of the Euphrates River, which was hatched by the pigeons. The poet Sappho described another origin of Helen: "People rumored that under the wild hyacinth flowers, Lida found an egg." From the cosmic egg to the Leda's egg, Helen experienced a transition from God to human identity.

Helen, as a gift that God gives to the mortal world has no difference from the nature of Pandora. Its catastrophic performance has two aspects: first, her origin was connected with "Zeus violence"; second, her "sexual desire" was connected with "Eros's violence", so as a gift, she could only bring misfortune.

Helen had a close relationship with the goddess Aphrodite, because Aphrodite promised her to the Prince of Troy and Helen was also closely related to the love god "Eros". She had a peerless love with Prince Troy. In Dante's *Divine Comedy*, she was sent to hell for this connection. Socrates called "the lust" a "tyrant", as René Giral said: "Desire was always linked to violence." However, Helen's "violence" was very different from her sister Clytemnestra: the bloodyness of the Agamemnon's bathroom was in stark contrast to the bed in the Tender Land of Paris. It turned out that it was not anger that could kill, love could also kill, but the former used "knife" while the latter used "laugh".

Although they were all raped, Helen's ending differs from her mother Leda. Leda could not live in humiliation and hang herself. Helen had a beautiful love with the hijackers after the initial violence of the hijacking. Helen did not break her own self, nor was she punished by the gods. Instead, she got eternal life and went to the world of bliss. The choices of Helen and Leda seem to imply a certain contradiction between "woman" and "violence".

As the daughter of Zeus, Helen revealed a kind of divinity, a kind of "otherness" that was different from human beings and this "otherness" also reveals the secret of reconciliation between women and men behind "rape". The most effective and direct way for a man to domesticate a woman "who was the opposite sex" was to use violence. The desire to be raped by "God" and the anger of being raped by "beasts" seem to reflect women's attitudes towards violence. The desire to be raped and the reconciliation with the rapist reflected the impulse of women to transcend reality and compromise with reality.

As an established order, Zeus's "violence" was "cruel", but also "sacred". Leda can't stand "cruel" and was not aware of "sacredness". Therefore, she chose death. Helen's "shameless wisdom" ended women's "desperate confrontation" with "violence" and subtly transformed this "violence" into their own "marriage". Men love and fear this kind of "shameless wisdom", but they could only conceal the hidden connivance under the contemptuous coat.

3. Gorgia, Aeschylus and Euripides' Helen

Gorgia, the wise school scholar, defended Helen's love in *Encomium of Helen* : he emphasized the inevitability of natural lust, saying that Helen's love belonged to the natural lust and is a last resort. Moreover, he praised Helen's "sacred beauty" because it provoked such a strong "sexual desire" and exchanged a "body" for the "corpse" of many men.

In Aeschylus's *Agamemnon,* the chorus saw Clytemnestra's hands stained with blood, first rebuked Helen: "For a woman, sacrificed so many men. Their lives were exhausted in the shadows." They called Helen "the hell of the ship, the hell of the city-state, the hell of the man."But the poet defended Helen by the mouth of Helen's sister: "You pour your anger at Helen, as if the corpse of Troy is her masterpiece. Forget it."

In the *Trojan Women* of Euripides, the wife of Priam, the queen of Troy, Hecube also rebuked the initiator of this war: "All that has suffered and would bear, was it for a woman and her bed?" Strangely, Euripides made another interpretation of Helen: The slut in *Trojan Women* turned into a virgin in *Helen,* which made us curious to Euripides' attitudes towards women.

Euripides' *Helen* described the story of a paragon of chastity who was waiting for her husband to return: Helen, who was robbed by Paris to Troy, just a phantom. The real Helen was brought to Egypt by the gods, hidden in the home of kind king Proteus. After the Trojan War, Menelaus drifted to Egypt, recognized Helen and fled together.

The plot of Euripides' *Helen* was incontrovertible and similar to the ancient legends that Herodotus reflected in Helen's story in Egypt. According to Herodotus's record in the second volume of *History*, Helen was abducted by Paris and was blown by the storm to the coast of Egypt on her way to Troy. King Proteus hated Paris's injustice and ordered him to leave Helen and the treasures for some time and was ready to return to Menelaus in the future. After the war, Menelaus discovered that Helen was not in Troy. He came to Egypt and Proteus returned Helen to him.

Euripides' *Helen* and Herodotus's narrative Shared two similarities: First, Helen has not been to Troy; Second, Helen's asylum was the Egyptian King Proteus. As for the plot that Helen moved from Sparta to Egypt and lived in the Egyptian royal palace, Euripides was not specifically mentioned in *Helen*. The use of two mythological traditions by Euripides was enough to illustrate the "truth" of "history": "the truth of history" was always outside of "history" and Helen's "phantom" was the "truth" of history.

II "Helen" and "History"

The question of "who was Helen" and "how did Helen become Helen" had shown the division between the history of analyticism and the history of positivism in the 20th century. Even though the new Hegelianism and the new historicism had the danger of slipping into "relativism" and "nihilism", Dilthey's "experience" and Croce's "all history was contemporary history", Collingwood's "All history is the history of thought" and the historical philosophy of Gadamer's "understanding or interpretation" still opened up new horizons for explaining the possibility of historical knowledge. The philosophical construction of "How did Helen become Helen" could not replace the historical research of "Who was Helen", just as the performance of Hamlet could not be played without the Danish prince, but it may be more important for exploring the collective imagination of human beings.

The reason why "tragedy" becomes a "tragedy" is related to the "event", but more importantly, it is related to the experience of the tragedy and the viewer of the tragedy. For a person who feels numb and has no tragic experience, the meaning of "tragedy" is far less important than the tragic spectator who witnessed this event. Similarly, if the pain and painful memories of Helen were limited to the Trojans and Greeks in Homer's writings, then the question of whom Helen was has lost the possible meaning. "Helen became Helen" because the pain and memory she brought constantly spurred the "living imagination" of later generations. Whether the epic of Homer or the tragedy of Euripides, as a symbol, "Helen" revealed the "truth" of "history".

Collingwood's "imagination" was an important means of "reappearing history". The "problem" that has been lost in "reconstruction" was the fog that has been set aside by history. Although Hayden White's "The essence of historical narrative was fiction" has been greatly criticized, he has followed the analysis of the "imagination" and "history" proposed by the masters of historical philosophy, or more precisely,the associated question related to the "historical narrative"could not be avoided. The "narrative" about Helen may not be "history" and it would never become "history", because as the accumulation of human collective imagination, "Helen" would always be active in the "history" that would not stop.

III "Helen's Name"

As a human being, the historical truth of Helen could not be tested, while as a name, Helen had achieved another "history of truth."The question that "Who was Helen" was not important for the history of human experience, what is important is the "name" of "Helen".The "name" made "Helen" a "denomination" which we cannot control, and the name makes us feel, seek and worship. The name generates the true meaning for us.

Umberto Eco, an Italian semiologist once wrote a best-selling novel, *The Name of the Rose*. Since then, the struggle between "rose" and "name" has become a lasting interest in academia. Shakespeare said: "We call the rose with another name and it would be as sweet as it is." This seems to imply a general understanding of the "name": "rose" was "real" because it could be "experienced", "name" was just a "title" but not a reality that could be experienced. However, was it really only the objects that could be experienced are real? Can "name" not be "real" experience? Did the fragrance of "Rose" really have nothing to do with its "name"? At the end of the novel, Eco wrote: "The old rose existed in its name and we only have this name." "Name" and "Rose" were two different "realities" and in the history of experience, the "name of the rose" as the title was more authentic than the "rose". Not only that, the true meaning of the "name" may just be the key to making "rose" a "rose".

In his book *Reminiscence*, Derrida pointed out that "name" was longer than "person", "the name begins his life to get along without him."The "name" as Derrida's "performative event" or Paul Ricoeur "the event of language" revealed the meaning of "Helen". The truth of the "name" is that "rose" is extended through the symbolic activity of "name" and that "rose" enters history as a "name". Helen's imagination and interpretation were contained in the "name" of "Helen", which made "truth eternal in fiction". As an "event", "Helen" fulfills Wittgenstein's philosophical proposition: "The meaning of the world was outside the world."

Asking "Who is Helen" is not to reveal the truth of history, but to understand the illusory history. The process of truth contained in the questioning of the "name" and "how Helen became Helen" was the way in which truth was revealed.

（张振宇译）

02　The Perpetual (M)other—Medea in Historical Interpretations

I　Medea's Motif in the Ancient Greek Myth

As one of the oldest motifs in the Western literature, Medea's story itself has become an eternal myth and a typical process of text-production through the re-narrations and re-interpretations in the different ages. If every "understanding" means "interpretation" and all history is the history of contemporary thought, it is of course more valuable to trace back the formation of the motif than any analyses of single texts so as to demonstrate its hermeneutic value in common.

From a Chinese scholar's point of view to trace back the motif will inevitably meet some difficulty caused not only by historical distance, but regional,cultural and lingual distance. However, perhaps it is these distances that make the fundamental human interrelationships visible and the understandings of different ages to these interrelationships conterminous. These interrelationships such as parents-children, man-woman, individual-society, moral-choice and the understandings towards them make it feasible to analyze the motif and its meaning-production.

II   The Hermeneutic History of Medea's Motif

The re-narrative tradition begins with Homer. Pindar's ode and Euripides' tragedy *Medea* are the representative works in the period when Greek literature prospered and Aristotle also made great remarks on it. In the Hellenistic and the Roman period, Apollonius, Ovid, Seneca and Chrysippus left rich legacy to this tradition. Dares, Dictys, Bocaccio, Chaucer and Christine de Pizan are the important writers who left the clear marks to track down the Christian ethical and moral rules in the middle ages and the Renaissance. The rewritings in the modern period have lots of entanglements not only with the Classical view of passion and glory but colonialism and feminism. Christa Wolf's novel *Medea-Stimmen* represents the echo of the motif in the post-modern context. The different re-narrations and reinterpretations of course reflect the social environment and thoughts of the different ages.

The re-narrations and reinterpretations of the motif formed a particular inter-texual chain in the Western tradition while Medea's "eros"and"identity" are the two main points which all interpretations focused on in the tradition.

From ancient Greece, the image of "Medea" can never stop to dispute about her "identity". Whatever an outsider,an abandoned wife, a witch or a woman, Medea as two symbols continuously excited the imaginations of the later interpretations. One symbol is her "political identity" and the other is her "sexual identity". If"sex"is more cohesive with subject, discourse and power, the structural relationships,then Medea's"sexual identity" is often her "political identity".Whereas through the reflection of her sex and character, her"political identity"always reveals a kind of challenge, subversion and "otherness".

In the eye of the Greek, Medea is a barbarian from Colchis and she is quite antipathetic to the Corinthian civilization and is difficult to be tolerated by the social formation in the period of transition, which can not be easily regarded as a kind of representative of the social concept.She may betray her father for her lover and kill her sons to revenge the lover when love has gone. Therefore, the outsider dooms an "(M)other" either to the matriarchy or to the patriarchy.

Whereas this"(M)other"and"outsider"to the established order and the Greek civilization has another "identity". In Pindar's ode, Medea is not only a woman but a Muse. In Euripides'tragedy, Medea is not only an abandoned wife but the descendant of Helios, the sun god. Thus when Medea challenged human's feelings and the moral system in the most cruel and extreme way, she seems to perform the functions of "Furies"and contain some logic and characteristics of "goddess".It is to say, no matter what kind of an "outsider" or "(M)other", Medea's identity bears some initial holiness, which dooms to a kind of "otherness" to human's norms. Nevertheless, in the collective imagination of human beings, it is this "holiness"that makes "(M)other" eternal.

From the princess of Colchis to the slave of Corinth and from a Greek goddess to a common woman dominated by eros, the process seems to satisfy the prevalent expectation. However, as time goes by, we gradually realize that the "obedience" of the character is the "loss".We can even say that what Medea obeys is not the so-called civilized "god to man" process but the possible phallus—logos—centric system. Wherefore, Wolf's Medea exhibits her special value for the subversion.

Medea is related to a kind of old emotional principle which is inconsonant with the rational order no matter she is a goddess or a woman. The"eros"she represents is not only the secret emotion hiding in human beings'hearts and the primitive, bloodthirsty instinct of humanity but a kind of feminine characteristic which is quite different from masculine authority and rational order. Even the"eros"which caused Medea's love and infanticide, is also related with the holiness non-rational order through this feminine characteristic.

Hence, Medea's "feminine characteristic" is always part of the"holiness" no matter in Greek mythology, Greek tragedy or Christian dramas in the mediaeval time. Maybe, it is the way we understand "holiness". Thereupon Medea's affection sometimes appears in the form of "ardor",sometimes in the form of"caritas","charity"even" agape". If Medea in Corinthian worship stands for"birth"and symbolizes"holiness", then the variance of the motif reflects man's quest for"holiness"in different ages.

III　The Hermeneutic Interpretation of Medea's Motif

Perhaps it is impossible to interpret the motif completely, but from Pindar's"outsider"to Wolf's subversive"voice"—from the view of female writers, with the ending by the conclusion of inheriting the Medea's motif, it is at least a kind of relative entelechy. The production and extension of the motif all the time aims at essentialism in different ages through the"otherness", and this is the vigor and charm of the various interpretations and for this reason, Medea can be an eternal "(M)other" to the phallus—logos—centric system and provide some possibility to escape from "the trap that to seek for subject when subject is destructed".

（杨慧译）

03　The Song of Siren—The Existential Predicament of Human Beings

I　The Legend of Siren

It is said that the Siren is the daughter of Achelous the river God, and is a beautiful fairy who was born from the blood of her father. In the early time, the document of the Siren was recorded in the *Odyssey* of Homer. Circe taught Odysseus to stuff ears of other partners with beeswax when they crossed the the channel of Messina. If he wanted to hear the beautiful voice, he firstly asked his companies to tie him on the mast with a rope. However, these Homer's descriptions about Siren are ambiguous. So many puzzles were left, such as, how many Sirens did he meet? What did Siren look like? Where was she born and where did she live? These questions are not surely clear in the epics of Homer. Actually, in the epics of Homer, all images of fairies are equivocal. Words of Homer's description about fairies are simple,which leaves much endless imagination to the later generations. Later, all changeable documents about the myth of Siren are based on this story to gradual evolution and supplement. After explaining that, the details of Siren's myth are constantly full. When filling the vacancy, the new story has new ambiguities and uncertainties, and the mythology will go on to be created.

Ⅱ   The Interpretations of Siren

Narrowly speaking, Siren only stands for the sea demon in the ancient Greek mythology. Widely speaking, Siren refers to the female sea demon. However, its connotation and image constantly are changing in the development of different times. In the 6th century B.C., the image of the sea demon, just like the dovelet, presented on the surface of potteries. In 490 B.C., the image of Siren, just like a bird with a human face, open mouth and singing, was carved on the Greek pottery. However, in this period, another image described Odysseus and Siren on the pottery has such a Siren: she had the human arms and breast, playing the zither or flute. In the 3rd century A.D., a popular fable named *Physiology* was delivered in the city of Alexandria, the sea demon was regarded as the evil animal. It was a female's body from head to navel, while the lower half was a body of a bird.

Why is Siren regarded as a monster with the body of bird and face of mankind? Is it because the sailor's imagination that they can often hear the beautiful sound of seabirds when travelling at the sea? Or is it because the later legend that Siren's mother is one of the Muses who have image of bird's body? There is another tale that Siren lived in the underworld. It is said that they were female companion of Persephone, daughter of Zeus and Demeter. After Persephone plundered by Hades as a queen, Sirens turned into birds with wings to look for and accompany Persephone. These kind Sirens, with kind and sweet voice, comfort the dead spectre. Their bodies are elves with wings, so they are often made as the burial objects with birds' bodies and humans' faces. However, according to another version named *Physiology* in the 7th century, the image of the Siren has changed— the Siren was described as a mixture with a woman, a bird and a tail of fish. In the 8th century, in a famous works written by a clergy, the Siren was firstly recognized as this image—a pure lady from head to navel with a scaly tail of fish. As for the evolution of fish tail, I am afraid it comes from the related imagination of people— sea fairies often appear in the ocean,so they have their tails just like fish. The image is also relative to fairies in other seas in Greek mythology—it is said that daughters of Nereus are fairies who lived in the sea, so the image of Siren is combined with that of fairies. In the art during the medieval age, the image of the sea demon was basically acknowledged as the lady with a tail. The image of the sea monster with two tails, in that times, appeared on some coins, even on the cross. However, the memory about bird's body has not disappeared completely. In the 13th century, in some versions of *Zoology*, the sea monster was bird's body with sharp claws and fish in their hands. Another image of the sea demon was a naked lady with a tail and two hands catching fish. In 1250, *the Animal Love Story* described it just like this, there were three different female monsters in the sea. The upper body of the first two was a woman, the lower body was fish; The upper body of the third was a woman, the lower body was bird. These three different Sirens can sing and play the instrument at the same time. The first one blows the bugle, the second one plays the harp and the last one shows her charming voice. The depict merged with the Siren's monster of the bird's body and human's face in the ancient Greek myth and that of the human's body and fish tail in medieval times. Nevertheless, it remained the charming features with the melodious music and singing of Sirens and fascinating characters.

The charming characters that Sirens possessed are not only their beautiful voices but also their bodies: long hair, plump breasts that can make men fall in love with them at the first sight. In order to address the mark that Sirens are streetwalkers, the artists who are from different regions also combined the image of "Babylonian Prostitute" to make them become a beauty with a mirror and comb in hands and golden long hair down. Meanwhile, the Christians also reinterpreted the mixed meaning of "fascinating", "dangerous", and "bones of the dead" about Sirens in *Odyssey*. It does not explain why the island of Siren is filled with white bone, nor how danger and death happened— "the island that the Siren lived is full of bones. And it is also terrible and gloomy. " As for the explanation about different meanings of the Siren in the later generation, it is the creation according to the writer's purpose. For example, the *Physiology* in the 3rd century was written by a Christian, and it was said that the Siren attracted men with the charming voice to make them feel sleepy, then rushed at them and ate them. The Siren directly killed men here. The best bait for the demon is a woman. The Siren marks the debauchery and indulgence. The bait of the Siren involves the mundane indulgence—letters, dramas, music and acrobats. The Siren is the obstacle to prevent Christians from approaching God. In Christians' opinion, the Siren almost equals with Satan. In the middle ages, the plot was interpreted by churchmen in *Odyssey*: sailors plugged their ears with cotton and did not hear the song of the Siren, which meant a Christian preferred to plug their ears rather than accepted the bait from the demon. Odysseus, like a Christ, carries a cross and bears the original sin. When facing all kinds of temptations of Satan who incarnated the Siren(including sweet songs), Odysseus can overcome the desire with will and faith. At this moment, the ship became a church and waves of the life swarmed in the sea, while this voyage sailed by Odysseus and his sailors meant trying to be close to the purpose of God. The sailing of Odysseus, is a *Journey to Heaven*, is a way of overcoming all kinds of obstacles to get to Heaven. In the middle ages, it was a common phenomenon to reinterpret Siren like this. Christians' opinion to Siren only paid attention to the part of temptations, even works of the literature written by Boccaccio and Dante were understood like this.

Under the influence of Christian asceticism, the Siren was a sign as carnal desire at this time. During this time, the image of Siren combined the form of "Babylonian Prostitute"—golden long hair, a mirror and a comb in hands. However, after the renaissance, the image of Siren in the literary works wiped off the pornographic form in the middle ages. Although inheriting the image with upper body of a beauty, long hair and the tail of fish, the Siren was always endowed kind personality, for example, the fairy tale named *the Little Mermaid* written by Andersen, was remembered as a good image in human's mind. By the 15th and 16th century, some naturalists did their best to find the Siren in the real life. Then they suppose that the image of Siren equaled with manatee, which made it more ugly.

Ⅲ   Reasons for Different Interpretations

The Siren, at first, has multiple images. Nevertheless, some of them gradually are faded away in the history, dispelled and forgot, even changed and manipulated. After choosing, misunderstanding during the middle ages, the Siren as a pornographic image with the features of carnal desire, lasciviousness and temptation was intensified. What factors made other legends about the Siren disappear? What made the image of the pornographic Siren stressed? Is it because Siren not recorded in the Book of God, or is it not decent? Or because the ascetics in the middle ages needed to flag a lewd and opposite image to educate common people as a discipline? The explanation in the middle ages set Siren as a symbol of desire and temptation. The Sirens were regarded as vulgar, lewd and flighty ladies. They always showed beauty and touching voices superficially and hid the devil with concealed intention, which could bring the disaster to human beings. When the sailors went through the island and heard their songs, they would be puzzled, feel sleepy and even die on the rocks. Actually, in the early time of Plato, some comedians put this pornographic Siren on the stage. In the 4th B.C., Palaeifathus, a writer in Greece, said directly: Sirens were streetwalkers! The elegance was only their surface, and beneath it lied devil, infidelity and death. In terms of this definition, Odysseus became a moral example of preventing the temptation. In fact, if the charming temptation of the Siren can be explained in this way, it exactly shows in *Odyssey* that the humanity can not resist the libidinal temptation because the partners of Odysseus have to plug their ears with the cotton. Once they heard the songs of Siren, they inevitably ran to Siren without fear and death. Even Odysseus, who is smart, rational and crafty, can not dispel the curiosity and longing for desire. As for Odysseus, he wanted to enjoy this desire, so he wanted to listen to the songs. He deeply knew that he could not overcome the carnal desire by himself, then he had to tie himself with the rope. Maybe the mast marks the justice and morality, the rope might symbolize the power of the reason. Even the moral models still need the rope and mast, this means the desire is so powerful. It is not special opinion that the Siren is defined the origin of the carnal desire and disaster. To punish human beings, Zeus once made a lady named Pandora. Actually, Pandora is a trap of Zeus. She comes to the world carrying a bottle filled with all kinds of disasters. Pandora is "a kind and cute girl who looks like an immortal goddess", which attracts both men and god. But Hermes "gives her a thick-skinned heart and cheating humanity." Pandora released disasters from the bottle, while herself was full of hungry sexual desire and appetite.

The definition of Siren is the same as Pandora's. The pornographic Siren, for the asceticism in the middle ages, was depicted so perfectly that people can not remember many available and original meanings of Sirens. Actually, there is another description of the Siren in the ancient Greek: the song of Sirens marks the seven heavens of the harmonious universe. This idea suggests that the music is the most ideal method to release the soul of mankind, and seven strings of a harp symbolize the seven heavens in the universe. Plato supposed that the philosophers designed eight rings in the universe, each ring had a sea monster, each Siren pronounced a sound, and eight sounds sang together for the harmony of the universe. The Siren here is close to Zeus. During the time of renaissance, Neo-platonists revered the songs of Sirens, which equaled with the feeling of spirits. In the works of Petrarch, the image of Sirens appeared with Zeus' again. The Siren can know the past and present, and also predict the future. Cicero said in *Theory of Purpose*, "It is neither their voice nor songs that captures the soul of sailors, but their utter knowledge of the truth. " During the period of Byzantine, scholars usually called "the sea Siren" each other, which equaled the title of "doctor". They often said that Homer himself was a "Siren". However, in the later time, the view of the "doctor Siren" did not seem to spread widely. And the interruption of the process was probably due to the extensively spread of pornographic Sirens in the middle ages.

IV Conclusion

When tracing the process of interpretations of Sirens, we find the footprint of human civilization: the history is the previous record of interpretations. What we see is not a legend or a kind of Siren. In the literature classics, in the story teaching orally, in the imagination of the sailors, in the conclusion of so-called researching by scientists, in the description of litterateurs and in the reproach of churchman. With Siren's image appearing and splitting in different forms, it is ridiculous that we find the essential Siren in the mist of a variety of Sirens. The meaning of Siren's myth is "different" here: different Sirens, different narrations, different purposes and different senses. In the endless explanation, we do our best to find "the real Siren", but maybe "the real Siren" does not exist utterly. Sirens, as the same as Muse, know the past, present and future. Because they keep pace with the civilization of human beings, then they have the memory of passing through the space and the ability of knowing everything.

（宣麒麟译）

04 The Phenomenological Value of Sound from the Myth of Narcissus

I The Significance of Sound

Kristeva criticized structuralism for imagining language as a static homogeneous structure, simplifying language to the level of logical proposition and to the level that can be grasped by reason at any time. Her semiotics reveals the basic heterogeneity of language and concerns about discourse and the subject of discourse.

II The Myth of Narcissus

There is another story in ancient Greek mythology that illustrates the sorrow that women are rejected by men: Narcissus is very handsome and always cares for himself. Echo fell in love with him, but found that she could not express her love in any other way except imitating his speech. Once, Echo crossed the mountains and shouted to him, "Let's merge with each other!" Echo ran to his place full of joy and was about to reach out his arms to hold him when he shouted, "Get your hands off me! I would rather die than let you possess me! " Since then, Echo has been living in the mountain forest, died, only the sound left. This voice does not have any validity in mainstream discourse, but can only reverberate between the valleys and cliffs. Sound is meaningful only when it is heard. The subject of sound is recognized by sound. This recognition is not only the authentication of others, but also the authentication of oneself. Various phonetic symbols are heard by the subject, and the subject should not be directly affected by the expressed activities beyond himself. "My words are alive, because it seems that they have not left me: they have not fallen out of me, out of my breath, into visible distance, they belong to me without interruption, and they belong to me unconditionally. Therefore, in any case, the phenomenon of sound is manifested as the sound of phenomenology. Through sound, the subject obtains a confirmation of existence, knowing that he is alive and making others feel alive.

Ⅲ The Phenomenological Value of Sound

The phenomenological value of sound is its transcendence over the dignity of any other signified entity. The "surface transcendence" of sound is always the reference as the ideal essence, that is, the expressed meaning directly goes to the things present in the expressing activity. This direct presence is tied to what the signified phenomenological "corps" which seem to disappear at the moment of its creation. Signifer refers to factors that already seem to be ideal. From the phenomenological point of view, it restores itself and transforms the secular opacity of its body into pure translucency. The disappearance of the sensible body and the disappearance of its externality are the direct presence of signifer itself for consciousness.

The factor is the most ideal reason in symbols because it has an accomplice relationship with the subject. When we speak, it has the phenomenological nature of the active process that we expect when we speak. Energized signifer refers to the intention of being absolutely close to me due to my breath and meaning. Living activity is to give life, to give vitality to the signifier body and to transform the body into an expression of "meaning". It is the soul of language. It is not separated from itself or from its own presence. It can point out the ideal object and the ideal meaning. This ideal object or meaning has not been encountered outside the ideality and the internality of self-being.

Voice endows the subject with vitality, and the active self-presence in the transparent spirit sets its own life internality: the subject of speech is heard now. This is the nature or normal state of speech. This involves the speech structure that the speaker expects: to discover the sensible form of the phenomenon and understand its inherent expression intention at the same time. If some accidents seem to refute the necessity of this teleology, then they will either be overtaken by some supplementary process or there will be no words. Silence and deafness both come. Deaf people can only take part in the discussion if they slip these activities into the form of words whose ultimate goal means that they are heard by those who make their voices heard. From the viewpoint of pure phenomenology, within the restoration, the process of speech has the vitality of pure phenomenology, which has suspended the natural standpoint and the existence of the world. The process of "being heard—speaking" is an absolutely unique type of self-influence. On the one hand, this process is carried out in the universal middle term. The signifier appearing in this process should be some ideality. People should ideally repeat these idealities or transmit them as the same ideality. On the other hand, the subject can be heard or speak to himself, and let himself be influenced by signifiers. This signifier is a signifier that the subject makes without turning according to the requirements of internality, the world or the general non-nature requirements.

There are no obstacles to the spread of sound in the world, precisely because it is produced in the world as a pure self-influence. This kind of self-influence may be the possibility of what people call subjectivity or self-reliance. However, without it, no parts of the world can be emerged. It is this universality that is structurally speaking and has the right to make any consciousness impossible as long as it leaves sound. Voice is the existence of consciousness of action that is close to self in common form. Sound is consciousness. To speak to someone may be to hear yourself and be heard by yourself. But at the same time, if people are heard by others, that is to say, they make others directly repeat in themselves in the form of "being heard—talking".

Aristotle described barbarians and slaves as "beings lacking language." This certainly does not mean that barbarians and slaves lack the ability to speak physically, but rather that they are deprived of the rights to make their statements meaningful. Women, groups with the same roles as slaves, have certainly lost their voices, and this process has been rationalized by the "law". Originally, the gods of "power" and "violence" were followers of Zeus' throne, symbolizing the tyranny of sacred power and the rampant irrationality. Derrida said: "discourse is everything, and text is dead." (There is nothing outside the text) Ancient women did not have text or interpretation of text-discourse. "A voice without writing is absolutely living and absolutely dead at the same time." Whether it is Hermes' letter to the gods or the church's exegesis, in quite a few cases, the reason why the "sutra" becomes the "sutra" is the result of interpretation. Therefore, the interpretation of classical activities often reflects a sense of power. In the long history of women, there is only voice without writing. Even if this voice is drowned out. Who makes them both alive and dead?

There is a feminist analysis that tends to human hermeneutics, emphasizing that women experience the world with different subjects or senses, and advocating the view that "discourse is gender-specific." The history of the male-dominated society is the history of the conscious inundation of women's voices, which makes women lose their subjectivity while this makes men feel deeply bored. Being bored means having nothing to say. One of the reasons why there is nothing to say is that no one listens to you. Since women, the other half of the world, are objectified, then men correspondingly lose listeners who can understand their own voices.

Voice is a way to confirm subjectivity. The absence of female voice not only makes women lose the value of existence, but also makes the significance of male existence questioned: meaning is highlighted in the relationship with others. Without the "other" of women as a whole, the male world has become a one-dimensional existence and an unrecognized narcissism. Christa Wolf's rewriting of Cassandra's and Medea's myths is to reveal the historical truth that women's voices have been drowned out and is an effort to make women talk again.

（茆博译）

05 Freedom, Justice and Death—The Symbolic Meaning of Antigone

I Introduction

Antigone (Greek: monster), a shocking name, starting with Homer's epic, through the rendering of Sophocles, through Hegel, Lacan, Martha Nussbaum, the analyses of many philosophers, such as Judith Butler, became the sword of Damocles over the human civilization and became a Big Dipper in the history of human social thought. It became the object of many disciplines such as philosophy, law, literature, ethics and psychoanalysis, especially feminism.

The writers saw the tragic beauty of heroic sacrifice from Antigone; the philosophers saw the collision of love and justice from Antigone; the jurists saw the conflicts between national law, natural law and human law from Antigone; politicians saw the opposition between human rights and sovereignty from Antigone; ethicists saw the incompatibility between incest and social order from Antigone; feminists saw the value of rebellion and resistance from Antigone.

Hegel used the example of "Antigone" when he talked about the fate of Socrates and praised her as "the most magnificent image that appeared on the ground". To become a subject of many disciplines, to become a topic of many people's comments, Antigone must be extraordinary. So, what charms did she have, which was worthy of interpretation for thousands of years, deserved the common concern of the West as well as China? That was the symbol, the symbol of Antigone— symbolizing freedom, justice and death. She was a symbol, representing resistance-rebellion against the order of the patriarchal society, the rationality of the patriarchal society, the system of the patriarchal society, and the rule of law in the patriarchal society, she was a symbol, representing the thinking—thinking about the rule of law in human society, the order of human society, the rationality of human society and the system of human society. Whether it was a symbol or an animal of thought, Antigone was a kind of existence that transcends reality.

II Plots of the Story

Oedipus, the king of Thebes, killed his father and married his mother and then has two sons and two daughters. One son was Polyneices, the other was Eteocles; one daughter was Antigone, another daughter was Ismene.Polyneices and Eteocles competed for the throne and fought each other. Polyneices encircled Thebes with the army of the father-in-law of Argos. At last two men died in the battlefield. Creon, the younger brother of Oedipus's mother (wife), Oedipus's brother-in-law (a little nephew) succeeded to inherit the throne of the city of Thebes. In order to punish the traitor, Creon ordered not to bury Polyneices, the offender. The daughter of Oedipus, Antigone, held a symbolic funeral for the dead brother, who secretly sprinkled a layer of soil on the body of the Polyneices. This act of Antigone challenged Creon's decree and caused her own death. The sister Ismene tried to persuade Antigone but was rebuked by Antigone. After Antigone was detained, Ismene said that she would go to die with her sister and was rejected by Antigone.

The reason for Antigone doing this was that even if her brother was a traitor, he should be buried, because it was the eternal unwritten law that the gods have made for the dead. Creon also found an excuse for Antigone, but Antigone did not give up her responsibility. Creon sentenced Antigone to death in anger and soon closed her to the tomb and let her die naturally.

Antigone's fiance, Haimon, son of Creon, went to his father and hoped that he could listen to the voice of the people. However, Creon not only insisted on his own way, but also rebuked his son. In the end, Haimon committed suicide for love and the mother of Haimon, the wife of Creon, also committed suicide. As a result, Creon really became a "loner" and was caught in extreme pain.

Ⅲ　Antigone's "Heroism Complex"

There are many interpretations in later generations about this motif derived from ancient Greek myth. One of the most famous is Hegel's interpretation and Hegel's interpretation has triggered more interpretations, including Holderlin, Heidegger, Derrida, Lacan and Irigary. The interpretations of Zizek, Judith Butler and Martha Nussbaum were particularly eye-catching. The interpretations of these later generations are carried out from different angles such as ethics, philosophy, psychoanalysis and feminism, therefore the meaning of this motif is unprecedentedly excavated and the human thought is further expanded on the basis of continuous enrichment.

Although the domestic research on Antigone is limited in the jurisprudential circle, the introduction of research on Antigone abroad has gradually broadened this field of research, especially Bernardette's research on classical philology. The introduction of Martha Nussbaum's literary research of ancient Greek ethics (philosophy) has led to the domestic reflection of the ancient Greek mythological motif of Antigone a new understanding of meaning.

In the process of combing the study of the "Antigone" motif, the first thing that could not be avoided was the myth of ancient Greece. In ancient Greek mythology, Antigone had the "heroism complex" that the ancient Greeks highly praised. In the cultural atmosphere of the ancient Greeks, "to be brave" and "the pursuit of honor" were always regarded by the ancient Greeks as "virtue". The reason why

Antigone was put into history and became "classic" lies in the virtue of her brave qualities and the "pursuit of honor". Although in Hegel's interpretation, Antigone's "bravery" and her "pursuit of honor" were somewhat stubborn and one-sided, she was still a heroine. Especially in the interpretation of feminism, Antigone was a model that dared to resist the patriarchal society and was a model that all women should follow.

In the later generations, all the praises of Antigone's "romantic complex" and the affirmation of Antigone's "Socratic martyrdom" come from the standpoint of ancient Greek mythology. However, in the interpretation of the original form of ancient Greek mythology, Antigone was not a representative of family ethical entities as it was located in Hegel's interpretation—because there was no "ethical entity" in the age of the story. Even the feminist interpretation of Antigone was also "biased" because feminist researchers believed that the antithesis between Antigone and Creon was the opposition between men and women. That was to say, Antigone in the interpretation of ancient Greek mythology was not like in Hegel's interpretation— "consciously brave"; likewise, Antigone in the interpretation of ancient Greek mythology is a "hero", but not a hero in feminist interpretation with consciousness of gender. In other words, the "Antigone's heroic complex" in the interpretation of ancient Greek mythology was only a simple "heroism complex" without any added meanings by later generations.

Restoring Antigone's "Heroic Complex" to the "Heroic Era", we would find that the opposition between Antigone and Creon was the opposition between men and women(Although they themselves did not have such awareness.) The factors that trigger this kind of opposition were the change of social form, the improvement of social system and the change of social concept.

On one hand it is the decline of family ethics, on the other hand it is the rise of city-state politics, but the relationship between them did not eventually form a stable pattern in terms of system or general social ideology. Antigone and Creon represented these two equally reasonable demands though unconsciously.

The story of Antigone occurred in the era of heroes (according to the records of ancient Greek mythology). The qualifier of "heroes" indicates that the city-states were not really established at the time and people were still limited to their natural feelings, that was, the family ethics they were used to. Even Sophocles's "Antigone" was difficult to accept Aristotle's point of view—this was a socio-political ideology after the establishment of the city-state: people were city-state animals, but city-states inherently ahead of and different from any other social group including the family.The political authority of the heroic era often came from those who were brave and noble and whose family, both has political authority noble bloodtie. But in the city-state, a political authority system has been formed, which was often formed by means of major political events, military conflicts or other unexpected events. The most famous event was Trojan War, which was almost contemporaneous with the story of Antigone.

In the Trojan War, Achilles showed an unstoppable "Heroic Complex", even if he would sacrifice his life for it. The same was true of Antigone. In the era of heroes, the emphasis on personal glory was particularly emphasized. Although this pursuit of honor sometimes seemed reckless (Antigone) and sometimes even fierce (Achilles), but this was the true state of life of the ancient Greeks. For Achilles, only the "honor" could be worthy of his noble origin—the son of the goddess of the sea; for Antigone, to resist the order of Creon was worthy of the noble status of her royal family members. In the era of heroes, only brave ones were noble, only noble people could become rulers—Antigone was convinced of this—so she refused Ismene's request and laughed at her. At this point, Antigone differed from Achilles: Antigone was a member of the royal family and Achilles was not, so Achilles pursues only "honor" but Antigone pursues not only honor but also dignity. In addition to the pursuit of "honor", she also paid attention to the nobleness of her behavior. In other words, Antigone believed that her behavior was noble, only she was worthy of the title of the royal family while Ismene was not worthy.

Under the condition that there was no strong and universally effective political and legal order in ancient times, this highly individualized personality could replace the political system. On one hand, this "hero's personal charm" was the guarantee of domination, but on the other hand, this "heroism" or "individualism" has become an obstacle to the political system of mature society, because it may have a strong conflict with national laws. First of all, a strong personal honor, or a hero's individual, was the exclusion of political order and bureaucratic system. In the era of worshiping heroes, people supported more of the sacredness of blood and the courage and charm of the individual. This was an ancient individualism built on the family. If the political and legal system has taken shape, then the character of this individual heroism would also resist, exclude and hinder the effective functioning of the system. The heroism of Antigone has confirmed this.

The heroism of Antigone was not only individualistic but also aristocratic. An ordinary person could not have this mentality. It was only in her previous living environment that she could cultivate her aristocratic mentality that ignored the consequences of behavior and was so arrogant. This was a fearless spirit, of course exciting, but not a wise action, especially for a growing city-state, which may be devastating.

The conflict between Antigone and Creon took place in the context of such a social change. At the beginning of the story, Antigone's family has collapsed. In a certain sense, what Oedipus did meant that the blood-stricken society had already broken. The meeting of the two brothers and swordsmen meant that the blood relationship has been unable to resolve the political conflict. In this social context, Creon represented the political system that was being formed and was not yet stable, while Antigone represented the decline of blood—stricken system which was still influential and would never disappear completely. In this sense, Creon represented a driving force of change, and Antigone represented a conservative force. Although "to be radical" and "to be conservative" didn't contain derogatory or complimentary meaning.

Although it was a "representative", in fact, both Creon and Antigone had no sober consciousness. That was to say, Creon did not realize that he represented the emerging political system and Antigone did not realize that she represented the blood-tie political system which was withdrawing from the historical stage. What Creon could be sure of is that what he did would consolidate the development of the city-state and consolidate his rule. What Antigone could be sure of is that what she did would preserve the ancient law. If Creon was more cautious, or Antigone was more sensible, if both of them were not stubborn in their own values or principles, then this tragic collision between the old and new systems could be avoided.

Antigone was tragic because the time of her past life has passed and would never come back. The era in which she lives now no longer needed heroes, nor did it allow the aristocratic mindset to exist (this was not to say that the nobility did not exist, but that the aristocratic spirit no longer existed). However, she was not aware of this. Creon was also tragic. He was driven by the pressure of social change, responsible for the city state and the future, although this responsibility was also beneficial to himself. But he was confronted by conservatives supporting the family ethics and ideology which have been established for a long time. It meant failure or even sacrifice. Therefore, although Creon has political power, which seemed to be very powerful, but this power was unstable during this transition period. He was just a tyrant.

Ⅳ Conclusion

Justice was also an unchanging topic. Since ancient Greek mythological era, there has been Athena representing justice; to the time of classical rationalism, there was also Socrates' determination of the virtue of justice. Justice was not only the appeal of philosophy, the goal of law, but also the means of politics. The pursuit of justice never left the history of human civilization. As a result, there was the trial of Orestes who killed his mother, there was the judgment of Socrates, there was also the death of Antigone. Justice was a banner which always guided the advancement of human society—philosophical justice, legal justice, political justice, moral justice. Human beings constantly revised their own thoughts and behaviors and constantly moved toward perfection. However, justice was also an excuse.It always tempted the advancement of human society—the justice of war, the justice of autocracy and the justice of persecution. Mankind constantly seek excuses for their own mistakes and find legitimate reasons for their greed. Therefore, it was the justice that Creon believed, the justice that Antigone believed and the justice that Socrates believed. What was justice? What kind of justice was public and universal?

Death, like freedom and justice, was also a constant topic. No one could get rid of its entanglement, and no one could escape its control. To be or not to be— the question that Shakespeare's melancholy Danish prince has been thinking and always confused that still made us think and puzzle us. For five hundred years, this question has been plaguing us, or when humans began to think, this question began to plague us. For this question, all kinds of people think in a variety of ways, all kinds of thinking have a variety of answers, but these various answers can not get rid of our confusions. Why? This is a paradox, this is the mystery of the Sphinx—this mystery will not disappear because of the Sphinx's suicide, because of the wisdom of Oedipus. We could choose death for freedom, or death for justice. However, we could not answer the question of justice, freedom and death.

Antigone was such a huge metaphor. In this metaphor, freedom, justice and death were closely intertwined—you had no way of distinguishing, freedom and death, justice and death, freedom and justice, but you knew very well that they were all embodied in Antigone. This was the eternal paradox, this was the eternal Antigone.

（张振宇译）

Chapter 3   The Ancient Greek City-state and Politics

01   The Founding of Ancient Polis System

I   The Civilization of the Mycenae

Homer's Epic depicted the civilization of the Mycenaean. The modern archaeology discovered the pottery, sculptures, tools, tombs, architecture of the Mycenaean and unearthed the city of Troy depicted in Homer's Epic. Archaeological evidence shows that the Mycenaean people were engaged in hackers, pirates, small-scale manufacturing and a little agriculture between the rich East and the wilderness of the Northwest. They plundered weak and backward neighbors, traded with powerful countries which weren't easy to plunder and sold weapons, slaves, wood, raw materials, metal tools, jewelry, spices and leather. Its trade network from eastern coast of Asia Minor Peninsula to the west coast of South Italy and Sicily, the French coastal region, Spain and even the British Isles. Like their descendants, the Mycenaean people failed to overcome difficult geographical conditions to build a unified empire and established many small kingdoms only on the Greek and Aegean islands. But the social management of those small countries has reached a fairly high standard. The government archives of Pylos found in Greece showed that the centralized rule of the royal family was achieved through a well-organized and complex bureaucratic system which managed tax collection, distribution of goods and religious life. And there were oversight agents to control corruption and correct administrative errors. This specialized institution obviously didn't belong to the agricultural society. These small countries were politically unrelated to each other, but they were highly consistent in language and culture, indicating that their business and cultural exchanges were very close. An expert on the history of western civilization commented on the achievements of the Mycenaean people. The civilization at its peak was more developed than the Greek civilization in the 6th B.C. The first half of the 6th B.C. was the Solon era in Athens and the second half was the time of the tyrant of Peisistratos.

II The Invasion of the Dorians and the "Heroic Era"

Around 1200 B.C., the end of the Shang Dynasty in ancient China, the 200-year prosperity of the Mycenaean civilization was suddenly interrupted. Some barbarian tribes who spoke another Greek dialect invaded from the north. They entered the Greek region. These tribes, known as Dorians, destroyed the Mycenaean civilization. Some Mycenaean people fled east to the "Attica flatland" (Attica was the area of Athens) which was not trampled by iron hooves, and the islands of the Aegean Sea and the coast of Asia Minor, such as the later revival base Ionian. The Trojan War broke out in the Aegean coast of Asia Minor around 1190 B.C. (the eve of the beginning of the Western Zhou Dynasty in ancient China). That was about an episode of the escape of the Mycenaean. In the four hundred years before the 8th B.C., Greece and the Aegean region fell into what the historians called the "dark ages". The ancient Greeks, who were descendants of the Dorian and the Mycenaean, were called "The Homer's Epic". It was the "heroic era", an era in which giants walked on the earth and left countless miracles. Archaeological findings showed that the links between the various tribal kingdoms in Greece were interrupted and different dialects and different pottery styles were formed. Since the two neighboring empires were also under aggression and chaos, the connection between Greece and the East was interrupted. The skills of writing have been lost, the majestic palace has collapsed, the Greek merchant ships on the Mediterranean have disappeared, commercial wealth has disappeared, and a large number of gold and silver products have ceased to appear in the tombs. The entire region has retreated to a simple and agricultural society. However, the Greeks who spoke different dialects still can communicate with each other, and the Mycenaean civilization hasn't been completely destroyed. Later, some important parts of the ancient Greek civilization were the replicas of the Mycenaean civilization. Sparta, representing the Dorian civilization, turned the descendants of the Mycenaean into slaves.

Ⅲ The Significance of Mycenaean Civilization

The rise and fall of the Mycenaean civilization has something in common with the history of other civilizations in the world: no matter what kind of political system was advanced or backward or pursued, military security was the ultimate guarantee. A kind of civilization that was incapable of maintaining its own security was a weak one. In other words, the rise and fall of the nation wasn't only related to the political system of civilization, but also to the continued possession of a strong military force. A political system that cannot maintain a strong military force was the one with major flaws.

Although it wasn't a perfect era, it was an era in which human beings could pursue freedom and publicity. People lived, not for worship, but for seeking, perceiving, thinking and self-realization. Therefore, Socrates of this era said: Unexplored life is not worthy. Although there was no modern technology in this era, its bright, pure and divine style of freedom was rarely seen in the history of mankind for thousands of years. Why is the Aegean Sea still so beautiful and blue today? Because on this vast sea surface, the eternal breeze has been telling Homer's heroic stories and legends of the gods.

Ⅳ Ancient Greek Social Structure and City Politics

The history of the Greek city-state politics is a history of heroic creation and a history of social structure of balance of class forces. In other words, it is the history created by the hero together with the people. When China entered the Spring and Autumn Period (722 B.C.), that was, in the late 8ᵗʰ B.C., the free farmer forces in Greece suddenly increased, interrupting the slow process of the aristocratic class expanding the arable land and turning the farmers into serfs. The sudden change in the contrast of class forces triggered a general political crisis in ancient Greece at the time.

The situation of traditional Chinese society was superior. It wasn't only a society where free farmers were the mainstay, but also a unified empire structure to support the development of civilization. Due to the traffic difficulties caused by geographical conditions, it was difficult for ancient Greece to form a large empire. However, due to the simple peasant living habits inherited from the dark period, a large number of small-scale peasant economy have always existed in the "dark ages" of Greece and haven't evolved into a subsidiary of aristocratic families like the developed empire in the Near East. The sudden increase in the number and power of free small farmers in ancient Greece was related to the widespread use of iron and to military inventions that emerged from colonial expansion.

The city-state wasn't a city at first, but a settlement based on tribal blood relations. Some settlements have gradually developed into commercial and official business centers and later appeared temples, other public buildings, and the Senate Square appeared. With different religious groups as the core, different city-states have their own special identity and the tribal blood consciousness has gradually faded. Then a spirit similar to today's patriotism appeared in the foreign war. To substitute religious superstition and individualism became the pillars of the cohesiveness of the ancient Greek city-states. The first and initial political consequences of the city-state were the disappearance of the king and the establishment of aristocratic rule. The "king" of the ancient Greek region was roughly equivalent to the chieftain, and bravery and family wealth were the basis of this position. However, this "king" was powerless to force the entire community to pay taxes regularly, with weak financial status and limited organizational capacity. After the advent of the heavy armored infantry era, the dominance of the "king" was gradually replaced by aristocratic groups. The second political consequence of the city-state was that the rule of the aristocratic oligarchy was challenged by its own factional contradictions and the heavy armored class. Individual autocracy was the simplest and most common solution and the authoritarian often opposed the noble class and was the most attractive to civilians. The third political consequence of the city-state was that citizens continued to seek the ideal form of government in order to build a stable and neutral public authority and recognized social justice at that time, the primary rule of law or the oligarchic rule was the result of their search. The fourth political consequence of the city-state was that all social and economic groups sought for government responsibility for their own interests, and the civilian society, which accounts for the majority of the population, has led to the emergence of direct democracy.

V　Conclusion

The political system of ancient Greece was diversified, which was related to the dramatic social changes with that era and to the different social conditions and historical traditions of the city-states and regions. People could comment on the merits and demerits of the system, but all the realities must have their causes. For social scientists, not all causes can be summarized by subjective will and values. Social composition was the reason why this wasn't subjective. Therefore, the preference for a certain political system may lead to the emergence or even establishment of such a system, but the same system cannot lead to the same result in different places.

（吴瑞丰译）

02　The Differences between Athens and Sparta

I　Introduction

Athens and Sparta were the two largest and most representative slavery city-states in ancient Greece. Comparing Athens and Sparta, on one hand, there are some similarities between them: firstly, they are the two most powerful city-states in ancient Greece; secondly, they are both small countries with few people. Because of geographical constraints, the development of Athens and Sparta was limited. Thirdly, they were both slavery states, and there was a noble slave-owner class in them, which had a great influence on the political system of ancient Greece. On the other hand, there are many differences between them. To know the differences between Athens and Sparta, you need to know how the two polis developed. Through the analysis of the development process of Athens and Sparta,

We would find many inspirations.

Ⅱ Formation of Athens and Sparta

Greek polis, represented by Athens and Sparta, experienced a period of prosperity in the 5th B.C. It declined gradually from the 4th B.C. As the polarization between the rich and the poor among citizens intensified, the relationship between citizenship and land became more and more relaxed, the contradictions among citizens'collectives increased, and the civil service system began to disintegrate. The conquest of Alexander, the Great of Macedonia in 338 B.C. and the enslavement of Greece by many kings in the Hellenistic era of 323-30 B.C. deprived most of the Greek city-states of their political independence, disintegrated the original collective citizens, and transformed them into local autonomous units under huge centralized jurisdiction.

1. Athens

Athens was located in the Attica Peninsula southeast of Central Greece. Around 1600 B.C., the Ionians entered Attica and lived a clan-tribal life, living with the local residents of Pelasgians. In Homer's era, the phenomenon of mixed living has become more and more serious, and class contradictions and social divisions have been aggravated. In order to adapt to this situation and change this situation, the legendary hero King Theseus reformed. He unified the divisive parts of the Attica Peninsula, established the Central Council and the Government of Athens to replace the local councils and governments, and formulated the first Constitution of Athens. Another important content of Theseus' reform was to classify domestic citizens into three levels: aristocrats, peasants and handicraftsmen. It stipulates that aristocrats hold office and enforce laws. Peasants and handicraftsmen have only one seat in the National Assembly and must not be in power. In this way, the distinction between aristocracy and citizenship (peasants and handicraftsmen) was obvious, laying the foundation for the aristocratic politics of Athens in the future. This reform actually reflected the historic transformation of Athens from tribe to state on the basis of class differentiation. Theseus was also regarded as the founder of Greek state. It was generally believed that this marked the beginning of Athens' national form. Around 700 B.C., Attica had formed a united slavery state centered around Athens. In the 8th B.C., the monarchy declined and the regime was ruled by clan nobles. Since 682 B.C., the consul has been elected once a year. In the 7th B.C., nine consuls were in charge of the Supreme administrative, military, judicial and religious affairs of the country.

2. Sparta

Sparta was located in the Laconian plain southeast of the Peloponnesus Peninsula. Its inhabitants were formerly Dorian and non-native. During the Mycenaean Civilization (about the first half of the 16th B.C. to the 12th B.C.), there was a country in Laconia. Around the 11th B.C., the Dorians invaded Laconia and destroyed the original country after a long struggle. The Spartans depreciated the local inhabitants of Spartan lands and wealth as "Pelasgians" (free people, with autonomy but without citizenship of Spartan city-states), suppressed the rebels who were dissatisfied with Spartan rule, and degraded their status as "Helots", also known as "Black Rovers" (agricultural slaves owned by Spartan collectives). About the 10th B.C., the Dorians established Sparta. The city consisted of five villages, which formed a new political center. Though it was called a city, in fact, it has neither walls nor decent streets. In the mid-eighth century B.C., Spartans colonized and invaded Mycenaean, in order to solve the shortage of land due to the intensification of social differentiation and population growth of Spartans themselves. Historically, it was called the First Mycenaean War (about 740 B.C. to 720 B.C.). As a result, the Spartans occupied the whole of Mycenaean and turned its inhabitants into Helot people. The encroached land was divided between Spartans and Pelasgians. Spartans were dispensed to into plains and Pelasgians to mountains. Around 640 B.C. to 620 B.C., the Mycenaeans could not endure slavery and oppression and held an uprising (historically known as the Second Mycenaean War). Though it was the heavy blow to Spartans, they still failed in the end.

Ⅲ   Differences between Athens and Sparta

Sparta and Athens, as two great city-states in Peloponnesus Peninsula, deserved to be two famous city-states in ancient Greece. They had strong military power, and each of them had established a military alliance to dominate Greece. They were typical slavery city-states, which were representative economically and politically.

They all attached importance to sports. Women took part in sports as men did. However, there were many differences between Sparta and Athens due to the specific geographical environment and historical conditions. This chapter discusses the differences of Athens and Sparta.

1. Economic Situation

The development of slavery economy in Greece can be divided into two types: Spartan type and Athen type. Sparta was located in the Laconia Plain, the south was sea-bound and surrounded by mountains on three sides, and the central part was irrigated by the Juroda River. The mild climate and fertile soil determine that Sparta was a city-state dominated by agriculture. Sparta also implemented land state ownership, using state-owned agricultural slaves, mostly from the inhabitants of captured and conquered areas. Although Athens was based on agriculture, its industry and commerce were relatively developed, and cash crops played an important role in agriculture. For example, grapes, olives and other crops; Athens mountain area was rich in mineral resources, such as marble, silver ore, pottery and so on, which provided great convenience for the development of handicraft industry in Athens. The source of slaves was also different from Sparta. They were mostly bought through the market and used in all aspects of social life.

As far as Greece was concerned, there were three situations in which slaves were used in agriculture at that time: first, Spartan state-owned slavery, in which all state-owned slaves Helots served as agricultural labor. Such slavery was often established by conquest. Secondly, the slaves were used in aristocratic farmland, it was the concentrated way of using private slaves in agriculture, but on a small scale and not very common. Thirdly, slaves were owned and used by farmers or small farmers, it was the most developed form of agricultural slave economy in this period. In addition, slaves were also widely used in handicraft industry, industry and commerce, mining and housework. This situation was more common in Athens and other city-states where industry and commerce were prospered. This reflected that the privatization of Greek society was more thorough at that time, and the principle of market exchange played a very important role in social life.

2. Political Situation

With regard to the development of Athenian democracy, there are three main stages:

(1) Break the descent and open the forerunner. The "Solon Reform" in 594 B.C. abolished all debts of Athenian citizens mortgaged by their own life, prohibiting the borrowing of debts by their own life, and forbidding the conversion of indebted civilians into slaves. The state paid money to redeem those who had been sold as foreign slaves because they were unable to pay their debts, and abolished the "61 Han" system (civilians were unable to pay their debts and had to cultivate land for debtors). There are different opinions about tax rates in academic circles at home and abroad. According to Aristotle's account, the tax rate is five-sixths, and they can only keep one-sixths. It is called "61 Han". This measure is historically known as the "Decree of Removing Taxes". Abolish the monopoly power of hereditary aristocrats, and no longer classify citizens according to their origin and the number of property. To establish 400-member council as permanent organs of the citizens' congresses and as the Supreme Administrative organs. To establish the Supreme Jury Court, and any citizen has the right to appeal. At the same time, a new code was enacted to replace Draco's harsh laws.

(2) Eliminate the property restrictions. The keratsini reform in 508 B.C. redistricted Athens and reorganized the whole Athenian tribal system; Established a "500-member council" to replace "400-member council" and opened it to citizens at all levels; Normalized the Civil Assembly and the People's Court Activities; Enacted the "Pottery Banishment Law"; Established the "Ten General Committees".

(3) The heyday. After the 5th B.C., especially after the Greco—Persian Wars, the democratic politics of Athens attained the heyday. From 443 B.C. to 429 B.C., Pericles was successively elected Chief General of the Athens Ten General Committee, and since then the "Pericles Age" has been created. Specifically, there are the following measures:All adult male citizens can hold all official positions; Establish the status of "Citizens'Congress", "Five Hundred Meetings" and "Jury Court";Remove the restrictions on acquiring the status of "Athenian Citizen". The democratic politics of Athens, represented by the Pericles, is an advanced political system in the ancient Greek city-state society. It is conducive to mobilize the enthusiasm and creativity of the citizens of the city-state and promote the progress

of social economy and culture.

Sparta, on the other hand, belonged to the aristocratic republic. The main political organs of the city-state included: (1) two kings. Each inherited by two royal families. The main power was in religion and military. In peacetime, he presided over state sacrifices and handled family law cases. In wartime, one king led the army and the other stayed. Because the two kings had equal power, they often restricted each other, which limited their sovereignty. (2) Presbyterian Meeting. The two kings were members, with other 28 members. The presbyters served for the whole life, and when they were vacant, they were selected from citizens over 60 years of age to make up for their vacancies. The Presbyterian Council prepared resolutions for the National Assembly, presided over criminal trials and handled state administrative affairs. (3) Citizens'Congress. It was composed of all Spartan male citizens over 30 years of age. Citizens may vote on bills and elect officials in the General Assembly, but they could not put forward bills. The way of voting in the National Assembly was generally based on the voice of the participants, so it may not be able to truly express the will of citizens. (4) Five Ombudsmen. Every Spartan citizen had the rights to be elected. It was said that the Ombudsman was an assistant judicial official of the king. Around the time of the conquest of Mycenaean, their power gradually increased, not only to supervise all the officials of the Spartan city-state, but also to try and even execute the king. Each time the king went out, two ombudsmen or inspectors accompanied him and supervised him on the spot. In order to suppress the numerous and highly resistant slaves, the Spartan city-state stipulated a strict system of civil military training. After the birth, the citizen's child was not allowed to be adopted until he or she has passed the physical examination. Boys left their families at the age of 7 and joined the children's company. They received preliminary organizational and disciplinary training, and strict military and sports training after the age of 12. When a man married in adulthood, he must live in a military camp, take part in meals and exercises, and not retire until he is 60 years old.

3. Women's Status

Women's Status in Athens was lower than that in Sparta. The loss of women's rights in Athens can be reflected by the change of their names. The term "Athenian" refers to an male adult who has acquired Athenian citizenship and the Athenian citizenship excluded women completely. According to the official documents of Athens, "Athenians and their wives and children".

It reflected that the Athenian women are "adherents" of adult male and this is guaranteed by Athenian law. In addition, in Athens, men were actively encouraged to learn how to read and write, but because women did not allow to participate in political affairs, Athenians believed that there was no reason for women to become educated people. Although some Athenian women were educated, the number was small. Among the educated people in Athens, the proportion of gender was very wide. Family was the basic unit of economic activities in ancient Athenian society, and also the main place for Athenian women's activities. Athenian women had no economic autonomy and could not manage or control their dowry or inherit any property. Athens law stipulated: "The law specifically forbids a minor to enter into any contract, or a woman to sign a contract with a price of more than one wheat doll." The most important duty of the Athenian wife was to have legal offspring for her husband and to ensure the continuity of the family. This was what made a wife different from other women.

Compared with Athens, Spartan women's education has improved slightly. In Sparta, boys were educated to be militias, so men had little time for cultural education. Girls spent most of their time with their mothers and other older women and did not have to take part in productive labor, so they had a lot of time to spend on education. In addition, two famous female poets were produced in Sparta: Megalostrata and Cleitagora. In addition, Sparta has a cultural overlap with Samos, Pythagoras'home town. According to Iamblichus, among of the 235 students of Pythagoras, 17 and 18 are women, one third of whom were Spartan women. It is worth mentioning that Spartans believed in Pythagoras as long as Pythagoras established a corresponding system for people's daily life, including dietary taboos and proper seasons for sexual intercourse. Spartans were familiar with the precepts of the whole social life and even the minor details of life. In Sparta, there is only one main task for all citizens, that is, to defend the country. Children's public education and men's life-long collective life, thus dispelled the family role of women. Women's function is to give birth to a strong baby for the country; to stimulate men with language and sex to die for the country. Spartan women will never mourn the death of their husbands because they have no fixed husbands. Leggs, the country's legislator, argued that monogamy was ridiculous. It is ridiculous that people try to choose strong and beautiful mating varieties for their pets, but they want to monopolize women to have children for themselves at home, even if the man has all kinds of defects and diseases. Therefore, in Sparta, only the strong have the rights to bear offspring. In terms of sexual relations, women not only have the initiative, but also their temporary husbands often give their wives to the strong. This is the so-called "co-wife system".

Generally speaking, in terms of women's social status, although in ancient Greek city-states, even in Athens, the low status of women was a common phenomenon. But in Sparta, women's social status was higher than that of other city states.It mainly reflected in some sections as followings: ①Spartan women enjoyed the rights of inheritance, they could have disposable property; ② Spartan women enjoyed the right to education; ③the weakening of the role of the Spartan family, liberated the absolute bondage of men to women; ④ the open sexual mind liberated women.

4. Educational condition

Athens's education emphasized that through physical, moral, intellectual and aesthetic training, the educatee could be trained to be a citizen with good physique, noble sentiment, extensive cultural attainment and intellectual development, multi-faceted interest and good speech, that is, "body and mind are both beautiful and good". Boys and girls before the age of 7 received physical and mental education at home. At the age of seven, boys attended privately charged Athens grammar and music schools, but they lived at home and attended school with servants. Grammar school was an enlightenment education, learning the basic knowledge of reading, writing and calculating. Music schools taught children to play musical instruments. They also taught Homer's epic and lyrics, accompanied by music for children to sing while playing, in order to cultivate students'sense of beauty, rhythm and melody.They attached importance to the musical education to cultivate the sentiment through music and foster the morality. Teenagers aged 12 to 13 attended gymnastics schools while studying in music schools. In addition to the five competitions of running, long jump, wrestling, discus throwing and bidding gun, the contents of education include swimming, dancing and boxing, so as to make young people strong, well-proportioned and healthy in shape, and to cultivate moral qualities such as toughness, courage and restraint. After graduating from music and gymnastics schools, young people aged 15-16 finish their basic education. Most of them were employed to earn a living. A few children of rich families could enter the national three-dimensional gymnasium to receive education of harmonious physical and mental development. Physical education was still dominated by pentathlon, but more attention is paid to running and wrestling. He also learned military techniques such as horse riding, archery and driving. In addition to teaching grammar, rhetoric and philosophy which are closely related to speeches, they also taught spiritual and aesthetic classes through playing, singing and dancing, and organized students to participate in practical activities such as religious sacrifices, social celebrations, public gatherings and court trials to carry out political and moral education. From the age of 18, those who have been examined as descendants of formal citizens could be promoted to Everby and receive two years of formal military training. Since then, he needed to serve in the city army for one year, learning to refit infantry training and weapon use. In the second year, he received a spear and a shield from the state, defended the frontier or learned to sail. When they reach the age of 20, they could participate in state affairs by obtaining formal citizenship through certain ceremonies.

Spartan education is mainly military education because of the hierarchy of Spartan society. Spartans of the first rank should rule the second and third ranks. If a few Spartans wanted to rule the majority of slaves and free people, they had to carry out the responsibility of militarizing the whole people and carry out military training. This also determined that Sparta's nature of education belonged to the integration of military and peasant education, that is, the education system had the purpose of training soldiers who are brave and good at fighting. Spartans were put to the test of life when they were babies. Their parents scrubed them with alcoholic spirits, and then let the elders check their health. Anyone who failed to stand the test or was considered weak by the elders was abandoned in the nursery. Seven-year-old boys enter the country's coaching institutes, and from then on they had to undergo the tempering of their hearts and bones to form the qualities of toughness, bravery, ferocity, brutality, alertness and obedience. The main form of training was fighting. The life system in the training center was very strict. The children were barefoot all year round, wearing only a single dress. They ate meals that were not enough for their stomachs during the day and slept on rough reed mats at night. Those who could tolerate or made a living by robbery would be rewarded. In addition to military sports training, music and dance were also Spartan ways of education. They believed that music can cultivate the spirit of worship and martial arts, dance could train and coordinate the rhythm of physical activity. They should also receive the moral education of slave owners regularly, and cultural knowledge was not valued. Eighteen-year-olds would receive regular military training. The Youth Corps should organize at least one military "exercise", that is, to surround, beat and kill slaves wantonly by means of sudden attacks at night, in order to exercise character and ability. Young people aged 20 or over should practice martial arts all the year round. They could not finish their education and training until they were 30 years old and became a real soldier and citizen. Sparta also adopted the same military and sports training methods for women, such as walking race, discus throwing, bidding gun, fighting and so on. For women, such training has another important significance, that is, to help strong women produce strong children after marriage.

According to the above educational situation in Sparta and Athens, we can draw the following conclusions: ①the educatee are different: Athens's democratic politics stipulates that the educated are all citizens of Athens, while Sparta's educated are only Spartans, the Pelasgians and the Helots have no rights of education. ②the contents of education are different: Athens's democratic politics stipulates the all—round education while Sparta pays attention to military training and physical exercise. ③ The purpose of education is different: Spartan military education is mainly for expanding territory to the outside world and suppressing slaves of the inside. Athens's education is for better development of the country and take this as the training goal. It needs to cultivate citizens with high quality, good quality, versatility and strong body.

Ⅳ Conclusion

Through analyzing the two big city-states, Sparta and Athens, we can draw a conclusion: Athens is an open and outward city-state with features of freedom,progress and democracy, which ultimately develops a big relative developed city-state in different aspects, such as politics,economy and culture and so on. While although the politics of oligarchy in Sparta is less open, tolerant and progressive as the democratic politics in Athens, it is recorded by western constitutional thinkers as the classic cases of investigating the constitutional institution in ancient Greek.

（吴瑞丰译）

03 The Influence of Zeus' Theogony on Western Politics

Ⅰ Introduction

Greek mythology was born in primitive times. It has been circulated for thousands of years because of its fairly complete mythological system and unique literary charm. When we come into contact with Western culture, we will inevitably encounter allusions in Greek mythology. Almost all the classical literary works we are familiar with involve Greek mythology, and some of them even draw directly from Greek mythology. Therefore, the influence of Greek Mythology on religion, philosophy, thought, custom, natural science, literature and art of the whole West and even human beings is beyond doubt. However, through the power transfer of the three generations of Gods in ancient Greek mythology, we can see the change of Greek political thought. At the same time, its ideological changes are fully reflected in the political reality of ancient Greece. This is not only a direct manifestation of the concept of animism, but also a reflection of the ancient Greeks on nature and social system.

II Establishment of Zeus Theogony

1. The First Generation Gods

As the first descendants of the God of Origin, Uranus, the God of the sky, was very powerful compared with other gods. He monopolized the rights of mating and reproduction with Gaia. His children often trembled when they saw him, and Uranus called them Titans, meaning nervous people.

There are twelve Titans. They are Oceanus (The giant river which surrounding the world. Thales, the first philosopher in ancient Greece who believes that water is the essence of all things, the land is floating on the water, and the great reflects the idea vividly), Tethys (the goddess of the sea, the wife of Oceanus), Hyperion (high altitude), Theia (goddess of light, the wife of Hyperion), Phoebe (Oracle goddess), Coeus (celestial movement, Phoebe's husband), Iapetus (soul), Mnemosyne (memory, Zeus's wife, the mother of nine Muses), Themis (Law and Justice, the wife of Zeus, the mother of the three goddess of time and the three goddess of destiny), Crius (celestial bodies), Rhea (space, the wife of Kronus), and Kronus (the husband of Time and Rhea). The narrow sense of the Titans is these twelve, and the broad sense of the Titans include all ancient gods.

2. The Second Generation Gods

Owing to Uranus's obsession with power and exclusive maternity rights with his mother Gaia, the children (12 Titans, 3 one-eyed giants and 3 hundred-armed giants) were all pushed into Gaia's stomach. Gaia was sad. She encouraged the children to rebel against their father. The Titans were horrified by the idea, but only the smallest Titan, Kronus, bravely agreed to their mother. Gaia handed him a sickle. When Uranus was ready to mate with Gaia, Kronus cut off Uranus's genitals with a sickle. Uranus floated to the highest place in the world in pain and cursed that Kronus would be overthrown by his own children. The genitals of Uranus fell into the sea, in which Aphrodite, the God of love and beauty, was born; the blood of Uranus formed the vengeance goddess and the giant.

Kronus became second king. But Kronus knew the strength of the one-eyed giants and hundred-handed brothers, believing that their existence was a potential threat to his throne. For this reason, he caught them and imprisoned in the hell of Tartarus, the creator of hell.However, he could not rest at ease because of his father's curse, "You will also be overthrown by your son like me." To avoid this curse, Kronus made a cruel decision: to eat all the new-born children.

Rhea had five children for Kronus and all the babies were swallowed after birth. So after she gave birth to her sixth child, she was determined to preserve the boy and named the boy Zeus. She wrapped a stone in cloth and pretended that it was a newborn baby. Kronus did not hesitate to swallow the stone in one gulp. So Zeus escaped, and he was brought up by his uncle and aunt, ocean god Oceanus and sea goddess Thetis of the Twelve Titans.

When Zeus grew up, he knew his life and was determined to save his brothers. He married Metis, the daughter of Oceanus and Thetis, and then obeyed his wife's plan to prescribe drugs to his father, Kronus, then Kronus spit out the children. They were Hestia, Demeter, Hera, Hades and Poseidon. Then the children were taken away and adopted by the Oceanus and the Thetis in time. Finally Zeus joined five elder gods, and began to fight back against Kronus.

Later Zeus listened to the advice of his cousin Prometheus and rescued the family of the Cyclopes and Hecatonchires who were trapped by Kronus. Cyclopes was the greatest forging master in the whole universe, and Hecatonchires could throw 100 huge stones at a time. The great power made Titans impossible to resist. With the help of the God of fire, Hephaestus, the Cyclops built a lightning spear for Zeus, created Trident for Poseidon, and built two forks for Hades. Finally, Zeus won the battle with the help of giants.

3. Establishment of Zeus' Theogony

After the great victory of the Titan War, Zeus and his brothers confronted with how to distribute the world's domination. Seeing the conflicts among them, Prometheus, full of wisdom, proposed that the rule of the world should be decided by lots. According to the result of the lottery, Zeus was given the sky and became the God of heaven. Poseidon was given the sea and became the God of sea, and Hades was given the underworld, and became the God of hell. As for the earth, through consultation, the three brothers shareed it. Then Zeus fulfilled his promise to make Hera the queen of heaven, and shared power to control Olympia and the sky.

Zeus then imprisoned Kronus and the defeated Titans in the prisons of the Underworld. In order to avoid their escape, Zeus ordered Poseidon to build bronze doors, windows and walls around the prison, and to keep Hecatonchires and Cerberus in charge.

Then the third generation of Gods get their way and established a new governing structure: the three brothers headed by Zeus, and they three ruled together. The theogony included twelve main gods: Zeus (the King of gods, the God of thunder), Hera (Queen of gods, the goddess of marriage and fertility), Hestia (stove and family goddess), Poseidon (God of sea), Demeter (the goddess of agriculture and harvest), Athena (the goddess of war and wisdom), Apollo (the God of light,music, prophecy and medicine), Artemis (the goddess of hunting), Ares (the God of war and violence), Aphrodite (goddess of love and beauty), Hephaestus (the God of fire and craftsman), Hermes (the messenger of the gods, and the God of thieves, travellers and merchants). A new system was formed in which twelve main gods jointly took charge of Mount Olympus.

It is worth mentioning that Homer's attitude towards Zeus is different from Hesiod's. *Iliad* has the following description:

O goddess, the anger of Achilles son of Peleus, that brought countless ills upon the Achaeans.

Many a brave soul did it send hurrying down to Hades,

and many a hero did it yield a prey to dogs and vultures: then Zeus's will would come true.

Homer called the anger of heroes, mutually violent massacres, and even the number of dead bodies that could not be buried as "Zeus's will", which clearly emphasized the noble honor represented by heroes. In the eyes of the ancient Greeks, "Zeus's will" was undoubtedly the supreme rule, but between the lines Homer's criticism of Zeus's behavior were clear.

However, Hesiod had another attitude in *Theogony*:

This is the will of the great Zeus.

That's what the son of Kronus wants.

Zeus's will can not be deceived or evaded.

It is easy to see from the words of Hesiod, *Theogony* as a poem, that the theme of the divine spectrum is the generations of gods, but it puts all the faith in Zeus above everything else, and praises him wholeheartedly.

Ⅲ The Influence of Zeus' Theogony on Western Political Thought

The study of ancient Greece is not confined to religion and mythology. It was directed to politics at the beginning, and tried to grasp the development of politics through a series of social and ideological innovations. With the birth of the city-state system as a form of collective life, the emergence of politics was associated with those conditions. Ancient historians outlined a kind of "myth-religion-politics" ideological system and immediately applied it to the construction of city-state. The power submission system within the family, the moral dignity of the ruler, the armed forces, the power monopoly of communicating with God and the monopoly of wealth itself make the city-state grow rapidly and advance continuously. And the role of myth in the construction of city-state power can not be underestimated. It is myth that endows the system constructed with divinity and strengthens the political power of city-state through this divinity.

1. Power transition

From the rule of Uranus in the first generation to Zeus in the third generation, the way of power transition is bloody and violent. As mentioned above, Uranus was violently overthrown by his son, Kronus, and Kronus was overthrown by his son, Zeus. This is a way of power alternation through violent resistance. In short, it is a way of "oppression-resistance-alternation-expulsion". Take the third generation God Zeus as an example, Kronus feared the curse of Uranus, swallowed all his children, and put great pressure on the new gods; the earth mother Rhea saved Zeus, and prepared for the later resistance; Zeus liberated all brothers and sisters, overthrew the oppression of Kronus, and established a new God system headed by himself; after the establishment of the new god system, Zeus again expelled and suppressed Titans.

Such a way of power transition is similar to the "tyranny" appeared in ancient Greek polis, or it can be called "myth version tyranny system". Kronus adopted Gaia's suggestion and replaced Uranus by Violence. Like Kronus, Zeus chose a violent revolutionary way. He first united the other gods, and then contacted the previous Titans to resist together. This also reflects the role of King archon in Athens.

Zeus overthrew his father's rule and established a new order of rule: the twelve principal gods of Olympia. In ancient Greek mythology, the twelve main gods constructed a power structure with "one core, three elements and twelve juxtapositions". That is to say, Zeus was the head of the Twelve Gods, the king of the gods; Zeus, Poseidon, and Hades, the most important parts of the world: the sky, the sea, the underworld, and the twelve Olympians gods were co-managed. In addition, when the Olympus gods discussed events or discussed a certain matter, they all jointly participated in the discussion to express their views, which more or less affected the formation of the Western parliamentary system. It is this kind of assembly system that has evolved into the parliamentary system of western countries after a long history. Taking the British constitutional monarchy as an example, the constitutional system in Britain is based on the position that the monarch is ruled by the law. Parliament is the centre of state power. According to the concept of "separation of powers", the legislative, administrative and judicial powers are separated and restricted. Under the leadership of the Cabinet, the functional organs of the state deal with state affairs. This is the first time that ancient Greek mythology developed the political ideals in western history.

In the period of Zeus' rule, the negation of power was indispensable. To a large extent, the basis of Zeus's rule was its powerful force. In mythology, Zeus was never overthrown. Even the secret of overthrowing Zeus that Prometheus mastered was cleverly solved by Zeus. Since ancient times, though, dangers have lurked during the founding of new rule, the ancient Greeks did not completely destroy Zeus that ruled by force, but created a better vision. This is Athena, a symbol of democracy and wisdom. Ancient Greeks endowed her with supreme force and incomparable wisdom. The setting of Athena reflected the conflicts between patriarchy and matriarchy society and their conciliation. It is worth mentioning that with the advance of democratic reform, the status of women in the city states has risen to a new level.

2. Democratic Thought

In ancient Greek mythology, Athena was the first woman to appear as a powerful force, and the ancient Greeks also gave Athena democratic strategy. In the ancient Greek concept, democracy could be realized by the use of intelligence and the support of powerful force. Athena had both these two qualities. Especially during the heyday of Greece, the commercial prosperity of Athens was inseparable from Athena worship. Athena is the goddess of art, craft and women's handwork. With the worship of Athena, to some extent, Pericles promoted the development of the handicraft industry in the period of administration, and greatly promoted the development of Commerce. So when Athena was set up as a perfect ruler, there was already a great element of democracy in it. It was a way of using force with intelligence, and the reality continued this imagination, making it a pioneer of democracy in the ancient world.

3. Concept of Contract

In ancient Greek mythology, the operation of all divine institutions was based on rules, which were observed and implemented with the consent and approval of the gods. Prometheus violated the conventions of the divine realm and gave fire to the world. Zeus trapped him on a rock in the Caucasus Mountains and was pecked by a hawk. This mapping to the real life of ancient Greece at that time was a kind of contract consciousness that ancient Greeks recognized and abode the common system. If someone violated this system, they would be punished. Parliamentary system in the political system of western countries is also based on this sense of contract to a large extent. When the Olympian gods encounter anything or situation, they will gather to discuss and consult countermeasures. All gods have the rights to express their opinions. In ancient Greek city states, there are places for public assembly. These places are also the convenings of the ancient Greek City Council. After continuous development and evolution, they formed the parliamentary system in western countries' political system.

From the mythological system mentioned above, it is clear that the Greeks'overall identity and internal negativity of the system, to a large extent, resulted in the social contract and common bipartisan discrepancy in the political parliament in western politics. Taking the theory of social contract as an example, social contract is the inheritance of social contract by the people of all social strata. This kind of social contract is the affirmation of the system contained in ancient

Greek mythology and the materialization of the political expression in ancient Greek mythology.

4. Women's Status

In ancient Greek mythology, female gods represented more reason and wisdom than male gods. The mother of the earth, Gaia, as one of the gods of creation, was born after chaos, representing creation and destruction, order and chaos; Muses, the goddess of art and science; Athena is in charge of painting, gardening, courtroom, and so on, and Athena, with wisdom incarnation, is also the goddess of military and force. Correspondingly, in the social life of ancient Greece, female priests were generally in charge of oracles. In this way, it seems that, in ancient Greeks, wisdom belonged to women. But with the progress of civilization, the status of women began to decline. Athens' degree of civilization is higher than Sparta, so the status of women is lower than Spartan women.

IV   Conclusion

Ancient Greece is the birthplace of western democracy, which is also the greatest contribution to world civilization. Shelley, the English poet said, "We are all Greeks. Our laws, our literature, our religion are rooted in Greece." The word democracy, which we have been talking about all along, originated in ancient Greek. For democracy in ancient Greece is a democracy on the basis of slavery, it has its limitations and narrowness. After the hindrance and interruption of theology politics in western Europe during the middle age, the theory and practice of democracy in ancient Greece provided a source of thought and inspiration for the democratic system in western countries since the Renaissance and laid the foundation for modern western political system.

Through the creation and development of ancient Greek mythology, the ancient Greeks had a great influence on western political culture and western humanism. From the above we can see that the ancient Greeks as early as the 9th to the 8th centuries B.C. has already had the ideology of political power. This earliest Greek mythological thought is not only full of ancient Greeks' ideas about political power, but also consistent with the description of modern political thought. The ancient Greek mythology together with the democratic politics of Athens laid a theoretical foundation for the modern western political system, and made indelible contributions to the establishment and development of other modern nation states.

（吴瑞丰译）

Chapter 4 The Ancient Greek Dramas

01 *The Cloud* of Aristophanes and the Sophists

I Introduction

Socrates was undoubtedly one of the greatest thinkers of ancient Greece and the most ethical sage of western culture. In the eyes of the public, he was always a shining image full of wisdom, justice, reason and morality. However, his good friend Aristophanes, a great ancient Greek dramatist, expressed his humorous expression to Socrates in a humorous way. The image has undergone a subversion, creating a Socratic image that is completely "unbelievable" to the public.

II Plots of the Story

1. The Admirers of Socrates

The son of Srisiades lived a life of luxury without knowing the frugality. He only knew horse racing and then he owed a lot of debt. In order to avoid to pay the debt, Srisiades asked his son to learn rhetoric in Socrates' "thinking place", because as long as you learned this technique, you could win in any debate, then you could avoid to pay the debt. In order to let his son learn such "injustices", Srisiades was also trying his best to please his son. This was undoubtedly the democratic politics poisoning social theory. But despite his bitterness, his son was not willing to go because he thought it was "indecent". It could be seen that although the son had bad habits, he still had a sense of morality and knew what was wrong. Here,

Aristophanes gave Socrates a subversion. He used the words of the father and son to ridicule that Socrates was actually teaching people how to argue, how to be immoral. And those were "the indecent thing".

2. The Institute of Socrates's Thought

Srisiades, who failed to persuade his son, finally slammed the door of the "thinking place". The disciples opened the door and introduced him the situation of the place. They also introduced him Socrates' recent achievements which were all ridiculous. The disciples of Socrates were bending over and bowing their heads to "study things on earth," just like a tetrapod. Aristophanes said: "If a person's observation of the world is confined to the material nature, then he loses the dignity of being a person walking upright." Srisiades found that when they were studying things on earth, their asses were facing the sky and now the vulgar part of the human body were in the light. Here the institute of thought was proved ridiculous and Socrates seemed like a moron.

3. The Appearance of Socrates

Socrates appeared, sitting in a hanging basket suspended in midair. It was indeed ulterior motives for Aristophanes to arrange the philosopher Socrates in the basket here. The philosopher Socrates, who just appeared, was ragged, barefoot and funny. Socrates thought that he was thinking about profound questions, so it was necessary to raise himself into the air. Socrates said that he was walking in the air, he was obsessing the sun.Is this not dangerous? How can the sun be obsessed? And how could Socrates dare to look at the sun? Socrates abandoned his god and he looked at his god. The philosopher hung in the air, mapping the philosophy that was getting farther away from life and the world, which shows philosophy is not worth mentioning. This is nothing more than a warning of Aristophanes to Socrates.

Ⅲ Socrates and Sophists

Throughout the drama, Aristophanes was satirical and criticized Socrates. Of course, this was a kind of criticism. He was also secretly reminding and warning Socrates of his thoughts. It would make him face a disaster. The early Socrates walked in the air, away from the earth, and didn't care about politics, but later Socrates began to return to the world, bringing philosophy back to the earth and began to pay close attention to politics.

Ancient Greek influential sophists include Protagoras (490 B.C.-421 B.C.), Gorgias (about 485 B.C. to 380 B.C.), Antiphon (470 B.C.-411 B.C.) and others. Among these wise men, Protagoras was considered to be "the most talented and creative of the wise," and "the theoretical leader of the wise school".

Plato was the enemy of the wise, but the young Socrates and the young Plato used to be typical wise men. Moreover, important philosophical propositions or educational issues, such as "the dialectics"of Socrates, "whether the virtues can be taught" and "pull philosophy from heaven back to the human world", have already been advanced in philosophers such as Protagoras.

IV   The Practical Philosophy of the Wise Man

The philosophy of the wise man was different from the natural philosophy of Thales. The natural philosophy of Thales only studied the natural ontology and didn't care about human affairs. The wise man was the first person to bring philosophy back from heaven to the world. In the past, people thought that "Socrates was the first person to bring philosophy back from the sky to the world." This statement was generally correct, because the young Socrates was a typical wise man. Young Socrates, like Protagoras, was a typical image of a wise man.Aristophanes's *Cloud* described the image of the young Socrates as a wise man. Aristophane's Socrates was completely different from Plato's Socrates. Aristophane's Socrates lived a typical wise life. Like wise men like Protagoras, the young Socrates taught young people "the eloquence", not for the purpose of pursuing the truth but for defeating others in the debate. Unlike wise men like Protagoras, adult Socrates began to pursue justice and truth and opposed secular morality and democratic politics in an outspoken irony. Socrates was later sentenced to death.

Plato's resentment and humiliation came from the experience of being a wise man when he was young and had a deep understanding of the philosophy of the wise. As he grew older, Plato took another path (absolute philosophy) and liquidated and self-criticized his past. Plato's resentment and opposition to the wise, mainly because the sophist's philosophy conformed to the democratic political life of the time while the democratic system was precisely opposed by Plato.

Authoritarian society suppressed speech because of advocating violence while democratic society attaches importance to debate because of advocating law. The emergence of the sophists in ancient Greece was precisely because the wise and the eloquent education provided by the sophists conformed to the needs of the democratic society at that time. The public, recurrent jury court created by Pericles has opened up one of the most talents of the Athenians suitable for its natural tendency to develop. This new judicial system promoted the development of the Athenian genius to the eloquence. At this time, not only those who wanted to be politically explicit must have a certain speaking ability but those ordinary citizens must also do this in order to defend their rights in court or refute the accusations of others. Regardless of whether it was used to achieve one's ambitions, eloquence was always the most practical talent and its importance was absolutely no less than martial arts or physical training. Therefore, the teachers who taught grammar and rhetoric, as well as the literati who wrote the speeches for others, began to increase and received unprecedented attention. Moreover the sophists also engaged in lobbying or diplomatic activities. The early sophists were noble, well-respected people who were often diplomatically appointed by the city councils they were in.

The sophists, philosophy was also supported and sponsored by Pericles (about 495 B.C. to 429 B.C.) in response to the needs of a democratic society. When Pericles was in power, he took sophists as honorable guest such as Protagoras and talked to them many times. Later, the democratic political system declined, the sophists was suppressed. The first important measure adopted by the "Thirty Tyrants" were to expressly prohibit the teaching of eloquence. Aristophanes had stabbed the Athenians for arguing because he felt that the atmosphere weakened the military power of the Athenians. Plato's attack on the sophists could also be seen as a criticism of democrats such as Pericles.

Socrates and Plato both were keen on the education of sophists and the education of eloquence. However, Socrates and Plato later turned to pursue the political philosophy of "the philosopher king" and the intellectual philosophy of absolutism. Plato thus criticized the philosophical relativism and subjectivism philosophy. Plato's critique of the sophists was first and foremost not only because of their differences on knowledge philosophy (absolutism and subjectivism) and political philosophy (democratic politics and philosophical king politics) but also because of jealousy and hatred. The sophists persuaded the outstanding young people to give up learning to others and switch to their own door. It was not a safe thing from the beginning. They won admiration and also attracted hatred. Many sophists suffered from the "burning books" disaster. Although they didn't suffer from "pit the Scholars", they were expelled for allegations of "disrespecting the gods" and "destroying the youth" (then Socrates was also sentenced to death by the same charges) . Protagoras was once expelled from Athens and his book was burned.

Because of Plato's "hostile description" of the wise school, sophists always has a bad reputation in the history of western philosophy. In his works such as *Protagora* (also translated as *The Wise* or *Intelligence*), *Gorgia* and *Tiataide*, Plato slanders the sophist philosophy in an exaggerated literary way.It makes the descendants generally contempt for the sophists and it makes the work of sophists not completely preserved and spread, leaving only fragments and vague abstracts. Influenced by Plato, the sophists was regarded as a "cheat swindler": Using the public's gullibility earned a lot of money; in the name of teaching morality, it actually teaches people to use a hypocritical speech, as well as advocating unethical use of opinions.

However, the sophists, especially Protagoras at that time could become Plato's "big enemy", which in itself shows that the wise school has enough strength to make Plato feel uneasy and fearful. After Plato, Hegel has more affirmation of the wise school in *The Lectures on the History of Philosophy*, but since Hegel regarded the philosophy of the sophists as "anti-thesis" against Thales' (about 624 B.C.-546 B.C.) natural philosophy and regarded the Plato philosophy as the "combination" after the natural philosophy (the topic) ,it has stipulated that Plato's philosophy was higher than and prior to the sophist's philosophy. However, Hegel's inclusion of sophists in the ranks of philosophers was an affirmation of sophists. After Hegel, there have been people who have made new comments on the sophists. For example, the British historian G. Grote's (1794–1871) *History of Greece* and the German scholar E. Zeller's (1814–1908) *The History of Ancient Greek Philosophy* make a completely different evaluation of the sophists from Plato. Russell (B.

Russell, 1872–1970) also stood on the side of the sophists in *History of Western Philosophy* and expressed dissatisfaction with Plato's hostility and defamation.

V The Opinions of Sophists

The core spirit of the sophist philosophy was mainly shown as empiricism (and scepticism, relativism). It was also because of the choice of empiricism and relativism philosophy that the sophists made a choice between "nature" and "custom" different from Plato's philosophy: Plato stood on the "nature" side, while the sophists paid more attention to the "custom" (secular moral law and politics). The first characteristic of the sophist philosophy was to express doubt and distrust of all dogmatism based on empirical observation. "The way it was experience-inductive."

Although the natural philosophy of Thales differs from Plato's philosophy in many aspects, the natural philosophy of the time and Plato's philosophy are consistent in one point: both emphasize super-experienced contemplation and pursue objective truth and both are consistently shown as dogmatism, objectivism and absolutism. In contrast, the sophist philosophy adheres to empirical observations and thus chooses the path of skepticism, subjectivism and relativism. Plato's philosophy believes that "things are understandable by our reason", while sophist philosophy insists that "things are things that our reason cannot understand." The so-called "incomprehensible" implies both have philosophical attitudes of "skepticism" and also means that people can only obtain "relative" truth or "limited" truth. "Protagoras saw all morality and law as relatively effective and the validity was only closely linked to the human society that produced these morals and laws and only that society believed that these morals and laws were good.... There was no absolute religion, no absolute morality, no absolute justice." He believed that "every question contains two opposites." He said at the beginning of *Truth or Basis*: "Man is the measure of all things, both the scale of existence of the being and the measure of non-existence." Hegel thought this was a "great proposition", " From now on, everything was revolving around this proposition.... All objective things existed only in the connection with consciousness; therefore, thinking was declared as the basic link in all truths; therefore, the subjective thinking was absolutely taken as the form." Protagoras further believed that any truth depends on consciousness, without any objective existence of self-sufficiency, "everything was only relative", "things for me was what it presented to me. For you was what it presented to you."

Protagoras' theory of relativity was itself a suspicion and distrust of all dogmatism. This skepticism further developed by Gorgia. In three parts of *On Nature*, Gorgia proposed his three arguments: Firstly, nothing exists; secondly, even if something existed, it couldn't be recognized; thirdly, even if it could be recognized, nor can it be said. These three propositions of Gorgia were constantly being recalled and quoted in later philosophy.

The second characteristic of the sophist philosophy was the introduction of evaluation criteria for physis and nomos, including ethical legal norms and real politics. The drama *Antigone* of Protagoras' peer Sophocles (496 B.C.–406 B.C.) attracted attention because of the conflict between nature and customs in this drama got a serious discussion. At the beginning of this drama, Antigone was placed in a dilemma: if she followed her unwritten law (natural law or divine law) to bury her younger brother, she would be executed because of rebellion against the national law; if she complied with the national law, she would be condemned by divine law. Then, the drama began with "human shackles": "Wonders are many, and none is more wonderful than man; he crosses the sea, driven by south-wind, making a path under surges that threaten to engulf him; and Earth, the eldest of the gods, the immortal, the unwearied, doth he disturb, plowing the field with the offspring of horses from year to year. And the merry birds, the savage beasts, and the fish of the sea, he snares in the meshes of the woven toils. Man is excellent in wit. He masters by his arts the beast in the wilds; he tames the horses of shaggy mane, he puts the yoke upon its neck, he tames the tireless mountain bull." This "human shackles"of sophocles wasn't only a praise of human civilization and rationality, but also a vigilance and irony of human civilization and rationality.

Between nature and customs, Plato's philosophy stands on the nature side, while the sophists pay more attention to customs. Although sophists generally adhered to the relativist standards of "Man is the measure of all things", it doesn't mean that they haven't any standards. It was precisely because the sophists believed that all man-made or secular morality and political system had no absolute legitimacy but relative legitimacy, they reminded people that there was a need for a temporary covenant. Even if such a covenant was temporary and modifiable, people must respect and abide by the ready-made morality and law after formulation and revision. Otherwise, society would become chaotic. The sophists discussed three sources of law: first, the law from God, this was the divine law. Second, the command from the power and the ruler, this was the will of power, reflecting the interests of the ruler (the strong). Third, from the agreement of the majority, this was a "social contract" that reflected the interests of the weak. Among the three, sophists often stood on the side of the social contract, and reminded people to be vigilant about the will of power. For example, Antwerp insisted on the equality of people and the social contract theory. He "used the contrast between nature and customs to classify the country as a social contract and treats morality and customs as a constraint on nature. He asserted in unambiguous terms that all people were equal. He condemned the distinction between the royal and the Greek barbarians, because this distinction is itself a barbaric statement." Gorgia suggested that "morality and law were formulated by the majority of the weak and they domesticated the strong who were like carnivores and pointed to the younger the justice. But nature and history were contrary to each other. When the strong saw this scam, they broke through these constraints and made themselves the masters of the weak. Delasumahos reminded people that the so-called law or justice may only reflect the interests of the strong. People often think that Delasumahos was opposed by Socrates and Plato for insisting on power justice. It was a matter of course that Socrates and Plato stood on the side of natural law against the concept of power justice. However, as a sophist, Delasumahos only pointed out the possibility of the concept of power justice in his theory but he himself wouldn't believe in the concept of power justice. The sophist responsibility was to win in the court debate. If Delasumahos insisted on the power justice in the court, he wouldn't be able to win.

In general, the sophist philosophy was the classical form of empiricism. Later empiricist philosophers such as Berkeley, Hume and Dewey all can be regarded as modern sophists. Beckley's existence is perceived, Hume denies all causal relationships, Dewey's "from absolutism to experimentalism", these are the modern echoes of the sophist philosophy. Even when Kant, who was awakened by Hume, proposed "self-containment", there was also an element of sophist philosophies. It is said that the reason why Protagoras was expelled was that he didn't respect God. He wrote at the beginning of *On God* "With regards to the gods, I couldn't know whether they exist or not; because there were many things that prevented us from getting this kind of knowledge." Kant's "things in themselves" and Protagoras' statement was exactly the same.

VI Conclusion

From the above analysis, we will have a general understanding of why Aristophanes criticized Socrates in *Cloud*. Whether Aristophanes' serious criticism of Socrates who is representative of all philosophers, or many thinkers who continue to participate in the struggle between poetry and philosophy after the Greek era, their ultimate goal is to explore the truth for human beings, to find a correct path and identify a correct leader. The continuous and repeated struggle between poetry and philosophy also shows how many contradictions and twists and turns are experienced in the process of exploring the truth. It is the attachment to the truth that has become the driving force for mankind to move forward, and any of these thinkers deserve the high respect of future generations.

（张振宇译）

02　The Mask of Socrates and Euripides'*Bacchae*

I Introduction

In *The Birth of Tragedy*, Euripides was considered as "the mask of Socrates" while Nietzsche did not like Socrates at all. Though Euripides had a great deal of similarities with Socrates for they lived in the same age, his poetic philosophy was quite different from the rationalistic philosophy. *Bacchae* fully revealed Euripides' rational thought on "rationality" and "irrationality".

II The Tragedy of Euripides

Euripides was born in a noble class with land, but became a poor after the Peloponnesian War, which made his tragedy contain a kind of civilian consciousness and democratic thought. Euripides was a pacifist who had annoyed the political authorities by exposing the truth behind the unjust war. Euripides was a humanitarian and a staunch supporter of democratic politics. He severely condemned the gender-based oppression that existed at the time and made a fuss for the women who were deeply bullied.

The tragedy of Euripides did not receive the same praise as Sophocles in his time. In his 50-year career, he won only four first prizes, while the contemporary Sophocles won twenty awards. The irony is that *Bacchae* was written in Macedonia after the poet was expelled from Athens and the award was won by his son after his death. Why was Euripides so unsuccessful and so successful?

III The Euripides' Philosophy

Euripides was skeptical: he wanted people to understand the truths they didn't want to understand and he imposed philosophical thinking on his tragedy. He was blasphemous because he put higher demands on people —these requirements were so powerful that you couldn't reach and couldn't wait and see.

Euripides had long been fascinated with philosophy and had heard a lecture on natural philosophy proposed by Anaxagoras. Anaxagoras proposed the eclipse principle, which clearly undermined the religious beliefs of Zeus and the poet was accused of Blasphemy and was expelled from Athens. Euripides defends Anaxagoras in *Medea*: "A minded person must not teach his children to be 'smart people' because people who were too smart will get useless bad name and also provoke local people's jealousy: if you propose a new doctrine, those stupid people would think that your words are too impractical and you are too unwise". Protagoras and Prodicus as poet's friends also gave him a profound influence: it is said that the former had read his paper on God in the poet's house: "I can not say whether there is God. There are many obstacles to this understanding: first, the object itself is not clear; next, the span of human beings is short." This paper was burned publicly and Protagoras was found guilty. Euripides often spreaded these new doctrines in the theater, so the political instigator Kleon has accused him of Blasphemy.

Euripides was deeply influenced by Socrates, Socrates' knowledge, especially moral knowledge, his god (demon; δαιμων), the sacred supreme god, in the era when the social morality was on the verge of collapse, seemed so important. Nietzsche said in *The Birth of Tragedy*: "Euripides was only a mask: the god who spoke through this mask was neither Dionysus nor Apollo, but a completely new pagan god. That was Socrates". However, it would rather say that the same historical conditions brought them together than say Socrates influenced Euripides. However, as a poet, Euripides was different from Socrates as a philosopher: the tragedy of Euripides fully embodied at the beginning of philosophy, how poetry expressed philosophical thinking in its own unique way.

Nietzsche worshiped Dionysus, who worshiped the mystery and temperament of life, so he naturally didn't like Socrates, the image of knowing the world. Nietzsche pointed out that the theoretical culture initiated by Socrates was rooted in an optimism and attempted to resolve the tragedy. "He believed that the world could be corrected with knowledge and life could be led by science". Although Nietzsche believed that the essence of tragedy was the opposition and reconciliation between the spirit of Apollo and the spirit of Dionysus, it was a combination of two spirits, but he actually preferred the latter. Nietzsche's extreme admiration for the Greek carnival culture and his extreme understanding showed that he did not fully understand the essence of the Dionysian spirit. The essence of this spirit has been fully recognized by Euripides as early as the 5th B.C.. Unfortunately, his understanding has always been dusted in the memory of history.

IV Ancient Greek and Roman Worship of Bacchus

Dionysus(Διονυσος) or Bacchus (Βακχος), was the patron of the grape growing industry and the wine industry. It was said that he traveled all over Greece, Syria, Asia, and India and along the way he taught people how to make wine. It was precisely because he had the characteristics of a rich god and could free people from the troubles and sorrows of life, so his worship was almost fanatical. This cult was accompanied by a carnival ritual in which believers reached an intoxicating position through wine, dance and songs. Especially the female believers, they were called "the madwoman of the god of wine". At that time, the folks also popularized the secret ritual ceremony for Dionysus. During the spring planting season, people dressed in sheepskin, wearing shofars, dressing up as a half-human and half-goat Satyrus (the follower of Dionysus) and formed a chorus. They sang the suffering of the god of wine in the earth and his regeneration around the altar. This primitive form of art which was called "the song of goats" was the predecessor of tragedy and the Greek word for "tragedy" was "the song of goats".

The tragedy *Bacchae* was created by Euripides based on the myth of Dionysus. Euripides once praised Dionysus in *Bacchae*: "He brewed liquid wine for humans, made up for the lack of nutrition and alleviated the sorrow of those poor people, when they drank enough wine; he also offered "Sleep", so that they forget the pain of the day and there was no good medicine to relieve the pain. He was a god, but he was buried on the ground to worship, to make people happy".

Russell compared the dionysia between the ancient Greeks and ancient Romans. He affirmed the former and denied the latter: in Greece, this kind of carnival was combined with solemn religious rituals and religious sentiments, so it looked both savage and beautiful, both crazy and sacred, full of mysterious colors purifying the soul. Russell believed that the indulgent songs and dances of the madwoman of Bacchus on the hillside were wild, but they were also a kind of transcending impulse to "escape from the burden and troubles of civilization to the beautiful world of non-human world, with the freedom of the breeze and the moon". But the Romans' Dionysian sacrifice was sinister: "The Italian Dionysian celebration was carried out at the crossroads and it was fanatical and debauchery. People worshiped the male genitals in the name of Liberl (Roman Dionysus). It was an extremely open and degenerate act". Livy also described the frenzied scene of the Roman Dionysian in a disgusting tone in *the History of Roman*.

The worship of Dionysus was primitive and rude. The spiritual fanaticism would realize in the madness of the flesh, as Nietzsche said: "The central point of these celebrations was a pure sexual marriage; It devastated every tribal patriarchal law which had been established. All these wild impulses were liberated in these opportunities until they reached the peak of a desire and violent feelings". So this madness was opposed by the aristocratic class that represented the principle of prudence at the very beginning.

V *Bacchae* of Euripides

Poetic philosophy was not necessarily "rational" and rational philosophy does not necessarily exclude "irrationality". *Bacchae* fully reflects Euripides'thinking about the dialectical relationship between rationality and irrationality. The philosophy of Euripides has been deeply influenced by the dualism. From the division of rationality and irrationality, it could be known that the mother Agaue (Αγαυη) was obviously the representative of irrationality and a fanatic of Dionysus; Son Pentheus (Πενθευς) was a representative of reason, a loyal supporter of Apollo; his grandfather Cadmus (καδμος) had both characteristics.

Pentheus was full of disgust on the Dionysian offering and called it a "failure": "Our women have gone out of their homes to participate in the false rituals of Bacchus, wandering around in the mountains... they sneaked into secluded places one by one to satisfy the man's desires and pretended to be a sacrificial woman, it was actually to put Aphrodite on top of Bacchus". Pentheus believed that the worship of Bacchus corrupted the morality of women with the passion of Aphrodite. Pentheus eventually died in the hands of irrationality, which was the result of rational contempt for irrationality.

The purpose of Dionysus to come to Greece was to punish the arrogance of rationality: "I only hate my mother's sisters—they shouldn't say that Dionysus was not born of Zeus (Zευς), they said crankily that Semele (Σεμελη) had an affair with the mortal, but attribute the fault to Zeus and said that it was Cadmus, who lied. They said arrogantly that Zeus killed her because she concealed the fact and told lies". Dionysus revenged because people didn't believe his holy bloodline. The implication here was that Dionysus represents irrationality. His existence was the existence which rationality would not ignore. If he was denied and despised, he would incur revenge. Dionysus was narrow-minded, revengeful and extremely cruel. "So I made their sisters mad. They were now insane and live on the mountains; I told them to wear my religious costumes".

As a counterbalance to the internal breeding of reason, irrationality restricted the arrogance of reason, but irrationality had its own paranoia. Agaue carried the results of the hunting—the son's head, frequently called for the winner of the victory, "With his help, she won only tears".

As a symbol of irrationality, Minotaur of Crete always looked at the rational civilization of human society: reason could never escape from its maze. The line of Ariadne was the only hope to get out of the maze: to treat irrationality couldn't rely on simple suppression and diversion was the right way.

The dialogue between Pentheus and Dionysus was classic, which reflected the ridiculous and self-righteous singularity of rationality and irrationality: "(Dionysus) Those who are always telling clever words to fools are often considered as fool". (Pentheus) "Did you firstly guide this God to come here"? "First to other places, all foreigners hold this teaching". "Because they are far less intelligent than the Greeks". "In this field they are smarter, even though they have different habits". When Pentheus was going to put Dionysus in the stable and pull the women who were "doing bad things" with him as slaves, Dionysus said: "It was your so-called non-existent god that would retaliate against you and punish your atrocities". "God's strength came slowly, but it would come, let the time advance, but they would finally capture the disrespectful people...recognizing the power of sacred things, acknowledging the constant habits and the beliefs that nature has established over a long period of time." The implication here was that rational contempt for irrational existence, its paranoia and arrogance would eventually lead to the revenge of irrationality: Dionysus put pentheus "into the confused madness, which made him nervous; because if he was clear-minded, he would not wear women's clothes. If he put it on, he would die in his mother's hand, he would know that Zeus's son was an authoritative god, the most kind but the most fierce to human beings".

VI Conclusion

The god of Euripides was a philosophical god. This god hated the self-righteousness of rationality, but also hated the indulgence and madness of irrationality. Despite being the representative of irrationality, Dionysus was very rational. He had carefully planned a play that not only punished the rationality of autocracy, but also punished the self-satisfaction of irrationality. Cadmus said to his daughter: "He (Pentheus), like you, did not respect this god. So God has brought you all together and involved you with him in the same disaster". The reason why grandfather said so because he was soberly aware that a new god had emerged. This true god was different from Dionysus in ancient Greek mythology. Although he was opposed to the rational spirit of Apollo, he was equally disgusted with the irrational blindness and ignorance. This new god was a combination of the spirit of Apollo and the spirit of Dionysus. He proved in a peculiar way that there was no boundary between rationality and irrationality. They were contained in each other's body and would transform each other in a specific situation. Indulgence would only lead to the destruction of people. Pentheus wanted to conquer this unconquerable god by force. The punishment of his will is death. Only those who sincerely believed in God according to their duties could live without any worries".

Socrates did not seem to practice his motto, the rule of "ηδεν αγαν", which was engraved in the Temple of Delphi. This was reflected in the tragedy of Euripides. However, Euripides' dialectical thinking on rational violence and irrational violence did not attract widespread attention. This was proved by the extremes of the ancient Roman carnival and Christian asceticism.

（张振宇译）

03　The Spirit of Tragedy—Greek and Post-Modern

Ⅰ　Introduction

As one of the highest literary forms, tragedy is well deserved, just as the piano is the king of musical instruments. Tragedy involves aesthetics, literary criticism, psychology and is closely related to religion and philosophy. In the two thousand and five hundred years of glory, tragic works are constantly emerging, and various arguments for studying tragedies can be found everywhere.

Ⅱ　The Tragic Works

Since ancient Greece, there have been a large number of tragic works represented by the three great tragedians—although most of these works have been lost or scattered today. To the ancient Roman era, there were Seneca's rewritings and retellings of the ancient Greek tragedies. Although the medieval period was not a stage of tragedy, religious drama has always been active in the life of Christians. The Renaissance was naturally the reappearance of ancient Greek civilization, during which Shakespeare's tragedy was the most attractive; During the period of classicism, Pierre Corneille and Racine were more admired the tragedy of ancient Greece and on the basis of it, they carried out reprocessing according to their own purposes. During the romantic period, the German romantics focused on ancient Greece. The creation of poetry was a reappearance of the ancient Greek glory. The works of Schiller, Goethe and Shelley should be the modern echoes of ancient Greek civilization. Unfortunately, the romantic Greek dream of the Greeks was actually a kind of self-expansion, far from the spirit of ancient Greece. After that, there was social tragedy, represented by Ibsen and Eugene O'Neill. It was a close combination of social tragedy and psychological tragedy. The 20th century was a changing century, which was extremely strange and its rapid changes make life grotesque and phantom. Therefore, absurd drama occupied the right to speak in literature, art even philosophy and history.

Ⅲ The Tragic Spirit

What makes tragedy a tragedy is an inner tragic spirit. The tragic sense comes from the pain of human life and the reflection of pain. In many tragic works, it often manifests the pain and suffering suffered by human beings in social practice due to external social and historical limitations, but only external pain is not enough to produce tragedy. Only the tragic spirit, that is, the sorrowful life experience of human beings, the conscious and inner tragic emotions of human beings can achieve tragedy. Throughout the history of the development of tragedy, we sorrowfully discover that the tragic spirit contained in the ancient Greek tragedy that truly made the ancient Greek tragedy eternal, constantly changing, constantly dissolving and dying in the evolution of history, although this cannot be generally accepted. Though it is just personal opinion, who can say that this view is completely absurd? After all, "a thousand readers have a thousand Hamlet in their eyes."

In his *Tragedy Psychology*, Mr. Zhu Guangqian humbly pointed out his book's position: "We would discuss in turn the extent to which aesthetic elements, maliciousness, compassion and morality could be considered when explaining the reasons for the pleasure of tragedy. An optimistic outlook on life and a pessimistic view of life, emotional mitigation, vitality, intellectual curiosity and other factors are all included. If possible, we would group these factors into some common standards. But since we recognized the diversity of causes, We don't need to stick to a certain dogma and distort the specific experience. We don't intend to cut the footsteps for the establishment of the theory. We would mainly discuss on the basis of specific facts and did not want to use any major premise of metaphysics. Our theoretical basis for the conclusion of tragedy did not want to use any tragedy theory to support some predetermined philosophical doctrine. Our method would be critical and comprehensive and the bad one was 'eclectic'."In *Tragedy Psychology*, Mr. Zhu Guangqian combed the works discussing tragedy. His main purpose was to present the views of various factions and focus on the problem of "tragic pleasure".

We must realize that this kind of combing work was a kind of value in itself, although this method of "compromise" was in order to avoid being attacked by peers and sounded a bit tricky, the "compromise" position was actually a position by itself. However, the position here was not "compromise": with the preference for ancient Greece and helplessness of the real life environment, I insisted on choosing a position, intended to express a view that tragedy belonged to ancient Greece.

After ancient Greece, Seneca of ancient Rome also left tragic works, but his tragedy had exaggerated the atmosphere of terror, so that the tragedy did not have the unique tragic spirit of the ancient Greek tragedy; the medieval religious drama was only wearing the mask of sorrow while expressing the essence of comedy; the tragedy of the Renaissance was full of a playful atmosphere; the tragedy of the classicism was more like a political preaching; the modern absurd drama was revealed in absurdity and boring. Therefore, no matter how hard the efforts of later generations, the unique tragedy spirit of the ancient Greek tragedy has gone forever, the unique beauty, the unique nobleness and the unique tragic strength.

Tragedy is related to "beauty". As a form of beauty, tragedy is an important category of aesthetics. Tragedy has a beauty, a cold and magnificent beauty. But what is the aesthetic characteristic of tragedy? This is an old but realistic issue. Since Aristotle until today, more than two thousand years have passed. We do not know how many philosophers and aesthetic masters have tirelessly studied and explored it and put forward various opinions and explanations. However, this problem is still ambiguous.

In summary, the research materials on tragedy can be divided into the following four types: first, the remarks made by the tragic poets themselves, such as Pierre Corneille's *Thesis, Preface*, Racine's *Preface*, Schiller's *On the Aesthetic Education of Man*, Hugo's *Preface to Cromwell* and other similar works—these articles generally defended the author's creative practice. Second, philosophers' discourse on tragic works, such as Aristotle's *Poetics*, Hume's *On Tragedy*, Rousseau's *On Dramas*, Hegel's *Aesthetics*, Schopenhauer's *The World of Will and Representation* and Nietzsche's *The Birth of Tragedy*. Third, the audience, readers, editors, commentators' remarks, such as Johnson's *The Complete Works of Shakespeare's Preface*, Diderot's *On the Contradiction of Actors*, Lessing's *Burger Drama Review*, Schlegel's *Drama And Literary Lectures*, Bradley's *On Shakespeare's Tragedy*, and James Agut's *British Drama Critics*. Fourth, the actors' remarks, such works are very limited, because actors rarely write books about their own performing arts but sometimes, some biographers indirectly write the actor's life experience and performance art. Mentioning their deductive works, Percy Fitzgerald's *David Galic* was typical of such information.

These different viewpoints and explanations highlight the characteristics of tragedy in dififerent era. The different manifestations and themes of the tragedy in each different period reflected the footsteps of human civilization, further thinking and confusion of human beings. However, some of these thoughts were fragmentary, such as the "preface", some are the feelings of the tragic writers themselves, such as Schiller's *Study of Aesthetic Education* and some are the philosopher's set of theories such as Hegel's *Aesthetics*, some focus on a certain subject and field such as Aristotle's *Poetics*, there is no complete analytical work. Mr. Zhu Guangqian's *Tragedy Psychology* made a useful attempt. He combed the views of different theoretical factions and then sorted them out, occasionally adding their own unique views but this work focused on "psychology". That was the aesthetic psychology of tragedy.

Of course, the "sublime" associates with the "tragic spirit". It can not be separated from the category of aesthetics. The "feeling" and "experience" associated with the "tragic spirit" can not be separated from the scope of psychology. However, the basic question is: What makes tragedy? Why the tragedy spirit is dissolved, why the tragedy belongs to ancient Greece, why there is no great and lofty tragedy in postmodern era, why Indians, Hebrews, Japanese, Chinese and Romans have no such thing as "great and noble tragedy"? All of these are related not only to the religions and philosophies of various nationalities and eras, but also to the ethical and philosophical ways of thinking of religions.

Thomas Kuhn proposed the concept of paradigm in *The Structure of the Scientific Revolution*(1962). As a scientific philosopher, Thomas Kuhn believed that the nature of structure determined that all interpretations, statements and theories must operate within a hypothetical, orderly framework, which was a paradigm. A major breakthrough in science was not just new inventions and discoveries, but the overthrow of an old paradigm and the creation of a new paradigm. As for literary criticism and literary theory, it was constantly introducing new paradigms and constantly introducing new interpretation theories. Take the study of tragedy as an example. Aristotle proposed the paradigm of Fault Theory. Hegel proposed the paradigm of self-disintegration and reconciliation of ethical entities. Bullard (British philosopher, logician, the representative of the Neo-Hegelianism) put forward the paradigm of the ultimate moral order. Nietzsche proposed the paradigm of the fusion of the spirit of Apollo and the spirit of Dionysus. Freud proposed the paradigm of the Oedipus complex, Jung and Northrop Frye proposed the prototype paradigm.

From Aristotle's "fault theory" to Hegel's "ethical entity theory", from Nietzsche's "the reconciliation of spirit of Dionysus and Apollo" to Freud's "Oedipus Complex",from Jung's "collective unconsciousness" to Frye's "prototype", only "Destiny" was the best paradigm for explaining the tragedy of ancient Greece. Explaining the rise and fall of the ancient Greek tragedy with "destiny " could clearly show the essence of the spirit of tragedy.

Ⅳ   The Tragic Spirit of the Ancient Greek

Tragedy stemmed from the predicament of human survival. The fear of the living situation and the fear of the impermanence of fate not only produced primitive religions, witchcraft, rituals, but also tragedies. In fact, the tragedy arises from the ritual of sacrifice. American drama critic Francis Ferguson said: "The Cambridge School of Classical Anthropologists has explained in great detail that the form of Greek tragedy follows the form of an ancient ritual to worship the god of vegetation or the growing season." Euripides's *Bacchae* clearly showed this. The famous British classical scholar Gilbert Murray studied in detail the process of the transformation of religious rituals into tragedies. Reina Friedrich also said: "The combination of imitation and religion has produced rituals and the ritual has produced drama. In the ritual, dramatic imitation and religious rituals form an indiscriminate combination; it was this combination that develops imitation into a refined stage, which made this complex art form of drama possible." It could be said whether it was ritual, religion, witchcraft or tragedy, it was born in the dilemma of human survival.

The fear of the natural environment gradually evolved into the awe of God and the fear of God. It not only bred religion but also bred tragedy. When talking about the nature of tragedy, Belinsky said that the end of the tragedy, "was always the destruction of the most precious hope in the human heart, the loss of life and happiness. This has produced its gloomy solemnity, its grand grandeur, tragedy covering the destiny, the destiny was the basic essence of the tragedy."

However, unlike religion, tragedy not only reflected people's fear, but also reflected people's resistance. Both were the exploration of the relationship between human and god, but tragedy and religion had embarked on different paths. In religion, people were required to be unconditionally awed God. In tragedy, in addition to the religious requirements of fearing God, human showed more heroic rebellion although this resistance also meant transcedence, it was sacred. Tragedy occurred and developed in the tension between God's fear and sacredness. The paradigm of destiny was the tension which was discussed. Therefore, the paradigm that runs through the argument was destiny. Destiny was the sword of Damocles hanging over the head of the ancient Greeks. It was a phantom wandering through the tragedy of ancient Greece. It was the foothold of the unique tragic spirit of the ancient Greek tragedy.

V   The Revival of the Spirit of Post-modern Tragedy

As for the tragedies of later generations, such as the tragedy of the Renaissance, although inheriting some of the spiritual traits of the ancient Greek tragedy, although it also reflected the survival dilemma of human beings, the color of destiny has faded. In the tragedy of the classicism, the color of destiny has disappeared. The survival dilemma of the people reflected in the tragedy was no longer a conflict between humans and gods, but between humans and the society or between humans and humans. More precisely, it is the conflict between the two societies, the conflict between reason and emotion, the conflict between interests and interests.

As for the social drama of the 19th century, it was a further extension of this tragedy, which more deeply reflected the conflict between humans and society and the conflict between humans and humans. If the peculiar tragedy of ancient Greece had signs of reappearance in post-modernism, it was probably because human reason has come to some end and the scientific spirit has reached a certain limit, as Nietzsche said: "If the ancient tragedy was dialectically, the impulse of knowledge and the impulse of scientific optimism have squeezed out its orbit. From this fact, it could be inferred that there was an eternal struggle between the theoretical worldview and the tragic worldview. Only when the scientific spirit was guided to its boundaries, the universal validity of self-sufficiency was proved by this boundary to be bankrupt, then we could count on the regeneration of the tragedy."

After two world wars, Hegel's human moral optimism was deeply questioned. The Jewish concentration camp in Nazi Germany and the Japanese massacre of the Chinese were vivid examples; they have experienced various achievements and crises brought about by scientific progress. The chemical weapons of the Japanese and the atomic bombs of the Americans are clear examples. People with scientific rationality began to rethink the optimism of science. Only at this time, the spirit of tragedy seemed to be recovering.

The absurd drama of the 20th century was the product of this reflection. However, the absurd drama of the 20th century was still missing something. Take *Waiting for Godot* as an example. There was no plot in this drama. There was no other actions except the funny, boring "waiting". Followed Aristotle's theory, this drama could not be called a tragedy. However, the theme of this drama waiting for "God" seemed to be the modern echo of the ancient Greek tragedy spirit. If the form determines the content, or the form itself was a kind of content, then there was no tragedy in postmodernism though the tragic spirit contained in the modern absurd drama seemed to respond to Nietzsche's still optimistic expectation.

The debate about whether there is a tragedy in Western modernity has not been conclusive until now. Scholars represented by Joseph Wood Kruch and George Steiner believe that there is no modern tragedy and writers represented by Albert Camus believe that there are also tragedies in modern times. In 1992, the famous American scholar Walter Kaufman's student Richard H. Palmer once again raised the question of whether there is tragedy in Western modernity in his book *Tragedy and The Theory of Tragedy*: "In a society which philosophy and religion lost the co-accepted standards, whether tragedy can exist."

The position here tended to the former, although the playwright represented by Albert Camus did express the return of some tragic spirit through absurd drama. However, in terms of form, postmodern drama cannot be called tragedy in the strict sense. In essence, the spirit of tragedy of postmodern drama was also far from the tragic spirit of the ancient Greek tragedy. The same was the desire and expectation of "God". The "God" in the ancient Greek tragedy was obviously different from the God in post-modern tragedy. Though both of them think of the relationship between human and god, the focus of the ancient Greek tragedy and the postmodern drama is different. Therefore, even if the absurd drama of the 20th century expressed the return to the spirit of tragedy on a certain level, it was only an effort at most.

VI   Conclusion

It could be said that tragedy was in the decline of modern times. Although Pierre

Corneille, Racine and Goethe still wrote tragedies, the conflicts between reason and emotions, emotions and responsibilities that supported the modern tragedy were no longer the tragic spirit that supported the tragedy of ancient Greece. There were no soils for tragedy in modern times. There are two reasons for this: First, the pagan spirit that nourishes the tragic spirit has been expelled by Christianity; second, the skepticism caused by the development of science has exhausted the function of faith. God is dead, what else is worth tangling? After that, no matter how ridiculous and tragic human life is, even if the modern absurd drama is so profound, tragedy as a supreme form of literary works no longer exists. What we have is only the indifference to life, so it is impossible to produce a "tragedy" based on "passion". The tragedy of Euripides does not have the "passion effect" like Sophocles because Euripides doubts more about the existence of God. For these reasons, modern people are considered to be unable to reach the realm of tragedy, or the realm of tragedy is beyond us.

From the perspective of popular culture, the traditional tragedy theory retained deep-rooted aristocratic prejudice and it had a bureaucratic contempt for modernity and ordinary life. However, according to the perspective of elite culture, the existing concept of tragedy has always been transcendent—a concept that transcends reality. A metaphysical concern does not signify the unlucky reality only. As Zhu Guangqian said: "Tragedy signified an idealized life."

In short, the ancient Greek tragedy reflected an ideal life that is higher than real life. For the Chinese and Romans who were too realistic, the tragedy was not the best literary form; the ancient Greek tragedy had an incomparable tragic spirit. The spirit of tragedy, the quality of constant thinking in confusion was not understood by Buddhists, Hebrews and other religious believers. Therefore, Indians and the Hebrews had no tragedy; it was even more impossible in modern times to have tragedy, because philosophy fundamentally destroyed the spirit of poetry no matter how incisive the views of Hegel, Nietzsche and Schopenhauer, they were always just critics rather than tragedians! Thus, the tragedy only belongs to ancient Greek.

（张振宇译）

Chapter 5   The Ancient Greek Philosophy

01   The Rewriting of the Myth of Eros and the Controversy between Poetry and Philosophy of Plato

Ι   Eros in Greek Myth

Eros was the god of love, better known by his Latin name Cupid, son of Aphrodite and Ares, took his place among the small gods of Olympus. He was represented as a little naked boy, with sparkling wings and he carried his bow and arrows wherever he wandered shooting his thrilling arrows mischievously. He inspired the passion of love and provided all nature with life and power of reproduction.The lovely naughty god had two kinds of arrows: the gold tipped arrows used to quicken the pulse of love and the lead tipped ones to stop it. Besides, he had a torch to light hearts. Though sometimes he was blindfolded. No man nor god, Zeus himself included, was safe from his tricks. Once the little naughty god was wounded by his own arrows and such burning love was awakened in his heart for the human maiden psyche that he disregarded the constant interference of his mother and got up his courage to beg Zeus for justice. Another famous story where Eros played an important role was the Argonautic expedition. Medea, daughter of King Aeetes, was wounded by Eros' arrows, took Jason's part in searching for the golden fleece and eventually became the hero's wife.

Eros' mother is Aphrodite, Venus in Roman myth. Venus was raised from the sea. It is said that at the beginning of the world, the Gaia goddess who ruled the earth and the Uranus who ruled the heavens gave birth to a group of giants. Later, the couple turned against each other, and Gaia ordered her son, Kronus, to hurt his father with a sickle. The genital of Uranus fell into the sea and stirred up the foam and Aphrodite was born. Aphrodite in Greek means bubble.

In Greek mythology, although she is promised to be given to Hephaestus by Hera, she has fallen in love with others many times: she commits adultery with the god of war and gives birth to five children; gave birth to Aeneas with the hero Angus. In the Homer era, she often accompanied the goddess of time, the goddess of beauty, and the son cupid. In Rome, she merged with the local fertile plant goddess Venus to become a goddess of harvest and love. Because she is the mother of Aeneas, she is regarded as the female ancestor of the family of Ulysses. Her early image was full of glory and radiance, and was often portrayed as a nude woman.

II   Rewriting of Eros Myth by Plato

The struggle of Plato's poetry and philosophy was not only an eternal struggle between poetry and philosophy, but also a struggle between the poets represented by Homer of ancient Greece and the newly emerging philosophers around the 5th B.C. The philosopher's rational thinking and the world defined by certain concepts are the liquidation and criticism of the former mythology, the traditional world of witchcraft thinking. This controversy not only meant the transformation of ancient Greek culture from the mythology of the witchcraft world to a rational world, but also an ancient cultural and political revolution. Under the discourse mechanism of this transformation, Plato's soul "memory" theory reverses the concept of the soul of witchcraft and reveals the transcendental rationality that can communicate with unemotional ideas in the human soul; Plato's "eros" theory has carried out a critical transformation of the mythical eros, forming a philosophical erotic desire and making "eros" tend to conceptual knowledge. Therefore, Plato's poetry— philosophy struggle has shown that Plato attempted to use the transcendental rationality that philosophy relies on to clean and transform the poetic intuition implicit in mythology and witchcraft, so that transcendental intuition can intuitively standardize poetic intuition and fit with it.

Utopia summarizes all the major issues that Plato has thought about human virtue and politics, poetry and education, precise science, philosophy and myth and show all the themes their positions in Plato's entire ideology. And in the ideal country, Plato repeatedly attacked, degraded poetry and severely expelled the poet in order to maintain the "justice"of the ideal city-state in his heart. Plato mentioned many times the "poetry—philosophy dispute"which has existed for a long time and believed that this "major struggle" was the key to determine the quality of a person.

"The ancient thing", which has existed since ancient times in the dispute between the poetry and philosophy in the book written by Plato, actually improved the status of philosophy, because philosophy was born far later than poetry. As early as the era described by Homer, poetry has been regarded as means of sacrificing and expressing emotions and judging tool for merits. As the earliest intellectual, the poet was both a historical accountant and an interpreter of the cosmology. He was not only the founder of primitive theology, but also the distributor of various knowledge and memory. Poetry reflected the "customs" of the city state, but this custom has now become "opinion" in the vision of philosophy.

In Plato's dialogue, the philosopher's attack on poetry was also unrelenting. In *Utopia*, Plato launched a fierce attack on poetry and poet from the perspective of "the wise man." He believed that poetry was the product of "a city with a high fever." The poet, as one of the non-essential populations was the cause of injustice and war. He satirized the poet like Homer who didn't understand the truth and despised by his own students. They weren't beloved by others and were displaced. He believed that all poets since Homer were only imitators of images of other virtues or other things they made, they didn't know the truth at all. At the same time, He thought that the poets didn't know anything other than imitating the other. If the music color of poetry was removed, the poets' language would become plain. He regarded the poets as a simple imitator, imitating the shadow two layers from the truth. The poets fattened, indulged bad feelings so Plato proposed to expel the poet who could only imitate from the ideal country he established orally. He put poetry and philosophy together and compared that poetry was not a serious thing and philosophy pursues truth. He believed that poetry would have a bad influence on the human mind system and philosophy itself was truth and order.

Plato's serious critique of poetry made people dare not believe that Plato was a man who loved to write poetry before he was the student of Socrates. He was especially good at writing tragic poems. However, in his work *Poetry*, Philip Sidney praised Plato as his most respected teacher, because among all philosophers, the most poetic was Plato. Plato was also a poetry expert. The first existing article in the history of Western literary criticism to discuss poetry and poet's writings *Ian* was written by Plato. In addition, from the philosophical text of Plato, his extensive reference to mythology, vivid dialogue, fluent and rich language, the poetic feature revealed in the words and sentences also reflect Plato's love of poetry.

This contradictory attitude towards the "poetry—philosophy dispute" was also reflected in Plato's critique of poetry in *Utopia*: the second and third volumes were only the requirements for the imitation of poem and poets, but in the last volume plato proposed to expel the poet from the ideal city-state. Although Plato launched a fierce attack on Homer, the originator of the tragic poems, he didn't deny Homer's position in the entire city-state and the wonderful descriptions and rich knowledge contained in Homer's works. On one side, plato insisted on expelling poets out of the city-state, on the other side, he allowed the poets to defend for themselves: "We probably also wanted to tolerate the poetry supporters—they were not poets themselves, just poetry lovers using prose to apologize that poetry was enjoyable and good for orderly management. We also had to listen to their defenses, because if they could explain that poetry was not only pleasant but also beneficial, it was clear that poetry was good for us.

It can be seen that Plato didn't completely deny the value of poetry. Nor did he really want to completely expel poetry and poet from the city-state. He never thought that human life could be perfect without the participation and embellishment of poetry. Poetry was God-given "pleasure". "Poetry was the "child" of skill. Poetry was the opponent of philosophy. Poetry was an effective means of seeking truth. The reason why Plato wanted to expel poetry and poet in *Utopia* was that the poems should be based on the political views of the construction of ideal city-state. In order to construct an environment suitable for the development of truth and philosophy, the imatating poetry should be got rid of because it had bad effect on the justice of the city state.

III   Conversion from Mythological-Poetic Thinking to Transcendental Rational Thinking

Plato's metaphysical discourse mechanism made him think of ideas more real than reality and the idea regulated the final certainty of all phenomena of reality. Therefore, philosophy as "love of wisdom" was to pursue the knowledge of a more real idea than reality, including the highest concept of beauty. The ideal world was a world of eternal certainty that was free from heterogeneity and phenomena. But the problem was that when such a pure concept of justice, goodness and beauty established, how does the mortal person relate to the idea itself which existed in the eternal world? Plato's solution to this problem is another revolutionary change in the dispute between poetry and philosophy: intellectual intuition transferred from the poetic intuition of mythological poetry and witchcraft.

Plato's appeal to knowledge and the resulting liquidation of the world created by mythology-witchcraft, first reflected in his dialogue. He was constantly asking his opponents of the debate not to give examples, but to define and pursue for the reliable, justified knowledge. In this case, on one hand, not only ancient Greek traditions such as mythology, poetry, witchcraft, but also people's habits and experiences were put in doubt; On the other hand, knowledge, argumentation, definition etc. were placed above the custom, experience, opinions, myths and witchcraft. In this sense, the philosophy from Socrates to Plato had the meaning of the political revolution with enlightenment.

In ancient Greece, in Socrates' idea, human wisdom was limited, so was to grasp the Platonic doctrine. There was no knowledge sturdily unless we completed the order to be like God. According to this, the philosophy of loving wisdom was the intuitiveness of Godhood in the soul to the idea. It needed to go away from the flesh through "death practice" to obtain the unity and the communication between the rational intuitiveness and the idea world.

In this sense, the dispute between poetry and philosophy is to get rid of the rheological and illusory world of phenomena and to return to a certain world that can be defined by the highest knowledge of ideas; it was to replace the perceptual descriptions of poetry and myth with conceptual knowledge, to replace poetic imitation or imagination with rational thinking. This made Plato couldn't see the value of the sensual beauty in poetry and art, because they were all emotional, seditious and imitative. Importantly, this discourse logic also made Plato reverse the traditional meaning of "poiesis". The original meaning of "poiesis" was "bringing forth" or "brings to appearance"or "opening". But in Plato there has been a reversal, "poiesis" has become "poetry", the latter was mainly an imitation, in opposition to real production. In this way, the nature of the original generation or generation of "poiesis" from the origin was invisible and became an imitation production. Poetry was placed in the position of making deceitful lies and the beauty of poetry could only be something that satisfied sensual pleasure, then it was rejected.

However, it should be noted that it was the discourse mechanism that enabled Plato to grasp the most beautiful concept of beauty, that is, a beauty that wasn't entangled with the practical needs of reality. This was crucial to the subsequent aesthetic development. Because it laid the core conceptual foundation that aesthetics was about to discuss. When a real concept was cast, the phenomenon associated with the concept revolves around the concept and enriches the connotation and extension of the concept. In this sense, the formation of a core concept implies a revealing exposure. Plato, through its metaphysical casting of the concept of beauty, transforms the sensational beauty which entangled in myth and witchcraft and lacked qualitative into an independent, self-identifying aesthetic ontology. In Plato's elaboration, this beauty itself is a kind of existing truth, a kind of commonality. In other words, Plato's metaphysical structure not only presented a clear, independent concept of beauty, but also deepened the relationship between beauty and truth. Although some scholars say that the discussion of beauty in Plato's dialogue cannot be seen as Plato's aesthetics, we still believe that Plato's discussion of beauty cannot be regarded as non-aesthetic though it is certainly part of his metaphysics because in the opposition of conceptual beauty and sensual beauty which Plato established, there is an implied way of thinking which from the former to the latter, that is, if the concept of beauty was justified, how can the sensual beauty in poetry and art have such connotation? If beauty itself was a kind truth and was the display of true knowledge, then how could art be related to such truth? That is to say, Plato's philosophy shows a way of correcting poetic intuition which exists in mythology and witchcraft through transcendental rationality. The correction which conceptual knowledge, the transcendental rationality made has been shown in Plato's theory of eroticism.

Ⅳ　Conclusion

Plato's dispute between poetry and philosophy wasn't to completely abolish poetry and art, but to liquidate the mythological poetry and imitation art that provides sensual illusions and sensual pleasures and reverse them to a true knowledge. From this perspective, we could understand what kind of poems Plato rejected and what kind of poetry and art plato hoped to create. That is to say, the dispute between poetry and philosophy implies a kind of real poetic and intuitive exploration that is veiled in the mythical witchcraft by transcendental reason.

In general, Plato's ideal lied in the fusion of poetry and philosophy. Of course, the fusion of poetry and philosophy in his mind is not only a combination of forms, but the complementarity between the two. On one hand, philosophy could use the expression of poetry to make philosophical speech more understandable and acceptable. On the other hand, the poet could extract the knowledge he needs from philosophy and enhance the power of reason in his thoughts. The ideal realm was that "the combination of poetry and philosophy to a certain extent brings a vigorous vitality to Plato's language art. Language can be 'sublimated' and can tell the profound meaning. Poetic philosophy talks about "maximizing the potential of language to reveal truth".

Objectively speaking, Plato's ideal of integrating poetry and philosophy was groundbreaking in the history of Western aesthetics, broadening people's academic horizons, and he has considerable insights on the understanding of many issues. However, this "interdisciplinary" thinking was discussed under the premise of not strictly defining poetry and philosophy and will undoubtedly lead to confusion of concepts and confusion of connotations. More importantly, Plato's criteria for evaluating literature and art were political standards. He fundamentally denied the art standard. Therefore, when affirming it, we should also recognize its limitations.

（张振宇译）

02　The Philosophy of the Era of Greek Tragedy

Ⅰ　The Death of God

The death of the metaphysical God marks the end of the philosophy, and the death of the incarnate God is the beginning of the religion. "The death of the God" expresses the real religion: not an authority over us, but a spirit among us.

"The death of the God" written by Nietzsche is the most complete criticism of the western metaphysics after the enlightenment. It is also the absolutely collapse for the logo-centrism and a thorough overturn for the Plato's tradition. He wanted to replace the philosophical tradition as a "system" with the philosophical tradition as "philosopher". He appealed the "Dionysian Spirit" to go against the "Apollo Spirit". He also wanted to pay more attention to the philosophical version to the Greek before Plato. However, although his return to philosophy had profound value and his effort to seek the truth was admiring, his path was still the style of the philosophy,that means the pattern of the Plato. It was sure that he sought the goal of the truth, but the method he sought was still the model of the philosophy. The issue here is: Is philosophy the only way to find the truth? Can the philosophical way really achieve its goal for seeking the truth? Criticized the tradition which he stood in it. Is his criticism really thorough? Is his criticism really effective?

Ⅱ　The Philosophy of the Era of Greek Tragedy

Nietzsche's "the death of the God " made us go back to the philosophy of the era of Greek tragedy. The Greek owned not only Socrates and Plato but also owned other tragic authors, Aeschylus, Sophocles and Euripides. Except Socrates who was written by Plato and Euripides who talked the philosophy on the stage, we also had Socrates who talked the philosophy with people in the street and Sophocles who did not discuss the philosophy. So what's the difference among them? If the philosophy had begun from Aristotle, maybe we could not understand Plato, let alone Socrates and the ancient civilization of the Greek before Socrates. "Firstly, the philosophy means a kind of life or the way of the life, a special way of the life in which the thought and speech take action." The philosophy is not a system but an "individuality" of philosophers. Nevertheless, the "individuality" of philosophers should refer to their unique understandings and attitudes of the life. Philosophers ' understanding of the life related to the meaning of caring the life and the attitude to the life generally embody the great of the humanity, therefore, the philosophy enlightened the nation and human beings. If the history of the philosophy turned into the systematic substituted philosophy, the result is that "the individual things would be buried inevitably." Although the system can be abandoned, the personality of the philosophers would have a deep influence forever. Comparing with the system, the character can be more valuable and more essential. The philosophy was not the knowledge but the method of the life. The purpose of the philosophy was not to seek the truth, which the scientific thought did. "The philosophy starts with the legislation of the greatness." The philosophy sought for something scared and useful. The interests and useful things were the scientific motivation. The philosophy was about the life—not the existence of our body, but the worth of the spirit. The philosophical concerning of the life is to concern the meaning of the life.

If the philosophy was also a kind of the way to the life, so what distinguishes the philosophy and the poem as the method of the life? If the philosophy was also a way of the life, why did Plato expel poets from the Utopia? There was no doubt that the poem was also a kind of the way of the life. Socrates once regarded Homer as an educator of all Greek. Herodotus once delivered that, before Plato, "Homer and Hesiod...taught the family property of the God to the Greece, including some of their names, rank and honors, skills and shapes they told. " By the description of the tree diagram of the God, Homer and Hesiod together worked out the way — a kind of the way organized and guaranteed by the God to the life for the political community so that it can help the nations and polis in Greece. The characteristics of heroes in the epics written by Homer, such as the courage, is regarded as the highest ethics of the life, and all the life guaranteed or embodied by the gods is regarded as "the best and the noblest life" [Plato: *Laws*(888b)]. It means that "poems" had a positive influence on the legislation and the establishment of the political institution. Compared with the philosophy, poetry can provide or consist more whole knowledge—two epics, *Iliad and Odyssey* written by Homer, covered all life of human beings.Therefore, if the philosophy wanted to purse the whole knowledge about people's life,it must learn from poetry. Therefore, on the one hand, Plato wanted to expel poets from the "Utopia", on the other hand, he also wanted to rebuild a statement with the "poetry" for the polis.

Plato regarded "poetry" as the object of criticism and he wanted to establish orders for the city-state with the "poetry". But what is the significance? Since the poems written by Homer are political, Plato, as a competitor, must write poems with characteristics of politics. Since Homer described a way of life for people who lived in the city-sate by his poems, Plato had to replace it with philosophical poetry. However ,Plato, as a poet himself, was determined to expel Homer with the form of "poetry". There were two reasons for it. One was the issue of limitation and rationality, the other was the shield to attack with the spear of the other. The philosophers required the whole wise or absolute knowledge. Nevertheless, only the god had the whole wise and absolute knowledge. The philosophers couldn't do it without depending the rationality. The language of the poetry was necessary for the philosophers. The rational words could not achieve the unlimited purpose. Even the philosophers seeking for the truth in their whole life cannot overcome the fundamental limitation of the rationality. Therefore, in *Utopia*, Socrates explained the truth of metaphysics by metaphor one after another, for instance, the sun, caves and so on. When it comes to the politics, the rules of political life can not only depend on the argument— because the argumentation can delay without limit, but the political issue can not wait to be solved. Thus, the legislative action of lawmaker can not completely rely on the rationality but to depend on the myth, the story and the allegory, in other words, which was the poetry. Hence, for the politics, the most important things are not the knowledge, argumentation, philosophy and the truth, but the ideas, the myth, the poetry and the lie. Therefore, it must happen to crash between the philosophers and the community of the city-state. So-called the "noble lie" told by Plato, was for the majority people—since the rationality was limited, since the majority people wanted to understand the arguments and foundation legislated by the philosophers without the rationality. Therefore, the most effective way that we can persuade and educate a lot of people with the "story". "Story" or (poetry) can be the best way for political education in the city-state. When the story spread generation by generation, when our descendants realized it sooner or later, a new type of custom and patriarchal system would be built. This kind of "story" was the "noble lie". "The noble story " was not always absolutely against the truth, which was the "correct idea". Although it was not the "correct idea", it was the suggestion that most of people can accept. The new poetry written by Plato was a kind of the "noble lie" like that. However, not all of "stories" and "lies" were noble. If writers slandered others or falsify the history on purpose, those kinds of "evil lies" can eventually bring negative influence for thousands of years.

The philosophy restarted after leaving the research of the physics and mathematics, which was "the second voyage " that Plato said through Socrates in the famous work named *Phaedo*. "The second voyage" of the philosophy had a tight relationship with the poetry. Therefore, Plato rebuilt the statement for the city-state in the way of poetry. If the epics of Homer were the classical poems, while the philosophical poems of Plato were the new style ones. The epics of Homer represented the custom life of mass and the life of patriarchal system that most of people lived in the city-state. While the philosophy of Plato represented a newly style of life that less people pursued the wisdom. The stipulation of Homer's epics was the philosophy—a kind of the political way of the life, which can be regarded as "the dispute between the Athens and Jerusalem within the Athens."Although both of them had the same point in the politics, the former was religionary and sensitive and the latter was philosophical and rational. The reason why Plato opposed Homer was that the epics of Homer embraced the "idea", relied on the "lust" and was located in the "cave", whose purpose was that "an evil political system was created in everyone's soul"(*Republic* 605b). Plato produced his dramas with methods of the literature and figures of speech, for instance, myth, metaphor, allegory and so on, to be against the classical epics of Homer with the newly style ones. Homer wrote Achilles,while Plato created Socrates as a new image of heroes.

Achilles lived for honor, Socrates died for justice; Achilles was the incarnation of the courage, Socrates was the model of the morality; Achilles was driven by the lust, Socrates was limited by the rationality. All in all, Plato expelled the poetry of Homer with his own poems.

The philosophy, in the era of Greek tragedy, was the beginning of the "dispute between the poetry and the philosophy", was also the ending of the "dispute between the poetry and the philosophy". The long-standing dispute between poetry and philosophy had led to the crisis of logo-centrism in the west for two thousands years. Returning to the dispute between poetry and philosophy was the way to solve it. There was an old saying that whoever starts the trouble should end it. Plato was regarded as the father in the rational philosophy in the west, so returning to Plato was the best key to solve the crisis of the logo-centrism.

Nietzsche criticized the western rational philosophy tradition of Plato, because in this tradition "poetry" had not any places. In the tradition of Plato's annotating for more than two thousand years, Plato's "dispute between poetry and philosophy" was understood as the conflict between the "poetry" and the "philosophy". however, the completely opposition of "philosophy" is not only the misunderstanding to Plato, but also the crisis of the human spirit for modern people which can not be worked out. The concerning to the meaning of the life in the center of philosophy inevitably pushed human to believe the metaphysics. However, the problem is that the metaphysics was not scientific and logical but visual and mysterious.— "the root of the concept about metaphysics was deeply covered in the some mystical senses ." The purpose of philosophy for Nietzsche's returning to the tragic era, was to overturn the tradition of Plato's annotating and misunderstanding for over two thousand years in the west.

Nietzsche had turned to the ancient Greek, pointing the philosophy in the tragic era, but his foothold was in the longer history. He recommended the Heraclitus even more—although Pythagoras and Empedocles were also praised, Heraclitus was even more isolated: because he surpassed the human beings, merged with the space and became the reality of the world and the truth and the deities that were immortal. "The world needs the truth forever, so it also needs Heraclitus forever, although Heraclitus does not need the world. " The reason why Nietzsche highly praised Heraclitus was that he firmly opposed to master the essence of the world by depending on the logic, which was obviously and deeply enlightened by Kant. Nietzsche believed that firstly the cognition of the philosophy to the essence of the world was the kind of the intuition, and the real way to achieve understanding was not the logic but the imagination. From the very beginning, Nietzsche took the metaphysics as the faith, intuition and imagination, not the science and logic. Therefore, Nietzsche especially recommends the ancient philosophers, such as Taylor and Heraclitus. He said, "When Taylor said that 'everything is water', the human beings can break through the worm-like touch and crawl of single science, predicted the final answers to the matters and overcome the general limitation of lower levels of cognition by the ability of prediction." From the viewpoint of Nietzsche, any deeply intuitions of philosophy can be presented by the scientific and logical way, which was only a method to express what we saw and also a poor means. Essentially, this was only "the transliteration that was metaphorical and unreliable in the different regions and languages." Taylor saw the unity of the existence, but he did not know how to describe and deliver his findings. In this issue, it not only involves the question of rational limitation, but also the question of the linguistic limitation. Therefore, he thought of "water",then he used it to express the most profound thoughts of the philosophy. There is no doubt that the image is poetical, so the language is. So the image not only awakens the feeling of the poetry, but also the imagination of the poems. Actually, there are no essential differences about things, no matter what the "water" of Taylor was, the "fire" of Heraclitus was, or the "atom" of Democritus was. When the scientific structure collapsed, the rest still remained. Among the rest, there was a kind of the motivation, even involved the hope of future which blossoms and fruits—" in fact, the rest things were the intuitions of 'the unity to the existence', which can form the faith of metaphysics that human beings could surpass the experiential world." If giving up this intuition, the philosophy would lose the source power of its existence.

Ⅲ　Conclusion

The ancient Greeks were a typical nation of philosophy, and their "to love wisdom tradition" was so famous. "Most saints were from other nations, while philosophers came from the Greek..., in other times and other places, philosophers were wanderers accidentally and lonely in the most hostile environment. They either hide their names or fight alone to live. Only in the Greek, can the philosophers not be accidental. " The Hellenes worked on the philosophy for not pursuing the knowledge. "With the concerning of the life and the need of life in the ideal, they limit the earnest for knowledge from a baby, then, they create the typical brain of philosophy." For concerning of the meaning of life, the Greeks had the "knowledge"—in Nietzsche's opinion, the reason why we lived the uncultured times was that we lost the concerns of the meaning of life. In the uneducated times, the philosophy was only bound to "the academic confessions for the lonely wanderers, the spoils of war for others, the secret room for the solitaries or the harmful chatter between the anility and the child. The Greeks are educated, because their health, only the health of a nation can endow the full rights of the philosophy. The ancient Romans were also healthy, but they can live without philosophy. The culture made the ancient Greeks have a kind of keen ability of discrimination and a kind of noble taste. "To define a nation, it is better to see in what ways they recognize to define and recommend these great persons rather than to see what great persons it has. " A lot of philosophers were in the ancient Greeks, and the Hellenes were proud of them. The philosophers look down upon everything, and they regard interests as a flash in the pan. The greatness of philosophers do not depend on the attitudes that human beings towards them, while the greatness of human beings depends on the philosophers. There is no greater pride of philosophers than that. There is no greater pride of the ancient Greeks than that. The philosophy, in the ancient Greek, was the pride for the ancient Greeks as well as the precious treasures for the whole mankind.

（宣麒麟译）

Part 2

Hebrew Traditions

Chapter 1   The History of *the Old Testament* Tradition

01   *Ecclesiastes, Lamentations* and the Tragic Past of Hebrews

I   Introduction

Hebrew civilization was born in Canaan, the Palestinian region today. About 1200B.C.-400 B.C., the Hebrews founded Judaism. They believed in God, and claimed that the Hebrews were the voters of God and had a contract with God. In the nearly 1000 years of history, the Hebrews have been constantly ravaged and displaced by war. Judaism has become the spiritual bond to maintain the Hebrew national consciousness. *Lamentations* deeply reflect the bitter and difficult history of the Hebrews, and their helplessness in the face of disaster. They hope to be saved and rebuild their homes by relying on their faith.

II   The History of Hebrews

The Hebrews were originally a branch of the Semitic tribe and were originally meant as "people crossing the river." Around 3000 BC, under the leadership of Jewish patriarch Abraham, Jews crossed the Euphrates River and Jordan River from Ur city and moved to Canaan, known as Hebrew. In 935 BC, the Hebrew kingdom was divided into the northern state of Israel and the southern state of Judea. The state of Israel was destroyed by the Assyrians in 722 B.C. In 972 B.C., Solomon, son of Jewish king David, came to power and built a temple in the capital Jerusalem. From then on, the temple became the center of Jewish power and symbol of faith. However, the Jews did not live in a stable life from then on. In the following hundreds of years, the Jewish state was continuously divided and occupied by many countries. The temple was even destroyed.

In 586 B.C., the Jewish state was overthrown by the kingdom of Babylon. Nebuchadnezzar occupied Jerusalem, the capital of the Jewish state, destroyed the Temple of Solomon and captured a large number of upper-class Jews to penal servitude in Babylon. In 538 B.C., the Persian empire conquered the kingdom of Babylon. the Persian empire repatriated the Jews imprisoned in Babylon and rebuilt the temple (the second temple) after the Jews returned to Jerusalem. the Persian empire allowed the Jews to establish theocracy under the premise of obeying the Persian rule, but the Jewish state at this time was not an independent sovereign state though it enjoyed autonomy. In 331 B.C., Alexander conquered Canaan and Judea was ruled by the Greek Empire. In the early days of Greek rule, Jews still enjoyed freedom of religion. After Antioch IV came to power, in order to stabilize the regime, he began to exercise high-handed rule over Jews and suppress Judaism. In 168 B.C., After Antioch IV issued the first order to destroy religion in human history. He openly declared Judaism illegal, ordered the abolition of all Jewish festivals, the burning of all holy books, the prohibition of Israeli circumcision and the observance of the Sabbath. He also abolished the religious taboos of all Israelis and ordered all Israelis to convert to Greek religion and worship the altar of Zeus Olympia in the Temple of Jerusalem. Violators will all be executed on the spot. In order to humiliate the Jews, they sacrificed pigs that were considered unclean by the Jews and even forced the Jews to eat pork. Under Antioch IV 's brutal rule, the Jewish people rose up and the Makabi Uprising broke out. After a long and arduous 25-year struggle, the Jewish nation finally liberated all of Palestine in 143 B.C. and achieved national liberation. Later the Roman Empire turned the Jewish region into a Roman province. After Rome captured Pakistan, Jews revolted against the Roman occupiers, but they were all brutally suppressed by the Roman rulers. In 135 A.D., the Jews revolted again and were defeated in the end. More than a century, the Roman rulers massacred 1.5 million Jews and finally dismissed all the remaining Jews. Jerusalem was completely razed to the ground, the Jewish regime ceased to exist, and the 2000-year wandering of Jews began.

Ⅲ *Lamentations of Jeremiah*

Lamentations of Jeremiah is a book of wisdom. This book consists of 5 chapters and records the lamentations of the Jews after Jerusalem and the temple were destroyed (586 years ago). It is generally believed that the *Lamentations* of Jeremiah was written by the prophet Jeremiah. it was written during the Babylonian conquest of Jerusalem in 586 B.C. This war was the beginning of the bitter history of the Hebrew people. the temple was destroyed. a large number of Hebrew residents were captured and sent to Babylon as slaves for half a century. history calls it "prisoners of Babylon." The former Jewish king state reached its peak in the era of David Solomon, and the people lived and worked in peace and contentment. Now that the city is in mourning, the Jewish people can only sing the lament of national subjugation tragically under the feet of the enemy.

This lament is not "personal sorrow", but "national sorrow" of the country's destruction. Its sorrow is far deeper than any sentimental work. There is no emotion more gloomy or shocking than the destruction of the country and the loss of people's home. In Hebrew's national memory, the pain of national subjugation magnified their inner pain to the extreme. However, the Jewish nation at that time was powerless to change the pain of national subjugation and the humiliation of power. In *Lamentations*, the Jews pointed the source of the war to the secular evil- "Jerusalem sinned grievously, so she has become mockery; All who honored her despise her, for they have seen her nakedness; she herself groans, and turns her face away." They think that "The Lord is in the right, for I have rebelled against his words." The Lord was angry and condemned to the world. Only through devout repentance can he "believe in salvation". This is a cry against the miserable world weakly. Hebrews have always claimed to be God's voters, but in reality, the Jewish region has always suffered from wars. The highest symbol of Hebrew belief, Solomon temple, was ruthlessly crushed by the enemy and the spirit of Hebrew was also destroyed. The contradiction between belief and reality led them to a basic concept to explain all human sufferings, namely "sin of human" and "punishment of divine".

Taking "God's will" as the absolute value standard of all behaviors, only trusting in the Lord and repenting completely can they change the tragic fate-this explanation can well bridge the desperate reality and the hopeful future, which is the inevitable need of spiritual liberation based on physical torture. Therefore, the *Lamentations* of Jeremiah is optimistic on the whole and conforms to the basic characteristics of general beliefs. The first few chapters of *Lamentations* describe the tragic situation in Jerusalem and God's punishment. The next few chapters turn to call on God to punish the invaders. "Pay them back for their deeds, O LORD, according to the work of their hands! Give them anguish of heart; your curse be on them! Pursue them in anger and destroy them from under the LORD's heavens."They prayed to be accepted by God again ,to be protected from difficulties and to return to their homes.

IV   Conclusion

The Hebrew nation is a nation that has suffered many hardships. It has suffered a lot from war and displacement. However, the Hebrews fought bravely with their tenacious faith and firm belief, eventually creating immortal classics and leaving an indelible spiritual mark on world civilization.

（徐秋月译）

02   Nationalism in *Old Testament*

I   The Belief of Monotheism

Hebrews have established the monotheistic faith since Abraham, which is best shown in the story of Abraham's sacrifice to Isaac: *Genesis* (22:1-18) tells the story of Abraham's sacrifice to Isaac. God tested Abraham. He said to him, "Abraham!" And he said, "Here I am." He said, "Take your son, your only son Isaac, whom you love, and go to the land of Moriah, and offer him there as a burnt offering on one of the mountains that I shall show you." So Abraham rose early in the morning, saddled his donkey, and took two of his young men with him, and his son Isaac; he cut the wood for the burnt offering, and set out and went to the place in the distance that God had shown him. On the third day Abraham looked up and saw the place far away. Then Abraham said to his young men, "Stay here with the donkey; the boy and I will go over there; we will worship , and then we will come back to you." Abraham took the wood of the burnt offering and laid it on his son Issac, and he himself carried the fire and the knife. So the two of them walked on together. Issac said to his father Abraham, "Father!" And he said, "Here am I, my son." He said, "The fire and the wood are here, but where is the lamb for a burnt offering?" Abraham said, "God himself will provide the lamb for a burnt offering, my son." So the two of them waled on together. When came to the place that God had shown him, Abraham built an alter there and laid the wood in order. He bound his son Isaac, and laid him on the alter, on top of the wood. Then Abraham reached out his hand and took the knife to kill his son. But the angel of the Lord called to him from heaven, and said, "Abraham, Abraham!" And he said, "Here am I." He said, "Do not lay your hand on the boy or do anything to him; for now I know that you fear God, since you have not withheld your son, your only son, from me." And Abraham looked up and saw a ram, caught in a thicket by its horns. Abraham went and took the ram and offered it up as a burnt offering instead of his son.

II Belief and National Identity

After Jacob wrestled with the angels, God changed Jacob's name to "Israel". Since then Jacob's descendants have been called Israelis. Although the Israelis still continue to believe in monotheism, in the polytheistic atmosphere in the land of Canaan, under the rule of the Egyptians and the subjugation of the Assyrians, the Israelis have gradually accepted the influence of polytheism and gradually deviated from their own belief tradition, or their belief is not so pure. However, after the subjugation of North Israel and the capture of Babylon and Persia, South Judah realized the importance of the purity of faith to maintain the nation and began to strengthen the power of faith in various ways. However, this effort could not escape the later Greek invasion. Jews either gradually became Greek in the Greek environment or began to go to the extreme of nationalism under the pressure of the Gentiles. Looking at the course of this development, we find that the Jewish faith is closely related to its national consciousness: whether it is for the Second Temple Judaism or for Rabbi Judaism.

The history of national subjugation after the "Babylonian prisoners" made the Jews more sensitive to the consciousness of national identity. Although the short reign of Persians and the loose policies of Alexander the Great and Ptolemy eased the sensitivity to some extent, the harshness of Seleucid dynasty further deepened the sensitivity; although the Hellenistic environment has gradually weakened the national consciousness of some Jews, especially the aristocracy, priests and vested interests among Jews, reforms of the reformist within Judaism have made some Jews (especially Pharisees) more sensitive. What is interesting here is that the hatred of the Pharisees towards the pro-Roman Herod family and the Jewish priesthood is not as good as their hatred towards Jesus. This shows that the so-called nationalism is sometimes just an excuse: the Pharisees are the main force of Rabbi Judaism, because after the destruction of the Second Temple, other tribes of the Jews such as Sadducees, Nazarenes and Zealots disappeared. The Pharisees thus developed a more sensitive nationalism. Then why is the Pharisee's nationalism complex not as good as that of the Zealots in Jesus' time? Are they targeting the reformer, Jesus, instead of Roman puppet government because of Jesus' accusation? Obviously, nationalism is sometimes just a tool used by a certain group of people for a certain purpose. Take the Macabies family as an example. The uprising of the Macabies family initially had a positive meaning of national liberation, but when the Hasmony dynasty was established, it also made great compromises and exchanges of interests with other races, which is enough to show the hypocrisy of the so-called nationalism in front of interests.

The dispute between North Israel and South Judah in the history of the Hebrew nation seems to be the best example of the narrow nationalism of the Jews. Even their brothers are constantly fighting, killing each other, and they are incompatible with each other. How can we talk about tolerance towards the Gentiles? From the reconstruction of the temple, the radical nationalism of the Jews has been continuously strengthened: from the prohibition of marriage between Jews and the Gentiles in *Nishimi* and *Ezra* to the subsequent revolution in *Macabies*, this tendency has intensified. Jews who suffered the pain of national subjugation began to reflect on their own history: some prophets bravely criticized the extreme and obstinacy of the Hebrews, criticized the corruption and depravity of the upper rulers, and called for religious tolerance, but others strengthened the Hebrew national consciousness and xenophobia. For example, Ezra, the high priest, is a narrow-minded nationalist: after returning to Jerusalem, Ezra's most important job was to rebuild the temple and reorganize the customs. Ezra thought that the Hebrews have not separated themselves from the peoples of the lands with their abominations, from the Canaanites, the Hittites, the Perizzites, the Jebusites, the Ammonites, the Moabites, the Egyptians, and the Amorites who were guilty, and his reaction was extremely fierce: "I tore my garment and my mantle, and pulled hair from my head and my beard, and sat appalled." (*Ezra* 9: 1-3).They pledged themselves to send away their wives, and their guilt offering was a ram of the flock for their guilt.(*Ezra* 10:19).During this period, the priests and the Jews renewed their pact and made the rest of the people swear that "We will not give our daughters to the peoples of the land or take their daughters for our sons."(*Nehemiah* 10:30) This practice of drawing a clear line with the Gentiles, while maintaining the Jewish lineage, has deepened the estrangement between different nationalities.

Jews are not only cut off from the Gentiles, but also cannot coexist peacefully with their kin. For example, the prophet Obadiah claimed to have been inspired by the Lord and cursed the Edomites because when Jerusalem was destroyed, the Edomites gloated and even helped to rob the victims and sell the refugees to the invaders. However, in fact, Edomites are descendants of Jacob's brother Esau. They live in Edom, because Edom is a mountainous country, so the people live in the mountains. But the Jews thought Edom was their old enemy and he asked the Lord to punish Edom (the book of *Obadiah*). The book of *Malachi* also begins by scolding the Edomites, and the religious thought is extremely narrow and there is no broad mind in it. The book of *Haggai* also shows narrow nationalism: Haggai hopes that the governor of Judah will be king and concentrate all his treasure in Jerusalem so that all the peoples of the world will worship the Lord there.

The prophets cursed the invaders such as Babylon and Assyria and looked forward to their destruction. For example, the book of *Nahum* accuses the king of Assyria and hopes for the destruction of Nineveh, "See, I am against you, says the LORD of hosts, and I will burn your chariots in smoke, and the sword shall devour your young lions: and I will cut off your prey from the earth, and the voice of your messengers shall be heard no more."(*Nahum* 2:13) The prophet who experienced the destruction of his country and his family not only poured his anger on the invader Assyria, but also spread to other so-called "enemies": "A jealous and avenging God is the LORD; the LORD is avenging, and wrathful; the LORD takes vengeance on his adversaries, and rages against his enemies... Bashan and Carmel wither, and the bloom of Lebanon fades. "(*Nahum* 1:2-4) The powerful empire that destroyed Israel and Judah is certainly hateful, and those who are not as economically powerful as their Jewish neighbors and do not believe in the Lord are also hateful to the Hebrews: "For Gaza shall be deserted, and Ashkelon shall become a desolation: Ashdod's people shall be driven out at noon, and Ekron shall be uprooted. Ah, inhabitants of the seacoast, you nation of the Cherethites! The word of the LORD is against you; O Canaan, the land of the Philistines, I will destroy you until no inhabitant is left."(*Zephaniah* 2:4-5) No violent uprising broke out in northern Israel under the Assyrian empire and in southern Judah under the Babylonian king, but the famous revolution in Macabies broke out in Seleucid dynasty. The reason is probably: Assyria and Babylon belong to Asian countries, their culture, religion and Hebrew are similar, and foreign rulers do not interfere with culture very much. The Greek culture is fundamentally different from Hebrew. The rulers interfere with the Hebrew religious culture and even use coercive means to oppress the Hebrew religious culture. For example, in the 2nd century B.C., Epiphanes IV of Antioch (175 B.C.-164 B.C.) strongly advocated Greek culture. He built an arena next to Jerusalem, set up a statue of Zeus in the temple of the Lord to be worshipped, offered pigs on the altar of the Lord, and banned Jewish circumcision. These cultural oppressions were more intolerable than political oppression, which led to the Macabies revolution in 165 B.C.

Christians are opposed to the extreme nationalism of some Jews, especially the early Christians, who include not only some Jews but also the Gentiles. If early

Christianity also included Jews (especially Jews living in the diaspora and Jews living among the Gentiles), then later Christianity was gradually occupied by the Gentiles (especially after Christianity became the Roman state religion). Although most Jews hold a nationalistic attitude, especially narrow and extreme nationalism, it is mostly manifested in the cultural field, but the Perpetrators turn this extreme nationalism into political action. However, this narrow and extreme nationalism has become a huge controversy within the early Christianity (the factions of Paul and John & the factions of Peter and Jacob) and has also become an important difference (even the main difference) between Christianity and Rabbi Judaism.

Ⅲ   The Consciousness of Voters

So, what made Hebrew, Israeli and Jewish people have such strong national psychology? That is "the identity of voters" and "the consciousness of voters". One thing is basic in the self-understanding of the Israelis: they are convinced that they are chosen by the Lord. God chose Israel, and Israel responded to God's selection through a special covenant. This is more deeply rooted in the pre-exile era than "monotheistic beliefs". In ancient stories and creed, this point is constantly reiterated: from Abraham being chosen by God to God agreeing to Abraham's land. (*Genesis* 12: 1-3 and 15: 1-6 describe the initial choice and God's consent to Abraham, and this is clearly stipulated in the form of contracts in 15: 17-21 and 17: 1-8) In *Deuteronomy*, we can see such a strong statement: "When the LORD thy God shall bring thee into the land whither thou goest to possess it, and hath cast out many nations before thee." (*Deuteronomy* 7: 1-7) The central part of Deuteronomy describes the sacred motive of the Lord to rescue Israel from Egypt and grant land to Israel's ancestors (*Deuteronomy* 6: 20-25;26: 5-10).

This consciousness of being chosen played an important role in the Judaism of the Second Temple. That is to say, the lesson of the destruction of North Israel and the fate of the exile of South Judah strengthened this voter's consciousness. Therefore, the voter's consciousness, together with the Temple and Torah, became the main pillar of the Judaism of the Second Temple. The emphasis on voter identity, the emphasis on the significance of the temple (Persians allowed Jews to rebuild the temple, and the prophet Ezra led the people to rebuild the temple, which has unusual significance for Jews: the second temple is more significant to Jewish national identity than Solomon's temple), and the reorganization of Torah (Jews exiled after the first temple was destroyed lost their place of worship, so they attached more importance to the written Torah tradition), which became the main pillar and belief support of Judaism in the second temple. These supports reconstructed the faith of the Jewish people in the post-exile era. Nationalism was strengthened during the Jewish period of the Second Temple, because the subjugation of North Israel (not objectively, but spiritually) had taught Jews a heavy lesson, so they realized the importance of faith and national identity to their nation-building. Ezra firmly opposes intermarriage (although this tradition has always existed in the history of the Israelis), thus eliminating the entangled people and land. The prophets warned the Jews with harsh words: Israel is a people chosen by God to be separated from others. Although this action of the prophets is understandable: Jews who have suffered from national subjugation will disappear into the dust of history like Samaritans if they cannot take extreme measures to safeguard their faith and national identity. However, this kind of voter consciousness and voter identity can easily lead to an ethnic superiority and extreme exclusiveness, which also became an important reason why Jews were later rejected by the western world.

Ezra's reforms put Torah at the heart of Israeli life again. Along with other basic features of Judaism in the Second Temple, the model of contractual legalism was greatly strengthened in the revolutionary era of Macabies. In the era of Macabies, the Israeli identity of the contractual and legal subjects was at stake (*Maccabees* I 1: 57;2: 27,50; *Maccabees* II 1: 2-4;2: 21-22;5: 15;13: 14). The response of some Jews to this crisis was expressed as "zeal for the law" and became the slogan of national resistance (*Maccabees* I 2: 26-27, 50, 58). Macabies's resistance to alien culture and ethnic assimilation stems from the belief that Israel's land and people are not just one of many, but the special selection of the one god. After the revolution in Macabies, selection, the intersection of contract and law are still the basic and continuous themes of Jewish self-understanding. Ben Sira should conform to the hypothesis of *Deuteronomy*: The Lord's kingship and his special election to Israel *(Deuteronomy* 32: 8-9; *Bisyllands* 17: 11-17). Bensirah was the first to call the divine wisdom of the universe "the covenant of the supreme god, the law Moses commanded us to obey as Jacob's legacy" (*Bensirah* 24: 23). The Book of Jubilee also strengthened the Jewish voters' identity and contractual identity. By repeating the contracts made by the Lord, the legal obligations related to them, and the special selection of the Lord for the Israelis, these works continuously strengthen the Jewish voters' awareness. As for the Quinlan community, all is the same.

Israeli (Jewish) adherence to the law will give rise to a natural, more or less unavoidable view: this uniqueness means privilege, that is, a privilege enjoyed by the nation chosen by a single god and given the law of contract. This is obvious in those narratives that ignore, deny and regard the Gentiles as sinners. This sense of privilege not only aroused the resentment of the Gentiles during the Hellenistic period, but also aroused the widespread hatred of the Jews in the Christian world. Even today, in the fierce Israeli-Palestinian confrontation, we cannot stand on Israel's side with absolute sympathy. For this hostility to the outside world, the Jews either closed their doors and turned a blind eye, or tried to beautify the Israeli (Jewish) tradition (sense of privilege). Faced with an increasingly powerful world of the Gentiles, Jews have to try to apologize for Israel's declaration (the chosen people of the one God) and these statements (regarding the Gentiles as sinners).

Israel's unique and privileged consciousness, which Judaism insists on, has created narrow and extreme nationalism of the Jewish nation. This sense of privilege gives Israelis (Jews) a sense of superiority, which, if in power, will become a tool to oppress the Gentiles. When the Gentiles are in power, this sense of privilege, as a part of Jewish self-understanding, occupies an important position in their view of their society and their view of the world. From the perspective of sociology, special selection and contractual legalism inevitably become the expression of Jewish uniqueness-especially the law and ritual practice, all of which strengthen the awareness of Jewish unique identity. In the Jewish law, apart from the law of not intermarrying with the Gentiles (mainly referring to the Ammonites and Moabites), there are three other points that clearly distinguish Jews from the Gentiles: circumcision, Sabbath and food laws. No matter from the inside of the Jews or from the outside of the Greek-Roman world, these three points are Jewish identity marks.

IV Conclusion

Since the initial selection, the meaning of the word "Judaism" has been continuously strengthened. The word "Judaism" combines the Jewish faith and the Jewish national consciousness more and more closely, but this strengthening has also brought about great negative effects. Israel's ethnic superiority and exclusiveness caused by this voter consciousness have become the reason for their exclusion. Thus, this ethnic identity is a double-edged sword: it can save the Jewish nation or destroy the Jewish nation (the genocide in Nazi Germany is naturally shameful, but shouldn't the Jews themselves reflect? However, unfortunately, this belief of the Jews has continued into our time, and the Israeli-Palestinian conflict is a witness. What is sadder is that this kind of extreme nationalism is not only reflected in the conflicts between Arabs and Israelis. Looking at the world situation, from the conflicts between Irish and English to the conflicts between Russians and other ethnic groups such as Ukrainians, the tendency of extreme nationalism has become more and more intense all over the world. It can be seen that the Holocaust in Nazi Germany during the Second World War is only a microcosm, and the lessons learned from Germany during the Second World War have not really been accepted by mankind. On the contrary, narrow nationalism is still being advocated by some scholars and exploited by some politicians, and world peace is still under great threat. From this point of view, Jews are the epitome of the whole human race, so to reflect on the history of Jews is to reflect on the history of the whole human race. To face up to the Jewish present is to face up to the human present.

（徐秋月译）

03 Cosmopolitanism in *Old Testament*

I YHWH in *Old Testament*

In the *Old Testament*, God is called "Lord" (also translated as Yahweh): the h in the middle of the Hebrew Yahweh was not pronounced, but later, for convenience, the silent h was pronounced as Ho and became Jehoweh. The Lord was the god of Midian in the south of Canaan, and was absorbed by the Jews in the south of Hebrews. Here we can see the trace of Moses taking a foreign woman as his wife and also accepting the religious beliefs of his wife. However, the Israelis in the north did not believe in the Lord at first. Their god was Elohim, the god of Canaan and Syria in the north. The Syrians and Hebrews are brotherly peoples, with many similarities in language, belief, thinking, nationality and customs. Moses gradually established his authority and ruling position in the 40 years he led Israel out of Egypt and in the wilderness. Moses ruled not only politically but also religiously. In order to facilitate ideological control, Moses used coercive means to make the "Lord" the god of national unity.

Compared with Jesus in the *New Testament*, the Lord in *the Old Testament* seems to be more hostile.Why are the "father and son" in *New testament* different from the *Old Testament*? There is always such a prejudice in the academic world: *The New Testament* represents a universal mind while *the Old Testament* represents a narrow national consciousness. Although this view reflects the general development trend of Christianity to form its own unique personality from Judaism, it ignores the Judaism as the source of Christianity and has opened the way for Christian universalism.

In fact, before Judaism was split into Rabbi Judaism and Christianity, there were multiple factors and there was no unified and standard Judaism. Especially in the Jewish period of the Second Temple, many different interest groups have their own religious views, and these religious sects or different ideological groups-Pharisees, Sadducees, Essenes, Peruvians-all had their own documents, such as *the Dead Sea Scrolls* which contained many Essenes documents. One of the most noteworthy ideas in post-exile Judaism is the "Second Isaiah" movement. Different from the exclusion of nationalism, the "Second Isaiah Trend" has a tolerant national spirit and religious consciousness.

The Hebrews, who had experienced the pain of subjugation and the humiliation of captivity, developed two completely opposite national concepts: one is to strengthen the original narrow national consciousness and form ultra-nationalism;

the other is to emphasize peaceful coexistence with gentiles and to build the ideal of world harmony under the blessing of "God." In the Prophets of the *Old Testament*, these two thoughts coexist, confront and complement each other, and form a unique landscape.

Ⅱ　Violence in *Old Testament*

Moses was a great founding hero, a military strategist, a politician, a religious scholar and a legislator, as well as a poet and an orator. In the 40 years he lived in Egypt's pharaoh's palace, he learned knowledge of literature, history, army and politics. During his 40 years in Midian's father-in-law's house, he learned about animal husbandry and religion. During his 40 years in the wilderness, he established his own political, military and religious rule. The establishment of any country is accompanied by violence-"legal violence". Moses' rule was also based on blood.600000 people marched in the desert, hungry and thirsty, and blocked by enemies, so not everyone was willing to follow Moses. Moses had to deal with not only the people's religious complaints: some worshipped the Golden Calf (the symbol of Egyptian polytheism); there were also complaints about life: "It is better not to leave Egypt"-in Egypt, at least there was meat to eat; What's more, Moses was facing rebellion: one of the Levites named Korah united 250 famous leaders such as Abilan and An to form a new group against Aaron as chief priest.

Moses' treatment of traitors was cruel: Moses melted the Golden Calf and ground it into powder for the Israelis to drink in order to deal with the religious rebellion. Moses did not allow those who complained about life to enter the promised land, but those who instigated the people to complain were all plague（*Exodus*:32:19-21）; as for the political rebellion, Moses' method was even more sinister: Moses assigned the descendants of the Levites to kill traitors among his own people.3000 people of Levites were killed that day. Moses asked Korah to bring a censer to the entrance of the holy tent the next day, and then announced their crimes. The ground under the traitors' feet split and engulfed the house of Korah and his conspirators. Then, David sent fire to 250 of his companions, and he also sent pestilence and killed 14700 people (*Numbers* 16: 31-35;47-50）.

Both the religious reform in Josiah and the compilation of the canon of the *Old*

Testament have laid a solid foundation for the unification and development of Judaism. Politics played a major role in the unification of the northern and southern religions in Israel: northern Israel was subjugated before southern Judah; North Israel intermarried with foreigners under the policy of national integration of the Assyrian king. South Judah was able to preserve its religion and culture under Babylonian rule. South Judah took over the country before North Israel and was responsible for the reconstruction of the temple. The priests of South Judah were responsible for compiling the canon of the *Old Testament*. Due to these objective reasons, "Lord" has taken the place of "Ilyushin" as the only Hebrew god, and North Israel has lost its dominant power of discourse since then.

From the history of the Hebrews, from the marriages of the ancestors of Israel such as Joseph and Moses, from Joshua's so-called "conquest of Canaan" story, from the relationship between southern Judah and northern Israel, especially from the fate of the two gods of Jehovah and Ilyushin, we have clearly seen the Jews' so-called "monotheistic" faith, the so-called "nationalism", the so-called pure bloodline and pure faith. Since the purity of blood, the purity of faith and the unity of the nation are all so-called, the Jewish people's ultra-nationalism complex is problematic. They should not have been so extreme. The so-called "purity" actually makes it easier for us to understand the reasons for the emergence of Jewish pacifism. Since ultra-nationalism is a deliberate propaganda, the idea of pacifism, which exists at the same time, is deliberately suppressed.

Prophets are the products of the times, so their thoughts are influenced by the thoughts of the times. The late prophets were disturbed by the Greek culture to the Hebrew culture, and they were furious. Therefore, the trend of thought in prophet literature also tended to nationalism. For example, the style of the front part and the back part of The Book of *Zacharias* are completely different. They are two completely different works: the former is prophet literature, and the latter is revelation literature. The former's era is clearly written (520B.C.-518B. C.) while the latter's is vague. According to textual research, it is a work of the early Macabies era. The biggest gap between the front and the back of the book of *Zechariah* is that the former holds the idea of world harmony while the latter holds the narrow nationalism. Since it was the time of the Hebrews' uprising against foreign rule, it is not difficult to understand their hatred of foreigners and the spread of this narrow nationalism. However, understanding does not mean identification, nor does it mean obliterating the real history. In other words, we can understand the causes of the ultra-nationalism of the Jews, but we cannot agree with this ultra-nationalism, and we cannot ignore the pacifism thoughts of the Jews contemporary with the ultra-nationalism.

III   Cosmopolitanism in *Old Testament*

History is the history of interpretation. From the compilation process of the *Old Testament* canon, we have seen how "historical materials" serve "politics", "religion" and "culture". First, the "Deuteronomy School" added its own religious views to the "historical materials". Second, the "Priest School" changed its views to the "historical materials". Then, the "history" of the Hebrews was determined by incorporating the views of the prophets into the "historical materials" in the later period. In the period of Samuel and Saul, and even in the period of David, the description of history is purely a narrative without religious prejudice or theological inclination. Later, these historical books were compiled by some moralistic and utilitarian historians and then became the classic historical books we read now. However, interestingly, there are still too many different voices in the *Old Testament* classics compared with the *New Testament* classics: if we carefully study the history books compiled after being imprisoned, especially the prophet books, we will find very different views. At the end of their imprisonment, people hope that the "angry god" will become the "merciful god" after their introspection and repentance. As a result, the Hebrew god's inherent name "Jehovah" has become the world's name "Lord" and "God". Now, take the second Isaiah movement as an example to look at Jewish pacifism.

The "Second Isaiah Movement" is guided by the ideas of some prophets represented by *Second Isaiah*. The *Second Isaiah* is a text attached to the book of Isaiah, and its style is completely different from the book of Isaiah, the son of Amos. It is presumed that the completion time of the book was a period from the time when Persia destroyed Babylon to the time when the temple was rebuilt. The ideological realm of *Second Isaiah* reached its peak among the prophets, upgrading from narrow nationalism to the idea of one world. The idea of world harmony in the "Second Isaiah" is influenced by the book of *Zacharias*, which was written between 520 BC and 518 B.C., so the book of *Second Isaiah* was written in the early 5th century after 500 B.C..

The reason why Christianity has developed into a universal religion is directly related to the idea of world harmony that has developed in Judaism. If we cut off the origin of Christianity and Judaism, we will also cut off the origin and development of Christianity. However, the thought of "Second Isaiah" advocates that the Hebrew nation has the bounden duty to liberate the world from evil, which also affects the Christianity of later generations and becomes the source of oppression in the Christian universal thought. Therefore, Christianity (especially Protestantism) is keen to preach in the world, hoping to act as the savior of the whole world. Christianity's idea of "world harmony" has its value in the sense of "universal" and "universal love", but it cannot be denied that this "harmony" itself has some compulsion. Therefore, it is of great significance for the ethnic and religious problems in today's society to fully understand the thought of "Second Isaiah" and analyze and learn from it in two parts.

This "second Isaiah" thought developed in Judaism is of great significance to Judaism itself and the two major religions developed from Judaism-Christianity and Islam. If both Christianity and Islam really originated from Judaism, if both Christianity and Judaism use the Bible (the Jewish Bible is different from the Christian Bible), the Jewish Bible includes only the *Old Testament*. The *Koran* of Islam and the *Old Testament* have many similarities) as the core of their beliefs, so they should not ignore the idea of world harmony in Judaism and the Bible classics and blindly and unilaterally emphasize the narrow nationalism in them. If these three major religions can check themselves and reflect on themselves, then all kinds of religious wars in history and ethnic wars caused by religious conflicts, as well as the religious conflicts and ethnic conflicts in the world that are still going on till now, will disappear. However, on the contrary, these nationalist bigotry and fanaticism caused by religious beliefs seem to have an increasingly popular trend. Under the encouragement of "anthropology", the advocacy of liberal nationalism and "multiculturalism", radical nationalism has prevailed and "human rights" and "humanity" have been completely abandoned. "Regionality", "Nationality" and "Minorities" have become the cover for unruly behavior and reverse behavior, for which we have to think deeply about "pluralism".

Amos was an important figure among all the prophets who led the "Lord" out of the Jewish community and toward the Gentiles. Amos, a Jew, went to the State of Israel to preach, breaking the long-standing ethnic boundary between South Judah and North Israel. Not only that, he also broke the national boundaries, preaching in Syria, Philistia, Edom, Sudan and other countries, breaking the narrow nationalism.

Among the Prophets, *Jonah* is the most universal one. *Jonah* is the fifth book of the twelve little prophets in *Old Testament*. It is very different from the other eleven books because it is not about the passionate words of the prophets, but about the stories of the prophets. Some people think that *Jonah* is not a prophet but a novel. The author's aim is to "censure" the Hebrew's hatred of foreign countries and nations at that time, advocating the open-minded thought of "Second Isaiah" and believing that the Hebrew's mission is to illuminate foreign people with their own beliefs. Together with Ruth, it is a masterpiece of early novels. As a representative of "narrow nationalism," Jonah, the prophet, is different from other prophets and is a negative image. God sent him to Nineveh to convey the message of God. He did not want to go and fled to Tarshish, which is opposite to Nineveh, because he did not want to see foreigners rescued. When God saw the repentance of Nineveh people, he was kind-hearted and unwilling to destroy the city. Jonah was angry. The "God" in Jonah is merciful, which is in sharp contrast to Jonah's narrowness, willfulness and violence. The author of *Jonah* inherited the tradition of the prophet Isaiah II, believing that God cares not only for Jews but also for all the people in the world he created. The theme of this book is that Israel's real mission as a people of God is to spread the good news of God's love among the Gentiles and break the narrow national and national boundaries of the past. From the three parallel comparisons in the book of *Jonah* (Jehovah and Jonah, Sailor and Jonah, Jonah and Nineveh), we can clearly see the idea of universalism, which "breaks through Israel's previous view that the salvation and creation of Yahweh are confined to Israel." First, pagan sailors were willing to call on Jonah's god "the Lord" in order to save Jonah's life, but Jonah was unwilling to save Nineveh's life, which formed a sharp contrast. Secondly, when Jonah announced to the Nineveh people that "Nineveh will be overthrown," the Nineveh king"removed his robe, covered himself with sackcloth, and sat in ashes." (*Jonah* 3:6) He also ordered all the people in the city to put on sackcloth and earnestly call on them. When God saw that they had left the evil way, he regretted not bringing the evil he had said to them. The comparison here is between Jonah and Nineveh people: the true repentance of Nineveh people and Jonah's exasperation are vivid. Jonah himself is a god's elector, so he can be willful and unrepentant. However, Nineveh people have the courage to admit their mistakes and strive for good. Which is right or wrong, be clear at a glance; Third, the compassion of the Lord is in sharp contrast to Jonah's cruelty: Jonah did not want to go to Nineveh to announce the news of God. Although the Lord was angry, he forgave him. Jonah did not want God to show mercy to Nineveh. He was angry and begged for death. The Lord did not punish him. Instead, he patiently explained with the example of the castor tree: "You did not plant or cultivate this castor plant. One night, one night dry dead, you still cherish; What's more, Nineveh is a big city, in which there are more than 120000 people who cannot distinguish between their left hand and right hand, and there are many livestock. Can I not cherish it? "

Although *Ruth* is not a prophet book but rather a novel, it reflects the thought of "second Isaiah" like *Jonah*. Ruth, originally a Moabite, was the great-grandmother of King David (1013B.C.-973B.C.), and her virtue was more commendable than that of the Hebrews. Through the two marriages of Moab women to Hebrews, the author criticizes narrow nationalism. In *Nehemiah* and *Ezra*, Jewish priests were forbidden to intermarry with foreigners in order to maintain the "purity" of blood and religious belief. This policy was opposed by many people. The author of *Ruth* probably passed on Ruth to oppose this policy. This shows that the thoughts of the imprisoned Israelis have changed greatly. In addition, there are also some thoughts in *Psalms* that reflect the world's harmony: for example, 46 articles, whose ideological realm goes beyond narrow nationalism and regards Jehovah as the power to rule the world; Another example is article 19, in which the poet praised the macro universe and made the Lord the Lord of all people in the world. Out of the primitive superstitious religion, out of the narrow national religion, this realm is the realm of "second Isaiah" at that time.

IV　Conclusion

The reason why the Bible has become an "eternal book" is precisely because it covers different thoughts and even conflicting thoughts. As the "living water of the source", the inclusiveness and heterogeneity of the Bible itself provide an excellent paradigm for freedom of thought and religious tolerance.

（徐秋月译）

04　The Tradition of Misogyny from the Myth of Pandora and Eve

I　Introduction

The tradition of misogyny in western society has a long history. From ancient Greece to postmodernism, the tradition of misogyny has always run through the historical development of western society. In prehistoric times, women were in a dominant position in matriarchal society. Engels once said: "Among all savages, among all the lower, the middle, and, in part, the higher barbarians, women occupy not only a position of freedom, but a position of high esteem." At the end of primitive society, matriarchal society began to disintegrate and social productivity developed, followed by changes in the economic status of men and women in the clan. Patriarchy gradually replaced matriarchy. Engels believed that in that age, any progress is meanwhile a kind of retrogress, because in that progress, some people's happiness is based on other's bitterness. The decline of women's status marks the formation of a private ownership society, and in a male-dominated society, it is women who are suppressed. The change of social form embodied in the field of ideology, and ideology must reinforce and maintain the change of social form in a specific pattern. Therefore, the male-dominated society achieves the purpose of maintaining the change of social form by compiling and manufacturing "stories".

Ⅱ   Pandora's Myth and Its Extension in Ancient Greek Society

Marcuse holds the view that civilized society is based on repression of eros or sex while the suppression of women's sex is more serious. As a result, Pandora's myth was appeared. In ancient Greece, where Hesiod lived, the land was barren, the population was increasing, the food was scarce and the life was hard. In addition to the dispute with his brothers over their property, it was easy to understand that Hesiod had a deep hatred for women. He regarded woman as a symbol of evil and greed.In order to punish Prometheus for stealing the fire of heaven, Zeus created Pandora who could satisfy all men's fantasies and sent her to the human world. Epimetheus gladly accepted the gift from the gods, despite his brother Prometheus's warning. Pandora is a symbol of beauty and temptation, and also a symbol of men's desire and power. From then on, there was a disaster on earth, and hope was forever left in Pandora's box. People are used to attributing all mens mistakes to Pandora's charm and her curiosity about the magic box, believing that woman is "Dangerous Beauty". Fundamentally speaking, men are afraid. They are afraid of both women and the unknown world, but they attribute all the faults to women. They define women negatively and believe it is women who influence and seduce men to make mistakes. Men's negation of women is actually an escape from their own defects.

This misogyny tradition deeply influenced the ancient Greek civilization. In the ancient Greek city-state system, women are in an extremely low position in society (of course, Sparta's situation was completely different from Athens's-ancient Greek society was made up of many city-states, and women's status varied greatly in different historical stages and city-states. The status of women is most typical in Athens and Sparta. Sparta was a slave-owner aristocratic autocracy, while Athens was a slave-owner democracy. Compared with Sparta, Athens had a higher level of civilization, where the status of women was lower). When discussing the city-state system, Aristotle said if the status of women is not stipulated well, half of the citizens' organizations will lack regulations as half of population are women in the city-state. He thinks that men are superior to women. Women are the defective and incomplete form of men. Men are born noble and women are born humble. Men are rulers, and women are ruled. In ancient Greece, the geographical conditions were poor, and the land was barren. The Greeks compared "land" to "the belly of a woman", which is the evident of humble status of women.

In all ancient Greek city-states, women did not enjoy political rights. In Athens, Women, known as "Athenian wives", are excluded from civil groups and belong only to family members and do not enjoy citizenship. Women's status was not even as high as before its democracy system in Athens was built. Solon has formulated a series of regulations on the behavior, diet, travel and marriage of Athenian women. He has also set up a "Women's Supervision Committee" to supervise Athens women's code of conduct in public. What's more, marriage of women is only a transfer of relationship from patriarchy to husband. Women exist in society as a private property of men and a symbol of ownership. Although the father of the bride will receive a dowry from the groom after the transfer of custody, the father of the bride will also prepare a very generous dowry, usually giving more than one-tenth of his family fortune. This is an "uneconomical business", when the financial condition of a family is not sufficient to pay the dowry, they won't want a daughter again. There are even some places where girls are drowned. After a woman gives birth to a child, the child can be raised by her mother before the age of seven, and the boy can go to school at the same age. However, the girl can only stay at home and listen to her mother's upbringing. The mother will educate the girl what she should have as a mother and a housewife in the future. The most ideal education of a girl is to educate her not to leave the house, to be cautious, to follow the rules, and to live a life in silence. Aristotle used Sophocles' verse to define a woman's good character, that is, "Quietness is woman's virtue."" According to the Athenians, a wife is only the head of a handmaid except for giving birth to children." Engels once said.

In Sparta, women have more opportunities to participate in city-state affairs because men have been fighting outside all year round. In the heyday of Sparta, many affairs were managed by women. The freedom of Spartan women was not allowed before, Spartan women resisted vigorously to fight against the constraints of the rulers, and finally they won the freedom within its scope. But the most important responsibility of Spartan women is to have children. In ancient Greece, women were forbidden to take part in sports and even watch them. Watching men's sports would be executed. However, during the same period of Sparta, women were allowed to participate in sports. Spartans believe that participating in sports can keep women healthy, and they believe that healthy mothers can give birth to healthy children, women's participation in sports depends on their reproductive value. Woman who lost their lives due to childbirth, her honor is equivalent to a soldier who died in the war, and she is qualified to erect a gravestone with inscriptions in front of her tomb. Almost all laws relating to women involve the birth of children, and those who remain single, marry late or are not properly matched will be punished accordingly. Spartan girls can receive the same training as boys, while Spartan women generally do not need to engage in productive labor under the public ownership, and their daily necessities are also provided by the ruling class, so they have more time and opportunities to receive cultural education in daily life.

Although the city-state society in ancient Greece attached great importance to reproduction and family, the women in the city-state did not receive due respect. In ancient Greece, the city-state society generally believed that the origin of children was the father, while the mother was only a tool for reproduction. In Greek mythology, women were even deprived of their reproductive rights. Athena was born from Zeus' mind, and Dionysus, the god of wine, was born from Zeus' thigh. Fertility can also be done by men, which shows that ancient Greece did not recognize women's reproductive ability. Whether Athens or Sparta, women mainly play the role of wife and mother. Although the standards are different, they are essentially the same and are always dominated by men. Judging from the religious status, whether Athens or Sparta, the religious status of women is higher than that of men. In fact, the high-level rights in religious affairs are still in the hands of men.

Ⅲ   Women in Biblical Tradition

From the creation of Adam and Eve by God in the *Old Testament*, we can see the position of women in the biblical world-Eve is a bridle bone taken from Adam and is an appendage of men. The original intention of God in creating Eve was to see Adam alone and said,"It is not good that the man should be alone; I will make him a helper as his partner." After Adam and Eve were created, God said to them, "Be fruitful and multiply, and fill the earth and subdue it; and have dominion over the fish of the sea and thing that moves upon the earth." God created Eve just to company with Adam, reproduce and help Adam manage the Garden of Eden. In the Garden of Eden, Eve could not resist the temptation of snakes. She was the first to taste the forbidden fruit and then let Adam eat it together. The original sin was committed by women, while men were led innocently. After God discovered it, he cursed people: snakes and women are opposite in life, "And I will put enmity between thee and the woman, and between thy seed and her seed; it shall bruise thy head, and thou shalt bruise his heel. I will greatly multiply thy sorrow and thy conception; in sorrow thou shalt bring forth children; and thy desire shall be to thy husband, and he shall rule over thee." Women will suffer greatly from pregnancy and childbirth, they will love their husbands and be subject to their jurisdiction. Men, on the other hand, will toil all their lives because they listen to women, "Because thou hast hearkened unto the voice of thy wife, and hast eaten of the tree, of which I commanded thee, saying, Thou shalt not eat of it: cursed is the ground for thy sake; in sorrow shalt thou eat of it all the days of thy life; "and they have to word hard to making a living until they return to dust. Women are punished for crimes, while men are punished for obeying women. Women are always endowed with the ability to control men's thinking and lure them to commit crimes. All the mistakes come from women, because women are always unable to resist temptation. Eve's fall led to human original sin. In essence, women's influence is only the direct cause, and men's own desire is the root cause of destroy.

Eve is Adam's "bone of bones, flesh of flesh". She was never an independent being, but a part of Adam. Eve exists to perfect Adam's life. This is the sorrow of women-from the original intention of Eve's creation to the curse of women, women are only accessories of men: Adam was created only because he was lonely, and after he was driven out of Eden, he had to suffer not only from pregnancy and childbirth, but also from the jurisdiction of his husband. Both Pandora in Greek mythology and Eve in the *Old Testament* are always negative images of women. They are beautiful in appearance, greedy in heart and full of lies, which eventually lead to evil for men. Looking at the *Old Testament* and the *New Testament*, we can also see the decline of women's status. There were five female prophets (Miriam, Deborah, Huldah, Noah, Isaiah's wife) in the *Old Testament*, while there was only one female prophet (Ana) in the *New Testament*, which shows that the status of women was greatly reduced.

IV The Tradition of Misogyny in Western Society

Kant said in the postscript of *On Gracefulness and Loftiness*, "Women narrow men's eyes. When a friend gets married, it is when you lose that friend. " For this reason Kant proposed that "One may not marry" and obeyed this principle all hiss life. In *On Gracefulness and Loftiness* Kant believed that men and women have different characteristics. Women are graceful while men are noble; Men are good at rational thinking while women are good at perceptual observation. "The beauty of female is only relative, while the beauty of male beauty is absolute. This is why all male animals are beautiful in our eyes, because they have relatively little temptation to our senses." It is precisely because of the essential differences between women and men that women have never been accepted by the philosophical world. He even sneered: "A learned woman should be able to grow a beard in theory." In Kant's eyes, women are only suitable for artistic senses. Once a woman sets foot in philosophy, she will lose her charm for men. In the era of his life, women are the second sex. He equated women with material things, and finally he chose to be lonely instead of getting involved in marriage. "When I need a woman, I can't support her, but when I can give her support, I don't need her anymore."

"Is it to find a woman? Don't forget to bring your whip." (Thus *Spake Zarathustra* written by Nietzsche) Nietzsche profoundly expressed his disdain for women. Nietzsche's early life was miserable. His father died early. In his childhood, he lived with his grandmother, mother and sister. Facing women, he felt sensitive and inferior. Nietzsche once had beautiful fantasies about women. He also had infinite desire for love. He was humble and shy in front of feelings. After being rejected repeatedly, he completely changed from being willing to be whipped by women to whipping to all women. Since then, Nietzsche's works have been full of denigration and criticism of women.Russel, in *A History of Western Philosophy*, hit the mark with a single comment, and said, " Nine out of ten women will make Nietzsche lose his whip, but he knows this well, he has to avoid women." Russell is a real playboy. He treats his feelings frivolously, and women are just playthings in his hands. Rousseau and Schopenhauer also have misogyny. Throughout the tradition of western society, the door of philosophy has never been opened to women, philosophy seems to have become the privilege of men, and women are neither welcome nor allowed to set foot in it. However, in life, women are still subservient to men, only regarded as a need and the existence of "the second sex".

V   Conclusion

Marx believed that women's liberation was the symbol of the liberation of all mankind. The changing status of women has witnessed the progress and changes of civilized society. Reconstructing feminism, correcting feminism's overemphasis on women's rights and weakening male chauvinism is the ultimate trend of feminism to realize real equality between men and women; what's more, deconstructing the limitation of male chauvinism and advocating the emancipation of women and the acquisition of women's rights is the only way to a civilized society.

（徐秋月译）

Chapter 2   The Literature of *the Old Testament* Tradition

01   Hebrews Have No Tragedy—The Interpretations of *Job*

I   Is *Job* a Tragedy?

It is difficult to cultivate tragic spirit for religions that have expectations for the afterlife and promise to reward the good and punish the evil. The tragic spirit comes not only from awe and fear, but also from confusion, loss, questioning and resistance. However fear and awe can only produce religious godliness. Only through questioning and resistance in awe and fear can a great and noble tragic spirit be created. In this sense, *Job* can barely be regarded as Hebrew tragedy, because it contains a spirit of questioning and resistance. In *Job*, what we see is no longer the fear and awe of the Hebrews towards the Lord, but Job's various doubts and questions about God. However, Job's questioning and asking are only limited to the ideological level and are not put into any action. Therefore, his questioning and asking are incomplete. Moreover, Job finally ended with the reconciliation between Job and God —Job realized his mistake, still converted to God devoutly and God forgave Job's disobedience, which obviously did not conform to the tragic spirit.

The tragic spirit is a feeling of fear of chaos, hatred of violence and resistance to repression. However, the Hebrews' national characteristics are incompatible with the tragic spirit. In Hebrew religious beliefs, the world is orderly and God is omniscient and omnipotent. Even if there was a great flood disaster, Noah's ark will save it. Even if Sodom and Gomorrah were to be destroyed, it was God's purposeful arrangement. Everything is subject to the principle of justice. All evil will be punished. People do not need to have free will, they do not need to resist, but they only need to obey God's will. In the Hebrew world, there is no fear of fate, no resistance to evil, because God has arranged everything. Also because of this, the Hebrews have no tragedy, because tragedy comes from thinking about fate and resistance to evil.

In the whole Bible (strictly speaking, the *Old Testament*), *Job* can be regarded as the most tragic one—Job bitterly questioned God's justice, Job painfully pondered his own fate, so he debated with his friends and put forward a series of questions about good and evil. If Job does not end with repentance, if Job does not end with a reward from God, if Job ends with a tragic ending, then *Job* may be called Hebrew tragedy. However, "Job" turned suddenly when it was about to reach the tragic concept, avoiding the tragic spirit with religious beliefs. God has given Job more cattle and sheep than before. God forgave Job's disobedience and decided not to test people's beliefs any more. In response, Job also responded with sincere repentance and stopped asking questions that puzzled Sophocles and Euripides. From then on, Job became more devout and offered more burnt offerings to God. God and Job reconciled. *Job* ends here. Everything is very satisfactory. Where did the tragedy come from?

II   Why do Hebrews have no Tragedy?

Job is one of the wisdom books in the *Old Testament* and the most difficult to read. The main question raised in *Job* is rather acute: Why do believers suffer? After a long debate, Job's intelligent friends could not answer this question. Job's friends even made serious mistakes—they believed that sufferings only come from people's crimes—and were blamed by God. In fact, the Lord did not give a positive answer to Job's question—because this is an extremely difficult question to answer: if God is just, why should he let the wicked go unpunished and the good suffer? If God is not just, why should we believe in Him? If God is omnipotent, why does he tolerate so many sins in the world and remain indifferent? If God is not omnipotent, why should we believe in Him?

In fact, theologians have argued for more than 2000 years on the issue of theodicy, and still have no satisfactory answer—perhaps there will never be a satisfactory answer. Therefore, the strategy of the Lord is circuitous: instead of answering Job's questions directly, he has put forward other questions that cannot be answered by human intelligence—such as the formation of the universe, the magical characteristics of animals, and unexplained mysteries of nature. Thus, Job succumbed to the power of god, and he took silence as a symbol of faith—but this surrender did not meet the intellectual needs of all people, just as enlightenment thinkers and scientists later did: they tried to answer the questions raised by the Lord.

Job could not answer the same question, so he went to believe. For Sophocles and Euripides, belief could not completely solve these problems—although they also had faith, but in their life time, traditional beliefs had been disintegrated, especially Euripides, deeply influenced by the Sophists, atheists and Socrates. Can't explain their confusion with faith: they even attribute all kinds of sins to the will of god: for example, Euripides's *Hippolytus* blames the goddess Aphrodite, *Hyon* blames Apollo, *the women of Troy* blames the three goddesses and Zeus—thus tragedy is born, which is not the reason why Nietzsche thinks tragedy is born—in fact, Nietzsche's antagonism between Apollo spirit and Dionysian spirit is still the result of enlightenment. His explanation of the origin of tragedy is philosophical and cannot fully explain the characteristics of ancient Greek tragedy.

Through *Job*, we can clearly see the characteristics of Hebrew's thinking: Hebrews are not allowed to write people like Sophocles wrote Oedipus, let alone gods like Aeschylus wrote Zeus and Euripides wrote Apollo! In *Job*, the Lord is supreme, all—knowing and all—powerful. In *Job*, we cannot find the gods described by the three tragic writers—greedy, cruel, lusty and jealous. To the Hebrews, the Lord is the creator of the universe, the master of all things and the source of justice. He cannot be questioned or resisted. Even if wisdom is as good as Job's, even if Job asks questions that even the Lord cannot answer, the final result is that Job repents in dust and fire and humbly gives himself to the Lord god.

Therefore, even if *Job* is full of lofty ideas, brilliant imagination, intense emotion and intelligent thinking, it is by no means a tragedy.

The Hebrew nation has no tragedy, because the spirit of questioning and resistance unique to tragedy has been dispelled in the Hebrew religious beliefs—even if Job asked so many questions and wanted to fight with death—but the final result is: Job repented of his questioning and humbled himself to the Lord god. *Job* is full of passion and imagination, full of wisdom and enlightenment, which is not inferior to or even slightly better than the tragedies of Sophocles and Euripides. However, Job's sharp questions and fierce resistance were finally dispelled. God answered Job's questions, and Job regretted his questioning. The dust settled: God gave Job more material benefits, and Job humbly bowed to the Lord.

In addition, the Hebrew belief in God is the ultimate value of the Hebrews, which dispels the fierce conflict between different values, and the fierce conflict between different values is the key to the formation of tragedy. Hegel has a detailed and full exposition of this, while Paul Tillich's *Cultural Theology* has a more in–depth explanation.

The tragic tragedy in ancient Greece was caused by the polytheistic beliefs of the ancient Greeks. Different beliefs lead to different values, and there must be violent conflicts between different values. In addition, the continuous alternation of new and old beliefs and different political systems will also lead to conflicts. Only when there is conflict can there be tragedy. Tragedy is born of conflict.

Firstly, polytheism led to tragedy. Take Euripides's *Hippolytus* as an example. Hippolytus incurred retaliation from the God of beauty for his contempt for the God of beauty Aphrodite. Hippolytus believed in Artemis, goddess of chastity (moon and hunting). He hated Aphrodite's bed and despised the frivolity and indulgence of the god of beauty. In the belief system of the ancient Greeks, the god of beauty occupied an important position. Although Aphrodite was an imported god from Asia Minor, this imported product gradually became one of the twelve major gods of the ancient Greeks. Some people believe in love, some believe in chastity; Some believe in Aphrodite, some worship Artemis, so conflicts are inevitable. Hippolytus is an example.

Secondly, the conflict of values caused by the alternation of old and new beliefs is also the cause of the tragedy. Take Aeschylus's *Prometheus Bound* and *Oresteia* as examples. In *Prometheus Bound*, Prometheus is an ancient god, Zeus is a new god, and conflict is inevitable in the change and alternation of the new and the old. Therefore, Prometheus fiercely resisted the rule of Zeus and became a tragic hero, which has been praised for generations. In *Oresteia*, Orestes killed his mother for avenge his father's death, which represented the idea of paternal system, while the Nemesis's pursuit of Orestes reflected traces of matriarchal system. At last Apollo, the God of Sun, entrusted Athena to judge the case. In the trial of the case, Athena represented a new generation of gods, while Nemesis's represented the old gods. Athena represents the interests of the patriarchal society while Nemesis represents the interests of the matriarchal society. Athena represents the social system of ruling the country by law while Nemesis represents the social system of blood revenge. The alternation of new and old will inevitably lead to conflicts, and conflicts are the best material for tragedies.

Finally, the conflict of values caused by the change of different political systems is also the cause of the tragedy. Take Sophocles' *Antigone* as an example. The values held by Antigone are the values of the ancient family system, while the values held by Creon are the values of the emerging country (city—state) system. Antigone's burial of his brothers is a requirement of the blood system, while Creon's punishment of traitors is a requirement of the city—state political system. The two different values will inevitably lead to fierce conflicts, and the conflicts have also created the heroic image of Antigone.

In a word, the violent conflicts of ancient Greek tragedies were caused by people's absolute and ultimate values. Because human beings are small and limited, they are always pursuing absolute and eternal values. Any value belonging to a person is relative and limited, and one cannot pretend to be the ultimate name, while one's intelligence always hopes to pursue eternity and infinity. Therefore, the ancient Greeks with the tradition of love and wisdom always like to regard their own value identity as absolute, and there is only one absolute and ultimate. When the worshipers of each value compete for "absolute", the outcome must be tragedy, destroying both others and themselves.

The question of "what is truth" is not a problem among the Hebrews, because "truth" means God and belief in God. However, in the history of Greek—Roman and even the whole history of western philosophy, the question of "what is truth" is a problem, which has been repeatedly raised, discussed and debated for more than 2000 years and has become an eternal problem. It can be said that the question of "what is truth" is a hermeneutic one. You can keep saying it, but you cannot find the ultimate answer.

Drama is entertaining, although it also has educational function. In ancient Greece, both tragedy and comedy had strong political implications, especially tragedy, which was a means of ruling the ruling class. However, political rule is, after all, externalized. Despite the political compulsion of watching tragedy in Pericles' time, it is only an external form. Compared with the Hebrew religious beliefs and moral rules, the political "coercion" suffered by the ancient Greeks because of watching the tragedy cannot really be regarded as coercion. Compared with the ancient Greeks, the coercion suffered by the Hebrews is incomparable—this kind of coercion is not only external, but also internal, not only tangible, but also intangible. The Hebrews have already internalized this kind of coercion into an inner drive.

In addition, drama is produced by the impulse of games and is the product of leisure life. Greeks (of course, Greek citizens,How can slaves have leisure?) living at ease (except for special periods such as the Hippocratic War and the Peloponnesian War), so there is enough time and mood to create a variety of forms of entertainment, while Hebrews live in exile, move from place to place, fight all the year round, and be ruled by different races. How can they be in the mood to experience happiness? In their literature, apart from lamentation or lamentation, as for *Song of Songs*, it is only a distant memory—recalling the glory of Solomon's time and the quiet life of the period when there was no occupation in history.

III Conclusion

As a result, the Hebrews formed devout religious beliefs and strong moralism in their bitter experiences. This devout religious belief and strong moralism do not allow tragedy to exist because tragedy is entertaining. The Hebrew religious and moral feelings do not allow them to transform pain and disaster into tragedy, which is the literary form. Therefore, the Hebrew created its own special artistic form— lamentation, of which the most famous is of course the *Lamentation of Jeremiah* written by the prophet Jeremiah.

（徐秋月译）

02   The Reading of *Song of Solomon* and the Asceticism

Ⅰ   Brief Introduction of *Song of Solomon*

The Hebrew name of *Song of Solomon* is *Sir has-sirim*, which means "the most beautiful song" and "the song of songs". *Song of Solomon* is a volume in the Book of Wisdom, the author of which is said to be King Solomon. It praises the love between Solomon and Shulamite, a beautiful shepherdess, and it describes the joy of a short meeting between men and women, and the feelings of farewell.

Song of Solomon is one of the most special classics in biblical literature, because it does not eulogize "the well-being of God" as enthusiastically as other works. In the whole text, there is even only one mention of the name of God, that is, "Set me as a seal upon your heart, as a seal upon your arm; for love is strong as death, passion fierce as the grave. Its flashes are flashes of fire, a raging flame" (*Song of Solomon*: 8:6)

Song of Solomon is a collection of folk love poems, which is very similar to *the Book of Songs* in China. However, compared with *the Book of Songs*, its language is more concise, lyrical and direct, and its words are simpler and more straightforward. It directly talks about the love between men and women. It is said that Solomon wrote 1,005 poems in his life. *Song of Solomon* is the most precious of all his works. The first sentence of the poem is: *"The song of songs, which is Solomon's. "* However, some people believe that *Song of Solomon* was written by someone else in Solomon's name. As for the love in *Song of Solomon*, it is traditionally believed to be King Solomon and Shepherdess Shulamite. In the vineyard, King Solomon, disguised as a shepherd, met Shulamite, who was in charge of the vineyard. The two attracted each other and fell in love at first sight. The shepherd promised that he would come back to marry Shulamite and said good-bye to Shulamite. After that, they longed for each other and suffered from lovesickness. In the end, Solomon fulfilled his promise and came to marry Shulamite. They held a grand wedding in the royal palace. Their love was finally brought to fruition, thus making a long story. There is another argument that Shulamite, the shepherdess, loved not Solomon but another young shepherd. Solomon wanted to marry Shulamite, so he tried to seduce Shulamite. However, Shulamite who deeply loves shepherd is loyal to her true love, and will never change her mind. In the end, Shulamite rejected King Solomon and waited for her shepherd. Finally, they got married. However, no matter what kind of statement, the theme of *Song of Solomon* remains unchanged, which is to praise the purity and joy of love and loyalty to love.

Song of Solomon has particularity that other scriptures do not have. Whether its content, theme, language style or writing structure, it shows its differences from other scriptures.

First of all, in terms of content, *Song of Solomon* is extremely abundant in content. It describes not only love but also natural scenery, as well as the combination of feeling and scene. The poem mentions various plants, flowers and fruits:mynh,narcissus, rose,lily,apple tree,cedar,pine,fig,grape,wood from Lebaron and so on. At the same time, a series of images such as vineyard, field, mount, streets, royal city and wedding banquet also appear in the poem, which depicting a lively scene of spring and autumn. The picture is lively and changing, and it changes smoothly, creating an atmosphere of freedom. On the theme, *Song of Solomon* has a different theme. *Song of Solomon* is the only collection of pure lovepoems about human love. Compared with biblical classics in the tradition, *Song of Solomon* puts the heavy theme and serious style of Christianity aside, but warmly praises secular love in a brisk and touching tone.

Secondly, *Song of Solomon* has an elegant and vivid writing style and passionate feelings. The author describes the feelings of men and women with the utmost tenderness."As an apple tree among the trees of the wood, so is my beloved among young men. With great delight I sat in his shadow, and his fruit was sweet to my taste...My beloved is like a gazelle or a young stag. Look, there he stands behind our wall, gazing in at the windows, looking through the lattice." (*Song of Solomon* 2:3,9) The shepherdess's joy when she met her beloved was well expressed: "How beautiful you are, my love, how very beautiful! Your eyes are doves behind your evil. Your hair is like a flock of goats, moving down the slopes of Gilead. Your teeth are like a flock of shore ewes that have come up from the washing, all of which bear twins, and not one among them is bereaved. Your lips are like a crimson thread, and your month is lovely. Your cheeks are like halves of a pomegranate behind your veil. Your neck is like the tower of David, built in courses; on it hang a thousand bucklers, all of them shields of warriors." The poet's depiction of the sensory world is meticulous and vivid, showing the beauty of the human body. The shape of the shepherdess in the poet's works is very lifelike and impressive.

Finally, the writing structure of *Song of Solomon* is extremely complicated-people are changeable, characters are changeable, and changes of scene are complicated. The whole poem is very short, with 117 verses, but it is the most difficult and attractive poem to explain. The characters appearing in the poem include Solomon, King, all the women of Jerusalem, warrior, Shulamitete and so on. The titles have changed from "my love", "my beloved", "my sister" to "my bride", "my spouse", "my perfect one", "prince's daughter"and so on. The transformation of characters and persons is extremely complicated, but in general it is a duet between Solomon and Shulamite, accompanied by the chorus of all the women in Jerusalem.

II *Song of Solomon* and the Asceticism

Song of Solomon is a classic Hebrew legend, but it was recognized as the Christian canon at the latest. The whole Bible is a classic work of Hebrews integrating history, geography, literature, culture and religion. *Song of Solomon* describes the theme of secular love, and is a masterpiece of supreme goodness and beauty which is full of fireworks of human desire for love. If *Song of Solomon* is not listed as the canon of Christianity, it will be a loss for Hebrew tradition and the most regrettable thing in the history of Hebrew culture. Since ancient times, the main line of religious tradition has been "asceticism", which has always been the case for both Christianity and Buddhism. However, if the *Song of Solomon* is put into the Christian canon system, it means that the "human love" praised in the *Song of Solomon* deviates from the "asceticism" of the Christian tradition. In particular, there have been many explicit depictions of the human body in the poem, such as "Your two breasts are like two fawns, twins of gazelle, that feed among the lilies" (*Song of Solomon* 4:5) which is enough to make the Christian priest's face changed greatly. Therefore, how to bridge this paradox has become the puzzle of the Christian scripture interpreters for centuries. How to interpret *Song of Solomon* and sublimate secular feelings into religious feelings has become an eternal paradox in the history of Christian theology and even in the history of biblical interpretation. In the end, the Christian scripture interpreters found a perfect solution, comparing the relationship between Solomon and the shepherdess to the relationship between human beings and the church. They regard the church as God's agent in the world. The church is the groom and followers are the bride. They use the pure and sacred marriage vows as a metaphor to guide the believers to love the church. In fact, there have been many descriptions of the relationship between God and mortals in the *Bible*, such as "Christ is the head, we are the body", "Christ is the true vine, we are the branches", "God said, My sheep listen to my voice, I know them, and they follow me." or "Believers say, 'The Lord is my shepherd, and I shall not want.'" The most noble statement is to express the relationship between God and mortals as holy marriage. In the Christian tradition, marriage is the most sacred of all earthly relationships. The interpretation of *Song of Solomon* is actually to use Christian religious logic to expound secular ethical matters.

In fact, from the perspective of Christian tradition, there was no difference between "soul" and "body" in the early religious ethics. When God created Adam and Eve, both of them were originally an organic whole. They were all made of clay. It was only because of God's "spirit" that they became human beings. The "spirit" and "flesh" are inseparable. If the "body" is regarded as dirty, it is also tarnishing "God's spirit". As a result, the history of Christian doctrine interpretation is divided: how to reach a compromise between secular life and religious abstinence has become a major problem in Christian doctrine interpretation. For the solution, the Christian scripture interpreters tried in the interpretation of *Song of Solomon*.

Although this paradox cannot be fundamentally solved, it at least alleviates the sharp conflict-Christianity does not fully advocate "heartless and no desire", but at the same time it also teaches believers not to indulge their passions too much. Instinctive repression will only lead to the other extreme, namely the persecution of witches in the Witch Searching Wave in Europe. Therefore, after being endowed with religious spirit, the theme connotation of *Song of Solomon* is integrated with the original Christian concept, that is, pure love of sanctification. Its essence is the infiltration of the original religious spirit into secular life.

Ⅲ Conclusion

Song of Solomon praises the pure and honest love of men and women. It deeply reflects the secular spirit of Hebrew civilization, but this dimension has been deliberately erased from the Christian faith. *Song of Solomon* experienced the canonization of the biblical system, and this earthly love was clothed with "sacred aura". Therefore, to realize the particularity of *Song of Solomon* means to realize the inheritance and transformation of Hebrew civilization in Christianity.

（徐秋月译）

03　The Pessimistic Thoughts in *Ecclesiastes*

Different from *Lamentations*, there are no cries or prayers in *Ecclesiastes*. It is only a deep expression of pessimism and despair, which reveals the illusion of life and the truth that everything is meaningless. The background of belief is optimistic and hopeful, because believers are promised a world after death. However, different from other books, *Ecclesiastes*, like *Songs of Songs*, belongs to the "alternative". The whole idea of *Ecclesiastes* is incompatible with the Hebrew belief tradition, and even contradicts each other. Especially in the beginning of *Ecclesiastes* "Vanity of vanities, says the Teacher, vanity of vanities! All is vanity", it reflects a strong sense of pessimism. If we compare the "vanity" of the *Ecclesiastes* with the "vanity" of Chinese Taoist thought, we will find very interesting similarities between them, but they both are also quite different at the same time.

If the *Lamentations of Jeremiah* seeks hope in suffering, then *Ecclesiastes* seeks wisdom in vanity. *Ecclesiastes* was written in 930 B.C. by King Solomon of Judea. Solomon calls himself "the preacher" in his poems, from which comes the *Ecclesiastes*. In fact, *Ecclesiastes* is more pessimistic than *Lamentations*. Although *Lamentations* was written in a hopeless situation in which the whole country was devastated, the Jews still firmly believed in the power of faith in the desperate situation, and they prayed that God would punish the enemy, at that time they still cherished hope of escaping from the bitter sea and reviving the nation. Therefore, the *Lamentations* is still optimistic in general. However, *Ecclesiastes* is on the contrary. It negates everything in this world, "I saw all the deeds that are done under the sun; and see, all is vanity and a chasing after wind." All things are illusory, and everything, new and old, will follow a principle -"return". "A generation goes, and a generation comes: but the earth remains forever. The sun rises and the sun goes down, and hurries to the place it rises. The wind blows to the south, and goes around to the north; rounds and rounds goes the wind,and on its circuits the wind returns. All streams run to the sea, but the sea is not full; to the place where the streams flow, there they continue to flow...What has been is what will be, and what has been done is what will be done; there is nothing new under the sun. Is there a thing of which it is said, See, this is new? it has already been, in the ages before us." Following the return of nature, human beings and animals "the fate of the sons of men and the fate of the beasts is the same", so there is no difference after death,"as one dies, so dies the other. They all have the same breath, and humans have no advantage over animals; for all is vanity." So the preacher questioned,"All go to one place; all are from the dust, and all turn to dust again. Who knows whether the human spirit goes upward and the spirit of animals goes downward to the earth?" Both man and beast will fall into nothingness, and the soul will not know where to go after death,"There is nothing better than that all should enjoy their work, for that is their lot; who can bring them to see what will be after them?"

This "vanity" has deeply influenced modern western philosophy, especially Schopenhauer and Nietzsche. From Schopenhauer's pessimism to Nietzsche's death of god, the root of western nihilism finally blossomed.

The "vanity" presented in *Ecclesiastes* is very similar to the "vanity" of Taoism in Chinese tradition, but Taoism pursues serenity and detachment, while *Ecclesiastes* is more pragmatic and it also emphasizes timely enjoyment in reality. *A Dream of Red Mansions* with Taoism as its background is a lament written by Cao Xueqin in the last days. The first chapter of its opening chapter has a *Won-Done Song*:

Men all know that salvation should be won.

But with ambition won't have done, have done.

Where are the famous ones of days gone by?

In grassy graves they lie now, every one.

Men all know that salvation should be won.

But with their riches won't have done, have done.

Each day they grumble they've not made enough.

When they've enough, it's goodnight every one!

Men all know that salvation should be won.

But with their loving wives won't have done.

The dalings every day protest their love:

But once you're dead, they're off with another one.

Men all know that salvation should be won.

But with their children won't have done, have done.

Yet though of parents found there is no lack.

Of grateful children saw I never a one.

Mean hovels and abandoned halls

Where courtiers once paid daily calls;

Bleak haunts where weeds and willows

scarcely thrive

Were once with mirth and revelry alive.

Whilst cobwebs shroud the mansion's gilded beams,

Fh.collage casement with choice muslin gleams.

Would you of perfumed elegance recite?

Even as you speak,

the raven locks turn white.

Who yesterday her lord's bones laid in clay.

On silken bridal—bed shall lie today.

Coffers with gold and silver filled:

Now in a trice a tramp by all reviled.

(Translated by David Hawkes)

In Taoism, everything in the world is nothing but vanity, all ostentation will vanish into thin air, and the origin of Tao is eternal and unique.

"Moreover I saw under the sun that in the place of justice, wickedness was there; and in the place of righteousness, wickedness was there as well…Again I saw all the oppressions that are practiced under the sun. Look, the tears of the oppressed-with no one to comfort them!On the side of their oppressors there was power-with no one to comfort them." *Ecclesiastes* also sees through all aspects of life and breaks the illusion of life, which is similar to *A Dream of Red Mansions*. Both of them criticize and satirize the ugly social phenomena mercilessly, but the difference is that *A Dream of Red Mansions* only saw despair but could not find an exit. In the end, the Jia family declined, Daiyu died with tears, Baoyu became a monk with an empty heart. The once famous noble family finally disappeared in the vast clouds of history. *A Dream of Red Mansions* vividly depicts the rise and fall of the Jia, Shi, Wang and Xue families. They are either fighting openly or secretly, or trying to preserve their sanity, or losing their way, or abandoning their love to escape from the world. All living beings run around and chase after each other, leaving behind only a sigh of "All fell." *Ecclesiastes* found a way to reconcile with the real world, that is, to have fun in time and find the light of life. However, this kind of enjoyment is not to promote indulgence, but to advocate "work is what you get": "whatever my eyes desired I did not keep from them, I kept my heart from no pleasure, for my heart found pleasure in all my toil, and this was my reward for all my toil…Go thy way, eat thy bread with joy, and drink thy wine with a merry heart; for God now accepteth thy works. Let thy garments be always white; and let thy head lack no ointment. Live joyfully with the wife whom thou lovest all the days of the life of thy vanity, which he hath given thee under the sun, all the days of thy vanity: for that is thy portion in this life, and in thy labour which thou takest under the sun." This kind of enjoyment is within its scope of the principle, but not "indulgence". Besides, exchanging "the joy of toil" for "the share of toil" is the simplest social distribution method. In the social reality of good and evil injustice, it is also the most balanced mode of social development.

Similar to *Song of Songs*, *Ecclesiastes* reflects deep secular concern. Although it is quite different from the style of the whole *Old Testament*, it is still included as a classic, reflecting the intervention and compromise of faith in secular life.

（徐秋月译）

Chapter 3　The Tradition of *the New Testament*

01　The Passion of Jesus—the Fragility of Sacred

I　Introduction

Christianity is the combination of Greek philosophical tradition and Hebrew belief. Rational philosophy helped Christian theology to achieve the goal of metaphysical thinking, while the touching point of Christianity is not the abstract manifestation but the passion of Jesus, the passion of amour and suffering. The religion restricted by meditation, will be reduced to slave of philosophy. It is the passion of Jesus that saves Christianity, or in other words, Christianity results from the passion of Jesus. The passion of Jesus is the foundation of Christianity. However, the passion of Jesus is the metaphysical construction of Jesus' Godhood or the historical record of Jesus' Manhood? Probably the narrative integrates history with imagination? Anyway, the passion is indispensable to the human ultimate care. And the crucial point of the passion, is just the fragility of Jesus, which bears the sacred.

II　The Pray of Gethsemane(Mount Olive) and the Death of Jesus

The Synoptic Gospels which tend to the historical narrative is very different from the *Gospel John* in the narrative of Gethsemane Incident and the death of Jesus. The narrative differences between the historical evidence of the Synoptic Gospels and the philosophic evidence of the *Gospel John*, also can be the proofs as dispute between the belief and the reason in the Christian Theology, or can be as a way to make up the fracture. Therefore, the four books of gospel can be "bell-tiers" or "bell-untiers". The narrative trait of mutual proving and mutual complementing also can be considered as mediation of debating between the belief and the reason.

It has a lot of fun to compare and contrast the four gospels' narrative of Jesus' arrest and his death. The narrative of the Synoptic Gospel's pray about Gethsemane (Mount Olive) is the same,while the *Gospel John* does not have this narrative in details. What's more, the four books of Gospel are different about the narrative of the Jesus' death. If the Jesus' incident is the true history, why there are four books of narrative? If the narrative about the Jesus' incident is fictional, why they are so similar? Are there any similarities behind the differences of the expression between the history and the Revelation?

III   The Four Books of Gospel: Differences and Complementaries

There is no classical text that we can meet purely and willingly. Every classic has a history of acceptance and understanding filled with contradiction. The diversities of the textual understanding and accepting make us confused: *the Gospel of Matthew* attracted the listeners who sought the life of fellowship in the Christian community, such as, the Mennonites, Amish and Church of the Brethren in the Religious Reform, *the Gospel of Luke* and *Acts* have different interpretations in the different Christian communities: the Pentecostalists resort to the Holy Ghost; political and liberation theologians persist in preference of the poor; the liberal Christian like Luke's complete description of Jesus; Barthes regarded it as realistic novels in the 19th century; *the Gospel of John* always attracted Mediation Group, mysticism, metaphysicians and theologians in the Christian tradition.

Although this kind of diversity of understanding is from different pre-understanding of different reader, the obvious reason is the complication of the text itself. The narrations of four books of Gospel are historical or fictional? Are they the realistic novels with the elements of history or the metaphors story of metaphysics with the property of fiction? Are the differences among four books of Gospel the mutual supplement of the witness of the histories or mutual supplement of the structure of narrations? Or both. As different eyewitness of the Jesus' event before and after the 1st century, the narrations from *Mathew*, *Mark*, *Luke* and

John are mostly same, which completely proves the historicity of Jesus, while the different narrative features and styles of four books of Gospel seem to the mutual supplement to the events of the history.

Maybe the inter-textuality and otherness which four books of Gospel show are just the path to go closely to Biblical canon: it also avoids the homoousia as Procrustean Bed. The Christian crisis does not only have the obvious traces in the modern times. Of course, in the modern time, the background of secularization is surely one of the root causes. However, from the time of Jesus' birth, Christianity has never separated from the conflict between Judaism and the newborn-Christianity, God's electorate and gentile, canon and heresy. "The best way for religion is a kind of power of fighting." This fighting not only exists in the relationship between religions and politics and ideology, religions and religions, but also exists in the different views in the inner part of the religions. It is this struggle that religions keep the active power and prevent the discourse of hegemony or totalitarianism. Maybe the stubborn power of Christian subversiveness is not from the natural science, evolution or the Enlightenment, but from inner part. Kierkegaard believed, the otherness included in the Christianity was "a bomb in the pleasure ground of theologians."

"The disclosure" of four books of Gospel, is special to challenge the fully understanding ,certainty and ultimately control and harness. This disclosure provides the possibility of the dialogue—between inter-texts, and between readers and texts. If we can not tolerate the problems that are different from ours, the dialogue can not happen. The four books of Gospel connect with each other. Because the dialogue is the tolerance to the diversity and otherness, while the diversity and otherness are just the true "possibility". This kind of possibility of understanding makes us finally find "the similarity of the difference"—the reason why Jesus changed from a preacher to a preached content. The reason why Jesus can be a "model" is not only the "diversity" of the morality between him and us, but also the "similarity" of the flesh.

IV   "I am who I am" and "the God of Love"

From that "I am who I am" in the *Old Testament* to " God's Abandoned Son" in the *New Testament*, the images of the God has changed a lot. Especially, took the Jesus' image of Nazareth as an example, in the past 2000 years, the image of Jesus became a sustainable "basic topic" in every age and a precious try of seeking meaning for human beings. Whitehead supposed, it is also valid if the relationship of the philosophy in one era and the image of Jesus in the same era is resersed: in every era, the way of describing Jesus was also a special key to understand that era. The changes of Jesus' images made the history of belief more complicated, but was a treasure for the cultural history.

Jesus was not YHWH—who had the great power and caused nine great disasters to Egyptian, and who butchered the "first born",the "I am who I am". Jesus did not become the God. Because, although his behaviors were the traces of the God, he did the trace of curing and saving people. Jesus was not the Lord—who made Jacob and Moses scaring: Jacob dreamed the high ladder in Birtley, after waking up, he said terribly:"How awesome is this place! This is none other than the house of God, and this is the gate of heaven." When summoned by the Lord, Moses shows the same fear:And Moses hid his face, for he was afraid to look at God."The compliance is a kind of necessity of the human souls." Simone Weil believed, although the compliance is the nutrition of the life, after all, it derived from the awe. Though both of them are beliefs, what are the differences between "the belief in the fear and shudder" and "the belief in the love"?

The prediction of Hebrew has a tight relationship between God's wrath and censure, between the people's awe and obedience. At Horeb Mount, in the temple of Isaiah and Ezekiel, Moses saw the God's wheel and moved by the fear: they experienced the incompatibility between the mankind and the God in the name of whole nations. In the transformational process from "the fear of the sin" to "the faith of the love", Jesus played a significant role. However, it was the Jesus' vulnerability as a man that made this "love" effective. If the God was only an holy Other so that he can not hear the prays of others; if the sinner was the object of prophets' condemnations, then he would not have the reason to pray. Love can grow in the love: the love of men recalls the love of the people and the belief of "the love" also recalls "the love" of the faith.

Paul Ricoeur, a philosopher, believes that "the death of the God" means the true religion: not an authority above us but a spirit in our hearts. Ricoeur said,"Once get over the existence of the idol, the image of father can be a symbol again." God is a father, which means the God goes out himself in order to the purpose of people. The philosophical theology of Paul Ricoeur stands out the love in the belief and the faith in the love: the God is the absolutely love not the completely authority. YHWH promised Abram, "I will bless those who bless you, and the one who curses you I will curse." However, Jesus made pray for everyone, "Love your enemies, do good to those who hate you, bless those who curse you, pray for those who abuse you." The theology of Tertullian not only formed the significance of Jesus' theology and teaching as a son of the God, but also clarified the cultural meaning of Jesus. Because Jesus was the terminator in the historical transformation. And it also was the new way to explain the history and a foundation of the new historiography.

V   "God's Abandoned Son": Fragility and Passion

In a secular context, the connection between the history of Christian thought and philosophy, between the history of the Christian church and Doctrine theology, gradually becomes weaker. While the significance of individual Jesus increasingly becomes remarkable. As an individual Jesus, we not only see the metaphysical thought and moral nobility, but also a clinging pursuit for a true man to the faith. From "I am Who I am" to "the God of love" the Christ has changed a lot. However, it does not mean that there is no similarity between them. Jesus is not the Lord, but is a prophet, a true man. Since Jesus is a prophet, he can not avoid the difficulties: It is no doubt for Jeramiah that a true prophet is unlucky. If Jesus is real, then he should accept the vulnerability of human beings —the entanglement of different kinds of love and sorrow.

Tennyhale, a theologian, believed: The passion of Jesus was necessary. Because the sorrow was the fate that the prophet can not avoid. The necessity of sorrows "derived from the fact that the purpose of the God must be realized in a blind and stubborn world." The fact of prophetic fate is so important. Because it endows the same characters of Jesus' followers. In *Acts*, the witness of Jesus conforms to the same mode.

In terms of the opinion from Kant, the Gospels show the concept and the ideality of the morality and perfectness, which is the model that we should be. This concept of human kindness and freedom is not only the truth in the literal meaning. For Kant, the ideality is effective in practice. That is to say, it encourages us to practise it in the rationality and morality. Kant pointed it obviously that the concept of the Christ was on the value not in the fact. The argumentation of Kant was that the symbol of Christ not the history of Jesus is rather important to the human freedom. The moral religion of Kant naturally led to discontent and argumentation of many theologians. However, one point is worth of affirming: Jesus is a moral model. Nevertheless, if Jesus had the characters without the humanity, then how did the moral model fulfill the moral practice?

At the beginning of *the Fragility of Goodness*, Nussbaum, a famous American scholar, cited Pindar's metaphor of "grape of vine" and Plato's *Drinking at Meeting*. As a modern stoics, Nussbaum's affirmation of the eroticism is intriguing: In the eye of the female scholar, the eroticism was just the power of this fragile beauty. People, will be powerful, beautiful, outstanding and noble , if they are fragile. Although, for souls of people, we feel so weary for our heavy body, but who can deny that it is the flesh that helps us to shoulder the sorrows and happiness of souls? In *Drinking at Meeting*, after Alcipiades finishing his statement about the brilliant view for the virtues of people, Socrates asked in an ironic tone, "What is a man?" Based on this, Nussbaum began her reflection on philosophy and ethics. She said: "With more learning of Stoic's ethics, I began to treat many topics discussed in early times with a new eye—especially for the essence of the emotion and the concept of people."

Jesus was not a "hero" in traditional sense, and he did not win by the battle; he also did not kill the fire dragon: "Compared with the history officially, he is not a ruler or conqueror with the military exploits. And his stories are suffering ones." The narrative of "passion" was about the fragile, suffering and self-denying narration. Unlike other heroes, Jesus did nothing about the safety of his existence and meaning of his life—but gave these to the God. The Gospel must be narrative, because it referred to ways of existence, which led to the suffering history. Preaching in its inner part must need the narrative. Because what the preacher preached and ways of living were involved in the suffering history, then the preacher became the content of being preached.

Although Augustine highly praised the Gospel of *John,* he also affirmed the humanity of Jesus. Because he was what we should look like, "Christian Jesus is mediator between the God and people. The reason is not his divinity but his humanity, not because he is the perfect origin of everything, but because he is the perfect purpose of everything." About 1200 years, after dying of Augustine, Pascal, a French scientist and Christian philosopher, inherited the mantle of Augustine, "Without understanding the human sufferings, only leads to pride. Without knowledge about the God and only understanding the human sufferings, we may feel despaired. However, the knowledge about Jesus forms the doctrine of the Golden Mean. Because we can find God's sufferings and ours on his body."

What's more, other phenomenon vividly expressed the position of Jesus' humanity in the culture and history: the worship of Virgin Mary. Although Nestorians denied the divinity of Mary(of course its "the two natures" was against the orthodox doctrine of "The Trinity"), and was listed as heresy, it was the praise of the Virgin Mother that Catholicism thrived especially in arts. "When losing the connection with Nazarene in admiring or speculating of the Christ for manifestation, Mary replaced him; she was human, compassionate and approachable. Therefore, thinking and praising for her is not based on the principle of 'Worship the God'."

The God who proved his existence in Jesus event was the God of love. The reality of God's love was also the central clue of human love and of being loved. For the inquiry of Jesus " Who am I?" Tracy maybe answered,"You are Christ, a symbol of the mode of love that exists in the world." Although the "Yale School" properly complained that "Jesus" here had already transformed the allegory of "common sense", did this general truth of humanity about the person of Jesus and his narrative (gospel) have the unique value in the human history?

Although Jesus "stoutly expected" his dead time and never shook his faith, it did not mean that the terminal time of the death had no sorrows. The Gospel presented the experience of the sin and suffering in the world for us. Before the happiness of reliving, it was filled with the suffering fear. For Tracy, this view more firmly revealed the truth of human existence: just as Van Gogh's suffering paintings were more true of contemporary experience than the undisturbed and the lightsome world revealed by Raphael's arts.

How can Jesus be sure and love this world he suffered? The pray of Gethsemane showed the Jesus vulnerability as an individual person. However this nobility of vulnerability was that, although the death was painful, the determination of Jesus' faith never shook. Bearing the sufferings with the fragile flesh and facing the criminal world with the encouragement of love was just the value as a person. Jesus' affirmation for creation had a stronger influence than his disavowal of sufferings. The meaning was more essential than ridiculous.

VI The Passionate Narrative of Gospel: The Experience and Practice of the Love

The possibility of the poem tempted its feeling. According to the view of hermeneutics, the text seemed to invite readers to recheck their lives in terms of the symbol which the text conveyed. The real entry point of Jesus' question, "You said who I am", was that it came up with a basic question and made a challenge for readers: Is this the way of living? If readers possessed stories of Jesus' passion, and found that the way of cross for his existence in the world lightened the readers' world, the readers encountered the gospel of enlightenment.

If the basic function of the proposition is to tempt feeling then as for stories about Jesus, the readers should pay more attention to its value of feeling than its reality. The textual world is endowed the image of readers. Although the biblical texts look like the "reality", they can also be interpreted as the true possibility which is in order to state readers' feeling of imagination. The hermeneutic is the way of understanding. Therefore, when readers follow the temptation and possess the meaning of texts, they also obtain the new type of the subjectivity. For Ricoeur, the important Jesus should not be the Jesus of Pennberg's history and the Jesus of Karl Barth enlightenment of the God, but historical Jesus that the Gospel invites readers to share. That is to say, the Gospel is a story about the human history. Actions yield to emotions. The change of subjectivity is more significant than the fluctuation of the soul.

The function of the Gospel not only expresses the new God, but also creates a chance for the new God. Many stories have a great effect on readers, even if events which they tell never happened. The image of Christian Jesus not only presents the original event of enlightenment, but also provides a chance for events of enlightenment in the later time. Therefore, for Tillich and Ricoeur, the narrative of Gospel has a function to prove and change lives. For Tracy and Ricoeur, the key point for Jesus' stories is that reading can treat their lives with a new way. Tracy expects that readers can find the expression of deepening faith and hope in the Gospel. However,in fact, it is not Jesus that changed structures in the world or something in the human essence, but we can see the world in different ways by Jesus' stories.

（宣麒麟译）

02　Jesus Event—History or Imagination

Ⅰ　Introduction

As the representative of "Chicago School", Paul Ricoeur's hermeneutics bears an evident mediating characteristic. What he tries to mediate is not only the split between philosophy and theology, but history and imagination. If Ricoeur's hermeneutics is philosophical, then biblical narrative is just a regional example of his philosophical hermeneutics; if Ricoeur's hermeneutics is theological, then biblical narrative is the frame of his theological hermeneutics. Anyway, biblical narrative takes a special role in Ricoeur's philosophical-theological meditation and narrative theory. The biblical narrative makes Ricoeur's philosophy framed in theology while his analysis on history and imagination of biblical narrative makes his theology promoted to a philosophical height. No matter philosophy or theology, interpretation is the essential characteristic of Ricoeur's meditation. History and imagination is always the embarrassment which hermeneutics encounters. The implications between history and imagination are made of two dimensions and three elements. The two dimensions are history itself and the narrative of history; the three elements are text, narrator and reader. Text is the medium to link narrator with reader, while narrative and reading themselves are a kind of interpretations.

Ⅱ　Biblical Narrative: A Symbol of General Truth?

An analysis for the gospel narrative of David Tracy and Ricoeur makes the story of Jesus itself become a symbol of universal truth. The gospel narrative was included in the type of "classics" of hermeneutics by Tracy, which made the gospel narrative not only connected with the theology but also had a tight relationship with the hermeneutics. This method of secularizing the religion and generalizing the theology, made the "Chicago School" vigorously attacked by the "Yale School". If the gospel reveals the universal truth about the human general experience, so what is the special significance of Jesus?

With this question in the mind, let us have a look at the basic criticism that Frey made the hermeneutics of Ricoeur. As we can know, the special function of poetry and literature that Ricoeur believed uncovers the new possibility. The guidance followed by Rudolf Bultmann, Ricoeur and Tracy believe that *the New Testament* provides understanding of readers themselves with a new possibility. However, this strategy of the hermeneutics needs pay for a price. Frey accused that Ricoeur and Tracy can not remain the "literal" reading of the gospel so that it failed for the Christian theology to keep the necessity of Jesus himself and his behaviour. How did this happen?

If the gospel is about the universal experience of the mankind and possibility, so the standpoint of hermeneutics from Ricoeur and Tracy will regard Jesus as "the main body with existing of ideology, in another words, his ego exist as 'understanding'." What happened about Jesus on earth in the story? It just serves as a foil to allow him to understand himself. Frey opposed that this kind of reading can not make a fair comment to the gospel and regarded it as a story of a person's behavior, personality and event in the world, while such reading lost the "theological" factors of the gospel—the behavior of the God as historical witness in Christianity.

Can not Jesus go on to play a necessary role as a messenger of understanding himself? Frey did not think so, because the gospel narrative presented in this plan is not the first individual ego, not the predicative subject, but "the mode-of-being" in-the-world, which is an example of the ego, and is the 're-presented' disclosed to 'understanding'". According to this narrative, the Jesus' role "is just an individual strengthening of a particular set of attitudes. " "Jesus" doesn't exist as a name of the major role in his story any more, but as a label of special mode in the consciousness, as the possibility of our own understanding. Frey thought that this reading of gospel narrative could not retain the central position of Jesus' story: "at most, from this point, the relationship between meaning—proving and affiliation of the individual and the subject in the story is weak. The worst thing is that this connection has been wiped off. " What the "Jesus" of individual subject happened is not equally important any more.

In the "Biblical Hermeneutics" of Ricoeur, "the final reference substance of allegory...is not the kingdom of the God , but is all reality of the human beings." Frey pointed, the intention of Ricoeur was to include Jesus' teaching about the kingdom of the God in the more general proving. However, the wrong way he did was the separation between the literal meaning of biblical narrative and the reference substance of the ideality and it made the biblical narrative declined.

III   History and Imagination: Two Modes of Narration

If philosophy is a kind of thinking of the existence of the human beings, then this thinking must be promoted by the different kinds of languages(including behaviors of the mankind and the history itself) of expressing the human beings' existence. The reason why narration can be praised by Ricoeur is that this kind of language can express the reality of the mankind most. The narration embodies the possibility of behaviors, possible ways of doing something and the possible "world". Maybe the narration can be taken as the summit of Ricoeur's academic thinking, because the narration can not only connect with language, hermeneutics, philosophy and anthropology, but also be the discussional confluence of three imaginary topics about the possibility, reality and creativity.

History and imagination, two modes of the narration, are the ways that the human history can be redescribed. Therefore, the history and imagination together build up "a systematic plan" of narration for the possibility of the human beings. And the narrative creation presents a lot of ways that we live. Besides, the possibility that narration presents is not only to provide the possibility for the individual, but also for the whole society and community. Through the history and imagination of narration, we make a voice to the objects of hope, this object is a form of the life for mankind, a form that we are longing for but have not achieved yet. By presenting a possible world or the existent way in time, by requesting readers to turn this world into theirs, the narration reaches a purpose of " volitive poetics" which Ricoeur was eager to for a long time.

The disputation between the history and imagination, is the embarrassment which thinkers in the west can not get over and the gap that historical philosophy and hermeneutics can not step over. From Croce's "All history is contemporary history", to Collingwood's "All history is the history of the thought", then to Hayden White's "The essence of the historical narration is the fiction", the limitation of the history and imagination absolutely have become unclear. Thinkers in the historical narration find the shadow full of imagination between the lines. The history leaves the space for the imagination, and the imagination bears the burden of history. Therefore, where is the boundary between the literary fiction and the historical imagination?

The best is the most dangerous, while "where the danger lies, there must be more salvation." Maybe the embarrassment of history or imagination, has just completed the journey of Ricoeur from philosophy to theology then to literature. It is also like the key in hands of Peter Rock to open the door of the heaven for Ricoeur's faith request. Therefore, the task of *Time and Narration* is doubled: the story is very similar with the fiction depending on the power of imagination to build the plot; on the other hand, he also needs embody that the fiction is very similar with the history in proving the real world about the human behaviors. We also see that, in Ricoeur's opinion, the history and the fiction make up two types of possible passions: the history reminds us what is possible, and the fiction reminds us what will be possible.

IV History or imagination of Jesus' Event

Ricoeur is a mediating thinker. He has a talent to choose the standpoint. It seems to be mutually exclusive, in his mediation, he would become compatible but independent. According to the view of Ricoeur, the obvious feature of the gospel is the combination between good narration and preaching of gospel. The gospel is a good narration to announce Jesus himself and his history. As a combination of narration and preaching of gospel, the gospel retains the Christian integrality and indissolubility of historical Jesus and faith. Ricoeur mediated the history about the biblical narrative and imagination. Actually, he also built up a kind of rationality between the Christ of faith and the historical Jesus.

Although historians take part in building the possible lab of the fiction, but the history still has an objective question. The epistemology of historians is different from other human sciences, it demands the double honesty of criticism(the historical study) and imagination (the use of narrative). The historical objectivity means that a conclusion of a historian should supplement with that from other historian. If these two kinds of narrative relate with the same world, so the gospel just presentes the history of Jesus' event in this way.

Actually the history tells us what has happened, but historians are inspired by the desire of criticism of the past. Historians just have the past "traces", while the past is absent at present. On one hand, these "traces" are chains of the thought and remind us that the past can not be possessed so that it is the existence which is unable to reach; on the other hand, these "traces" are a guidance of historical study. The duty of judging "traces" in the past and the response to what has happened in practice make the history still keep the limitation from the fiction.

Historian can not describe but re-describe. In Ricoeur's opinion, the history is just like a metaphor, a structure of imagination: historians invent the image that can represent the past. Like the host of metaphor, historians are not copying but inventing. Historical narrative is a kind of creative imitation.

As for many philosophers, the fiction does not involve something absent, but includes something unreal. Ricoeur believed that it was a kind of real slander. Ricoeur pioneered the special cognitive function of the fiction: he found it through inventions. The fiction requests us to hang the attention for the real world and pay attention to the other world: "In this situation of no agreement,we do our best to try new views, new values and new ways of existing. The imagination maybe the competition of the freedom. " Historians discover the door to achieve the possible truth: "the 'real' story in the past reveals the present potential."

The truth of the fiction can be embodied in reading. When the world of texts encounters with that of readers, the fiction will become a reality. Therefore, readers' "appropriation" for the fictional world of texts is the necessary condition that the fiction turns into the reality. Reading mediates the fictional world of texts and the real world of readers, which is the special place where the possible world of texts and the real world overlap. No matter how ontological position the world of texts enjoys, it always remains in a state of suspicion until it is read and "appropriated". The fiction comes from the real world by its influence, that is, the transformation of life and morality. Therefore, Ricoeur did not explore the fictional truth by the theory of proving, but through the theory of influence. The fiction has enlightened and transformational power. The fiction makes reader release from the daily life and have a new criticism for the reality and ourselves. In other words, the connection between the fiction and reality is a kind of application and appropriation not proofs. Following Gadamer, Ricoeur found that the history could influence us by reading in a large part. The possibility of opening up from the history must be appropriated by the imagination.

V   Conclusion

If a nation has neither a story nor a history, they will have no past and future. The narrative gives us a historical sense and endows us an identity. Ricoeur said, in fact, an individual identity in itself is narrative, which is in heart. To understand who we are is to be able to follow our stories. The narrative provides the significant relationship between self-sustainability and fragmentation for us. One implication of narrative identity is that we must be "readers" for our own lives. One way to make sense of who we are is to tell ourselves in roles of other stories and histories. If so, these narrative "rebuild" our lives. From the beginning of his philosophical career, Ricoeur denied the privilege of direction examination of Descartes' consciousness. Man, this subject is neither self-transparent nor illusory: it is the existence of time that needs to be understood and the "trace" of its existence: "Therefore, at the same time, it also becomes readers and writers for our own lives." The identity of narrative has an influence in the social strata. Whether the individuals or groups, they form their identities with certain narrative, which become their story or history. Ricoeur said, it is by telling stories of certain basic events that the Biblical Israelis become a historical group.

（宣麒麟译）

03   Cosmopolitanism in *New Testament*

I   Introduction

At the beginning of the era, Christianity is actually a fusion of Greek and Hebrew cultural traditions. Christianity inherits the Hebrew culture through the Jewish classics and receives the penetration and impact of Greek culture due to the historical and regional stipulation. In order to gain the approval of the ruling class and the Romans, the early godfathers generally adopted two effective strategies: one is to demonstrate the common point between Christianity and Roman government in order to obtain the protection of the state machine; the second is to find the similarities between Christianity and Greek philosophy in order to enrich and spread their beliefs with more rigorous philosophical concepts. However, in terms of its essence, Christianity's fusion of the two ancient traditions is first reflected in its rebellion and renewal of the old beliefs. Therefore, the propositions of "transcending the world" and "justification by faith" of Jesus and Paul are its real starting point.

II   Cosmopolitanism in *the New Testament*

There are two sources of cosmopolitanism in the *New Testament*: one is the cosmopolitanism in Greek philosophy, especially the cosmopolitanism in the late Stoics in Roman times; The second is the tradition of ethnic integration and cultural exchange inherence in Hebrew tradition, especially the peaceful ideas that have emerged among Jews during the period of being captured. For Jesus, it is the latter that has a greater influence, while for Paul, it is the former. In fact, during the period of being captured, narrow nationalism and pacifism came into being at the same time, and the Prophets of the *Old Testament* have a lot of evidence to show this. If the Hebrew's greatest effort is to reverse the value system of Greek culture or make Greek culture a subsidiary of Hebrew culture, then Christianity tries to merge the two traditions, and in this integration, Greek culture has actually changed from a subsidiary status to a dominant status.

In fact, before the formation of the *New Testament*, Alexander's Philo talked about God's "megapolis" and the city of human beings in his works such as *Politicians*. Philo's efforts to integrate cosmopolitanism in the *Old Testament* with cosmopolitanism in the Greek-Roman world greatly inspired the authors of the *New Testament*. It was the founders of early Christianity, represented by John and Paul, who really combined the two traditions. They integrated the cosmopolitan theology in the *Old Testament* and the cosmopolitan philosophy in the Greek-Roman world, hoping to use it as the philosophical support of Christian belief. It is commendable that the authors of the *New Testament* drew on the essence of Hebrew and Greek traditions to form Christian cosmopolitan theology on the basis of criticizing the narrow nationalism of the *Old Testament*.

The Gospel of *John* is the most prominent one in the Gospels for the fusion of the two traditions. The beginning of the Gospel of *John* is not only the best explanation of universalism, but also the best witness of the fusion of the two traditions: "In the beginning was the Word, and the Word was with God, and the Word was God...And without him not one thing came into being...In him was life; and the life was the light of all people...The true light, which enlightens everyone, was coming into the world."(*John* 1:1-9) In this passage, the first thing we feel is "the light of cosmopolitanism", which illuminates all the people born in the world, not just the "voters". As a result, the uniqueness of "Israel" in *the Old Testament* no longer exists, the light of God illuminates all the people, and God's love and redemption are given to all the people, thus the superiority of Jews no longer exists.

The Gospel of *John* changed the Lord with Jewish appearance into "Word", "light", "logos" and the light of universal reason and life, which brought Christian theology into the category of cosmopolitanism.

Jesus' religious reform inherited the precious tradition of the Second Isaiah Movement. He challenged the boundaries of God's people, redefined the "righteous" and "sinners" and brought those excluded groups into his own scope of salvation. All these showed the hope of pacifism and cosmopolitanism. "Mountaineering and Training the Masses" is considered as the cornerstone of Christian ethics, and many of its comments are about Jesus' criticism of the narrow nationalism of Jews. In response to the narrow revenge mentality of the Jews, "An eye for an eye, and a tooth for a tooth" and "love your neighbor and hate your enemy", Jesus taught,"Do not resist an evildoer. But if anyone strikes you on the right cheek, turn the other also...Love your enemies and pray for those who persecute you." (*Matthew* 5:38-44)Jesus' cosmopolitan thought is fully reflected in this sentence, "for he makes his sunrise on the evil and on the good, and sends rain on the righteous and on the unrighteous." (*Matthew* 5:38-44) The change of Jesus' image of the God of Israel has laid a solid foundation for the cosmopolitanism of Christianity. In *the Old Testament,* the Lord is often portrayed as a military commander with terrible majesty, short temper and narrow mind. He not only punishes the enemies of Israel, the Egyptians and the Philistines, but also shows no mercy for the rebellion of the Jews. However, with the change of Jesus, God changed from a national God to the common Father of all mankind. And this heavenly father's temper has also improved, becoming amiable and tolerant. In Jesus' heart, the Jews did not have any privilege. Women, sinners and Samaritans who had been discriminated before were all the targets of his redemption. Therefore, in the belief system of Jesus, the object of salvation has changed from a group to a single person, which is exactly the same as the emphasis of cosmopolitanism in Greek philosophy on the individual. The two most important commandments of Jesus are "to love God" and "to love others as yourself", which fully shows the difference between Jesus' cosmopolitanism and Jewish narrow nationalism. The last commandment of Jesus to his disciples after his resurrection is also full of cosmopolitanism, "All authority in heaven and on earth has been given to me. Go therefore and make disciples of all nations."*(Matthew* 28:18-19)

Paul further expanded the logic of Jesus' gospel-the good news of Jesus brought not only "the just" but also "the sinner", while the good news of Paul brought not only "the sinner" but also "gentile sinners". In *Romans* 2: 10-11, Paul clearly said, "But glory and honor and peace for everyone who does evil, the Jews first and also the Greek. For God shows no partiality."Another example is *Romans* 4: Abraham, as an example of faith, his devotion to faith is not shown by the special mark of circumcision. Again, in *Romans* 9: 6-12, Paul reiterated the characteristics of divine calling or divine selection-regardless of race or physical signs. In *Romans* 11, Paul claimed that the hope of the last days is not only on Jews, but also on Gentiles.

If the Gospel recorded more cosmopolitan thoughts of Christian founders, then

Acts recorded more cosmopolitan practices of early Christians. *Acts* vividly records the missionary activities of the first generation of apostles in fully implementing Jesus' cosmopolitanism, and depicts the picture of the first generation of apostles spreading Christianity to all parts of the world, especially to the surrounding Mediterranean (Christianity and Judaism were not formally divided at that time, Christianity belonged to the heresy of Judaism) with indomitable will. The main clue is the story of how the apostles spread the gospel from Jerusalem to "in all Judaea, and in Samaria, and unto the uttermost part of the earth" (*Acts* 1:8), which is full of hardships, difficulties and even the cost of life. For example, Stephen, in order to spread Jesus' universalism, argued with the Jews and refuted all the people speechless. All this made the Jews angry from embarrassment, so they bribed the bad guys to give false testimony and accuse Stephen. Finally, Stephen was pulled out of the city and stoned to death. Another example is Peter, who was arrested twice by the Jewish government and later captured by Herod. He will be executed after Passover. After miraculous protection, he escaped from prison and saved himself.

As for Paul, his sufferings are even more incredible: he has not only made three overseas expeditions and distressed for many times, covering Palestine, Asia Minor, Mediterranean islands, Greece and Rome, but also has written many books that systematically explain Christian cosmopolitanism. In response to the Jewish viewpoint of "justification by law", Paul proposed the viewpoint of "justification by faith", which expanded the scope of Christ's redemption to all those who believe in Christ-this abolished the Jewish practice of defining national identity and belief identity by law, broke the unbridgeable boundary between Jews and Gentiles, and developed the narrow nationalism of Jews into a loving universalism. In order to remove the stumbling block of Moses' law, Paul tactfully bypassed Moses and returned to Abraham: Abraham was not circumcised, and he did not know the law of Moses, but this did not prevent him from justification, which shows that all people can do so and justification is not limited to Jews who follow the law.

In Paul's letters, cosmopolitanism can be seen everywhere. For example, *Corinthians* I (12: 12–27) said, "For just as the body is one and has many members, and all the members of the body, though many, are one body, so it is with Christ.

For in the one Spirit we were all baptized into one body—Jews or Greeks, slaves or free—and we were all made to drink of one Spirit."Again, as *Ephesians* (2: 11-15) says,"So then, remember that at one time you Gentiles by birth, called 'the uncircumcision' by those who are called 'the circumcision' —a physical circumcision made in the flesh by human hands—remember that you were at that time without God in the world. But now in Christ Jesus you who once were far off have been brought near by the blood of Christ."

In Paul's universal thought, Jesus' teaching of love has become the basic feature of Christian theology: "Love is patient; love is not envious or boastful or arrogant or rude. It does not insist on its own way; it is not irritable or resentful; it does not rejoice in wrongdoing, but rejoice in the truth. It bears all things, believes all things, hopes all things, endures all things. Love never ends." (*Corinthians* I 13:4-8)This is a love that knows no borders, no race, no social status, no poverty, this is an unconditional love, this love is completely different from the love of narrow Jewish compatriots, and it is also different from the love of "from near to far" in Chinese Confucianism, this is a universal love, and it is love beyond all boundaries.

In contrast, *Revelation* is full of narrow nationalism and bloody vendetta scenes, and God's judgment is everywhere. God is still the God of hosts who is always angry and often punishes. Therefore, *Revelation* was finally included in the *New Testament* and its canon status has long been questioned.

（徐秋月译）

04　Exclusiveness in *New Testament*

I　*The City of God* of Augustine

Although the Christ absorbed the concept of Stoic School's cosmopolitanism in the early time, it constantly deviated from the world spirit that the concept advocated in the later development. And this deviation left a foreshadowing in the beginning of the original doctrine. For the classification of the profane state and the divine nation—"Pay to Caesar what belongs to Caesar and God what belongs to

God", the crowds who did not believe the God were expelled from the God, which was not similar in the way that the Judaism as its predecessor distinguished the identity with the custom of religious belief and circumcision, but achieved the same influence—two different identities extremely were produced by the standard of believing God or not. However, the emotion of extremism generated by the status' distinction was no less harmful than the influence produced by ultra-nationalism. For Augustine's interpretation of "City of God" made the world city become a community of including the certain special crowds again. Augustine made a clear point that people who loved the God were chosen as citizens in the city of the God.

Ⅱ Anti-semitism

However, actually, the exclusiveness of the Christ was first to be embodied in the exclusion of "Jews", while antisemitism became an invisible feature of the Christ in the process of development for nearly two thousand years. For the Christians, the issue that who were the God's people related the self-understanding and self-origination of the Christianity. If not breaking between the Christ and Judaism but integrating in the same pattern, this issue was not a problem. However, several announcements of the Christ had a fiercely conflict with the Judaism in the 1st century A.D., and then the concept of "Israel" had been renewed and spread. Spreaded With the terminal divorce of ways, this issue was more sharp so that we can not avoid. Who were the people of the God? All of Jews? Or were Jews who had joined the Christianity (the Judaism of the eschatology)? And including the Metics? What about the Jews who did not believe Jesus as Messiah and seemed to be impossible to change? Did the Christianity take over Israel? Did "new Israel" surpass the old Israel? In the 2nd century A.D. , this issue became more complicated. The Christians felt that they were the third race—Jews and Metics became "them", while only the Christians were "themselves" and only the Christianity was real Israel. The growing consciousness of Christians' identities stimulated the antisemitism. A boring fact for a long time was that the Catholicism did its best to distinguish from the Judaism and always rejected the Jews—in the original several centuries, this trend was obviously interpreted in *Homily Against the Jews* of Chrysostom. The most ironic meaning was the Christianity began to resist the Jews and ethnocentrism of Jewish Christian; however, Christianity regarded itself as an independent "race"at the same time, and started a different kinds of racialism. In the racism of the Christianity, the Christians tried their best to classify from "Jews", which was the advocation that Paul once extremely rejected.

As for Christianity, whether they can realize this exclusiveness and narrow-mindedness or not, and they also can get over them, which was afraid to go back Jesus again. Jesus challenged the boundary of the God's people—it was the central opinion that he preached, which was a hint and a challenge for all sects in the Christianity. Many sects all faced a challenge, including not only among of the sects, even in the branches of sects, which regarded them as "righteous persons" and distinguished them from "sinners". Not only between sects, but even among branches of sects, there was a challenge they faced—these branches always regarded them as "righteous persons" and classified them from "sinners". Nowadays, the way that they excluded other religions with a flag of the God's will prevailed in the inner section of the Christianity, whether they were fundamentalists of Vatican or the ones of Protestantism. Therefore, Jesus' attitude to this criticism had an equally influence both before and now.

III The Power of the Church

For thousands of years, the argumentation of the theological philosophy of the Christianity centred on the status of "theology" and "philosophy", while the Christian church only paid attention to the power of "universal authority of politics" and "universal church", but the emphasis on church's features of the cosmopolitanism gradually declined, despite the regional community ideologically included all people. Simply, the disputation was between the universe world and the church in now days, while not between the locality and cosmopolitanism. In this way, the cosmopolitan trend of improvement involved in the Christian thought in the early period, was constantly forgotten instead of the limitation of identities, that was, the distinction between the spiritual and non-divine, which made the Christianity trap into the provinciality of its predecessor Judaism again. The provinciality in the Christianity became more and more serious in the later development, until the religious war and persecution in the period of religious reform developed to an alarming extent.

In the early period, the Christian church was persecuted, especially under the emperors' ruling of Nero and Trajan and many martyrs were sacrificed for their "belief". The spirit of "protecting religion" for these martyrs, were capable of evoking praises and tears. However, this oppressed history was worthy of historical reflecting—because after one thousand years, this religion once undergone by the persecution became the biggest persecutor in the European history. In the year of 313, Constantine, a great emperor, admitted the legal status of the Christianity. In 392, Theodosius, an emperor, even took it as a national religion. In the long time of Middle Age, the Christianity naturally had a significant influence in the inheritance of the thought and culture, as well as the construction and consolidation of the social institution. However we could not ignore the forbiddenness of the thought and the abusement of the social authority.

In 476, the collapse of the Western Roman and the invasion of the Germanic nation, made the society trap in a chaotic situation so that the Greek—Roman civilization was in danger. However, the churchmen of Christianity shouldered the responsibility as enlightened teachers. Because, at that time, only churchmen mastered the Latin and Greek as a tool of presenting the Greek—Roman civilization. The churchmen of the Christianity were required to learn the language of barbaric ethnic groups and made a preaching in the virgin places. Therefore, in this way, the establishment of the feudal system in the western Europe had a principle foundation, as well as the Christianity had been the greatest feudal lord who occupied a lot of lands with controlling of authority and thought. "The Middle Age of the darkness " referred to the much unknown that we had at this time. However, in the most situation, "darkness" always means the ignorance controlled by the thought, and even worse, it was the persecution governed by this extremely controlling.

History, was always easy to forget. Or that was, we chose to forget consciously, which was the "selective" obliviousness. Superficially, the Christianity came out from Judaism so that the doctrine of "justification by faith" had already made the Christians get rid of the conciousness of "Jewish ethnic identity". However, the new type of "identity" was constantly emphasized. The word of "status" , was translated "identity" in English. And originally, it meant "unity". Therefore, the status of Christians could not exist without the identification, which was to pursue the shadow of "unity". Why did the "status" have to need this "unity"? Was it because the "heretics" threaten the "unity"? However, the "heretics" always existed, which was not inevitable. Even if there is the "heretic tribunal", it can not be completely expelled. As a result, wars and conflicts went on.

IV The Exclusiveness of the Christianity

The "exclusiveness" of the Christianity mainly focused on four sections: firstly, to exclude the "heresy" distinguished from the "orthodoxy" (including two parts: on the one hand, the exclusiveness of "heretic thought" different from the "orthodox thought", on the other hand, the exclusiveness of "heretic sects different from the "orthodox church"); secondly, to exclude the classics of "canons" (including the *Apocrypha*, *Pseud-epigraphy* and *Dead Sea Scrolls*); thirdly, to exclude the Darwinism, scientism and historicism of opposing "orthodoxy" described as "the creation thought" and "mysterious manifestation"; fourthly, to exclude other religious beliefs (such as the Islam, Buddhism and the thought of Chinese Confucianism). If the first two parts were in the situation of "strengthening the defence" for the inner sections of the Christianity, and the latter two parts were in the condition of "adopting a closed-door policy" for the out sections of the Christianity.

V Conclusion

The cosmopolitanism that *the New Testament* hold was surly a kind of the historical progress. Under the background of the Hellenization, the Christianity reflected the limitation of the Jewish, and positively made reformation to deal with the circumstance of the Hellenization and the metics with the attitude of openness and tolerance, which was a progress. However, this process was limited. Because the Christianity (particularly in the late development) had an exclusive impact on other religious beliefs (such as the thought of Islam,Buddhism and Confucianism in China), at least on the aspects of religious doctrine and etiquette. Take an example, for the aspects of doctrines, Christianity had a large conflict to the view about "salvation" with that in Buddhism and Confucianism. For Christian followers, the "salvation" was carried out by the God so that non-followers could not be saved. For the Christian Church, "No grace out of the Church", whether the thought from Christians and the Christian Church or not, the non-Christians and non-Churchmen felt a kind of oppression in their heart. For the Buddhists who pursued the idea of "becoming a Buddhist immediately", and who believed that people can get into realm of the Buddha by "racking their brains" and "doing good things to accumulate the virtue" would be deprived of the "hope". For the Confucians who believed themselves and depended on their rationality and morality to become "sages and men of virtue", a kind of behavior of "justification by faith" was not "initiative" for non-Christians but a kind of "passivity". Another example for conflicts is etiquette. In the late Ming Dynasty and the early Qing Dynasty, the spread of Catholicism was successful and smooth, which was beneficial to communicate in the aspects of culture between the western country and China. However, during the time of Kangxi, the two sides finally made a division about "the battle of etiquette". For Chinese people, the worship of "heaven and earth, ancestor, monarch and teachers" can not be abolished; while for Christianity, kneeling down any "idols" except God was not permitted. Then the tragic conflicts were utterly occurred between this "One God" of the Christian tradition and the belief of "polytheism" in the Chinese tradition and Confucian morality. Therefore, what we can see was another aspect of the Christian cosmopolitanism: if the cosmopolitanism was based on the standards of the Christian principles, and then it would lose the original meaning and become a kind of new oppression. Christianity which came out from the nationality of the Jewish, became a kind of world religion because of its universal value. However, with later gradual improvement of the Christian theology, this cosmopolitan constantly deteriorated and also generated the same narrow-mindedness as the original Jewish, which is really a pity.

（徐秋月译）

图书在版编目（CIP）数据

西方文化中的两希传统／杨慧著. -- 北京：社会
科学文献出版社，2020.8
ISBN 978 - 7 - 5201 - 7027 - 7

Ⅰ.①西…　Ⅱ.①杨…　Ⅲ.①文化史 - 古希腊②犹太
人 - 文化史　Ⅳ.①K125②K124

中国版本图书馆 CIP 数据核字（2020）第 139111 号

西方文化中的两希传统

著　　者／杨　慧

出 版 人／谢寿光
责任编辑／高　雁
文稿编辑／韩宜儒

出　　版／社会科学文献出版社（010）59367226
　　　　　地址：北京市北三环中路甲 29 号院华龙大厦　邮编：100029
　　　　　网址：www. ssap. com. cn
发　　行／市场营销中心（010）59367081　59367083
印　　装／三河市龙林印务有限公司

规　　格／开本：787mm × 1092mm　1/16
　　　　　印张：23.5　字数：360 千字
版　　次／2020 年 8 月第 1 版　2020 年 8 月第 1 次印刷
书　　号／ISBN 978 - 7 - 5201 - 7027 - 7
定　　价／98.00 元

本书如有印装质量问题，请与读者服务中心（010 - 59367028）联系